Clement Mansfield Ingleby

Shakespeare's centurie of prayse

A history of opinion on Shakespeare and his works

Clement Mansfield Ingleby

Shakespeare's centurie of prayse
A history of opinion on Shakespeare and his works

ISBN/EAN: 9783742867155

Manufactured in Europe, USA, Canada, Australia, Japa

Cover: Foto ©Thomas Meinert / pixelio.de

Manufactured and distributed by brebook publishing software (www.brebook.com)

Clement Mansfield Ingleby

Shakespeare's centurie of prayse

Shakespeare's Centurie of Prayse;

BEING
MATERIALS FOR A HISTORY OF OPINION
ON SHAKESPEARE AND HIS WORKS,
A.D. 1591—1693.

BY
C. M. INGLEBY, LL.D.

Second Edition,
REVISED WITH MANY ADDITIONS,
BY
LUCY TOULMIN SMITH.

NEW SHAKSPERE SOCIETY
ALEXANDER MORING, L^{TD.}
The De La More Press
32 GEORGE STREET, HANOVER SQUARE, LONDON, W.

TO

MRS F. J. FURNIVALL

This Edition is Dedicated

(BY PERMISSION OF DR. INGLEBY)

IN TOKEN OF

AFFECTIONATE REMEMBRANCE AND ESTEEM

BY

LUCY TOULMIN SMITH.

TABLE OF CONTENTS.

		PAGE
FORESPEECH ...		vii—xiii
PREFACE TO SECOND EDITION		xiv—xxi
PERIOD I. 1592—1616		1
PERIOD II. 1617—1641	...	123
PERIOD III. 1642—1660	...	241
PERIOD IV. 1660—1693	...	311
APPENDIX A.	1. PASSAGES MISTAKEN FOR ALLUSIONS	421
	2. ALLUSIONS IN SPURIOUS WORKS	426
APPENDIX B.	SHAKESPERE'S INFLUENCE ON OTHER WRITERS	427
	ENGLAND'S PARNASSUS	430
APPENDIX C.	DESCRIPTION OF "THE NEW METAMORPHOSIS"	440
APPENDIX D.	SUPPLEMENTAL EXTRACTS	449
GENERAL INDEX		461
INDEX TO SHAKESPERE'S WORKS REFERRED TO IN EXTRACTS		469

FORESPEECH

TO THE FIRST EDITION.

ALL is not "Prayse" that is celebrated in the ensuing pages : but the prevailing character of the parts may fairly be allowed to give designation to the whole. The experience of the two years during which the editor has been engaged upon this work has prepared him for the discovery that many links in the chain of allusion to Shakespeare have been omitted. It were surely unnecessary for him to have undertaken such a work to convince himself of his liability to oversight and error. Yet as surely, if he had the conceit of regarding himself as *nothing if not critical*, and worse than nothing if not accurate, as being beyond, not indeed the possibility but the danger, of making mistakes, there is no surer help for his malady than the attempt to execute a complete catena of extracts relating to one man, stretching through a century of obsolete or obsolescent literature. The editor never rightly estimated the difficulty of making an exact copy or a perfect collation, to say nothing of other and greater difficulties that infest this kind of work, until he had partly executed *Shakespeare's Centurie of Prayse.* At its commencement he felt confidence in his ability to make the collection nearly exhaustive : but as it received, from time to time during the process of printing, fresh accessions of material, he gradually allowed resignation to usurp the place of hope, and looked no longer for "the praise of perfection."

Should this book reach a second edition, it may, by renewed researches, be rendered very nearly complete. The editor does not expect that much retrenchment is possible. The number or doubtful extracts included in it does not exceed half a dozen. But it is impossible to doubt that there is yet much gleaning to be done on the less frequented fields of the relative literature.

With all its defects, the *Centurie* is certainly far in advance of anything of the kind that has hitherto been attempted. Garrick's collection, the first that was made, was exceedingly meagre; and those of Drake and Malone not much more extensive. The extracts given in the last chapter of Book IX and the first of Book XI of Knight's *Shakspere Studies* are a mere selection to serve a purpose, and are sometimes inaccurately given. The late Mr. Bolton Corney, the Rev. Alexander B. Grosart of Blackburn, and Mr. George Dawson of Birmingham, have, each at a different time, projected a *History of Opinion* on Shakespeare and his works: but all their designs were either frustrated or delayed, and were not executed. Dr. Grosart's *Contemporary Judgments of Poets*, announced four years ago, seems to have shared the same fate; but it will some day, we hope, be carried out.*

Incomplete as the ensuing collection must be, it is sufficiently extensive to afford both positive and negative evidence as to the estimation in which Shakespeare was held by the writers of the century during which his fame was germinating; viz., 1592—1693. It is, in fact, praise, and in some few cases dispraise, and not yet fame, that is shown in the subsequent testimonies. They bear witness to *subjective* opinions, preparing the way for the *objective* judgment which has seated Shakespeare on the Throne of Poets. The absence of sundry great names with which no pains of research, scrutiny, or study could connect the most trivial allusion to the bard or his works (such, *e. g.*, as Lord Brooke, Lord Bacon, Selden, Sir John Beaumont, Henry Vaughan, and Lord Clarendon) is *tacitly* significant: the iteration of the same vapid and affected compliments, couched in conventional terms, from writers of the first two periods,—comparing Shakespeare's "tongue," "pen," or "vein," to silver, honey, sugar, or nectar, while they ignore his greater and distinguishing qualities, is *expressly* significant.

* [Dr. Grosart tells me, May, 1879, that his "intended booklet on 'contemporary opinions' is still in the future." L. T. S.]

It is plain, for one thing, that the bard of our admiration was
unknown to the men of that age, though it is undeniable that his
supremacy in some important respects was at length recognised by
Ben Jonson, and subsequently by Milton and Dryden. How could
it well be otherwise? Men of genius, like them, could no more be
blind to the genius of Shakespeare than could Wagner and Gounod
be insensible to the orchestral excellence of Mendelssohn. Differing
as the editor does from many of the conclusions of Mr. Gerald
Massey, he is the more pleased to find himself at one with him
here.* Assuredly no one during the "Centurie" had any suspicion
that the genius of Shakespeare was unique, and that he was *sui
generis*—*i. e.*, the only exemplar of his species. Those who ranked
him very high compared him to Spenser, Sidney, Chapman, Jonson,
Fletcher, and even lesser lights, and most of the judges of that
time assigned the first place to one of them.

We do not look for Shakespeare's name in books on poets and
poetry which were issued before 1593, when his *Venus and Adonis*,
"the first heir of [his] invention," was issued: so that we are not
surprised at the silence of William Webbe (1586), George Puttenham (1589), Sir John Harrington (1591), Sir Philip Sidney (1595),
and Lodge (1596). Shakespeare could hardly have been known
to any of them. But the case is otherwise with works of the same
character issued as late as 1596, the year in which was published
Thomas Lodge's *Wits Miserie and the Worlds Madness*, where,
among the "divine wits" named, we do not find the name of
Shakespeare. Similarly in 1598 was published Edward Guilpin's

---

* In allusion to Spenser's *Teares of the Muses*, Mr. Massey writes thus:

"But we may safely say that no man living in 1590 . . . . ever saw
Shakespeare as the 'man whom Nature's self had made to mock herself, and
truth to imitate.'"

And again—

"Harvey's lusty *réveille* and Ben Jonson's eulogy notwithstanding, it is quite
demonstrable that Shakespeare's contemporaries had no adequate conception of
what manner of man or majesty of mind were amongst them. We know him
better than they did!" *The Secret Drama of Shakespeare's Sonnets, &c.* 1872.
pp. 511 & 528. Nevertheless, Harvey's allusion referred to here, is to Nash and
not to Shakespere.

collection of satires called *Skialethia:* the sixth of which contains the names of Chaucer, Gower, Daniel, Markham, Drayton, and Sidney,—but not that of Shakespeare. Ben Jonson, writing some forty years later, makes the same remarkable omission in one part of his *Discoveries* (*Præcipiendi modi*); he remarks that "as it is fit to read the best authors to youth first, so let them be of the openest and clearest" (ed. 1630, p. 160); and he distinguishes how Sidney, Donne, Gower, Chaucer, and Spenser should be read, —but does not mention Shakespeare. Nash seems to have divided the palm between Spenser and Peele; but he wrote a little too early for Shakespeare. Richard Carew assigns the first place to Sidney, in which judgment he was, perhaps, influenced by their early friendship at Oxford. Davison and a host of others set an extravagant value on Daniel. The elder Basse, Taylor (the ferryman), and Edward Phillips seem to put Spenser and Shakespeare on an equality. Spenser himself, Webster, and Camden, after enumerating various contemporary poets, apologetically give the last place to Shakespeare, the two former employing the proverbial phrase "last not least," or an equivalent. It would be hard to find any grudge or unfairness towards him in all this dealing: on the contrary, if by many he was ignored, he was ignored with other poets of good repute, and assuredly by many he was considered as a formidable rival to Spenser and Sidney in one branch of the art, and to Lilly, Peele, Chapman, and Jonson in another. Such praise was indeed most inadequate; but it would reverse the order of nature if a poet were to attain to fame *per saltum,* to be recognised for what he is, and appreciated at his true value, before such lapse of time as is sufficient for the formation of a ripe and objective school of criticism. If, as Mr. Charles Knight concludes, "he was *always* in the heart of the people" (*Shakspere Studies*, 1851, p. 504), that fact speaks more for Shakespeare as a showman than for Shakespeare as a man of genius. Doubtless he knew his men; but assuredly his men did not know him. The drift of his plays was in a manner intelligible, or they would not have been entertaining, to the penny-knaves who pestered the Globe and Blackfriars Theatres. But his profound reach of thought and his unrivalled knowledge of human nature were as far beyond the vulgar ken, as were the higher graces of his poetry. It is to men of sensibility and education that Shakespeare appeals as a man of genius; and it is to the literate class we must look for the impress of that genius.

Amidst the discordant voices of praise and of blame, the echoes of antiquated compliment mingled with the pedantic censure * and fanatic eulogy of later times, it has been difficult to bring sobriety of judgment and purity of taste to bear on Shakespeare's writings. We are at length slowly rounding to a just estimate of his works; and the time seems to be at hand when men of culture will attribute to the object of their admiration a much higher range of powers than were requisite for the production of the most popular and successful dramas in the world.

A few words in conclusion on the notices which constitute this catena. Of course it begins with the earliest known allusions to Shakespeare, viz., those in 1592. In strictness it should end before the publication of the first systematic critique on Shakespeare: for the inclusion of all such would be to reprint a library. Now "Dryden," as Samuel Johnson says (*Life of Dryden*, prefixed to *Works*, ed. 1811, vol. i. p. lix.), "may be properly considered as the father of English Criticism, as the writer who first taught us to determine upon principles the merit of composition:" and Dryden's only systematic essay on Shakespeare is the Preface to his own *Troilus and Cressida*, printed in 1679. But having given so many of Dryden's remarks on Shakespeare, the editor thought he was justified in reprinting, in an abridged form, that remarkable essay, which in the quarto of 1679 occupies fifteen pages. He has so far, then, departed from his prospectus, and included in his collection a formal and lengthy criticism. That being so, Dryden's essay will serve to make his position the clearer: to exhibit an exceptional sample of the work he professes to exclude, and thus to bring home to every reader the necessity of the rule which excludes works of that class. After Dryden, the first formal critics are Rymer and Dennis. The work of Rymer which Dryden refers to in the Preface to *Troilus and Cressida* is that from which we have given the only extracts referring to Shakespeare, viz., *The Tragedies of*

* I here used 'censure' purposely to draw the word back to its catholic use, as on p. 129.

the last Age considered and examined by the Practice of the Ancients, 1678. His *Short View of Tragedy*, 1693,* and *The Impartial Critick* of Dennis, 1693, and all subsequent publications are excluded. Yet through the editor's decision to admit every work of Dryden's which deals with or alludes to Shakespeare, this catena extends into the year 1693 ; for the *Epistle to Sir Godfrey Kneller* was written in that year : and thus he is enabled to include the important letter of John Dowdall to the Rev. Edward Southwell. This pre-critical century naturally divides itself into four periods : the *first* extending from the earliest allusion to Shakespeare till his death in 1616 : the *second* from his death to the outbreak of the Civil War in 1642 : the *third* from the closing of the theatres to the Restoration : and the *fourth* extends from the return of the Merry Monarch to the rise of criticism. After this Shakespeare's fame as a classic really began. We are commencing with that century when rumour had hardly begun her work, and when his poems were read, and his plays seen, as matters which belonged to the age, and not as " works " for all time.

The editor has excluded from the catena all documentary notices of Shakespeare ; for, besides being foreign to its scope, they are sufficiently numerous and extensive to form a considerable volume by themselves.†

In garnering so large a harvest he has received kind and efficient help from many friends. He has usually gone to the fountain-head for the extract employed : but when occasional impediments—as distance, pre-occupation, or sickness—hindered him in this, he relied on the copy or collation of a friend. For such work he is chiefly

* [I have added two short extracts from Rymer's "Short View" in a note, to explain the design of his books, and the reference to them by Motteux. L. T. S.]

† Perhaps the most curious of these is one of the answers of Shakespeare's granddaughter, the widow of Thomas Nash, to a suit preferred by Edward Nash (*Chancery Proceedings*, N. N, 17, No. 65) ; where we read that New Place was "the Inheritance of William Shakespear the Defend[ts] Grandfather whoe was seized thereof in Fee simple long before the Defend[ts] marriage wth the said Thomas Nashe." This answer is dated April 17, 24 Caroli. As James died March 26, 1625, the 24th year of Charles *would have* ended on March 27, 1649 ; but it *actually* ended on January 30, 1649, by the king's decapitation ; so that the date of the answer is April 17, 1648. (Quoted in the Appendix to Staunton's *Life of Shakespeare*, Works, vol. i. p. lv.)

indebted to W. S. W. VAUX, Esq., F.R.S., and to W. B. RYE, Esq., the Keeper of the Printed Books of the British Museum. To J. O. HALLIWELL-PHILLIPPS, Esq., F.R.S., he is indebted for many references which he would otherwise have overlooked, and for having so liberally placed at his disposal the wood-cut (fac-simile) forming the frontispiece to the large-paper copies. He owes to his lamented friend, the late HOWARD STAUNTON, Esq., a felicitous amendment of the head-title, and three valuable extracts. His thanks are also due to Mr. C. EDMONDS and Mr. R. K. DENT (both of Birmingham) for numerous extracts, and to the Rev. H. A. HOLDEN, LL.D., for revising those of his notes which deal with the learned languages.

C. M. INGLEBY

Valentines, Ilford,
Oct. 16th, 1874.

PREFACE TO THE SECOND EDITION

DR. INGLEBY having generously offered to present a new impression of his book to the New Shakspere Society, provided the Committee found an editor to do the work of revision, I was asked to undertake it, under the supposition that verification of the quotations and the insertion of some new extracts would be a simple matter and fulfil the needs of a new edition. But as I went on I found that very much more than this was required; a critical knowledge of nice points, the weighing of evidence for and against different dates, a considerable knowledge of bibliography, an intimacy with the present state of Shakesperian criticism, and beyond all a wide acquaintance with Elizabethan literature to which I could lay no pretensions, were the needful qualifications for such a task. I can therefore but ask my fellow-members of the New Shakspere Society to be lenient if in my fulfilment of the work they find some errors or omissions, unavoidable with the utmost care in a work of this character.

Dr. Ingleby, in placing the work unreservedly in my hands, gave me a large number of new extracts and notes that he had collected; references, indications, or extracts have been sent in by several correspondents and friends; many are supplied from my own reading. The number of quotations in text and notes is thus increased from about 228 to 356, and the works referred to in the Appendices have grown from 25 to 41. In every case I have carefully tested the date, going back to the earliest editions (except in one or two instances where these were not accessible); where the date at the

PREFACE TO THE SECOND EDITION.

head of the extract differs from that of the edition, the reason is usually given in the note : the date of each manuscript quoted has also passed under examination. Every extract and reference in text, note, or appendix has been collated by myself twice with the original, except with regard to about twenty books at Oxford, which I had not the opportunity of examining more than once, and about a dozen more which Mr. George Parker of the Bodleian has been good enough to collate. The full references given will enable the student to refer to the originals for himself.

Having thus got as near to the actual penning by each author as possible, the extracts are arranged in chronological order ; what may be lost by not grouping those from one writer together (which easily may be recovered by referring to the pages under each name in the Index) may be compensated by the consecutive view of these indications of opinion thus gained. In about twenty-five instances it is somewhat doubtful whether there is an allusion to Shakespere or to any of his works intended, and, following the suggestion of Mr. Furnivall, an asterisk of warning is affixed to each ; these, however, form but a small proportion of the whole ; three of them have been rescued from "mistaken" allusions (see Appendix D) ; four remain doubtful out of the half-dozen which were considered so in the first edition (those on pp. 1, 7, 13, 98), and the rest have been inserted as affording various points of interest.

As the plan of this book is that it should contain all notices of Shakespere or his works, direct or implied, to be found in print or in manuscript within the hundred years from 1592 to 1693, it will be seen that the extracts illustrate, besides the chronological order of the literary and public estimate of Shakespere's merits, the following groups of facts ;—

1. References to Shakespere personally.
2. Direct mention of his plays or poems.
3. Quotation of a well-known line or character.
4. The imitation or appropriation of phrases, lines, and passages.
5. Record of times and places where his plays were seen or acted.

The first three of these groups speak for themselves ; they are all of them "Allusions." Under the first we have, besides those

xviii   PREFACE TO THE SECOND EDITION.

about which there can be no mistake,* the consideration of several of early date which do not mention Shakespere by name, but which are of the highest interest, if they can be shown to refer to him. The Third Letter of Gabriel Harvey is now considered by Mr. R. Simpson and Dr. Ingleby to allude to Nash and not to Shakespere, it is therefore relegated to the Appendix of "mistaken allusions" in this edition. Both of the supposed allusions by Edmund Spenser have been carefully re-examined, and the true identification of that in the "Tears of the Muses" appears to be settled by the most recent investigation.

The fourth class of extracts belongs really to the subject of the Influence of Shakespere on the literature of the century. Dr. Ingleby gave indications of several writers who exhibit this in a minor degree in an Appendix to the first edition, to which a good many more instances of the same kind are now added. But, inasmuch as public approval must be shown by that admiration of phrases and expressions which adopts or imitates, as indeed in one sense such appropriation may be said to be the highest praise, it appeared well to include in the text the more prominent of the examples that have come under my notice. In a few cases Shakespere and his imitator are placed side by side, to show the closeness of the parallel, or as we should now say plagiarism. Such passages are not indeed "Allusions," but they are an important part of the Materials for a history of opinion on the Poet. The field in this department is probably not nearly exhausted, I cannot hope to have given all the imitations that the century produced.

The writings which record for us either by official accounts,

---

* In 1870 Mr. Spedding edited for the Duke of Northumberland a manuscript of Lord Bacon's *Conference of Pleasure*, on the front leaf of which is written a list of several titles, among them *Richard the second* and *Richard the third*. It is inferred that these are meant for the titles of Shakespere's plays because the word "Shakespeare" is found eight or nine times among the scribblings of an idle pen which cover the rest of the page. A fac simile of this leaf is given in the book. The date of the manuscript leaf has been cautiously expressed by Mr. Spedding as between 1596 and 1780! The hand-writing seems to declare that it is near the beginning of that period, and if, says Mr. Spedding, it was not later than the reign of Elizabeth, "it is probably one of the earliest evidences of the growth of Shakespeare's *personal* fame as a dramatic writer" (p. xxiii). Though the uncertainty renders this testimony insignificant, it is worth a mention here.

private letters, or gossipping diarists the actual performance of Shakespere's plays are not the least interesting and valuable. The pity is they are so few! But we get Simon Forman's help to the date of the *Winter's Tale;* the testimony of Merrick, Phillipps, and Lambard to the acting of *Richard II* for the Essex conspirators of 1601; and the performances at Court in the second Period as shown by Lord Stanhope and Sir Henry Herbert. The great popularity of many of the plays, altered or unaltered, in the Restoration Period appears from theatre-loving Pepys and St. Evremond, while a curious fact regarding *Macbeth* and its "improvement" has come to light through the country report of Thomas Isham. In connection too with this group are the interesting glimpses which we get of the stage practice of the early actors of *Hamlet* in the *Elegy on Burbage* * and in John Raynold's *Primerose;* and the notices of the burning of the Globe theatre in 1613 during the performance of *Henry VIII*, given by Thomas Lorkins and the Sonnet on the pittifull burning, &c. (See Appendix D.)

To make the general view of the references to plays and poems during the century apparent at a glance, a second Index is added, of Shakespere's writings cited or alluded to in the extracts, distinguishing between those referred to before the closing of the theatres in 1642, and those after that date. With this should also be taken the results obtained from *England's Parnassus*, 1600, and Poole's *English Parnassus*, 1657 (pp. 430 — 439), the former of which especially shows the great appreciation of *Venus and Adonis* and *Lucrece.*

On the whole an extended knowledge of the sentiments of our fore-fathers, both in the Jacobean and the Restoration periods, shows that they had a keener appreciation of the merits of the great Master's works, and a more ready wit for their reception, than we in these days are inclined to give them credit for. Emerson's careless assertion that there is a "unique fact in literary history, the unsurprised reception of Shakespeare; the reception proved by his making

---

* Since the passing of the text through the press, Mr. Furnivall informs me that there are several MSS. of the Elegy known to exist in the collection of the late Sir Thomas Phillipps at Cheltenham, and at Warwick Castle. I am unable, however, to give any information as to which version they belong.

his fortune, and the apathy proved by the absence of all contemporary panegyric" (*English Traits, Essay on Literature*), is not borne out by the real facts; abundant examples of contemporary notice and praise prove that the reverse of apathy was the truth. "It is absurd," says Chas. Bathurst, speaking of a later time (*Shakespeare's Versification*, 1857, p. 153), "to suppose that people did not feel Shakespeare, because they did not talk perpetually, as we do, and write dissertations." When we consider the bare state of the early stage and the absence of scenic effect and accessories, the fact that Shakespere died a rich man is itself a testimony to the immense popularity of his dramas in a play-going age, which trusted to the imagination excited by the language delivered, and the gesture of the actors. That Hamlet, Richard III, Falstaff, and Justice Silence rapidly attained a personality among the people is amply shown by the allusions; and the delight taken in *Romeo and Juliet*, *Venus and Adonis*, and *Lucrece*, to mention no others, is shown in the references, very many in number, which occur before 1642, as well as by the indication of *England's Parnassus*. That he never died out of regard, but lived on in spite of the Puritan suppression, appears not merely from the attempts at Drolleries taken from his plays shown us by Kirkman and Cox, but from the evidence of such as Thomas Fuller, Cleveland, and Sir Richard Baker, the unwilling voice of Prynne, and even the plagiarist who wrote *Vindex Anglicus*. After the Restoration his fame, carried on by Davenant and Betterton, continued and increased; it was modified, a different class of faculties was appealed to, but Shakespere was present and recognised through all changes, till the growth of criticism came in to vindicate his higher claims.*

* Shakespere service, if not worship, is now acknowledged over the world, witness the publication of Shakesperean and Elizabethan works in Russia, a Shakespere Society in Moscow, the recent translations of Shakespere into Portuguese, Chinese, Bengalee, &c. &c. It may be interesting to note that this volume contains the earliest notices known at present of Shakespere from the pens of our German and French brethren. Wurmsser, the Secretary of the Prince of Wurtemburg, records a visit to the *Globe* to see *Othello* in 1610; Morhoff's reference to Shakespere's name in 1682 (p. 342) does not fore-cast the great adoption of the poet by his countrymen; though the indications of knowledge of some of Shakespere's plays abroad early in the century seem to show that the Germans were not slow to appreciate him. The notices from St. Evremond and Motteux are those of Frenchmen resident in this country.

PREFACE TO THE SECOND EDITION. xxi

This volume may be of use in a double sense ; besides its original purpose it will supply a collection of trustworthy copies of many passages which give important data in fixing the chronology of the plays. I would also call attention to the cautionary value of the Appendix A ; having not only fallen into a pit-fall myself, but having seen scholars whose learning and judgment might have ensured them against a false reference do the same, some pains have been taken with these instances that the canons of criticism have rejected. Not the least of the difficulties I have found, which must be well known to Shakespere scholars, is the distinguishing between a genuine and a supposed imitation; the enthusiast or the unwary setting down as taken from Shakespere, a verse, a phrase, or an idea, which on further knowledge may prove to be a proverb quoted by Shakespere himself, a current expression of the Elizabethan day common to all, or an idea which formed part of the contemporary philosophy or stock of knowledge. Examples of the proverb may be found on p. 423, of current phrases on pp. 82, 155, of a common idea on pp. 54, 423, and 428.

In Appendix C will be found a description of a manuscript of some interest, though not of great importance to Shakesperean studies, which seemed to fall into a useful place in this volume. The last Appendix, D, is occupied by a few extracts which came in too late for insertion in their places in the text. The whole will be found embodied in the General Index. This is perhaps the place to make two supplementary notes, one on the rare book called *Ratsey's Ghost* (p. 67). I searched for the First Part of this tract in vain ; for a sight of the second, I am indebted to the Rev. F. Ponsonby, late Hon. Librarian of Lord Spencer's Library at Althorpe. The following entries on the Stationers' Register, 2 May 1605, "A book called *the lyfe and death of* GAMALIEL RATSEY *a famous theefe of Englande executed at Bedford* 27 *marcij* 1605," and 31 May 1605, " A booke called Ratsey's ghoste or the Second parte of [his] lif with the reste of his mad Pranckes," &c., show, however, that there was a first part published. Secondly, Dr. Ingleby writes that the suggested emendation of Marston on p. 77, which is due to Dr. Nicholson, was partly anticipated by C. W. Dilke in his "Old English Plays" (vol. ii. p. 222), who prints the line, however, without any note to show that it is altered.

PREFACE TO THE SECOND EDITION.

For the spelling of Shakespere's name throughout this volume Dr. Ingleby is in no way responsible. I should have hardly thought it necessary to say this, but having unintentionally erred against Dr. Ingleby's wish (which I did not know till the work was too far advanced to make a change), that his use of *Shakespeare* should be continued in this edition, it may be clearly understood that the error, if any, of using the form *Shakespere* is my own. It is needless here to enter into the controversy as to the right spelling, the evidence afforded by the only manuscript signatures that are at present known being uncertain, and variously read by the best experts.

I have carefully preserved the spellings (including of course the various forms of Shakespere), punctuation, italics, however absurd, and capital letters of the originals in all quotations, with two exceptions to be noted immediately. It was the practice of the 17th century to print proper names in italic (or in a type equivalent to this), which was so consistently adhered to that it becomes a fact of value in conjectures such as that concerning Wapping and Whipping on p. 294, but that the italicizing all sorts of words irrespective of emphasis or sense was apparently felt to be meaningless, is shown, for example, by the lines by Mayne and West (pp. 212, 214), printed in 1638, which were reprinted in the 1687 edition of Cleveland's Works (and falsely attributed to that author), innocent of such italics. The only exceptions to a strict reproduction of originals is, in deference to the wish of Dr. Ingleby, the printing of *u* and *v*, *i* and *j*, according to modern usage throughout; and the capital initials to trivial words (adjectives, adverbs, &c.), which are sown broad-cast throughout many of the prints of the last part of the 17th century, are omitted in the extract from Margaret Cavendish (p. 332), and in one or two of those from Dryden. For the rest, no pains have been spared to attain accuracy, though in a work in which the *minutiæ* are almost endless, there are sure to be a few errors to mar perfection.

My initials are affixed to all fresh notes and passages inserted; but it was not necessary thus to distinguish (because it was impossible) all small alterations or corrections. For the facts of this volume I am responsible, the arrangement into periods and the notes unsigned are Dr. Ingleby's. The initials or names of several friends who have kindly supplied me with notes or criticisms on points on which they had special knowledge are given at the end of those notes. To these gentlemen my best thanks are due, and especially to Dr. Brinsley Nicholson, who has read through the whole of the proof-sheets, and to whose kind encouragement I am greatly indebted. Of Dr. Ingleby's support and courtesy I cannot speak too highly, all the more that I have been compelled to arrive at several conclusions entirely different from his. My warmest thanks belong to Miss Maria Latreille, a lady whose unwearied patience and knowledge of books have been of the greatest assistance, freely given, in tracking out many a rare edition, and in hunting up many a difficult passage. Besides the obligations which are referred to as they occur in their places, I beg to offer my acknowledgments to many valued friends and correspondents : to Professor Dowden, Dr. Nicholson, Mr. C. Elliot Browne, Dr. G. Kingsley, Mr. H. Littledale, and Professor Paul Meyer, for the loan or gift of books, as well as for suggestions and for information ; to Mr. P. A. Daniel and Rev. J. W. Ebsworth for much kind help; to Mr. Halliwell-Phillips, Dr. Grosart, Mr. Aldis Wright, Mr. W. G. Stone, Mr. Spedding, Mr. W. Chappell, Mr. Furnivall, Rev. H. P. Stokes, Dr. J. Jusserand, and others, for various references, extracts, or obliging answers to inquiry. It is a pleasant duty to acknowledge the consideration and sympathy evoked by efforts made for the name of him whose works have made "the whole world kin."

LUCY TOULMIN SMITH.

Highgate, London;
May 30, 1879.

*EDMUND SPENSER, 1591—1594.

And there, though laft not leaft is *Aetion*,
A gentler fhepheard may no where be found:
Whofe Mufe, full of high thoughts invention,
Doth like himfelfe Heroically found

Colin Clouts come home againe. 1595. *sign.* C 2. [4*to.*]
(*See New Shakspere Society, Allusion-Books, I. pp.* xxiv, 168.)

That Spenser's stanza on Aetion really refers to Shakespeare is established by the fact that no other heroic poet (*i. e.* historical dramatist, or chronicler in heroic verse) had a surname of heroic sound Jonson, Fuller, and Bancroft have similar allusions to our bard's warlike name. Mr. J. O. Halliwell-Phillipps remarks that "the lines seem to apply with equal propriety to Warner": (Life of Shakespeare : 1848 : p. 142.) But Warner is not an heroic but a premonitory name.

Malone's two attempts (Ed. 1821, vol. ii, p. 274) to explain the meaning of Aetion are equally unfortunate. He seems not to have known that $'Aετίων$ was a Greek proper name, borne, in fact, by the father of Cypselus of Corinth, and by two famous artists. It should be written Aëtion, and pronounced (like Tiresias in Milton) with accents on the first and last syllables. Its root is surely $άετος$, an eagle ; and it is, therefore, appropriate to one of "high thoughts" and heroic invention.

Three verses in *Colin Clout's come home againe,* viz. those on Amyntas (who is Ferdinando Earl of Derby), must have been written after April 16, 1594, when Lord Derby (formerly Lord Strange) died. Todd and others have inferred from this that the poem, which was first printed in 1595, was really written in the preceding year : and that in the date, 27 December, 1591, appended to the dedication, 1591 is a press-error for 1594. We adopted this view ; but we are now convinced that Spenser had finished the first draft of his poem in December, 1591, and subsequently amplified it. Some have seen a discrepancy between the date appended to that dedication, and that appended to the dedication of *Daphnaida,* January 1, 1591 : but if, as Mr. Hales believes, the latter work be alluded to in the former, January and December, 1591, must be the Gregorian or historical dates, the year beginning with the former and ending with the latter month. This supposition of the use of dates, unusual at that time. is supported by Spenser's division of the year in his *Shepherd's Calender.*

[I have placed the date above doubtfully, because the stanza quoted may have been one of the amplifications. —L. T. S.]

ROBERT GREENE, 1592.

Base minded men al three of you, if by my miferie ye be not warned: for unto none of you (like me) fought thofe burres to cleave: thofe Puppits (I meane) that fpeake from our mouths, thofe Anticks garnifht in our colours. Is it not ftrange that I, to whom they al have beene beholding: is it not like that you, to whome they all have beene beholding, fhall (were ye in that cafe that I am now) be both at once of them forfaken? Yes, truft them not: for there is an upftart Crow, beautified with our feathers, that with his *Tygers heart wrapt in a Players hide*, fuppofes he is as well able to bumbaft out a blanke verfe as the beft of you: and being an abfolute *Johannes fac totum*, is in his owne conceit the onely Shake-fcene in a countrie. O that I might intreate your rare wits to be imployed in more profitable courfes: & let thefe Apes imitate your paft excellence, and never more acquaint them with your admired inventions. I know the beft hufband of you all will never prove an ufurer and the kindeft of them all wil never proove a kinde nurfe: yet, whilft you may, feeke you better Maifters; for it is pittie men of fuch rare wits, fhould be fubject to the pleafures of fuch rude groomes.

In this I might infert two more, that both have writ againft thefe buckram Gentlemen; but let their owne works ferve to witneffe againft their owne wickedneffe, if they perfever to maintaine any more fuch peafants. For other new commers, I leave them to the mercie of thefe painted monfters, who (I doubt not) will drive the beft minded to defpife them; for the reft it fkils not though they make a jeaft at them.

Green's Groats-worth of Wit; bought with a Million of Repentaunce. 1596. *Reprinted from Mr. Huth's copy by New Shakspere Society, All-sion-Books, 1. p.* 30. (See also *Introduction* to that vol., p. ii.)

The three "base-minded men" whom Greene thus addresses on his death-bed have been identified as Marlowe, Nash, and Peele. That Shakespeare was the "upstart crow," and one of the purloiners of Greene's plumes, is put beyond a doubt by the following considerations: (1) That there was no such a word as *Shake-scene* (i.e. a tragedian : cf. Ben Jonson's lines,
"to heare thy Buskin tread,
And shake a Stage",
and also a passage in *The Puritaine* (1607, sign. Fi) where Pye-boord says, "Have you never seene a stalking-stamping Player, that will raise a tempest with his toung, and *thunder* with his heeles"). (2) That the line in italics is a parody on one which is found in *The True Tragedie of Richard Duke of Yorke*, 1595, and also in Shakespeare's *Henry VI*, Part III, Act I, sc. 4, viz. :
"Oh Tygers hart wrapt in a womans hide."
(3) That Marlowe and Robert Greene were (probably) the joint authors of *The two Parts of the Contention* and of *The True Tragedie*, which furnish Parts II & III of *Henry VI* with their *prima stamina*, and a considerable number of their lines.

Shakespeare, as the "upstart crow," seems to be one of those alluded to by "R. B. Gent." in *Greene's Funeralls*, 1594 (Sonnet ix, sign. C), where he writes :
"Greene, is the pleasing Object of an eie :
Greene, pleasde the eies of all that lookt uppon him.
Greene, is the ground of everie Painters die :
Greene, gave the ground, to all that wrote upon him.
Nay more the men, that so Eclipst his fame :
Purloynde his Plumes, can they deny the same?"
The strange terms huddled upon the players by poor Greene are paralleled by what we find in other works of the time : e. g.,
"Out on these puppets, painted images," &c.
The Scourge of Villanie, by J. Marston, Sat. VII.

"'Good manners,' as Seneca complaines, 'are extinct with wantonnesse, in tricking up themselves men goe beyond women, men weare harlots colours and doe not walke, but jet and daunce,' hic mulier, hœc vir, more like Players, Butterflies, Baboones, Apes, Antickes, then men."—Burton's *Anatomy of Melancholy*, 1621. [4to.] Part 3, sec. 2, memb. 2, subs. 3, page 571. (Ed. 1676, p. 295.)

As to the extract from *The Groat's-worth of Wit*, knowing no edition earlier than that of 1596, we have followed the text of that. A copy is in the library of Mr. Henry Huth. Greene died in Sept. 1592, and as Chettle's *Kind Hart's Dreame*, which alludes to this book, was registered in December 1592, *The Groatsworth of Wit* must have been printed before that date. (See next extract.) The British Museum Library has copies of the editions of 1617, 1621, and 1637. The two copies in the Bodleian Library are of the editions of 1621 and 1629, the former of which, by a very common error of the press, reads "Tygres head," instead of "Tygers heart."
or Tygres

HENRY CHETTLE, DEC., 1592.

Ile ſhew reaſon for my preſent writing. * * About three moneths ſince died M. Robert Greene, leaving many papers in ſundry Booke ſellers hands, among other his Groatſworth of wit, in which a letter written to divers play-makers, is offenſively by one or two of them taken ; and becauſe on the dead they cannot be avenged, they wilfully forge in their conceites a living Author, and after toſſing it to and fro, no remedy, but it muſt light on me. * * * With neither of them that take offence was I acquainted, and with one of them I care not if I never be : The other, whome at that time I did not ſo much ſpare, as ſince I wiſh I had, for that as I have moderated the heate of living writers, and might have uſde my owne diſcretion (eſpecially in ſuch a caſe) the Author beeing dead, that I did not, I am as ſory, as if the originall fault had beene my fault, becauſe my ſelfe have ſeene his demeanor no leſſe civill than he exelent in the qualitie he profeſſes : Beſides, divers of worſhip have reported his uprightnes of dealing, which argues his honeſty, and his facetious grace in writting, that aprooves his Art.

Kind-Harts Dreame. [n. d. 4to.] *To the Gentlemen Readers, p.* 2. Reprinted in *Allusion-Books, New Sh. Soc., I. pp. viii,* 38.

[The manuscript of the *Groatsworth of Wit* must have been put into Chettle's hands for publication, for he goes on to say after the above extract, that he copied it out, "Greene's hand was none of the best," and it could not be read by the licenser ; "but in the whole booke" he (Chettle) put "not a worde in." The "one of them" referred to by Chettle is Marlowe, "the other" appears to be Shakespere. L. T. S.]

Kind-Harts Dreame is undated : but the address "To the Gentlemen Readers" and the entry in the Stationers' Books, 8th December, 1592, prove that the tract was written between the date of Robert Greene's death and December in the same year, i. e. 1592. It was, probably, published in the following year. We were under the impression that the British Museum copy which we used was not the firſt edition. We are now disposed to believe that it is.

THOMAS NASH, 1592.

How would it have joyed brave *Talbot* (the terror of the French) to thinke that after he had lyne two hundred yeares in his Tombe, hee fhould triumphe againe on the Stage, and have his bones newe embalmed with the teares of ten thoufand fpectators at leaft, (at feverall times) who, in the Tragedian that reprefents his perfon, imagine they behold him frefh bleeding !

Pierce Penilesse his supplication to the Diuell. 1592. *Sign. F* 3. [4*to.*]

We have here doubtless an allusion to the play of *Henery the vi* mentioned in *Henslowe's Diary* (March 3, 1591-2 : Shakespeare Society's print, 1845, p. 22) : and this may or may not be identical with the *First Part of Henry the Sixth* in the Folio Edition of Shakespeare, 1623. Whether Shakespeare had any share in this latter play is, to say the least, problematical. Nash's work was reprinted, from the *first* edition of 1592, for the Shakespeare Society in 1842 under Mr. J. P. Collier's superintendence. That gentleman reprinted it again from the *second* edition of 1592, for his series of " Miscellaneous Tracts," generally known as his *Yellow Series*, in 1870. Many variations occur in the second edition. The extract above given from the first, is the same in both editions.

Anonymous, 1594.

In *Lavine Land though Livie loſt*
There hath beene ſeene a *Conſtant* dame :
Though *Rome* lament that ſhe have loſt
The *Gareland* of her rareſt fame,
    Yet now we ſee, that here is found.
    As great a *Faith* in *Engliſh* ground.

Though *Collatine* have deerely bought,
To high renowne, a laſting life,
And found, that moſt in vaine have ſought,
To have a *Faire* and *Conſtant* wife,
    Yet *Tarquyne* pluckt his gliſtering grape,
    And *Shake-ſpeare*, paints poore *Lucrece* rape.

Commendatory verses prefixed to Willobie his Avisa. 1594. Sign. A iiij.
Reprinted in Allusion-Books, New Sh. Soc., I, pp. xxxi, 170.

*HENRY WILLOBIE, 1594.

Cant. XLIIII.

Henrico Willobego.   Italo-Hispalenfis.

H. W. being fodenly infected with the contagion of a fantafticall fit, at the firft fight of *A*, pyneth a while in fecret griefe, at length not able any longer to indure the burning heate of fo fervent a humour, bewrayeth the fecrefy of his difeafe unto his familiar frend W. S. who not long before had tryed the curtesy of the like paffion, and was now newly recovered of the like infection; yet finding his frend let bloud in the fame vaine, he took pleafure for a tyme to fee him bleed, & in fteed of ftopping the iffue, he inlargeth the wound, with the fharpe rafor of a willing conceit, perfwading him that he thought it a matter very eafy to be compaffed, & no doubt with payne, diligence & fome coft in time to be obtayned. Thus this miferable comforter comforting his frend with an impoffibilitie, eyther for that he now would fecretly laugh at his frends folly, that had given occafion not long before unto others to laugh at his owne, or becaufe he would fee whether an other could play his part better then himfelfe, & in vewing a far off the courfe of this loving Comedy, he determined to fee whether it would fort to a happier end for this new actor, then it did for the old player. But at length this Comedy was like to have growen to a Tragedy, by the weake & feeble eftate that H. W. was brought unto, by a defperate vewe of an impoffibility of obtaining his purpofe, til

Time & Neceffity, being his beft Phifitions brought him a plafter, if not to heale, yet in part to eafe his maladye. In all which difcourfe is lively reprefented the unrewly rage of unbrydeled fancy, having the raines to rove at liberty, with the dyvers & fundry changes of affections & temptations, which Will, fet loofe from Reafon, can devife &c.

H. W.

H. W.

What fodaine chance or change is this,
That doth bereave my quyet reft?
* * * * *
But yonder comes my faythfull frend,
That like affaultes hath often tryde,
On his advife I will depend,
Where I fhall winne, or be denyde,[whether]
 And looke what counfell he fhall give,
 That will I do, where dye or live.[whether]

Cant. XLV.

W. S.

Well met, frend Harry, what's the caufe
You looke fo pale with Lented cheeks?
Your wanny face & fharpened nofe
Shew plaine, your mind fome thing miflikes,
 If you will tell me what it is,
 Ile helpe to mend what is amiffe.

What is fhe, man, that workes thy woe,
And thus thy tickling fancy move?
Thy droufie eyes, & fighes do fhoe,
This new difeafe proceedes of love,
 Tell what fhe is that witch't thee fo,
 I fweare it fhall no farder go.

A heavy burden wearieth one,
Which being parted then in twaine,
Seemes very light, or rather none,
And boren well with little paine :
  The fmothered flame, too clofely pent,
  Burnes more extreame for want of vent.

So forrowes fhrynde in fecret breft,
Attainte the hart with hotter rage,
Then griefes that are to frendes expreft,
Whofe comfort may fome part affwage :
  If I a freud, whofe faith is tryde,
  Let this requeft not be denyde.

Exceffive griefes good counfells want,
And cloud the fence from fharpe conceits ;
No reafon rules, where forrowes plant,
And folly feedes, where fury fretes,
  Tell what fhe is, and you fhall fee,
  What hope and help fhall come from mee.

CANT. XLVI.

H. W.

Seeft yonder howfe, where hanges the badge
Of Englands Saint, when captaines cry
Victorious land, to conquering rage,
Loe, there my hopeleffe helpe doth ly :
  And there that frendly foe doth dwell,
  That makes my hart thus rage and fwell.

CANT. XLVII.

W. S.

Well, fay no more : I know thy griefe,
And face from whence thefe flames aryfe,

It is not hard to fynd reliefe,
If thou wilt follow good advyſe :
   She is no Saynt, She is no Nonne,
   I thinke in tyme ſhe may be wonne.

Ars vetoratoria At firſt repulſe you muſt not faint,
Nor flye the field though ſhe deny
You twiſe or thriſe, yet manly bent,
Againe you muſt, and ſtill reply :
   When tyme permits you not to talke,
   Then let your pen and fingers walke.

Munera (crede mihi) placant hominesq; deosq ; Apply her ſtill with dyvers thinges, [Ply]
(For giftes the wyſeſt will deceave)
Sometymes with gold, ſometymes with ringes,
No tyme nor fit occaſion leave,
   Though coy at firſt ſhe ſeeme and wielde,
   Theſe toyes in tyme will make her yielde.

Looke what ſhe likes; that you muſt love,
And what ſhe hates, you muſt deteſt,
Where good or bad, you muſt approve, [whether]
The wordes and workes that pleaſe her beſt :
   If ſhe be godly, you muſt ſweare,
   That to offend you ſtand in feare.

Wicked wiles to deceave witles women. You muſt commend her loving face,
For women joy in beauties praiſe,
You muſt admire her ſober grace,
Her wiſdome and her vertuous wayes,
   Say, t'was her wit and modeſt ſhoe, [show]
   That made you like and love her ſo.

You muſt be ſecret, conſtant, free,
Your ſilent ſighes & trickling teares,

Let her in secret often see,
Then wring her hand, as one that feares
 To speake, then wish she were your wife,
 And last desire her save your life.

When she doth laugh, you must be glad,
And watch occasions, tyme and place,
When she doth frowne, you must be sad,
Let sighes & sobbes request her grace :
 Sweare that your love is truly ment,
 So she in tyme must needes relent.

*Willobie his Avisa, or the true picture of a Modest Maid and of a chast
and constant wife. In hexamiter verse. The like argument wherof
was never heretofore published.* 1594. [*4to.*] *Sig. L i, back.
Reprinted in Allusion-Books, I, New Sh. Soc., p.* 169.

Henry Willobie's W. S. is referred to Shakespeare on two distinct grounds : (1) Because W. S. appears in this "imaginary conversation" as a standard authority on Love ; and assuredly Shakespeare was *the* amatory poet of the day, and, to judge by his Sonnets, "had tried the curtesy of the like passion," and had come unscathed out of the ordeal. [Compare also his counsel to the wooer in the poem No. XIX, beginning, "When as thine eye hath chose the dame," of the Passionate Pilgrim, to which Willobie's verses bear a strong and curious resemblance in metre, subject, and treatment, L. T. S.] (2) Because it is said that this W. S. "in vewing the course of this loving Comedy determined to see whether it would sort to a happier end *for this new actor, then it did for the old player*," with other theatrical imagery specially applicable to a player and dramatist. Assuredly, no other contemporary poet of the same initials, whether lyrist or dramatist (and five or six might be named), had any claim to this distinction.

[SIR] W[ILLIAM] HAR[BERT], 1594.

You that to fhew your wits, have taken toyle
In regift'ring the deeds of noble men ;
And fought for matter in a forraine foyle,
As worthie fubjects of your filver pen,
Whom you have rais'd from darke oblivion's den.
You that have writ of chafte Lucretia,
Whofe death was witneffe of her fpotleffe life :
Or pen'd the praife of fad Cornelia,
Whofe blameleffe name hath made her fame fo rife,
As noble Pompey's moft renoumed wife :
 Hither unto your home direct your eies,
 Whereas, unthought on, much more matter lies.

Epicedium. A funerall Song, upon the vertuous life and godly death of the right worshipfull the Lady Helen Branch.
Signed, W. Har.
Reprinted in Sir Egerton Brydges' Restituta (1815), *vol. iii. pp.* 297–299, *also in Allusion-Books, I, New Sh. Soc., p.* 177.

This *Epicedium* is of uncertain authorship. Sir Egerton Brydges assigns it to Sir William Harbert (*Restituta*, vol. iii. p. 298). The lines—

"You that have writ of chaste Lucretia,
Whose death was witness of her spotlesse life :"

seem to refer to Shakespeare's poem. The line—

"Hither unto your home direct your eies"

recals two lines (163, 164) in *Lycidas ;* where, by the way, Milton implicitly compares Lycidas with Melicert (Palæmon), invoking the dolphins to waft his body into port.

*MICHAEL DRAYTON, 1594.

Lucrece, of whom proude Rome hath boafted long
Lately reviv'd to live another age,
And here ariv'd to tell of *Tarquins* wrong,
Her chaft deniall, and the Tyrants rage,
Acting her paffions on our ftately ftage.
  She is remembred, all forgetting me,
  Yet I, as fayre and chaft as ere was She.

*The Legend of Mathilda the chast, daughter to the
Lord Robert Fitzwater.* 1594. *Sixth Stanza.*
(*See Allusion-Books, I, New Sh. Soc., pp. xxxi,* 178.)

Shakespeare's *Rape of Lucrece* was published in the same year as Drayton's *Matilda* (the above passage is found in the editions of both 1594 and 1596). Heywood's drama of the same name did not appear till 1608. The fifth line seems to imply a dramatic representation : and, in confirmation of this view, we find almost the same words in Drayton's *Mistress Shore to Edward IV.* (England's Heroical Epistles, 1598, p. 73) :

" Or passionate Tragedian, in his rage
Acting a love-sicke passion on the stage."

[But this very line, taken literally, appears to offer strong proof that Drayton did not here refer to Shakespeare's Poem of *Lucrece*. L. T. S.]

ROBERT SOUTHWELL, 1594(?).[1]

This makes my mourning Mufe refolve in teares,
This theames my heavie penne to plaine in profe;
Chrift's thorne is fharpe, no head His garland weares;
Stil fineft wits are 'ftilling Venus' rofe,
In Paynim toyes the fweeteft vaines are fpent;
To Chriftian workes few have their talents lent.

*   *   *   *   *

O facred eyes! the fprings of living light,
  The earthly heavens where angels ioy to dwell,

*   *   *   *   *

Sweet volumes, ftoard with learning fit for faints,
  Where blifffull quires imparadize their minds;
Wherein eternall ftudie never faints
  Still finding all, yet feeking all it finds:
How endleffe is your labyrinth of bliffe,
Where to be loft the fweeteft finding is!

Saint Peters Complaint, with other Poemes. The Authour to the Reader, 1595. [4to.] (*Grosart's Ed.*, 1872, *pp.* xii, xc, 9, 25.)

---

[1] Southwell was executed Feb. 20, 1594/5.

[The allusion in the first of these stanzas is to *Venus and Adonis;* the two next contain, as pointed out by Dr. Grosart, the application to the spiritual eyes of Christ of the idea contained in the humorous thesis on women's eyes maintained by Biron in *Love's Labours Lost*, Act IV. sc. iii. L. T. S.]

W[ILLIAM] C[LARKE], 1595.

<small>All praise worthy.
Lucrecia
Sweet Shakspeare.
Eloquent Gaveston.
Wanton Adonis.
Watsons heyre.
So well graced Anthonie deserveth immortall praise from the hand of that divine Lady who like Corinna contending with Pindarus was oft victorious.</small>

Let divine *Bartaſſe*, eternally praiſe-worthie for his weeks worke, ſay the beſt thinges were made firſt: Let other countries (ſweet *Cambridge*) envie, (yet admire) my *Virgil*, thy petrarch, divine *Spenſer*. And unleſſe I erre, (a thing eaſie in ſuch ſimplicitie) deluded by dearlie beloved *Delia*, and fortunatelie fortunate *Cleopatra*; *Oxford* thou maiſt extoll thy courte-deare-verſe happie *Daniell*, whoſe ſweete refined muſe, in contracted ſhape, were ſufficient amongſt men, to gaiue pardon of the ſinne to *Roſemond*, pittie to diſtreſſed *Cleopatra*, and everliving praiſe to her loving *Delia*:

> *Polimanteia, or the meanes lawfull and unlawfull to judge of the fall of a commonwealth, against the frivolous and foolish conjectures of this age, etc.* 1595. *sign. R* 2, *bk.* [4*to.*]
> (*See Allusion-Books, I, New Sh. Soc., pp. xxxii,* 180.)

On the title-page of the Grenville copy of *Polimanteia*, 1595, is a pencil note, in the well-known handwriting of Mr. J. P. Collier, which runs thus: "Q if the notice of Shakespeare in this book be not the oldest known." This query must have been long ago answered in the negative by the querist himself. Mr. C. Elliot Browne, in a note on the side-note (*Notes and Queries*, 4th S. xi. 378), falls into the same error. Shakespeare's *name* occurs in a work printed in 1594. (See before, p. 6.) The construction of the side-note is not (as Mr. Halliwell read it in his *Life of Shakespeare:* 1848: p. 159) that "all praise worthy Lucretia [of] sweet Shakespeare," but that "All-praiseworthy [is the] Lucretia [of] sweet Shakespeare." In fact the epithet is used just above of Du Bartas; and Spenser applies it to nine of his heroines in *Colin Clout's come home again.* Mr. C. E. Browne would also identify "Watson's heyre" with "Sweet Shakespeare," and give him "Wanton Adonis," as well as "Lucretia." Others contend that the "heyre" was Henry Constable. Probably, it was on the strength of this side-note that the late Rev. N. J. Halpin arrived at the rather hazardous conclusion that Shakespeare was a member of "one (or perhaps more) of the English Universities." See his *Dramatic Unities of Shakespeare*, 1849, p. 12, *note.*
[The "Cleopatra" here mentioned is Daniel's, published in 1594; he addressed his prefatory verses to the Countess of Pembroke, to whom W. C. refers in the margin. L. T. S.]

JOHN WEEVER, 1595.

Ad Gulielmum Shakespeare.

Honie-tong'd *Shakespeare*, when I faw thine iffue,
I fwore *Apollo* got them and none other,
Their rofie-tainted features cloth'd in tiffue,
Some heaven born goddeffe faid to be their mother ·
Rofe-checkt *Adonis* with his amber treffes, [cheeked]
Faire fire-hot *Venus* charming him to love her,
Chafte *Lucretia* virgine-like her dreffes,
Prowd luft-ftung *Tarquine* feeking ftill to prove her :
Romea-*Richard;* more, whofe names I know not, [Romeo.]
Their fugred tongues, and power attractive beuty
Say they are Saints, althogh that Sts they fhew not
For thoufands vowes to them fubjective dutie :
They burn in love thy childrē *Shakefpear* het thē,[heated]
Go, wo thy Mufe more Nymphifh brood beget them.

Epigrammes in the oldest cut, and newest fashion. A twise seven houres (in so many weekes) studie. No longer (like the fashion) not unlike to continue. The first seven. John Weever. 1599. [12mo.] *The 4th week : Epig.* 22, *sign. E* 6.
(*See Allusion-Books, I, New Sh. Soc., p.* 182.)

[From Malone's copy in the Bodleian.]

The children of Shakespere's muse *het* or heated themselves with love; so Chapman says of Hero, that

"Her blushing het her chamber."

Hero and Leander, Third Sestyad (Chapman's *Works*, 1875, volume of Poems, p. 73, col. 2)

THOMAS EDWARDES, 1595.

Poets that divinely dreampt
  * * *

Collyn was a mighty fwaine,
In his power all do flourish,
We are fhepheards but in vaine
  There is but one tooke the charge,
By his toile we do nourifh,
  And by him are inlarg'd.

He unlockt *Albions* glorie,
He twas tolde of *Sidneys* honor,
Onely he of our ftories,
  Must be fung in greateft pride
In an Eglogue he hath wonne her,
  Fame and honor on his fide.

Deale we not with *Rofamond*,
For the world our fawe will coate,
Amintas and *Leander's* gone,
  Oh deere fonnes of ftately kings,
Bleffed be your nimble throats
  That fo amoroufly could fing.

Adon deafly mafking thro,
Stately troupes rich conceited,
Shew'd he well deferved to
  Loves delight on him to gaze
And had not love her felfe intreated,
  Other nymphs had fent him baies.

> Eke in purple roabes diftaind,
> Amid'ft the Center of this clime,
> I have heard faie doth remaine,
>   One whofe power floweth far,
> That fhould have bene of our rime
>   The onely object and the ftar.
>
> Well could his bewitching pen,
> Done the Mufes objects to us
> Although he differs much from men
>   Tilting under Frieries,
> Yet his golden art might woo us
>   To have honored him with baies.

L'Envoy to *Cephalus and Procris*. 1595. Unique copy in Peterborough Cathedral Library. Reprinted for the Roxburghe Club by Rev. W. E. Buckley, 1878, pp. 61, 62.

[Edwardes here speaks of the poets under the names of their best known works at that day. The mighty swaine *Collyn* is Spenser, he who sang of *Colin Clout*, and glorified Albion in the *Faerie Queen*, and gave an Elegy to Sidney. Samuel Daniel wrote the poem of *Rosamond;* Thomas Watson published his Latin poem of *Amintas* in 1585; and the *Hero & Leander* of Kit Marlowe was entered on the Stationers' register, 28 Sept. 1593, a few months after he died. (It came out, completed by Chapman, in 1598. See *Works of George Chapman: Poems, &c.*, with Introduction by A. C. Swinburne, 1875, p. 58.)

The verse devoted to *Adon* is another of the early tributes that are found to the great popularity Shakespere's *Venus and Adonis* attained at once. It reached seven editions between 1593 (the date of first publication) and 1602, two of which belong to the latter year. (See Mr. C. Edmonds' reprint from the Isham copy of 1599, Editor's Preface.)

The two stanzas referring to "one whose power floweth far" I insert, but he has not been identified. L. T. S.]

Anonymous, 1596.

Sophos. See how the twinkling Starres do hide their borrowed
    ſhine
As halfe aſham'd their luſter ſo is ſtain'd,
By *Lelia's* beauteous eyes that ſhine more bright,
Than twinkling ſtarres do in a winters night:
In ſuch a night did *Paris* win his love.
  Lelia. In ſuch a night, *Æneas* prov'd unkind.
  Sophos. In ſuch a night did *Troilus* court his deare.
  Lelia. In ſuch a night, faire *Phyllis* was betraid.
  Sophos. Ile prove as true as ever *Troylus* was.
  Lelia. And I as conſtant as *Penelope.*

      Wily Beguilde, 1606, *sign. I, back.*
    (*In the Bodleian, Malone,* 226. *Part of the leaf torn off.*)

[The unknown author of this play seems to imitate Shakespere's *Romeo and Juliet* and *Merchant of Venice* in several places. This dialogue would surely never have been written but for the moonlight rhapsodizing of Lorenzo and Jessica, *Merch. of Venice*, Act V. sc. i. The *Merchant of Venice* was probably written in 1596 (see Dowden's *Shakspere Primer*, p. 96). The first edition of *Wily Begvilde* came out in 1606, but Mr. Furnivall states that there is no doubt, on account of the allusions in it to the taking of Cadiz, that it was on the stage in or soon after 1596; though he has shown that there is no real ground for the old theory that Nash referred to it in his *Have with you to Saffron Walden* (printed 1596; sign. 24, back), where he makes *Respondent* say of Anthonie Chute—"But this was our *Graphiel Hagiels* tricke of *Wily Beguily* herein" (see *Notes & Queries*, vol. iv. 1875, p. 144; vol. v. p. 74. *Wily beguily* was a current phrase, meaning the wily man beguiled, or, as we should say, the biter bit. L. T. S.]

RICHARD CAREW, 1595-6.

Adde hereunto, that whatſoever grace any other language carrieth in verſe or Proſe, in Tropes or Metaphors, in Ecchoes and Agnominations, they may all bee lively and exactly repreſented in ours: will you have *Platoes* veine? reade Sir *Thomas Smith*, the *Ionicke?* Sir *Thomas Moore*. Ciceroes? *Aſcham, Varro? Chaucer, Demoſthenes?* Sir *John Cheeke* (who in his treatiſe to the Rebels, hath compriſed all the figures of Rhetorick. Will you reade *Virgill?* take the Earle of Surrey. *Catullus? Shakeſpheare* and *Marlows*[1] fragment, *Ovid? Daniell. Lucan? Spencer, Martial?* Sir *John Davies* and others: will you have all in all for Proſe and verſe? take the miracle of our age, Sir *Philip Sidney*.

The Excellencie of the English tongue, by R. C. of Anthony Esquire to W.C. Inserted by W. Camden in the second edition of his Remaines concerning Britaine, 1614, p. 43. [4to.]

(*See Allusion-Books, I, New Sh. Soc. p.* 183.)

---

[1] Printed *Barlows* in original, but unquestionably a mistake for *Marlows*.

FRANCIS MERES, 1598.

As the Greeke tongue is made famous and eloquent by *Homer, Hefiod, Euripedes, Aefchilus, Sophocles, Pindarus, Phocylides* and *Ariftophanes*; and the Latine tongue by *Virgill, Ovid, Horace, Silius Italicus, Lucanus, Lucretius, Aufonius* and *Claudianus*: fo the Englifh tongue is mightily enriched, and gorgeouflie invefted in rare ornaments and refplendent abiliments by fir *Philip Sidney, Spencer, Daniel, Drayton, Warner, Shakefpeare, Marlow* and *Chapman.*

* * * * *

As the foule of *Euphorbus* was thought to live in *Pythagoras*: fo the fweete wittie foule of *Ovid* lives in mellifluous & honytongued *Shakefpeare*, witnes his *Venus* and *Adonis*, his *Lucrece*, his fugred Sonnets among his private friends, &c.

As *Plautus* and *Seneca* are accounted the beft for Comedy and Tragedy among the Latines? fo *Shakefpeare* among ye Englifh is the moft excellent in both kinds for the ftage; for Comedy, witnes his *Gētlemē of Verona*, his *Errors*, his *Love labors loft*, his *Love labours wonne*, his *Midfummers night dreame*, & his *Merchant of Venice*: for Tragedy his *Richard the 2. Richard the 3. Henry the 4. King Iohn, Titus Andronicus* and his *Romeo* and *Iuliet*.

As *Epius Stolo* faid, that the Mufes would fpeake with *Plautus* tongue, if they would fpeak Latin: fo I fay that the Mufes would fpeak with *Shakefpeares* fine filed phrafe, if they would fpeake Englifh.

* * * * * *

As *Ovid* faith of his worke;

Iamque *opus exegi, quod nec Iovis ira, nec ignis,*
Nec poterit ferrum, nec edax abolere vetustas.

And as *Horace* faith of his; *Exegi monumentum ære perennius;
Regalique ; situ pyramidum altius ; Quod non imber edax ; Non
Aquilo impotens possit diruere ; aut innumerabilis annorum series
&c fuga temporum:* so say I severally of sir *Philip Sidneys,
Spencers, Daniels, Draytons, Shakespeares,* and *Warners workes;*

* * * * *

As *Pindarus, Anacreon* and *Callimachus* among the Greekes;
and *Horace* and *Catullus* among the Latines are the best Lyrick
Poets: so in this faculty the best among our Poets are *Spencer*
(who excelleth in all kinds) *Daniel, Drayton, Shakespeare, Bretton.*

As . . . . so these are our best for Tragedie, the Lorde
Buckhurst, Doctor *Leg* of Cambridge, Doctor *Edes* of Oxforde,
maister *Edward Ferris*,[1] the Authour of the *Mirrour for
Magistrates, Marlow, Peele, Watson, Kid, Shakespeare, Drayton,
Chapman, Decker,* and *Benjamin Johnson.*

* * * * *

... so the best for Comedy amongst us bee, *Edward* Earle of
Oxforde, Doctor *Gager* of Oxforde, Maister *Rowley* once a rare

---

[1] [It was George Ferrers who wrote six of the historical poems in the *Mirrour for Magistrates,* four of which appeared in the first edition of 1559 ; two more came out in the edition of 1587 ; three of these bore the title of Tragedy, though none of them were plays. It is singular (see Wood's *Athen. Oxon.,* i, 340, 445) that Puttenham, writing in 1589, and Meres in 1598, both appear to have made the same mistake, of naming Edward Ferris (or Ferrers) for George Ferrers. Puttenham says (*Arte of English Poesie,* 1589 (4to.), p. 49 ; Arber's Reprint, p. 74) that " Maister *Edward Ferrys*" "wrate for the most part to the stage, in Tragedie and some-times in Comedie or Enterlude, wherein he gave the king [Edward VI] so much good recreation, as he had thereby many good rewardes." None of the plays of either George Ferrers or Edward Ferrers appear, however, to be now in existence. Edward Ferrers died in 1564, George in 1579. Meres may have intended to mention them both in the sentence given above. G. Ferrer's name was not on the title of the *Mirrour* in the edition of 1587, and his initials only were attached to his portions of the work. But that Puttenham really meant George, and not Edward, seems to be shown by the words of Stowe, who says, " George Ferrers gentleman of Lincolns Inne, being lord of the merry disportes all the 12 dayes [of Christmas, 1553, at Greenwich]: who so pleasantly and wisely behaved himselfe, y^t the K. had great delight in his pastvmes." *Chronicle,* ed. 1615, p. 608. L. T. S.]

Scholler of learned Pembrooke Hall in Cambridge, Maifter
Edwardes one of her Maiefties Chappell, eloquent and wittie
*John Lilly, Lodge, Gafcoyne, Greene, Shakefpeare, Thomas Nafh,
Thomas Heywood, Anthony Mundye* our beft plotter, *Chapman,
Porter, Wilfon, Hathway,* and *Henry Chettle.*

* * * * * *

. . . fo thefe are the moft paffionate among us to bewaile and
bemoane the perplexities of Love, *Henrie Howard* Earle of Surrey,
fir*Thomas Wyat* the elder, fir *Francis Brian,* fir *Philip Sidney,* fir
Walter Rawley, fir *Edward Dyer, Spencer, Daniel, Drayton,
Shakefpeare, Whetftone, Gafcoyne, Samuell Page* fometimes
fellowe of *Corpus Chrifti* Colledge in Oxford, *Churchyard,
Bretton.*

> *Palladis Tamia. Wits Treasury, Being the Second part of Wits
> Common wealth.* 1598. [12mo.] *Fols:* 280, 281-2, 282, 283, 284.
> (*Reprinted in Allusion-Books, I, New Sh. Soc. pp. xxiii,* 151.)

Of these extracts from Meres' *Palladis Tamia,* the second has been
repeated *ad nauseam,* while the other five have been usually ignored. One
matter of interest in the second extract is the mention of a play by
Shakespeare under the name of *Love Labours Wonne.* If this be a superseded
or an alternative name for one of those included in our "canon," it is
important to identify it, as affording some addition to the scanty evidences
on which we have to determine the chronological order of the plays. Farmer
identified *Love Labours Wonne* with *All's well that ends well;* and his dictum
has been acquiesced in by many critics. The Rev. Joseph Hunter gave
the preference to *The Tempest,* which, for his purpose, had to be antedated
some ten or a dozen years; and Mr. A. E. Brae, in his *Collier, Coleridge
and Shakespeare,* advocates the claims of *Much ado about Nothing.* But as
that play was entered on the Stationers' Books on August 23, 1600, Meres
could hardly have referred to it. Professor Craik argued in favour of *The
Taming of the Shrew* (*English of Shakespere,* 1865, Proleg. II. p. 8, note).
The German critics Emil Palleski, E. W. Sievers, and W. Hertzberg, also
take this view. (See Tieck and Schlegel's translation of Shakespere,
published by the *Deutsche Shakespere Gesellschaft,* 1871, vol. ii. p. 355.)

The language of the first extract from Meres, which was quoted by Singer
(Pref. to *Hero and Leander,* 1821, pp. xiii, xiv), recalls two lines in Ben
Jonson's magnificent eulogy of Poetry in the first edition of *Every Man in
his Humour:*

> "But view her in her glorious ornaments,
> Attired in the majestie of arte," &c.

FRANCIS MERES, 1598.

*Michael Drayton (*quem toties honoris & amoris cauſa nomino*)* among ſchollers, ſouldiours, Poets, and all ſorts of people, is helde for a man of vertuous diſpoſition, honeſt converſation, and wel governed cariage, which is almoſt miraculous among good wits in theſe declining and corrupt times, when there is nothing but rogery in villanous man, & when cheating and craftines is counted the cleaneſt wit, and foundeſt wiſedome.

Palladis Tamia. Wits Treaſury, Being the Second part of Wits Commonwealth. 1598, *fol.* 281. [12*mo.*]

We have here an expression quoted from the *First Part of Henry IV*, Act II. sc. iv, where Falstaff says :
"You Rogue, heere's Lime in this Sacke too : there is nothing but Roguery to be found in Villanous man."
The *First Part of Henry IV* was entered on the Stationers' Register, Feb. 25, 1597-98.

R[OBERT] T[OFTE], 1598.

Loves Labour Loſt, I once did ſee a Play
Y-cleped ſo, ſo called to my paine.
Which I to heare to my ſmall Ioy did ſtay,
Giving attendance on my froward Dame :
　My miſgiving minde preſaging to me ill,
　Yet was I drawne to ſee it 'gainſt my will.
　　*　　　*　　　*　　　*
Each Actor plaid in cunning wiſe his part,
But chiefly Thoſe entrapt in Cupid's ſnare ;
Yet All was fained, 'twas not from the hart,
They ſeemde to grieve, but yet they felt no care :
　'Twas I that Griefe (indeed) did beare in breſt,
　The others did but make a ſhow in Ieſt.

The Months Minde of a Melancholy Lover, divided into three parts. By R. T. gentleman. 1598. [8º.] *sign. G 5. In the library of Mr. Henry Huth.*

(*See Allusion-Books, I, New Sh. Soc. p.* 184.)

As to the date of *Love's Labours Lost*, see after, p. 62 ; it was first printed in 1598.

RICHARD BARNFEILD, 1598.

A Remembrance of some Englifh Poets.

Live *Spenfer* ever, in thy *Fairy Queene*:
Whofe like (for deepe Conceit) was never feene.
Crownd mayft thou bee, unto thy more renowne,
(As King of Poets) with a Lawrell Crowne.

And *Daniell*, praifed for thy fweet-chaft Verfe:
Whofe Fame is grav'd on *Rofamonds* blacke Herfe.
Still mayft thou live: and ftill be honored,
For that rare Worke, *The White Rofe and the Red*.

And *Drayton*, whofe wel-written Tragedies,
And fweete Epiftles, foare thy fame to fkies.
Thy learned Name, is æquall with the reft;
Whofe ftately Numbers are fo well addreft.

And *Shakefpeare* thou, whofe hony-flowing Vaine,
(Pleafing the World) thy Praifes doth obtaine.
Whofe *Venus*, and whofe *Lucrece* (fweete, and chafte)
Thy Name in fames immortall Booke have plac't.
    Live ever you, at leaft in Fame live ever:
    Well may the Bodye dye, but Fame dies never.

Poems in Divers humors.[1] 1598. [4*to.*]   *Sign*. E 2, *back*.

---

[1] [This tract is fourth in a volume of which the first tract only bears Barnfeild's name: signatures begin afresh with the second tract, they do not run on throughout (my error in *Sh. Allusion-Books*, I, New Sh. Soc. p. 186). L. T S.]

JOHN MARSTON, 1598.

A hall, a hall,
Roome for the Spheres, the Orbes celeſtiall
Will daunce *Kemps Iigge*. They'le revel with neate iumps
A worthy Poet hath put on their Pumps.

  * * * *

Luſcus, what's playd to day? faith now I know
I ſet thy lips abroach, from whence doth flow
Naught but pure *Iuliat* and *Romio*.
Say, who acts beſt? *Druſus* or *Roſcio* ?
Now I have him, that nere of ought did ſpeake
But when of playes or Plaiers he did treate.
H'ath made a common-place booke out of plaies,
And ſpeakes in print : at leaſt what ere he ſayes
Is warranted by Curtaine plaudeties.
If ere you heard him courting *Leſbias* eyes ;
Say (Curteous ſir), ſpeakes he not movingly,
From out ſome new pathetique Tragedy ?
He writes, he railes, he ieſts, he courts what not,
And all from out his huge long ſcraped ſtock
Of well-penn'd playes.

   The Scourge of Villanie. 1598. *Satyre* 10. (*Humours.*)
   Sign. *H* 3, *back.* 16mo.
  [Malone's copy in the Bodleian.]

  (*See Allusion-Books, I, New Sh. Soc. pp. xxxi·, 187.*)

[*Romeo and Juliet* was first printed in 1597, but was probably performed a year sooner. (See Dowden's *Shakespere Primer*, p. 83.)
The first lines above contain a common phrase of the day, "A hall! a hall!

give room!" See *Rom. and Juliet*, Act I. sc. v : "A hall! a hall! give room and foot it, girls." So also Davies of Hereford has, "A hall, my masters, give Rotundus roome" (*Scourge of Folly*, Epig. 10, ed. Grosart, Chertsey Worthies Library, pp. 9, 66). L. T. S.]

"Kemp's jigge" was one of those diversions, of combined singing and dancing, of which several were written and performed by him and Tarlton. (See Dyce's Introduction to Kemp's *Nine days wonder*, p. xx, and Collier's *Memoirs of Actors*, Shakespeare Society, 1846, pp. 100—102.) The "worthy poet" was Sir John Davies, the author of *Orchestra or a Poeme of Dauncing*, 1596.

"Roscio" was a *sobriquet* of Burbage, which convinces Mr. Gerald Massey that John Davies' epigram, entitled *Of Drusus his deere Deere-hunting* (No. 50 in *The Scourge of Folly*), was meant to allude to Shakespeare's *escapade* at Charlecote or Fulbroke. To help his case, however, Mr. Massey has to omit the epigram and to alter its title. (*The Secret Drama of Shakespeare's Sonnets unfolded*, 1872: Supplemental Chapter, p. 40.) Besides, Davies does not apply Roscius solely to Burbage; he has "To the Roscius of these times, Mr. W. Ostler," in *The Scourge of Folly*, Epigram 205.

JOHN MARSTON, 1598.

A man, a man, a kingdome for a man,!
Why, how now, curriſh, mad *Athenian*?
Thou Cynick dogge, ſee'ſt not ſtreets do ſwarme
With troupes of men?

The Scourge of Villanie. 1598. *Satyre* 7. (*A Cyniche Satyre.*)

Reprinted by Mr. J. O. Halliwell in Marston's Works, Library of Old Authors, 1856, *vol. iii, p.* 278.

(*See Allusion-Books, I, New Sh. Soc. p.* 188.)

The first line is a parody on the well-known line in Shakespeare's *King Richard III*, literally quoted by Marston in his *What you Will*, 1607, Act II, sc. i. (See after, p. 77.) The speech had probably attracted popular attention, and seems to have already become a fashionable cant phrase. (See also Brathwaite, 1615, after.) Marston also parodies the same line in his *Parasitaster, or the Fawne,* 1606:

"A foole, a foole, a foole, my Coxcombe for a foole!" (*Sign. H* 3, *bk*),

where, too, we find another line taken almost literally from *Richard III*, Act I, sc. i:

" Plots ha' you laid? inductions, daungerous." (*Sign. C* 3, *bk.*)

[In this same *Cyniche Satyre* Marston repeats the part phrase "a man, a man!" three times, but it is as a forcible sneer, to open a new phase of his subject, it is not used in the sense of Shakespere's call.

Richard III was first published in quarto in 1597, but was probably written as early as 1593. (See Dowden's *Shakespere Primer*, p. 78.) L. T. S.]

GABRIEL HARVEY 1598 or after 1600?[1]

The younger fort take much delight in Shakefpeare's Venus and Adonis; but his Lucrece, and his tragedy of Hamlet, Prince of Denmarke, have it in them to pleafe the wifer fort. 1598.

Manuscript Note in Speght's Chaucer [now lost; see Allusion-Books, I, New Sh. Soc. pp. xxii, xxiii]. First printed in Johnson and Steevens' Shakspeare, 1773. (Reed, xviii, 2; Boswell's Malone, vii, 168 · Drake, ii, 391, &c.)

---

[1] We are unable to verify Steevens' note, or collate his copy: for the book which contained Harvey's note (a copy of Speght's *Chaucer*, 1598) passed into the collection of Bishop Percy; and his library was burnt in the fire at Northumberland House. [Malone, who saw the volume, doubted whether the note was written by Harvey before 1600 (Boswell's *Malone*, ii. 369). He does not, however, say whether the date, 1598, is really written at the end of the note and in Harvey's hand. L. T. S.] The editors of the Clarendon Press edition of *Hamlet* (Preface, p. ix) remark: "Steevens attributed to the note the date of the book; but Malone has shown that, although Harvey may have purchased the volume in 1598, there is nothing to prove that he wrote the note till after 1600, in which year Fairfax's translation of Tasso, mentioned in another note, was published."

The First Quarto of *Hamlet* was printed in 1603.

BEN JONSON, 1599.

Saviolina. What's he, gentle Mounfieur *Briske?* not that Gentleman?
Fastidius. No Ladie, this is a Kinsman of Iustice *Silence.*
(Act V. sc. ii.)

* * * *

Marie, I will not do as *Plautus* in his *Amphitryo* for all this, (*Summi Iovis caufa Plaudite;*) begge a *Plaudite* for Gods fake; but if you (out of the bountie of your good-liking) will beftow it, why, you may (in time) make leane *Macilente* as fat as *Sir John Fall-ftaffe.*

(Second " Catastrophe or Conclusion " to the play, sign. Q 4, back.)

Every Man out of his Humor. 1600. [4to]

["This Comicall Satyre was first acted in the yeere 1599."—*Jonson's Works*, 1616, vol. i. p. 176.

The speech of Mitis in the same play, Act III, sc. ii, suggesting that the argument of the comedy might have been based on cross-wooings, has been supposed to be a hit at *Twelfth Night*. But that play is not placed earlier than 1600, as its probable date.

The *First* and *Second* Parts of *Henry IV*, in which Justices Silence and Shallow appear, were probably both written before Feb. 25, 1597-98, when the *First Part* was entered on the Stationers' Register. L. T. S.]

*JOHN LANE, 1600.

When chaſt *Adonis* came to mans eſtate,
Venus ſtraight courted him with many a wile;
Lucrece once ſeene, ſtraight *Tarquine* laid a baite,
With foule inceſt her bodie to defile :
   Thus men by women, women wrongde by men,
   Give matter ſtill vnto my plaintife pen.

Tom Tel-Troths Message, and his pens Complaint. 1600, *p.* 43.
(*Reprinted by the New Shakspere Society*, 1876, *p.* 132.)

SAMUEL NICHOLSON, 1600.

Parallel Passages.

Acolastus.	*Shakespere.*
Or wher's the soules Atturney, when the hart.	the heart's attorney. (*Ven. and Ad.* l. 335.)
Being once corrupted, takes the worser part? (p. 12, l. 185.)	But with a pure appeal seeks to the heart Which once corrupted takes the worser part (*Lucrece*, l. 293).
O woolvish heart wrapt in a womans hyde (p. 16, l. 265).	O tigers heart wrapt in a woman's hide (3 *Henry VI*, I. iv).
Thus all askaunce thou holdst me in thine eye (l. 300).	For all askaunce he holds her in his eye (*Ven. and Ad.* l. 342).
Hence idle words, servants to shallow braines, Unfruitfull sounds, wind-wasting arbitrators,	Out idle words, servants to shallow fools, Unprofitable sounds, weak arbitrators! Busy yourselves in skill-contending schools:
Your endles prattle lessens not my paines His suite is cold, that makes you mediators (l. 559).	Debate where leisure serves with dull debaters: To trembling clients be you mediators (*Lucrece*, l. 1016).
Witnes faire heauens she, she, 'tis onely she, That guides this hand to give this wound to me (l. 647).	She utters this: 'He, he, fair lords, 'tis he, That guides this hand to give this wound to me (*Lucrece*, l. 1721).
A prettie while this prettie creature stoode Before the engin of her thoughts began (l. 853).	A pretty while these pretty creatures stand (*Lucrece*, l. 1233). Once more the engine of her thoughts began (*Ven. and Ad.* l. 367).

CENTURIE.

Acolastus.	Shakespere.
Heart-slaine with lookes, I fell upon the ground,	Or like the deadly bullet of a gun,
Her meening strooke me ere her words were done,	His meaning struck her ere his words begun,
As weapons meet before they make a sound,	And at his look she flatly falleth down,
Or as the deadly bullet of a gunne (p. 62, l. 1369).	For looks kill love and love by looks reviveth (*Ven. and Ad.* l. 461).
And pining griefe still thinkes it treble wrong	For lovers say, the heart hath treble wrong
When heart is barr'd the aydance of the tongue (l. 1433).	When it is barr'd the aidance of the tongue (*Ven. and Ad.* l. 329).

Acolastus his after-witte. By *S. N.* 1600. Reprinted by Rev. A. B. Grosart, 1876. *Introduction, pp. xiv—xxi.*

[The quotations here given are but a few out of many passages in Nicholson's *Acolastus*, in which the author has, like Robert Baron fifty years later, woven into his own verse quotations and recollections from Shakespere's Poems. Dr. Grosart and Dr. B. Nicholson, setting aside the accusation of literary theft and impudence in this striking use by the lesser poets of the ringing words of the greater, explain that "precedents of high excellence were much more looked to in those days, and copyings and imitations were not merely more common but allowed, especially when the sources were in all hands, and so 'plagiarism' out of the question. . . . Those familiar with Nicholas Breton and Samuel Daniel find frequently and silently introduced into their own poems [*i. e.* the poems of those authors] well-known sonnets and lines of others." Introd. p. xxi. L. T. S.]

THE ESSEX REBELLION, 1600:
EXAMINATIONS.

Sir Gelly Meyricke 17th Feb. 1600.

The Examination of Sr Gelly merick Knyght taken the xvijth of Februarij, 1600. He fayeth that vpon Saterday laft was fennyght he dyned at Gunter's in the Company of the L. monteegle, Sr Chriftoffer Blont, Sr Charles percye, Ellys Jones, and Edward Buffhell, and who elfe he remembreth not and after dynner that day & at the mocyon of Sr Charles percy and the reft they went all together to the Globe over the water wher the L. Chamberlens men vfe to play and were ther fomwhat before the play began, Sr Charles tellyng them that the play wold be of harry the iiijth. Whether Sr John davyes[1] were ther or not thys examinate can not tell, but he fayd he wold be ther yf he cold. he can not tell who procured that play to be played at that tyme except yt were Sr Charles percye, but as he thyncketh yt was Sr Charles percye. Thenne he was at the fame play and Cam in fomwhat after yt was begon, and the play was of Kyng Harry the iiijth, and of the kyllyng of Kvng Richard the fecond played by the L. Chamberlen's players

Ex. per   Gelly Meyricke
J. Popham
Edward Fenner

MS in the Public Record Office. Domestic State Papers, Elizabeth, Vol. 278, No. 78. (Mrs. Green's Calendar, 1598-1601, p. 575.)

---

[1] Misread Danvers in the Calendar.

Auguftine Phillipps 18 *Feb.*, 1600.

The Examination of auguftyne phillypps fervant vnto the L Chamberlyne and one of hys players taken the xviijth of Februarij 1600 vpon hys oth

He fayeth that on Fryday laft was fennyght or Thurfday Sr Charles percy Sr Jofclyne percy and the L. montegle with fome thre more fpak to fome of the players in the prefans of thys examinate to have the play of the depofyng and kyllyng of Kyng Rychard the fecond to be played the Saterday next promyfyng to gete them xls. more then their ordynary to play yt. Wher thys Examinate and hys fellowes were determyned to have played fome other play, holdyng that play of Kyng Richard to be fo old & fo long out of vfe as that they fhold have fmall or no Company at yt. But at their requeft this Examinate and his fellowes were Content to play yt the Saterday and had their xls. more then their ordynary for yt and fo played yt accordyngly

 Ex. per   Auguftine Phillipps
J. Popham
Edward Fenner

     MS. in the Public Record Office. Domestic State Papers, Elizabeth, Vol. 278, *No.* 85. (*See Mrs. Green's Calendar*, 1598-1601, *p.* 578.)

[The above examinations were thus summed up in the Report of The Trial printed from Le Neve's MS. :—

"And the story of *Henry IV* being set forth in a play, and in that play there being set forth the killing of the King upon a stage; the *Friday* before Sir *Gilly Merrick* and some others of the Earl's train having an humour to see a play, they must needs have the play of *Henry IV*.

"The players told them that was stale, they should get nothing by playing of that, but no play else would serve; and Sir *Gilly Merrick* gives forty shillings to *Philips* the player to play this, besides what soever he could get." (The Trial of Sir Christopher Blunt, Sir Gilly Merrick and others, for High Treason, 5 March, 1600. F. Hargrave's *State Trials*, 1778, vol. vii. column 60.) I have not succeeded in tracing Le Neve's MS., it does not appear to be in the British Museum, and Mr. J. Nicholson, the courteous Librarian of Lincoln's Inn, informs me that it is not in the Library under his charge (to which Hargrave's MSS. and books were originally assigned). But the examinations of Merrick and Phillipps show that what seemed to be the error of *Henry IV* instead of *Richard II*, as the name of the play, is so in the original. The account given of this trial in Camden's Annals (ed. Hearne, 1717, p. 867) has it as follows,—"exoletam Tragœdiam de tragica abdicatione Regis Ricardi secundi in publico theatro coram conjurationis participibus data pecunia agi curasset."

Richard II was published in Quarto in 1597 and 1598, the Deposition scene (ll. 154—318 of Act IV. sc. i) was not printed till 1608, though, from the allusions in the lines before and after the omission, which are in the Quarto of 1597, it is clear that this scene must have been in the original play; it was probably struck out on account of its political significance. That there is room for doubt whether the play ordered by Sir Charles Percy was Shakespere's *Richard II*, or another on the same subject, is seen by Professor Dowden's comment, "that this was Shakespere's play is very unlikely" (*Sh. Primer*, 1877, p. 87).[1] But Mr. Hales (*Academy*, Nov. 20, 1875), endorsed by Mr. Furnivall (*Leopold Shakspere*, Introd. p. xxxvi), asks that "considering the facts that the company employed by the Essexians was that to which Shakespere belonged, and that the play asked for answers in description to Shakespere's *Richard II*, can we hesitate to believe that the play was indeed Shakespere's?" See App. D, *Lambard*. L. T. S.]

---

[1] See also Clark and Wright's *Richard II*, Clarendon Press Series, 1869, p. v,—"it is certain that this was not Shakespeare's play."

CHARLES PERCY, 1600?

Mr. Carlington:

I am heere fo peſtred with coutrie bufineſſe that I ſhall not bee able as yet to come to London : If I ſtay heere long in this faſhion, at my return I think you will find mee fo dull that I ſhall bee taken for Juſtice Silence or Juſtice Shallow, wherefore I am to entreat you that you will take pittie of mee, and as occurrences ſhall fearue, to fend mee fuch news from time to time as ſhall happen, the knowledge of the which, thoutgh perhaps thee will not exempt mee from the opinion of a iuſtice Shallow at London, yet I will aſſure you, thee will make mee paſſe for a very fufficient gentleman in Gloceſtrſhire. If I doe not alwaies make you anfwere, I pray you doe not therefore defiſt from your charitable office, the place being fo fruitfull from whence you write, and heere fo barren, that it will make my head ake for invention, but if anything happen heere that may bee unknown unto you in thofe parts, you ſhall not faile but to heare of it. I pray you direct your letters to thee three cups in breed-street, where I haven taken order for the fending of them down: And fo in the mean while I will ever remain

your aſſured friend
Charles Percy

Dumbleton in Gloceſtſhire
this 27 of December

You need not to forbeare fending of news hither in refpect of their ſtalenes, for I will aſſure you, heere they will be very new.

MS. Letter in Public Record Office, Domestic State Papers, Elizabeth, Vol. 275, No. 146.

[The late Mr. Richard Simpson left an unprinted note on this letter which I here give as it stands :

"As this letter was part of the papers seized upon the companions of Essex in his attempt upon London, the date of it may be any year before 1602.

" Sir Charles Percy, 3rd son of Henry 20th Earl of Northumberland, married one of the family of Cocks, and through her was lord of Dumbleton in Gloucestershire, near Campden, and not far from Stratford-on-Avon. He was with Essex in Ireland, and accompanied him in his fatal ride into the City in Feb. 1601. He was the man who bespoke the play of *Richard II.* at the Globe on Saturday, Feb. 7, 1601. He was evidently one of Shakespere's admirers, perhaps one of his friends. Through him the dramatist may have got some of the vivid stories about the Percies in 1 *Henry IV.* Possibly he may be ' chaffed ' in the passage where Falstaff asks what Master Dumbleton says to his satin, and is told that he wants better assurance than Bardolph." L. T. S.]

"ONE FRIEND TO ANOTHER," 1600—1610.

For I muſt tell you I never dealt so freelie with you, in anie ; and, (as that excellent author, Sr. *John Falſtaff* ſayes,) what for your buſineſſe, news, device, foolerie, and libertie, I never dealt better, ſince I was a man.

> *A Collection of Letters made by Sr. Tobie Matthews, Kt.* 1660, *p.* 100. "*One friend to another, who showes much trouble for the miscarriage of a letter.*"

Countess of Southampton to Earl of Southampton.

Al the nues I can ſend you that I thinke wil make you mery is that I reade in a letter from London that Sir John Falſtaf is by his Mrs. Dame Pintpot made father of a godly milers thum, a boye thats all heade and veri litel body ; but this is a ſecrit.

> *Postscript to a letter, without other date than "Chartly 8th July," printed in the Appendix to* 3*rd Report of the Historical MSS. Commission, p.* 148.

[I put these two extracts together, as they both show the wide-spread popularity of Falstaff, even to the familiar personation of him : the late Mr. Simpson believed that they refer to Shakespere himself under the name of Falstaff (*Academy*, Feb. 6, 1875). The names and circumstances of many of the writers of the letters in Matthews' collection point to the approximate date of the first extract. L. T. S.]

SIR WILLIAM CORNWALLIS, 1600.

" Malicious credulitie rather embraceth the partiall writings of indifcreet chroniclers, and witty Play-Makers, then his [Richard III's] lawes and actions, the moft innocent and impartiall witneffes.

＊　　＊　　＊　　＊　　＊

Yet neither can his blood redeem him [Richard III] from injurious tongues, nor the reproch offered his body be thought cruell enough, but that we muft ftil make him more cruelly infamous in Pamphlets and Plays.

Essayes of Certaine Paradoxes. 1617. *Second edition. The Prayse of King Richard the Third. Sign.* C 3 *and D* 3. [*In the Bodleian.*] *Reprinted in a Collection of Scarce and Valuable Tracts, by Lord Somers*, 2nd *ed.* 1810. *Vol.* 3, *pp.* 321, 328.

[Mr. Elliot Browne pointed out the first extract given above, in the *Athenæum*, 13 Nov. 1875. The title of this second impression of *Essayes of Certaine Paradoxes* does not contain the addition "in prose and verse" said to belong to the edition of 1600. It is quite a different work from Cornwallis' *Essayes*, which passed through several editions. I have not been able to find a copy of the edition of 1600, but give the date on the authority of *Lowndes' Bibliog. Manual*, Bohn's edition, vol. iv. p. 2312. L. T. S.]

JOHN WEEVER, 1601.

The many-headed multitude were drawne
By *Brutus* ſpeech, that *Cæſar* was ambitious,
When eloquent *Mark Antonie* had ſhowne
His vertues, who but *Brutus* then was vicious?
Mans memorie, with new, forgets the old,
One tale is good, untill anothers told.

The Mirror of Martyrs, or The life and death of Sir Iohn Oldcastle Knight, Lord Cobham, 1601. *Stanza* 4, *sign. A* 3, *back.*

[In *Plutarch's Lives,* on which Shakespere founded his *Julius Cæsar,* there is no speech by Brutus on Cæsar's ambition; and though in Appian's *Chronicle of the Roman Wars* (englished in 1578) speeches on the killing of Cæsar are put into Antony's mouth[1] (see extracts in *Transactions of the New Shakspere Society,* 1875-6, pp. 427—439), yet none fit the words above, which must allude to those in Shakespere's play. F. J. F.]

---

[1] [Anthony's oration in Appian's Chronicle was quoted at length by Charles Gildon in his *Remarks on the Plays of Shakespere,* appended to his edition of Shakespere's Works, 1714, vol. ix, p. 336. L. T. S.]

ROBERT CHESTER, 1601.

LOVES MARTYR :/ OR,/ ROSALINS COMPLAINT./ *Allegorically /hadowing the truth of Loue,/* in the conſtant Fate of the Phœnix/ *and Turtle./* A Poeme enterlaced with much varietie and raritie ;/ *now firſt tranſlated out of the venerable Italian* Torquato/ Cæliano, by ROBERT CHESTER./ With the true legend of famous King *Arthur,* the laſt of the nine/ Worthies, being the firſt *Eſſay* of a new *Brytiſh* Poet : collected/ out of diuerſe Authenticall Records./ *To theſe are added ſome new compoſitions, of ſeuerall moderne Writers/ whoſe names are ſubſcribed to their ſeuerall workes, vpon the/ firſt ſubieƈt : viz.* the Phœnix and/ Turtle./ *Mar :—Mutare dominum non poteſt liber notus./* LONDON/ Imprinted for E. B./ 1601./

HEREAFTER/ FOLLOVV DIVERSE/ Poeticall Eſſaies on the former Sub-/ieƈt ; viz : the *Turtle* and *Phœnix./* *Done by the beſt and chiefeſt of our/* moderne writers, with their names ſub-/ſcribed to their particular workes :/ *neuer before extant./* And (now firſt) conſecrated by them all generally,/ *to the loue and merite of the true-noble Knight,/* Sir Iohn Saliſburie./ *Dignum laude virum Muſa vetat mori./* MDCI

[The first of these is the entire title to Chester's poem of 1601, mentioning "some new compositions of seuerall moderne Writers" upon the first subject treated of by Chester. The next is the secondary title to those "new compositions" (at p. 165, so mis-paged for 169), a collection of short poems in which Shakespere's *Phœnix and Turtle* and *Threnos* (lament over the dead) first appeared. The names or quasi-names subscribed to the poems are, Vatum chorus, Ignoto, William Shake-speare, John Marston, George Chapman, and Ben : Johnson.

The unsold copies of *Love's Martyr* were issued in 1611, with a different principal-title, which omitted all mention of the supplementary poems. The book has lately been reprinted by Dr. Grosart from the late Rev. Thos. Corser's copy of the edition of 1601, for his fifty subscribers and for the New Sh. Society, 1878 ; with an Introduction arguing that the Phœnix was Queen Elizabeth, and the Turtle dove the Earl of Essex. This theory has been strongly protested against. L. T. S.]

*ROBERT CHESTER, 1601.

To the kind Reader.
Of bloudy warres, nor of the facke of *Troy*,
Of *Pryams* murdred fonnes, nor *Didoes* fall,
Of *Hellens* rape, by *Paris Troian* boy,
Of *Cæsars* victories, nor *Pompeys* thrall,
Of *Lucrece* rape, being rauifht by a King,
Of none of thefe, of fweete Conceit I fing.

R[obert] Ch[ester].

Loues Martyr: or, Rosalins Complaint, sign. A 4, back.
1601. *Reprinted by Rev. Dr. Grosart,* 1878, *and by the New Sh. Society,* 1878-9.

This is the first of the two stanzas by which Chester introduces his poem to the reader. (See I. C.'s lines, after; p. 57.)

[We here find the author of *Lucrece* associated with Homer and Virgil, or more probably with those English writers who sang of all these classical subjects. (It is sufficient to recall Barbour's and Lydgate's Poems on Troy; Lydgate's *Falls of Princes*, followed by the popular collection of histories in verse in *The Mirour for Magistrates*, both of which went through several editions in the sixteenth century. The story of Pompey was also set forth by Thomas Kyd in his tragedy of *Cornelia*, 1594.) It is true that Chaucer and Lydgate in fragments of larger works both sang of Lucrece, as did Ovid; but that Chester more probably referred to Shakespere seems shown, (1) By the fact that his was the only separate poem on the subject. (2) By the recent publication of the *Rape of Lucrece* (1594), which, following on the previous excellence of *Venus and Adonis* (1593), had at once made its mark. (3) Because Chester calls Shakespere one of "the best and chiefest of our moderne writers," evidently from these two poems as I think, for in those days "a mere playwright" was hardly considered a true poet. (4) Because Chester was under an obligation to this chief poet, having obtained from him and adjoined to his *Love's Martyr* a *Phœnix and Turtle* poem "never before printed" and probably written at Chester's entreaty. (5) By the reminiscences in Chester's otherwise poor poem of Shakespere's wordings, and especially of his rhythm. B. N.]

JOHN MANNINGHAM, 2 Febr. and 13 March, 1601.

At our feaft wee had a play called Twelve Night, or what you will, much like the commedy of errores, or Menechmi in Plautus, but moft like and neere to that in Italian called *Inganni*. A good practife in it to make the fteward beleeve his lady widdowe was in love with him, by counterfayting a letter as from his lady, in generall termes, telling him what fhee liked beft in him, and prefcribing his gefture in fmiling, his apparaile, &c., and then when he came to practife making him beleeve they tooke him to be mad.

   * * * * * *

Vpon a tyme when Burbidge played Rich. 3. there was a Citizen greue foe farr in liking with him, that before fhee went from the play fhee appointed him to come that night unto hir by the name of Ri: the 3. Shakefpeare overhearing their conclufion went before, was intertained, and at his game ere Burbidge came. Then meffage being brought that Rich. the 3^d was at the dore, Shakefpeare caufed returne to be made that William the Conquerour was before Rich. the 3. Shakefpeare's name William. (*Mr. Curle?*)

Diary of John Manningham, of the Middle Temple, and of Bradbourne, Kent, Barrister-at-Law, 1602-1603. *Harl. MS.* 5353, fos. 12 bk, 29 bk. Edited by John Bruce, for the Camden Society, 1868, pp. 18 and 39.

[Rev. J. Hunter in his *New Illustrations of Shakespeare*, 1845, vol. i. pp. 391, 393, tells us that there were two Italian plays bearing the title *Gl'Inganni* (The Cheats), one by Nicholas Secchi, printed in 1562, the other by C. Gonzaga, 1592. A third, a comedy entitled *Gl'Ingannati*, 1585, is the nearest of all to Shakespere's *Twelfth Night*. L. T. S.]

As to the second extract, we will add to it one from John Earle's *Microcosmographie; or, a Peece of the world discovered in Essayes and characters*, 1628, 22. *A Player.* (*sign. E* 4):

"The waiting women Spectators are over-eares in love with him, and Ladies send for him to act in their Chambers,"

only remarking that the difference of rank between ladies and citizen's wives was strongly marked in those days.

The story is given on the authority of "*Mr. Curle,*" i. e. the Mr. E. Curle whom Manningham so often cites. But the name has been tampered with in the MS. (fo. 29 *b*), to make it appear *Toole* (or *Tooly*, the actor). A dark line has been drawn over the top of the C, to suggest a T; and similar touches are seen in the two succeeding letters. Accordingly Mr. J. P. Collier (*History of Eng. Dramatic Poetry*, **1**, 332) gives the name as *Tooly*. Mr. John Bruce, reading the name so touched up, gives it as *Touse*, a name which does occasionally occur in the *Diary*. He again mistakes the name on the next page.

The same story, in a somewhat different shape, is quoted by Mr. Halliwell from the Saunders Manuscript. (*Life of Shakespeare*, 1848, p. 196-7, note.)

W. J., 1601.

I dare here fpeake it, and my fpeach mayntayne,
That Sir Iohn Falftaffe was not any way
More groffe in body, then you are in brayne.
But whether fhould I (helpe me nowe, I pray)
For your groffe brayne, you like I. Falftaffe graunt,
Or for fmall wit, fuppofe you Iohn of Gaunt?

The Whipping of the Satyre. 1601, *sign.* D 3. 12*mo.* [*At Bridgewater House, and Crynes* 865 (*Bodl. Libr.*).]

Mr. J. P. Collier (*New Particulars*, &c., 1836, p. 68) remarks on this allusion, "'Small wit' means here *weak understanding*, which certainly is not a characteristic of Shakespeare's John of Gaunt." But W. J. does not make "small wit" a characteristic of John of Gaunt, any more than he makes "gross brain" a characteristic of Sir John Falstaffe. All he does is, with a humorous pun on *gross*, and with another on gaunt (*i. e.* John of Gaunt, John the thin), to suppose a fanciful proportion between the body and the mind.

Anonymous, 1601-2.

Ingeniofo. What's thy judgment of * * *William Shakefpeare*.

Judicio. Who loves *Adonis* love, or *Lucre's* rape,
His fweeter verfe containes hart robbing life,
Could but a graver fubject him content,
Without loves foolifh lazy languifhment.
Act I. sc. i.

* * * *

Kempe. Few of the univerfity pen plaies well, they fmell too much of that writer *Ovid*, and that writer *Metamorphofis*, and talke too much of *Proferpina* & *Iuppiter*. Why heres our fellow *Shakefpeare* puts them all downe, I and *Ben Jonfon* too. O that *Ben Jonfon* is a peftilent fellow, he brought up *Horace* giving the Poets a pill, but our fellow *Shakefpeare* hath given him a purge that made him beray his credit :

Burbage. Its a fhrewd fellow indeed : I wonder thefe fchollers ftay fo long, they appointed to be here prefently that we might try them : oh, here they come.

* * * *

Bur. I like your face, and the proportion of your body for *Richard* the 3. I pray, M. *Phil*. let me fee you act a little of it.

Philomufus. "Now is the winter of our difcontent,
Made glorious fummer by the fonne of Yorke."
Act IV. sc. v.

The Returne from Pernassus ; or the Scourge of Simony. 1606, *sign. B* 2, *back; G* 2, *bk ; G* 3, *bk*. [4*to.*]
(*Reprinted in Mr. Arber's English Scholar's Library*, 1879.)

Judicio's censure on Shakespeare's Poems is reiterated by John Davies of
Hereford : see after, p. 96; and justified by Peele, Machin, Heywood, and
Freeman : see pp. 75, 80, 81, and 106.

If we except such anthologies as Allot's *England's Pernassus*, Bodenham's
England's Helicon, and his *Belvedere*, all issued in 1600, we may venture on
the assertion that these two lines from *Richard III* constitute the earliest
acknowledged quotation from Shakespeare.[1]

The passage, "O that Ben Jonson is a pestilent fellow; he brought up
Horace, giving the poets a pill;" alludes to Jonson's *Poetaster*, Act V, sc. iii
(1602). The subsequent remark, "but our fellow Shakespeare hath given
him a purge, that made him beray his credit," is mysterious. Where did
our bard put Jonson to his purgation? Assuredly neither Stephano nor
Malvolio could have been a caricature of Jonson, who was neither a sot nor
a gull. [On the other hand Dr. Nicholson points out that Malvolio is
gulled solely through his overweening vanity, the very characteristic of
Jonson, and thinks that there is no character in Shakespere which, in various
ways, so well stands for Jonson. L. T. S.]

Two imprints of *The Returne from Pernassus* were published in 1606.
We have followed the text of the second : the first omits the word "lazy"
in the sixth line. [Though the date of publication is 1606, it was probably
written and acted at Christmas, or New Year, 1601-2. Mr. Arber has gone
carefully into this point, and shows (in his reprint, 1879) that several contemporary references point to this. In the scene of the examination on the
almanac [sign. E, back] C and D are taken as the dominical letters; now
D and C are the letters for the year between 25 March, 1601, and 24 March,
1602 (1601-2, old style). In other scenes (sign. F 3 and E 4, back) we
have references to Ostend and to the Irish troubles; the siege of Ostend by
the Spaniards began 5 July, 1601; the English succours arrived there under
General Vere, 23 July, 1601; General Vere departed on 7 March, 1602 (new
style). (See *A True Historie of the Memorable Siege of Ostend*. Translated
from the French by Ed. Grimeston. London, 1604. pp. 6, 7, 139.) The
fighting in Ireland extended over several years, but the references to the
queen scattered through the play fix it to a date before her death, which
occurred in March, 1603. The date of this play is important, in its bearings
upon the relations between Shakespere and Ben Jonson. See APPENDIX
A, *Mistaken Allusions, Jonson's Poetaster*. L. T. S.]

---

[1] But parodies on well-known lines and unacknowledged quotations
occur several times before this date, as in Greene, 1592; Meres, 1598;
Marston, 1598; Nicholson, 1600. (See before, pp. 2, 24, 29, 33.)
[L. T. S.]

THOMAS DECKER, 1602.

Ad Lectorem.

Inſtead of the Trumpets ſounding thrice, before the Play begin : it ſhall not be amiſſe (for him that will read) firſt to beholde this ſhort Comedy of Errors, and where the greateſt enter, to give them inſtead of a hiſſe, a gentle correction.

(*Sign. A* 4, *back.*)

*   *   *   *

Horace. I have a ſet of letters readie ſtarcht to my hands, which to any freſh ſuited gallant that but newlie enters his name into my rowle, I ſend the next morning, ere his ten a clocke dreame has rize from him, *   * we muſt have falſe fiers to amaze theſe ſpangle babies, theſe true heires of Ma. Juſtice Shallow.

Asinius. I wod alwaies have thee ſawce a foole thus.

Satiro-Mastix, or the untrussing of the Humorous Poet. 1602, *sign. E* 3. [4*to.*]

[Decker places three things at the beginning of this play, a few Latin lines *Ad Detractorem,* an address " To the World," and a list of errata headed by the above witty lines *Ad Lectorem.*

A slight allusion to *Henry IV.* (See before, p. 31, *note.*)

The *Comedy of Errors* (written ? 1589, Furnivall ; or 1591, Dowden) was firſt published in the First Folio of 1623. L. T. S.]

*THOMAS MIDDLETON, 1602.

Fontinelle. Lady, bid him whoſe heart no ſorrow feels
Tickle the ruſhes with his wanton heels :
I've too much lead at mine.
(Act I. sc. i ; sign. A 4, back.)

Camillo. And when the lamb bleating doth bid good night
Unto the cloſing day, then tears begin
To keep quick time unto the owl, whoſe voice
Shrieks like the belman in the lover's ears.
(Act III. sc. i ; sign. E.)

Blurt, Master Constable, or the Spaniard's Night-walke, 1602.

[Middleton's sorrowful Frenchman, bidden to dance, closely follows the expression in *Romeo and Juliet,* Act I. sc. iv,

"Let wantons, light of heart
Tickle the senseless rushes with their heels."

The second extract might, as Dyce says, recall the line in *Macbeth,* Act II, sc. ii,

"It was the owl that shriek'd, the fatal belman
Which gives the stern'st good night."

But *Macbeth* was probably written later, in 1606. Another play by Decker and Middleton jointly, bears traces of Shakespere's influence. *The Honest Whore,* 1604, has a passionate passage which seems moulded on that speech of Constance in *King John,* Act III, sc. i, which begins, "A wicked day, and not a holyday." It runs :—

"Curst be that day for ever that robb'd her
Of breath and me of bliss ! henceforth let it stand
Within the wizard's book, the calendar,
Mark'd with a marginal finger, to be chosen
By thieves, by villains, and black murderers,
As the best day for them to labour in.
If henceforth this adulterous, bawdy world
Be got with child with treason sacrilege,
Atheism, rapes, treacherous friendship, perjury,
Slander, the beggar's sin, lies, sin of fools,
Or any other damn'd impieties,
On Monday let 'em be delivered."
(Middleton's Works, ed Dyce, 1840, vol. iii, p. 9.)

Two or three other lines in the same play contain phrases made use of by Shakespere ; Reed believed that Shakespere imitated Middleton in *Othello,* Act III, sc. iii, 1. 341. See Dyce, vol. iii, p. 56, also pp. 79, 213. See also after, Appendix B, as to Middleton's *Witch.* L. T. S.]

T[HOMAS] A[CHERLEY], 1602.

Whilſt that my glory midſt the clouds was hid,
Like to a Jewell in an Æthiop's eare.

The Massacre of Money. 1602. *Sign. B* 2.

[In his poem Acherley here borrowed an idea and a line from *Romeo and Juliet* ·
"O, she doth teach the torches to burn bright!
It seems she hangs upon the cheek of night
Like a rich jewel in an Ethiope's ear." *Act I. sc. v.*
L. T. S.]

*MICHAEL DRAYTON, 1603.

Such one he was, of him we boldly ſay,
In whoſe rich ſoule all ſoveraigne powers did ſute,
In whom in peace th' elements all lay
So mix'd as none could ſoveraignty impute,
As all did governe, yet all did obey,
His lively temper was ſo abſolute,
  That t' ſeemd when heaven his modell firſt began,
  In him it ſhowd perfection in a man.

The Barrons Wars in the raigne of Edward the second, 1603. *Stanza* 40, *p.* 61.

[The *Barons Wars* was an enlargement of *Mortimeriados*, an historical poem published by Drayton in 1596, and the above passage is one among the fresh additions. In four following editions the stanza remained unchanged, but in that of 1619, canto 3, stanza 40, he altered it thus:

"He was a Man (then boldly dare to say)
  In whose rich Soule the Vertues well did sute,
In whom, so mix'd, the Elements all lay,
  That none to one could Sou'raigntie impute,
As all did gouerne, yet did all obay;
He of a temper was so absolute,
  As that it seem'd, when Nature him began,
  She meant to shew all, that might be in Man."

(I am unable to see a copy of the edition of 1619, but give this on the authority of Mr. Aldis Wright.)

Julius Cæsar was produced by 1601 (as fixed by Weever's *Mirror of Martyrs*, before, p. 42), and these lines nearly resemble the description of Brutus,—

"His life was gentle, and the elements
So mix'd in him that Nature might stand up
And say to all the world 'This was a man.'"—*Act V. sc. v.*

But though some have supposed that Drayton here borrowed from Shakespere, Mr. Aldis Wright, supported by Mr. Grant White, has pointed out that "the old physiological notion of the four humours which entered into the composition of man, their correspondence to the four elements, and the necessity of an equable mixture of them to produce a properly-balanced temperament, was so familiar to writers of Shakespeare's day that in giving expression to it they could hardly avoid using similar if not identical language." (Clarendon Press edition of *Julius Cæsar*, 1878, pp. vii, 203.) This is well illustrated by Mercury's description of Crites in a play of Ben Jonson's, acted in 1600—" A creature of a most perfect and divine temper. One, in whom the humours and elements are peaceably met, without emulation of precedencie :   *   '   in all, so compos'd and order'd, as it is cleare, *Nature* went about some full work, she did more than make a man, when she made him." (*Cynthia's Revells*, Act II, sc. iii.) Many examples confirming the same thing are given in Skeat's Notes to *Piers Plowman*, Part IV, pp. 216, 217, Early English Text Society, 1877; and in the Note to Tale XXXV. (Add. MS. 9066) of *Gesta Romanorum*, ed. Herrtage, E. E. T. S., 1879.

See other instances of similar concurrence of Shakesperian phraseology, after, I. M., 1623, *note*. L. T. S.]

*HENRY CHETTLE, 1603.

Nor doth the filver tonged *Melicert*,
Drop from his honied mufe one fable teare
To mourne her death that graced his defert,
And to his laies opend her Royall eare.
   Shepheard, remember our *Elizabeth*,
   And fing her Rape, done by that *Tarquin*, Death.

       Englandes Mourning Garment. [*Anon. n.d.* (1603.)
      4*to.*] *sign. D* 3.
      Reprinted in Allusion-Books, I, New Sh. Soc., 1874,
      pp. xiii, 98.

   Strictly speaking, *Englandes Mourning Garment* is undated and anonymous. But *The order and proceeding at the Funerall, &c.* (which follows the main work), has the date of Queen Elizabeth's burial, "28 of April, 1603;" and the postscript thereto, "To the Reader," is signed "Hen: Chetle."

   It is probable that Chettle had more rhyme than reason in calling Shakespeare *Melicert*. No allusion could have been intended to the story of Palæmon.

Anonymous, 1603.

You Poets all brave *Shakſpeare, Johnſon, Greenɩ,*
Beſtow your time to write for Englands Queene.
Lament, lament, lament you Engliſh Peeres,
Lament your loſſe poſſeſt ſo many yeeres.
Returne your ſongs and Sonnets and your ſayes :
To ſet foorth ſweete *Elizabeth*[a]*'s* praiſe.
    Lament, lament, &c.

<small>*A mournful Dittie, entituled Elizabeth's loſſe, together with a welcome for King James.* [*Anon.* n.d. *Heber Collection of Ballads and Broadsides in poſſession of S. Christie Miller : see Shakespere Allusion-Books, p.* 117 *(New Shakspere Society,* 1876).]</small>

The Green mentioned here is Thomas Green, not the more famous Robert. The author of this ballad is unknown. It was first noticed by Mr. J. P. Collier in his Edition of Shakespeare, 1844, vol. i, p. cxciv, note.

*I. C., 1603.

Of *Helens* rape and *Troyes* befeiged *Towne*,
Of *Troylus* faith, and *Creſſids* falſitie,
Of *Rychards* ſtratagems for the engliſh crowne,
Of *Tarquins* luſt, and lucrece chaſtitie,
Of theſe, of none of theſe my muſe nowe treates,
Of greater conqueſts, warres, and loves ſhe ſpeakes.

Saint Marie Magdalens Conversion. 1603, *sign. A* 3. [4*to.*]

[These lines, cast in the same mould as Chester's, before, p. 44, contain a more certain allusion to Shakespere than these, inasmuch as they may refer to three of his works. *Troilus and Cressida* is believed to have been out in 1603, though not printed till 1609 (Dowden's *Sh. Primer*, 127, 128). *Richard III* was first printed in 1597, *Lucrece* in 1594. L. T. S.]

JOHN DAVIES OF HEREFORD, 1603.

Players, I love yee, and your *Qualitie*,
As ye are Men, *that* paſs time not abuſ'd:
c W. S. R. B.   And ᶜſome I love for ᵈ*painting, poeſie,*
d Simonides saith, that painting is a dumb Poesy, & Poeſy a speaking painting.   And ſay fell *Fortune* cannot be excuſ'd,
That hath for better *uſes* you refuſ'd:
Wit, Courage, good ſhape, good partes, and all *good,*
As long as al theſe *goods* are no *worſe* uſ'd,
Roscius was said for his excellency in his quality, to be only worthie to come on the stage, and for his honesty to be more worthy then to come theron.   And though the *ſtage* doth ſtaine pure gentle *bloud,*
Yet ᵉ generous yee are in *minde* and *moode.*

Microcosmos. The Discovery of the Little World, with the Government thereof. 1603, *p.* 215. [4*to.*]
Reprinted by Rev. A. B. Grosart, in the Chertsey Worthies Library, 1878.

Just as Drusus and Roscio are associated by Marston (see before, p. 27), so here we find W. S. and R. B. [Shakespere and Richard Burbage] in company; and the text of both passages is sufficiently explicit to show whom Davies had in mind. Possibly, too, in the former he had been thinking of Hamlet's description of the player's vocation.

WILLIAM CAMDEN, 1603.

Thefe may fuffice for fome Poeticall defcriptions of our ancient Poets; if I would come to our time, what a world could I prefent to you out of Sir *Philipp Sidney, Ed. Spencer, Samuel Daniel, Hugh Holland, Ben. Johnfon, Th. Campion, Mich. Drayton, George Chapman, Iohn Marfton, William Shakefpeare,* and other moft pregnant witts of thefe our times, whom fucceeding ages may juftly admire.

Remaines concerning Britaine (1st *edition*). 1605. [4*to.*]
Poems, p. 8.

[The Epistle Dedicatorie is dated "From my Lodging xii Iunii, 1603. Your worships assured M. N." Though Camden did not publish his *Remaines* till 1605, he must have had it in manuscript before he could get his friend "M. N." in 1603 to write an Epistle dedicatory for it. L. T. S.]

* T. M., 1604.

Whereupon entered mafter Burfebell, the royal fcrivener, with deeds and writings hanged, drawn, and quartered for the purpofe * * * (p. 569.) Well, this ended, mafter Burfebell, the calves'-fkin fcrivener, was royally handled, that is, he had a royal put in his hand by the merchant. And now I talk of calves'-fkin, 'tis great pity, lady Nightingale, that the fkins of harmlefs and innocent beafts fhould be as inftruments to work villany upon, entangling young novices and foolifh elder brothers, which are caught like woodcocks in the net of the law . . . . . (p. 572.)

* * * * * * *

I appeared to my captain and other commanders, kiffing my left hand, which then ftood for both (like one actor that plays two parts) * * Neverthelefs, for all my lamentable action of one arm, like old Titus Andronicus, I could purchafe no more than one month's pay for a ten month's pain and peril (p. 590.)

Father Hubburd's Tales: or the Ant, and the Nightingale. 1604. [*Second edition, 4to.*]
Reprinted among the *Works of Thomas Middleton* by Rev. A. Dyce, 1840, Vol. V, *pp.* 547—603, *from which these extracts are taken.*

[The second edition of this tract (copies of which are in Bridgewater House, and in Malone's collection in the Bodleian) was "*Printed by T. C. for William Cotton, and are to be solde at his Shop neare adjoyning to Ludgate.*" "The first edition," says Mr. Dyce, "in which several verses and the whole of 'The Ants Tale when he was a scholar' are omitted, made its appearance during the same year in 4to, entitled *The Ant and the Nightingale: or Father Hubburds Tales. London Printed by T. C. for Bro Bushell, and are to be solde by Jeffrey Chalton, at his Shop at the North doore of Paules.* * *
"Mr. J. P. Collier (*Bridgewater House Catalogue, p.* 199 [see *Bibl. Cat.* i, 537]) mentions it as the *second* edition; but a careful examination of both the impressions has convinced me that it is the *first*" (vol. v. p. 549). Dyce assigns the tract to Thomas Middleton on account of "expressions which remind us strongly of his dramatic dialogue" (Preface, vol. i. p. xviii), as well as the signature T. M. Mr. W. C. Hazlitt thinks the author was

Thomas Moffat. But if Mr. J. P. Collier is right in identifying T. Moffat of the poem on *Silkworms* in 1599 with Dr. Mouffet, and this Dr. Mouffet is the man that wrote the *Theater of Tracts* in Topsell's *Fourfooted Beasts* and dedicated it to Q. Elizabeth (see Rowland's preface), then the style of these books shows he is not our T. M.

The first passage, referring to a scene at the lawyer Prospero's, where a young man had signed away his estate, may perhaps be taken as a recollection of Cade's speech in 2 *Henry VI*, Act IV, sc. ii.—

"*Dick*. The first thing we do, let's kill all the lawyers.

Cade. Nay, that I mean to do. Is not this a lamentable thing, that of the skin of an innocent lamb should be made parchment! that parchment, being scribbled o'er, should undo a man? Some say the bee stings; but I say 'tis the bee's wax, for I did but seal once to a thing, and I was never mine own man since."

On the second passage, that on *Titus Andronicus*, Dyce says: "See the tragedy so called, which, though now printed among the works of Shakespeare, was assuredly written by some other dramatist—probably, by Marlowe. In Act III, sc. i, Aaron cuts off the hand of Titus; and in Act V, sc. ii, the latter says,
"How can I grace my talk,
Wanting a hand to give it action?"

The *Tales* have other passages which may possibly be echoes of Shakspere, but most likely are not: the poet's "carnation silk riband" and the "remuneration" he did not get, p. 602, have these terms in common with Costard's "How much carnation ribbon may a man buy for a remuneration?" *L. L. Lost*, III, i.

"kings in that time
Hung jewels at the ear of every rhyme," p. 599,

may refer to Romeo's rhapsody; the battle and "points.. once let down" to Poins's joke on Falstaff in 1 *Henry IV*, II. iv. 238-9: "the submissive flexure of the knee," p. 566, to Henry V's "flexure & low bending" (IV. i. 272), and Hamlet's "crook the pregnant hinges of the knee," &c., but all these were no doubt common to the Elizabethan world. And we surely cannot adopt the suggestion (*Athenæum*, Sept. 14, 1878) that the passage on p. 374, praising the *nest* of boy-actors at the Blackfriars,[1] was a recollection of the "aery of children" sneered at by Shakspere (in a passage of *Hamlet* not in the Quartoes, but first printed in 1623), when we find that T. M. applies the term *nest* also to "a *nest* of ants," who typify man (p. 562), "a whole *nest* of pinching bachelors," p. 577, and "my honest *nest* of ploughmen," p. 580. F. J. F.]

---

[1] "if his humour so serve him, to call in at the Blackfriars, where he should see a nest of boys able to ravish a man," p. 574. [Compare, too, Jonson's "nest of antiques," *Bartholomew Fair*, Induction, leaf 3. L. T. S.]

SIR WALTER COPE, 1604.

Sir,
 I have fent and bene all thys morning huntyng for players Juglers & Such kinde of Creaturs, but fynde them harde to finde, wherfore Leavinge notes for them to feeke me, burbage ys come, & Sayes ther ys no new playe that the quene hath not feene, but they have Revyved an olde one, Cawled *Loves Labore loft*, which for wytt & mirthe he fayes will pleafe her excedingly. And Thys ys apointed to be playd to Morowe night at my Lord of Sowthamptons, unlefs yow fend a wrytt to Remove the Corpus Cum Cauſa to your howfe in ftrande. Burbage ys my meffenger Ready attendyng your pleafure.

Yours moft humbly,

WALTER COPE.

Letter dated "From your Library," written by Sir Walter Cope, addressed " To the right honorable the Lorde Vycount Cranborne at the Courte." Endorsed: 1604, Sir Walter Cope to my Lord. Hatfield House MSS. See Third Report of the Royal Commission of Historical Manuscripts. 1872. p. 148.

["The quene" here mentioned is Anne of Denmark, the Queen of James I. *Loves Labours Lost* was first published in 1598 (4to.), "newly corrected and augmented." It is supposed by many critics to be Shakespere's first play, written about 1588-90. L. T. S.]

I. C., 1604 circa.

Who'e're will go unto the preffe may fee,
The hated Fathers of vilde balladrie :
One fings in his bafe note the River Thames
4 Shal found the famous memory of noble king *Iames ;*
Another fayes that he will, to his death,
Sing the renowned worthineffe of fweet *Elizabeth,*
So runnes their verfe in fuch difordered ftraine,
8 And with them dare great majefty prophane,
Some dare do this ; fome other humbly craves
For helpe of Spirits in their fleeping graves,
As he that calde to *Shakefpeare, Iohnfon, Greene,*
12 To write of their dead noble Queene ;
But he that made the Ballads of oh hone,
Did wondrous well to whet the buyer on :
Thefe fellowes are the flaunderers of the time,
16 Make ryming hatefull through their baftard rime.
But were I made a judge in poetry,
They all fhould burne for their vilde herefie.

Epigrames. Served out in 52 *severall Dishes for every man to tast without surfeting.* (*From Malone's Copy in the Bodleian Library.*) *Epig*. 12, *sign. B.* [*n. d.* 12*mo.*]

The compiler is indebted to Mr. J. O. Halliwell-Phillipps for this curious epigram, which was overlooked by Malone's continuator. Malone saw in this epigram an allusion to *Englandes Mourning Garment.* (See p. 55.)

[It is difficult to fix the date of the epigram. Line 4, speaking of the "famous memory" of James, seems to point to the time of his death, March 1625 ; but the printer of the volume, G. Elde, died before 13th November, 1624. Line 11 refers to the *Mournful Dittie,* before, p. 56, and this, coupled with the possible reference to *England's Mourning Garment,* and with the appearance of ballads on the death of Essex (1601-2), containing the burden of O hone !, make it probable that 1604 is the approximate date. See *Allusion-Books,* I, New Sh. Soc. pp. xxi, 122, *note.* L. T. S.]

ANTHONY SCOLOKER, 1604.

It[1] should be like the *Never-too-well read Arcadia*, where the *Profe* and *Verce* (*Matter* and *Words*) are like his *Miftreffes* eyes, one ftill excelling another and without Corivall: or to come home to the vulgars *Element*, like *Friendly Shakefpeare's Tragedies*, where the *Commedian* rides, when the *Tragedian* ftands on Tip-toe: Faith it fhould pleafe all, like Prince *Hamlet*. But in fadneffe, then it were to be feared he would runne mad: Infooth I will not be moone-ficke, to pleafe: nor out of my wits though I difpleafed all.

(Epistle to the Reader.)

* * * *

[Daïphantus in love] To quench his thirst:
Runs to his Inke-pot, drinkes, then ftops the hole,
And thus growes madder, then he was at firft.
    Taffo, he finds, by that of *Hamlet*, thinkes
        Tearmes him a mad-man than of his Inkhorne drinks.
Calls Players fooles, the foole he judgeth wifeft,

* * * *

Puts off his cloathes; his fhirt he onely weares,
Much like mad-*Hamlet*; thus as Paffion teares.

(sign. E 4, back)

Daiphantus, or the Passions of Love. 1604. [4to.] Reprinted for the Roxburghe Club in 1818.

---

[1] "It," that is, an "Epistle to the Reader," should be like, &c.

[The last two lines give a curious glimpse of how Hamlet appeared on the stage in Shakespere's day; the writer probably means that he wore nothing over his shirt, or, as we should say, appeared "in his shirt-sleeves." L. T. S.]

Anonymous, 1604.

Sig. Shuttlecock.

Now *Signiors* how like you mine Hoft? did I not tell you he was a madde round knave, and a merrie one too: and if you chaunce to talke of fatte Sir *John Old-caftle*, he wil tell you, he was his great Grandfather, and not much unlike him in Paunch if you marke him well by all descriptions.

> *The Meeting of Gallants at an Ordinarie: or, The Walkes in Powles.* 1604, *sign. B* 4, *back.* [*Unique copy in Bodleian Library. Edited for the Percy Society by J. O. Halliwell, in Early English Poetry, vol. v.* 1841, *p.* 16.]

See as to Oldcastle and Falstaff, *note*, after, p. 269.

JOHN MARSTON, 1604.

[Enter Mendoza]
Celſo   Hee's heere.
Malevole   Give place.
Illo, ho, ho, ho! arte there, old true peny ? [Exit Celſo.
Where haſt thou ſpent thy ſelfe this morning ?   I ſee flattery in
thine eyes, and damnation i' thy ſoule.   Ha ye huge Rascal !

The Malcontent, Act III. Sc. iii.

Cf. *Hamlet*, I. v. ll. 118, 150. [This and similar quotations show the fame and reputation of Shakespere, being popularly known lines quoted or imitated for the purpose of causing a good-humoured laugh at their misappropriation. Malone (vol. ii. p. 356) long ago said that Marston has in many places imitated Shakespere, and that this is the case, any one, with a previous moderate knowledge of Shakespere, who reads his plays, will at once acknowledge. B. N.] (See note after, p. 77. See other extracts from Marston, pp. 27, 29 : also Appendix B.)

[Two editions of *The Malcontent* appeared in 1604, the second augmented by Marston, with an Induction by Webster. The above quotation is from the first edition.

In Webster's *Induction* Sly begins a speech, much like Osric in *Hamlet* (Act V. sc. ii), with the phrase, "No, in good faith, for mine ease."

Hamlet was entered on the Stationers' Register in July, 1602, but was not printed (quarto) till 1603. See, however, Gabriel Harvey's note, before, p. 30. L. T. S.]

Anonymous. About 1605.

Get thee to London, for if one man were dead, they will have much neede of fuch a one as thou art. There would be none in my opinion fitter then thyfelfe to play his parts: my conceipt is fuch of thee, that I durft venture all the mony in my purfe on thy head, to play Hamlet with him for a wager. There thou fhalt learne to be frugall (for Players were never fo thriftie as they are now about London) & to feed upon all men, to let none feede upon thee; to make thy hand a ftranger to thy pocket, thy hart flow to performe thy tongues promife: and when thou feeleft thy purfe well lined, buy thee fome place or Lordfhip in the Country, that growing weary of playing, thy mony may there bring thee to dignitie and reputation. * * * Sir, I thanke you (quoth the Player) for this good counfell, I promife you I will make ufe of it, for, I have heard indeede, of fome that have gone to London very meanly, and have come in time to be exceeding wealthy.

> *Ratseis Ghost, or the second Part of his madde Prankes and Robberies.* [*n.d.* 4*to. Unique copy in the Althorp Library. Sign. B* 1.]

[This tract bears no date, but it is found in a volume of contemporary binding with several other tracts of 1603, 1604, and 1605. L. T. S.]

Here, too, we find Burbage and Shakespere associated, as they were by Marston and by Davies: "if one man were dead" identifies the former; while, "some that have gone to London," &c., unmistakeably points to the latter.

We might have quoted as a pendant to this extract the following from *The Returne from Pernassus*, 1606 (played 1602, see before, p. 49) :

> *Studiofo.* Fayre fell good *Orpheus*, that would rather be
> King of a mole hill, then a Keysars slave :
> Better it is mongst fidlers to be chiefe,
> Then at [a] plaiers trencher beg reliefe.
> But ist not strange this mimick apes should prize
> Unhappy Schollers at a hireling rate.
> Vile world, that lifts them up to hye degree,
> And treades us downe in groveling misery.
> *England* affordes those glorious vagabonds,
> That carried earst their fardels on their backes,
> Coursers to ride on through the gazing streetes,
> Sooping it in their glaring Satten sutes,
> And Pages to attend their maisterships :
> With mouthing words that better wits have framed,
> They purchase lands, and now Esquiers are made.
> *Philomusus.* What ere they seeme being even at the best,
> They are but sporting fortunes scornfull jests.
> *Stud.* So merry fortune is wont from ragges to take,
> Some ragged grome, and him some gallant make.
>   (Actus 5, scena 1 ; Sign. G 4, back.)

[But Shakespere never was an Esquire, he was in his Will plain *William Shackspeare gentleman*. (See for example the extract from Edm. Howes, 1614.) In his day the distinction was real. See Sir Thomas Smith, quoted in *Transactions* of New Sh. Soc., 1877-9, Part I, pp. 103, 104. L. T. S.]

* GEO. CHAPMAN, BEN JONSON, J. MARSTON, 1605.

Enter Hamlet a foote-man in haste.
Ham. What Coachman? my Ladyes Coach for fhame; her ladifhips readie to come downe.

Enter Potkinn, a Tankerd beare.
Pot. Sfoote *Hamlet;* are you madde? whether run you nowe, you fhould brufhe vp my olde Miftreffe?

Enter Syndefye.
Syn. What *Potkinn?* you muft put off your Tankerd and put on your blew coat and waite upon miftris Touchftone into the countrie. ⁕ ⁕

Enter Mistress Fond & Mistresse Gazer
Fond. Come fweete Miftreffe *Gazer,* lets watch here, and fee my Lady *Flafhe* take coach. ⁕ ⁕ ⁕
Fond. Shee comes, fhe comes, fhe comes.
Gaz. Fond. Pray heaven bleffe your Ladifhip.
Gyrtrude. Thanke you good people; my coach for the love of heaven, my coach! in good truth I fhall fwoune elfe.
Ham. Coacn? coach, my Ladyes coach.

⁕ ⁕ ⁕ ⁕

G jr. I marle how my modeft Sifter occupies her felfe this morning, that fhee can not waite on me to my Coach, as well as her mother!

Quick silver. Mary Madam, ſhee's married by this time to Prentiſe *Goulding;* your father, and ſome one more, ſtole to church with 'hem, in all the haſte, that the colde meate left at your wedding, might ſerve to furniſh their Nuptiall table.

Eastward Hoe, Act III, Sc. ii. 1605, *sign.* D and Ɔ i, *back.*

[The unusual name Hamlet,[1] the question "are you madde?", the frequent references to the coach (possibly in reference to the anachronism committed by Shakespere in making Ophelia call for her coach, Act IV. Sc. v), and the reference to the cold meate for the nuptial table, all seem to shew that Shakespere's *Hamlet* was here pointed at. *Eastward Hoe* was played by the Children of her Majesty's Revels, that "aeyry of children" of whom Rosencrantz speaks, and who, by Shakespere's own confession, had driven his company to travel in the country. Syndefie's call upon Potkinn to wait upon Mistris Touchstone into the country may be the Children's out-cry of triumph at having thus beaten their rivals, a suggestion which gains its point from this, that Mistris Touchstone, the mother who has successfully helped her scheming daughter to marry above her station, is immediately turned upon by that daughter and made to defer to her. The only passages in which Marston might be said to sneer at Shakespere are these allusions to and parody on *Hamlet*, and a stage direction, also in *Eastward Hoe*, Act I. Sc. i., "Enter . . . Bettrice leading a Monkey after her." Bettrice is a dumb character, who never speaks nor does anything else. Hence Dr. B. Nicholson believes she is simply introduced to ridicule "Beatrice leading apes to Hell" in *Much Ado about Nothing*, and a dumb "Hero's Mother" in the same play. The name of Bettrice is never mentioned, and therefore she would be Bettrice to the spectators only because she would be dressed like Shakespere's Beatrice.

Eastward Hoe was "made by" Chapman, Jonson and Marston. It is quite probable therefore that these allusions were not from Marston's pen, they may be from Jonson's. L. T. S.]

---

[1] It is perhaps worth noting that Hamlet, as a Christian name, was otherwise not unknown in the sixteenth century. "Hamlet Rider" occurs in the Muster Roll of Calais, about 1533—1540. *Cotton MS. Faust.* E VII, *fo.* 76 (in the British Museum).

WILLIAM DRUMMOND OF HAWTHORNDEN, 1606 & 1611.

Bookes red be me, anno 1606

* * * * *

Romeo and Julieta, tragedie. [1597, 1599.]

* * * * *

Loues Labors Loft, comedie. [1598.]

* * * * *

The Paffionate Pilgrime [1599.]

* * * * *

The Rape of Lucrece [1594, 1598, 1600.]

* * * * *

A Midfommers Nights Dreame, comedie. [1600.]

* * * * *

Table of my Englifh bookes, anno 1611.

* * * * *

Venus and Adon. by Schaksp. [6th and 7th ed. 1602.]

The Rap of Lucrece, idem. [two eds. in 1607]

* * * * *

The Tragedie of Romeo and Julieta

          4^d. Ing

* * * * *

A Midfumers Night Dreame.

Extracts from the Hawthornden Manuscripts, by David Laing, Archæologia Scotica, vol. iv. Edinburgh. 1831-2. *pp.* 20, *note,* 21.

[It is curious that after 1606, the first year in which Drummond gives a list of his year's readings, up to 1614 when they end, there is no other mention of Shakespere than those above. It is also curious, especially when one looks to the dates of the editions, that all should have been read (except the *V. and Ad.*) in the one year of 1606. B. N.] [Young Drummond was however, staying in London in the summer of 1606, whence he went abroad, not returning till 1609, the bent of his studies would therefore naturally follow his place of residence for the time. (See *D. Masson's Life,* 1873, pp. 11, 14, 18.) He paid fourpence for *Romeo & Juliet,* the only one of Shakespere's books to which he marks a price. L. T. S.]

JOHN FLETCHER, 1607.

Count. Lazarello, beſtirre thy ſelfe nimbly and ſodainly, and here me with patience.

Laza. Let me not fall from my ſelfe; ſpeake I am bound to heare.

Count. So art thou to revenge, when thou ſhalt heare the fith head is gone, and we know not whither.

(*Act II. sc. i.*)

* * * *

It comes againe; new apparitions,
And tempting ſpirits: Stand and reveale thy ſelfe,
Tell why thou followest me? I feare thee
As I feare the place thou camſt from: Hell.

(*Act III. sc. i.*)

The Woman-Hater. 1607. [4*to.*] *Sign. D* 2, *D* 4.

[See the dialogue between the Ghost and Hamlet (*Hamlet*, I. sc. v.), two lines (6, 7) in which Fletcher has here quoted,—

"*Ham.* Speak; I am bound to hear.
Ghost. So art thou to revenge, when thou shalt hear." L. T. S.]

Anonymous, 1607.

Fabell. What meanes the toling of this fatall Chime,
O what a trembling horror ftrikes my heart!
My ftiffened hayre ftands vpright on my head,
As doe the briftles of a porcupine.

The Merry Divel of Edmonton. 1617, *sign. A* 3, *back.*

[Fabell makes this exclamation at the approach of the evil spirit Coreb, with whom he has covenanted for his soul. So the ghost tells Hamlet—

"I could a tale unfold whose lightest word
Would harrow up thy soul," and make
"each particular hair to stand on end
Like quills upon the fretful porcupine." (*Act I. sc. v.*)

Evidently the author of the *Merry Divel of Edmonton* had this in his mind, though he did not, like Marston, acknowledge that he made his puppet "speake play scrappes" (see after, p. 77).

The author of this play is unknown, though Kirkman (*Exact Catalogue of Comedies, &c.*, 1671, p. 9) attributed it to Shakespere. It was entered on the Stationers' Register, 22 Oct. 1607, the first edition being printed in 1608. L. T. S.]

THOMAS DECKER, 1607.

Jupiter feeing *Plutus* difperfing his giftes, amongft none but his honeft brethren, ftrucke him (either in anger or envie) ftarke blind, fo that ever fince hee hath play'de the good fellowe, for now every gull may leade him up and downe like *Guy*, to make fports in any drunken affemblie, now hee regards not who thrufts his handes into his pockets, nor how it is fpent, a foole fhall have his heart nowe, as foone as a Phyfition : And an Affe that cannot fpell, goe laden away with double Duckets from his *Indian* ftorehoufe, when *Ibis Homere*, that hath layne fick feventeene yeeres together of the Vniverfitie plague, (watching and want), only in hope at the laft to finde fome cure, fhall not for an hundred waight of good Latine receive a two penny waight in filuer, his ignorance (arifing from his blindnes) is the onely caufe of this Comedie of errors.

> *A Knights Coniuring done in earnest: difcouered in iest.* 1607. *Chapter VI., sign. F* 4, *back. Reprinted for the Percy Society, Early English Poetry, vol. v. pp.* 52, 53.

[This may be taken as proof that the *Comedy of Errors* was at least still in mind in 1607. L. T. S.]

GEORGE PEELE, ? 1607.

How he ferved a Tapfter.

George was making merry with three or foure of his friends in Pye-corner, where the Tapfter of the houfe was much given to Poetry: for he had ingroffed the Knight of the Sunne, *Venus* and *Adonis,* and other Pamphlets which the ftrippling had collected together.

Merrie Conceited Jests of George Peele. (*Earliest known edition,* 1607.) [*Bodleian* Ith *Tanner* 734, *p.* 19. *Date cut off. Works, by Rev. A. Dyce.* 1828. *Vol. II. p.* 213.]

[It is believed that George Peele died in 1598. There is little doubt that the collection of "Merrie conceited Jests" was published shortly after, though the earliest recorded edition is of 1607. The book is of little authority; Peele was a scholar, though a needy scrupulous man, and the use of his name to father such a book finds a parallel in a worse book assigned to the great Scottish scholar and statesman, George Buchanan. (See Dyce's edition of Peele's Works, 1828, vol. i. p. viii.) L. T. S.]

WILLIAM BARKSTEAD, 1607.

But ſtay my Muſe in thine owne confines keepe,
  & wage not warre with ſo deere lov'd a neighbor,
But having ſung thy day ſong, reſt and ſleepe
  preſerve thy ſmall fame and his greater favor:
His Song was worthie merrit (*Shakſpeare* hee)
ſung the faire bloſſome, thou the withered tree
  Laurell is due to him, his art and wit
  hath purchaſt it, *Cypres* thy brow will fit.

Mirrha, the Mother of Adonis; or Lustes Prodigies. 1607.
Last stanza. [4to.] *In the Bodleian Lib.* Malone, 393.)
Reprinted by Dr. Grosart in Poems of William Barksted,
1876, *p.* 65.

JOHN MARSTON, 1607.

Ha he mount[s] *Chirall* on the wings of fame.
A horſe, a horſe, my kingdom for a horſe,
Looke the I ſpeake play ſcrappes.

What You Will. Act II. Sc. i. 1607,
sign. C i. [4to.]

[*Richard III*, Act V. sc. iv, l. 7. (See before, p. 29.) It is possible that the first line of this extract contains two printer's errors, "he" for "ile" (the old way of printing "I'll"), and Chirall for Chevall; the line would thus run,—
"Ha, Ile mount Chevall on the wings of fame."

The *s* would not then be required to help out "mount;" and Marston, mounting Pegasus in writing his Satire, naturally calls out for "A horse," &c. It should be noted, however, that the play is unusually well printed, in better type than many of the quartos of the time. L. T. S.]

W. S. 1607.

in ftead of a Iefter, weele ha the ghoft ith white fheete fit at upper end a' th Table.

The Puritaine, or the Widdow of Watling-Streete.
1607, sign. H, back. [4to.]

A slight allusion to the ghost of Banquo in *Macbeth*.

Macbeth was probably written in 1605-6, though not printed till the first Folio of 1623.

[Mr. Fleay (*Shakespere Manual*, 1876, p. 20) considers that *The Puritan* "is filled with allusions to Shakespere." He only instances, however, the above line, and a portion of Act IV. sc. iii, as being imitated from *Pericles*, Act III. sc. ii, the scene of the recovery of Thaisa. But we have no earlier date for *Pericles* than 1608, when it was entered on the Stationers' Register.

In Beaumont and Fletcher's *Knight of the Burning Pestle*, 1613 (written 1611), Jasper, personating his own ghost, threatens the Merchant,—

"When thou art at the Table with thy friends
Merry in heart, and fild with swelling wine,
Il'e come in midst of all thy pride and mirth,
Invisible to all men but thy selfe,
And whisper such a sad tale in thine eare,
Shall make thee let the Cuppe fall from thy hand."

(*Act V. sc. i; sign. I* 3.)

Mr. Aldis Wright points out that this too may be a reminiscence of the ghost of Banquo (*Macbeth, Clarendon Press Series*, p. viii.). L. T. S.]

CAPTAIN KEELING, 1607.

September 5 [At "Serra Leona"] I fent the interpreter, according to his defier, abord the Hector, whear he brooke fast, and after came abord mee, wher we gave the tragedie of Hamlett.

[Sept.] 30. Captain Hawkins dined with me, wher my companions acted Kinge Richard the Second.

31. I envited Captain Hawkins to a ffifhe dinner, and had Hamlet acted abord me : wch I permitt to keepe my people from idlenes and unlawfull games, or fleepe.

Narratives of Voyages towards the North-West in search of a Passage to Cathay and India, **1496** *to* **1631**. *Edited by Thomas Rundall, for the Hakluyt Society,* 1849, *p.* **231**.

[The above extract is printed by Mr. Rundall from "the journal of the *Dragon* (Captain Keeling), bound with the *Hector* (Captain Hawkins) and the *Consent* towards the East Indies." The original was among the East India Manuscripts.

The first quarto of *Richard II* was published in **1597**. L. T. S.]

THOMAS HEYWOOD, 1607.

Bowdler. I never read any thing but *Venus* and *Adonis*.
Cripple. Why thats the very quinteffence of love,
If you remember but a verfe or two,
Ile pawne my head, goods, lands and all 'twill doe.
Bow. Why then, have at her.
Fondling I fay, fince I have hemd thee heere,
Within the circle of this ivory pale,
Ile be a parke.
Mall Berry. Hands off fond Sir.
Bow. —And thou fhalt be my deere;
Feede thou on me, and I will feede on thee,
And Love fhall feede us both.
Mall. Feede you on woodcockes, I can faft awhile.
Bow. Vouchfafe thou wonder to alight thy fteede.
Crip. Take heede, fhees not on horfebacke.
Bow. Why then fhe is alighted.
Come fit thee downe where never ferpent hiffes,
And, being fet, ile fmother thee with kiffes.

The Fayre Mayde of the Exchange. 1607, *sign.* G 3. [4*to.*]

Heywood is quoting stanzas 39th and 3rd of *Venus and Adonis*; but the lines—
"Feed thou on me, and I will feed on thee,
And love shall feed us both,"
are not Shakespeare's, but Heywood's parody; and "Come, sit thee down," is an error for "Here come and sit." Machin also is quoting stanzas 39th and 3rd; and he also misquotes from both: "on dale" should have been "in dale," "when those mounts are" should have been "if those hills be," and "Here sit thee down," is inaccurate. That Shakespeare may have disseminated a first draft of his poem, differing from that known to us, is, perhaps, countenanced by the *variæ lectiones* in the old copies of Shakespeare's Poems: especially considering that we know one stanza of the *Rape of Lucrece* (quoted in the *Second Period*, Sir J. Suckling, 1636) which is not only different, but in a different measure from ours.

JARVIS MARKHAM AND LEWIS MACHIN, 1608.

Veloups.[1] This is his chamber, lets enter, heeres his clarke.

President. Fondling, faid he, fince I have hem'd thee heere,
Within the circuit of this Ivory pale.

Drap. I pray you fir help us to the fpeech of your mafter.

Pre. Ile be a parke, and thou fhalt be my Deere.
He is very bufie in his ftudy.
Feed where thou wilt, in mountaine or on dale;
Stay a while, he will come out anon.
Graze on my lips, and when thofe mounts are drie,
Stray lower, where the pleafant fountaines lie.
Go thy way thou beft booke in the world.

Ve. I pray you, fir, what booke doe you read:

Pre. A book that never an Orators clarke in this kingdome but is beholden unto: it is called maides philofophie, or *Venus and Adonis*. Looke you, gentlemen, I have divers other pretty bookes.

Drap. You are very well ftorde, fir; but I hope your mafter will not ftay long.

Pre. No, he will come prefently.   *Enter* Mefhant.

Ve. Who have we heere? another Client fure, crowes flock to carkaffes: O tis the lord *Mefhant*.

Me. Save you, Gentlemen; fir is your mafter at any leafure?

Pre. Heere fit thee downe where never ferpent hiffes,
And being fet ile fmother thee with kiffes.
His bufineffes yet are many, you muft needes attend a while.

The Dumbe Knight. 1608, *sign. F.* [4*to.*]

We here find Machin quoting almost the same passages from *Venus and Adonis* as Heywood. See the last extract, p. 80.

CENTURIE.   G

* JOHN DAY, 1608.

Joculo. But Madam, doe you remember what a multitude of fifhes we faw at Sea? aud I doe wonder how they can all live by one another.

Emilia. Why foole, as men do on the Land, the great ones eate up the little ones.

* * * * * * *

Polymetes. What ominous news can *Polimetes* daunt? Have we not Hyren heere?

Law Tricks, a comedy, 1608, *signs. B* 3 *and F* 2.

[Mr. A. H. Bullen (*Athenæum*, Sept. 21, 1878) points out that John Day here copies a part of the Fishermen's talk in *Pericles*, Act II. sc. i.—

"3 *Fish.* Master I marvel how the fishes live in the sea.
1. *Fish.* Why, as men do a-land, the great ones eat up the little ones."

Pericles was entered on the Stationers' Register on 20 May, 1608*. Day's *Law Tricks* was entered on the Register 28 March, 1608.

George Wilkins' novel, *The Painfull Adventures of Pericles*, which appeared in the same year, "in great measure founded upon " Shakespere's play, says Dr. Dowden (*Shakespere Primer*, 1877, p. 145), gives the same passage in a different form, " Againe comparing our rich men to Whales, that make a great shew in the worlde, rowling and tumbling up and downe, but are good for little, but to sincke others : that the fishes live in the sea, as the powerfull on shoare, the great ones eate up the little ones." (Prof. Mommsen's reprint, Oldenburg, 1857, p. 27. Fourth chapter.)

Pistol's exclamation "Have we not Hiren here?" (2 *Hen. IV*, Act II. sc. iv.) is also used by Day ; it seems to have been a popular " play-scrap,"

---

* *Pericles*, of which Shakespere probably wrote only the main parts of the last three acts, was printed in quarto in 1609 (twice), and was reprinted from the sixth quarto of 1635 in the second issue of the Third Folio of Shakespere's Plays, 1664. See Furnivall's *Introd.* to the *Leopold Shakespere*, 1877, p. lxxxviii (where 1644 is a misprint for 1664); and the *Cambridge Shakespere*, 1866, Vol. I, p. xxvii ; vol. IX, p. ix.

one of the current phrases of the day ; Dyce considers that it was probably taken by Shakespere as well as by other writers from George Peele's lost drama, *The Turkish Mahomet and Hiren the Fair Greek* (ed. of Shakespere, 1864, vol. iv. p. 344, note). Steevens gives the quotation as occurring in Massinger's *Old Law*, T. Heywood's *Love's Mistress*, and *Satiromastix* (Malone and Steevens' *Shakespere*, 1821, vol. xvii. p. 83). It is also found in Chapman, Jonson, and Marston's *Eastward Hoe*, Act II. sc. i, spoken by Quicksilver, who is constantly quoting scraps of plays. William Barksted published his Poem *Hiren, or the faire Greeke* in 1611. See Dr. Grosart's Reprint of the Poems of W. Barksted, 1876. L. T. S.]

JOHN DAVIES OF HEREFORD, 1609.

<small>* Stage plaiers.</small> Some followed her [1] by *acting all mens parts,
　　　　　　Thefe on a Stage fhe rais'd (in fcorne) to fall:
　　　　　　And made them Mirrors, by their acting Arts,
<small>† Shewing the vices of the time.</small> Wherin men faw their † faults, thogh ne'r fo fmall:
<small>‡ W.S.R.B.</small>　Yet fome fhe guerdond not, to their ‡ defarts;
　　　　　　But, otherfome, were but ill-Action all:
　　　　　　Who while they acted ill, ill ftaid behinde.
　　　　　　(By cuftome of their maners) in their minde.

The Civile Warres of Death and Fortune, [*being the "Second Tale" in the volume of which " Humours Heav'n on Earth" is the first*]. 1609, *p.* 208, stanza 76. [*sm. 8vo.*]
Reprinted by Rev. A. B. Grosart in the Chertsey Worthies Library, 1876, *p.* 37.

---

[1] The "her" is Fortune. For W. S, and R. B., see John Davies, quoted before, p. 58.

SAMUEL ROWLANDS, 1609.

In a new mould this woman I will cast,
Her tongue in other order I will keepe,
Better she had bin in her bed afleepe,
Then in a Taverne, when those words fhe fpake;
A little paines with her I meane to take:
For fhe fhall find me in another tune,
Between this February and next June:
In fober fadneffe I do fpeake it now,
And to you all I make a solemne vow,
The chiefeft Art I have I will beftow
About a worke cald taming of the Shrow.

Whole Crew of Kind Gossips. 1609. p. 33.
Reprinted by the Hunterian Club, 1876.

[This is part of the answer of the fifth of the "Six honest Husbands" who are all accused by their wives or "Gossips." He was "complained on by his wife to be a common Drunkard."

The old play of *The Taming of A Shrew*, on which Shakespere's play is founded, was printed in 1594; his play of the *Taming of the Shrew* was not printed till 1623, but it seems most likely to have been written not later than 1597. L. T. S.]

THOMAS THORPE, 1609.

TO . THE . ONLIE . BEGETTER . OF.
THESE . INSVING . SONNETS.
M^r. W. H. ALL. HAPPINESSE.
AND . THAT . ETERNITIE.
PROMISED.
BY.
OVR. EVER-LIVING . POET.
WISHETH.
THE . WELL-WISHING .
ADVENTVRER . IN .
SETTING.
FORTH.

T. T.

Shakespeare's Sonnets. 1609. [4to.] *Dedication.*

The entry of this edition of the Sonnets in the Stationers' Registers runs thus :

20 Maij [1609]

Thomas Thorpe. Entred for his copie under thandes of master Wilson and master Lownes Warden a Booke called SHAKESPEARES sonnettes.

1609.

A never Writer to an ever Reader. NEWES.

Eternall reader, you have heere a new play, never ſtal'd with the Stage, never clapper-clawd with the palmes of the vulger, and yet paſſing full of the palme comicall; for it is a birth of your [that] braine, that never under-tooke any thing commicall, vainely: And were but the vaine names of commedies changde for the titles of Commodities, or of Playes for Pleas; you ſhould ſee all thoſe grand cenſors, that now ſtile them ſuch vanities, flock to them for the maine grace of their gravities; eſpecially this authors Commedies, that are ſo fram'd to the life, that they ſerve for the moſt common Commentaries of all the actions of our lives, ſhewing ſuch a dexteritie and power ot witte, that the moſt diſpleaſed with Playes, are pleaſd with his Commedies. And all ſuch dull and heavy-witted worldlings, as were never capable of the witte of a Commedie, comming by report of them to his repreſentations, have found that witte there, that they never found in themſelves, and have parted better-wittied then they came; feeling an edge of witte ſet upon them, more than ever they dreamd they had braine to grinde it on. So much and ſuch favoured ſalt of witte is in his Commedies, that they ſeeme (for their height of pleaſure) to be borne in that ſea that brought forth *Venus.* Amongſt [Venus & Adonis] all there is none more witty then this: And had I time I would comment upon it, though I know it needs not, (for ſo much as will make you thinke your teſterne well beſtowd) but for ſo

much worth, as even poore I know to be ſtuft in it. It deſerves
ſuch a labour, as well as the beſt Commedy in *Terence* or *Plautus*,
And beleeve this, that when hee is gone, and his Commedies out
of ſale, you will ſcramble for them, and ſet up a new Engliſh
Inquiſition. Take this for a warning, and at the perrill of your
pleaſures loſſe, and Iudgements, refuſe not, nor like this the
leſſe, for not being ſullied, with the ſmoaky breath of the
multitude ; but thanke fortune for the ſcape it hath made amongſt
you. Since by the grand poſſeſſors wills, I beleeve you ſhould
have prayd for them rather then beene prayd. And ſo I leave
all ſuch to bee prayd for (for the ſtates of their wits healths) that
will not praiſe it.—Vale.

Address prefixed to Troilus and Cressida. [*Some copies only of the first issue of* 1609. *First 4to.*]

[There is here an ingenious and delicate allusion, after the far-fetcht faſhion of the day, to one of Shakeſpere's previous pieces, i. e. *Venus and Adonis*, when the writer ſpeaks of Shakeſpere's comedies having ſo much of the ſalt of wit that they ſeem to be born in the ſea that brought forth Venus. L. T. S.]

Anonymous, 1609.

Amazde I ftood, to fee a Crowd
Of *Civill Throats* ftretchd out fo lowd;
(As at a *New-play*) all the Roomes
Did fwarme with *Gentiles* mix'd with *Groomes*,
So that I truly thought all Thefe
Came to fee *Shore* or *Pericles*.

Pimlyco or Runne Red-Cap. Tis a mad world at Hogsdon. 1609. [4*to.*] *Sign. C i, line* 6.
[*Malone* 299 (*Bodl. Libr.*)]

The play referred to under the name of "Shore" may be one by Henry Chettle and John Day, *circa* 1599, entitled *Shore's Wife*. It is mentioned by Henslowe in his *Diary* (1603), Shakespeare Society's Edition, p. 251; Beaumont and Fletcher, in *The Knight of the Burning Pestle* (Induction, 1613, probably written 1611), speak also of a Play on the same story: the Wife says,—

"I was nere at one of these plays as they say, before; but I should have seene *Jane Shore* once,"

and Christopher Brooke in *The Ghost of Richard the Third* (*His Legend*):

"But now her fame by a vild play doth grow."

(*Fuller Worthies Library*, 1872, p. 94.) The play is not extant.

[The play referred to as "Shore" may be one by T. Heywood, printed in 1600, entitled *The first and second parts of King Edward the Fourth, &c.* It contains the whole history of Jane Shore. P. A. D.]

The first edition of *Pericles* came out in 1609. See before, p. 82.

BEN JONSON, 1609.

Moroſe. Your knighthood * * * ſhall not have hope to repaire it ſelfe by *Conſtantinople, Ireland,* or *Virginia ;* but the beſt, & laſt fortune to it Knight-hood ſhall bee, to make *Do, Teare-ſheet,* or *Kate-Common* a Lady : & ſo, it Knight-hood may eate.

Epicæne ; or, The Silent Woman, Act II. sc. v. end. 1609. [4to.]

[Doll Tear-sheet, of the Second Part of *Henry IV*, was long in the popular mind. See extract from Ligon's *Voyage*, in 1657. L. T. S.]

EDMUND BOLTON, 1610.

The Choife of Englifh. As for example, language & ftyle (the apparell of matter) hee who would penn our affaires in Englifh, and compofe unto us an entire body of them, ought to have a finguler care ther of. For albeit our tongue hath not received dialects, or accentuall notes as the Greeke, nor any certaine or eftablifhed rule either of gramer or true writing, is notwithftanding very copious, and fewe there be who have the moft proper graces thereof, In which the rule cannot be variable: For as much as the people's judgments are uncertaine, the books alfo out of which wee gather the moft warrantable Englifh are not many to my remembrance, of which, in regard they require a particuler and curious tract, I forbeare to fpeake at this prefent. But among the cheife, or rather the cheife, are in my opinion thefe.

Sr Thomas Moore's works

* * * * *

George Chapmans firft feaven books of Iliades.

Samuell Danyell.

Michael Drayton his Heroicall Epiftles of England.

Marlowe his excellent fragment of Hero and Leander.

Shakefpere, Mr Francis Beamont, & innumerable other writers for the ftage; and preffe tenderly to be ufed in this Argument.

Southwell, Parfons, & fome fewe other of that fort.

> [*Hypercritica; or a Rule of Judgment for writing or reading our histories. Addresse the fourthe.*][1] § 11. *Concerning Historicall language and Style. An Enumeration of the best Authors for written English. Rawlinson MSS. (Oxford). p. 13. D 1. (formerly Misc. 1.)*

---

[1] [The part of the title between [ ] is taken from Haslewood's reprint, it is not found in the MS.

Edmund Bolton's treatise long remained in manuscript, and was firft printed by Dr. Hall, in 1722, at the end of *Nic. Trivetium Annalium Continuatio.* Mr. Joseph Haslewood reprinted it, together with what he considers the original outline of "Addresse the fourthe" from the Rawlinson MS. This outline differs considerably from the printed text, in it Bolton could show his high opinion of Shakespere's language, and could press him and other stage writers into his service for "the most warrantable English;" but he thought differently when he wrote his fuller work, and the mention of Shakespere and Beaumont is there left out. (See Haslewood's *Ancient Critical Essays upon English Poets and Poesy*, 1815, vol. ii. pp. 221, 246.)

The date 1610 is given to *Hypercritica* on the authority of a note by Antony Wood; it might possibly be that of the outline, but is probably too early for the final version, in which he cites Bishop Montagu's edition of King James's works, which came out in 1616; he sums up the fourth address as "Prime Gardens for gathering English : according to the true Gage or Standard of the Tongue, about 15 or 16 years ago." L. T. S.]

HANS JACOB WURMSSER VON VENDENHEYM, APRIL 30, 1610.

Lundi, 30. S. E[minence]. alla au Globe, lieu ordinaire ou l'on Joue les Commedies, y fut reprefenté l'hiftoire du More de Venife.

> *Journal of Prince Lewis Frederick of Wirtemberg, Representative of the United German Princes to France and England, in* 1610. *Written by his Secretary Wurmsser.* (*British Museum. Add. MS.* 20,001, *fo.* 9, *back.*) *Printed in W. Brenchley Rye's England as seen by Foreigners.* 1865. *pp. xciv—xcix, cxii, &* 61.

It is not improbable that "cosen garmombles" in the first quarto (1602) of the *Merry Wives of Windsor* (called "Cozen-Jermans" in other editions) is a direct reference to Count Mompelgard (in French Montbéliard), Duke of Wurtemberg, who visited England in 1592, and the visit of whose second son to the Globe Theatre is here recorded by his secretary.[1] In fact, Garmomble is Mombel-gar by metathesis; and the designation of the Duke as "cosen" is an evident allusion to Queen Elizabeth's letters to him. In the play the plural "cosen garmombles" seems to be a generic term for the suite of the Duke. In the compiler's opinion, Mr. W. B. Rye has perfectly identified the allusions in the *Introduction* of his capital work, *England as Seen by Foreigners*, 1865, p. lv; and a more interesting bit of Shakespearian illustration has never been recovered than the first visit of the Duke to London, Windsor, Maidenhead and Reading, in 1592. (See, also, Halliwell's reprint of the First Sketch of the *Merry Wives of Windsor*, for the Shakespeare Society, 1842, *Introduction*, pp. xii—xiv.)

---

[1] [It seems rather strong to call this a "direct reference" in a play published in 1602 to a visit which happened ten years before. Dr. Dowden, however, considers that "such an event would be remembered" (*Sh. Primer*, p. 104). Some think that Shakespere was alluding to a gang of cozeners or sharpers who may have been personating the Duke's followers. L. T. S.]

JOHN DAVIES OF HEREFORD, About 1611.

To our Englifh Terence, Mr. Will. Shake-fpeare.

Some fay (good *Will*) which I, in fport, do fing,
Had'ft thou not plaid fome Kingly parts in fport,
Thou hadft bin a companion for a *King ;*
And, beene a King among the meaner fort.
Some others raile ; but, raile as they thinke fit,
Thou haft no rayling, but, a raigning Wit :
 And honefty *thou fow'ft, which they do reape ,*
 So, to increafe their Stocke *which they do keepe.*

> *The Scourge of Folly, confisting of Satyricall*
> *Epigramms and others, &c. About* 1611.
> [8*vo.*] *Epig.* 159, *p.* 76.
> *Reprinted by Rev. A. B. Grosart, in the Chertsey*
> *Worthies Library, Davies' Works, p.* 26.

The commencing lines may refer to a fact related in a letter from John Chamberlaine to Winwood, dated December 18, 1604.

"The Tragedy of *Gowry*, with all the Action and Actors hath been twice represented by the King's Players, with exceeding Concourse of all sorts of People. But whether the matter or manner be not well handled, or that it be thought unfit that Princes should be played on the Stage in their Lifetime, I hear that some great Councellors are much displeased with it, and so 'tis thought shall be forbidden." (Winwood's *Memorials*, 1725, ii. 41.)

[It seems likely that these lines refer to the fact that Shakespere was a player, a profession that was then despised and accounted mean. For evidence of this feeling see before, pp. 3, 58, and after, Sir Richard Baker's Chronicle, 1643. L. T. S.]

*LODOVIC BARREY, 1611

PARALLEL PASSAGES.

Lodovic Barrey.	*Shakespere.*
Now to the next tap-house, there drink down this, and by the operation of the third pot, quarrel again (*Act II. sc. ii; sign.* C 3, *bk*).	He enters the confines of a tavern * * * and by the operation of the second cup draws on him the drawer (*Rom. and Jul.* Act III. sc. i. l. 6).
Dash, we must bear some brain (*Act II.; sign.* D 3).	Nay, I do bear a brain (*Rom. and Jul.* Act I. sc. iii. l. 29).
Is there no trust, no honnesty in men? (*Act II.: sign.* D 2.)	There's no trust, no faith, no honesty in men (*Rom. and Jul.* Act III. sc. ii. l. 86).
He stirreth not, he moveth not, he waggeth not (*Act IV.; sign.* G 2).	He heareth not, he stirreth not, he moveth not (*Rom. and Jul.* Act II. sc. i. l. 16).

Ram Alley, or Merrie-Tricks, a Comedy, 1611.

[Mr. Fleay in his *Shakespeare Manual*, 1876, p. 19, says that this "play is one continuous parody of Shakespere," and that it contains, besides the above, allusions to *Hamlet, Othello, Much Ado about Nothing*, &c. L. T. S.]

JOHN DAVIES OF HEREFORD, *About* 1611.

Another (ah, Lord helpe) mee vilifies
With Art of Love, and how to fubtilize,
Making lewd *Venus*, with eternall Lines,
To tye *Adonis* to her loves defignes :
Fine wit is fhew'n therein : but finer twere
If not attired in fuch bawdy Geare.
But be it as it will : the coyeft Dames,
In private read it for their Cloffet-games :
For, footh to fay, the lines fo draw them on,
To the venerian fpeculation,
That will they, nill they (if of flefh they bee)
They will thinke of it, fith *loofe* Thought is free.

*Papers Complaint, compil'd in truthfull Rimes
Against the paper-spoylers of these Times.* [*In
the Volume containing The Scourge of Folly,
and other poems. About* 1611. *p.* 231.] [4*to.*]
*Reprinted by Rev. A. B. Grosart in the Chertsey
Worthies Library, Davies' Works, p.* 75.

The first line here quoted is thus given by Drake (who follows Brydges *Censura Literaria,* 1808, vol. vi. p. 276) in his *Shakespeare and his Times,* vol. ii. p. 30 :

"Another (ah, harde happe) me vilifies
With art of love," &c.

SIMON FORMAN 1611.

In Richard the 2 at the glob 1611 the 30 of Aprill.
(fo. 201.)
In the Winters Talle at the glob 1611 the 15 of maye
(fo. 201 *b.*)
Of Cimbalin King of England
(fo. 206.)
In Mackbeth at the glob 1610 the 20 of Aprill
(fo. 207.)

Forman MSS. Ashmolean 208. *In the Bodleian Library.*

[Dr. Forman began this "Bocke of Plaies and Notes therof *per* Formans for Common Pollicie" a few months before his death (he died September 1611); it consists of a thin paper folio, of which only six pages are filled with notes on the four plays indicated by the above heads; he got no further. The "notes" are nothing more than a short relation of the story of what he saw, and are in no way critical. They have been printed by Mr. J. P. Collier, "New Particulars regarding the Works of Shakespere," 1836, pp. 6—26: by Mr. Halliwell, who also gives facsimiles of them, in his Folio edition of Shakespere's Works, 1853—65, vols. viii. p. 41; ix. p. 8; xiv. p. 61; xv. p. 417: and in the *Transactions* of the New Shakspere Society, 1875-6, Part II, pp. 415—418.

The description of *Richard II.* shows that the play seen by Dr. Forman was not Shakespere's play of that name. See Halliwell as above, Vol. ix. p. 8, also Dr. E. Dowden's *Shakespere Primer*, p. 87.]

* J. M., 1600—1612.

who hath a lovinge wife & loves her not,
he is no better then a witleſſe ſotte;
Let ſuch have wives to recompenſe their merite,
even Menelaus forked face inherite.
Is love in wives good, not in huſbands too?
why doe men ſweare they love then, when they wooe?
it ſeemes 't is true that W. S. ſaid,
when once he heard one courting of a Mayde,—
Beleve not thou Mens fayned flatteryes,
Lovers will tell a buſhell-full of Lyes!

*The Newe Metamorphosis, or A Feaste of Fancie, or
Poeticall Legendes.* Brit. Mus. Add. MSS. 14,824,
14,825. 3 vols. 4to. Vol. I. Pt. II. p. 96 (old No.).

[The first volume of this MS. bears the date 1600 on the title-page. The work, however, was added to, emended, and probably continued from time to time; in the second volume (in which the above extract occurs) is a passage which puts the date of part of it at least as late as the end of 1612, the date of Prince Henry's death and Princess Elizabeth's marriage.

"But H. vntymely in his prime of yeares
  must hence departe, & passe through funerall fyres
  iust at that tyme when gieatest ioye's intended
  at bright E's nuptials, with all mirth portended." (p. 215, old nos.)

The author's name is quite conjectural; he says (I. leaf 4, b):

"My name is Frenche, to tell you in a worde
  yet came not in with Conqueringe williams sworde."

See further on this manuscript, Appendix C. L. T. S.]

The W. S. above must stand for a name which gives two trochees (like William Shākespeāre), and is, probably, identical with the W. S. in *Willobie his Avisa*, before, pp. 7—11. It is not wonderful that the concluding couplet is not found in Shakespeare's works, seeing that it is quoted as a conversational impromptu. [Polonius' advice to Ophelia contains an expansion of the idea found in them. See *Hamlet*, Act I, sc. iii. ll. 115—120, 127. L. T. S.]

THOMAS HEYWOOD, 1612.

Here likewife, I muft necessarily infert a manifeft injury done me in that worke,[1] by taking the two Epiftles of *Paris* to *Helen,* and *Helen* to *Paris,* and printing them in a leffe volume, under the name of another, which may put the world in opinion I might fteale them from him;[2] and hee to doe himfelfe right, hath fince publifhed them in his owne name: but as I muft acknowledge my lines not worthy his patronage, under whom he hath publifht them, fo the Author[3] I know much offended with M. *Jaggard* that (altogether unknowne to him) prefumed to make fo bold with his name.

An Apology for Actors. 1612. *Epistle " To my approved good Friend, Mr. Nicholas Okes,"* [*the printer*] *at the end.*

---

[1] That worke, "my booke of *Britaines Troy.*"
[2] *i. e.* the printer of *Britaines Troy.*
[3] Shakespere.

[" *The Passionate Pilgrim,* by W. Shakespeare, was first publisht in 1599... The *Pilgrim* is a collection, made by the piratical publisher, William Jaggard, of some genuine Sonnets, &c., by Shakspere, Richard Barnfield, Bartholomew Griffin, Christopher Marlowe, and other writers unknown, got from divers printed books and other sources. Thirteen years afterwards, in 1612, the same pirate Jaggard reprinted *The Pilgrim* as Shakspere's, and put into it, under Shakspere's name, and to his disgust, two poems by Thomas Heywood, for which the latter publicly reproacht Jaggard " (as above).—Furnivall, *Introd. to the Leopold Shakspere,* p. xxxv. Only eleven out of the twenty-one songs in the collection are certainly or possibly Shakespere's. (See Dowden's *Shakespere Primer,* p. 111.) L. T. S.]

JOHN WEBSTER, 1612.

Detraction is the fworne friend to ignorance : For mine owne part I have ever truly cherifht my good opinion of other mens worthy Labours, efpecially of that full and haightned ftile of maifter *Chapman:* The labor'd and underftanding workes of maifter *Johnfon:* The no leffe worthy compofures of the both worthily excellent Maifter *Beamont* & Maifter *Fletcher:* And laftly (without wrong laft to be named), the right happy and copious induftry of M. *Shake-fpeare,* M. *Decker,* & M. *Heywood,* wifhing what I write may be read by their light : Protefting, that, in the ftrength of mine owne judgement, I know them fo worthy, that though I reft filent in my owne worke, yet to moft of theirs I dare (without flattery) fix that of *Martiall.*

—non norunt, Hæc monumenta mori.

The White Divel. 1612. [*4to.*] *Dedication (last paragraph).*

JOSEPH FLETCHER, 1613.

He di'd indeed not as an actor dies
To die to day, and live againe to morrow,
In shew to pleafe the audience, or difguife
The idle habit of inforced forrow :
    The Croffe his ftage was, and he plaid the part
    Of one that for his friend did pawne his heart.

His heart he pawnd, and yet not for his friend,
For who was friend to him, or who did love him?
But to his deadly foe he did extend
His deareft blood to them that did reprove him,
    For fuch as tooke his life from him, he gave
    Such life, as by his life they could not have.

Christe's Bloodie Sweat, or the Sonne of God in His Agonie.
1613. *p.* 31. [4*to.*]
Reprinted by the Rev. A. B. Grosart in the Fuller Worthies'
Library, 1869. *p.* 177.

This is perhaps the most curious allusion to a work of Shakespeare's made during his lifetime :
          "the part
   Of one that for his friend did pawn his heart"

was assuredly the part of Antonio, in the *Merchant of Venice.* That play was probably written in 1596, it was entered on the Stationers' Register in 1598 and 1600, and published in 1600 in two editions, the first by James Roberts, the second by Thomas Heyes.

THOMAS LORKINS, 1613.

London this laſt of June 1613.

No longer ſince then yeſterday, while Bourbege his companie were acting at ye Globe the play of Hen : 8, and there ſhooting of certayne chambers in way of triumph; the fire catch'd & faſtened upon the thatch of ye houſe and there burned ſo furiouſly as it conſumed the whole houſe & all in leſſe then two houres (the people having enough to doe to ſave themſelves).

Letter from Thomas Lorkins to Sir Thos. Puckering. Harl. MS. 7,002, fo. 268.

[Another contemporary account of the burning of the Globe theatre says that the play going on at the time was a new play called *All is true*. (See Furnivall's *Introduction to the Leopold Shakspere*, p. xviii.) "Chambers" were small cannon or mortars. **L. T. S.**]

LORD TREASURER STANHOPE, 1613.

The Accompte of the right hono*u*rable the Lo*r*d Stanhope of Harrington, Trea*fu*rer of his Maje*ft*ies Chamber, for all *f*uch Somes of money as hath beine receaved and paied by him within his O*t*fice from the fea*ft*e of St. Michaell Tharchangell, Anno *Regni* Regis Jacobi Decimo (1612), untill the fe*n*fte of St. Michaell, Anno *Regni* Regis Jacobi undecimo (1613), conteyning one whole yeare.

Item paid to John Heminges uppon lyke warra*nt*, dated att Whitehall ix° die Julij 1613 for him*f*elf an*d* the re*ft* of his fellowes, his Maje*ft*ies *f*ervauntes an*d* Players for pre*f*entinge a playe before the Duke of Savoyes Emba*ff*adour on the viij*th* daye of June, 1613, calle*d* Cardenna, the *f*ome of vjli. xiijs. iiijd.

Item paid to John Heminges uppon the Cowncells warra*nt* dated att Whitehall xx° die Maij 1613, for pre*f*entinge before the Princes Highnes the L*a*dy Elizabeth and the Prince Pallatyne Elector fowerteene *f*everall playes, viz: one playe called Fila*ft*er, One other called the Knott of ffooles, One other *Much adoe abowte nothinge*, The Mayeds Tragedy, The merye dyvell of Edmonton, *The Tempe*ft, A kinge and no kinge/ The Twins Tragedie/ *The Winters Tale*, Sir John *ff*al*f*ia*ff*e, *The Moo*r *of Venice*, The Nobleman, *Cæfars Tragedye*,/ And one other called Love lyes a bleedinge, All w*hi*ch Playes weare played with-in the tyme of this Accompte, viz: paid the *f*ome of iiij*xx* xiijli. vjs. viijd [£93 : 6 : 8]

Item paid to the *f*aid John Heminges uppon the lyke warra*nt*, dated att Whitehall xx° die Maij 1613, for pre*f*entinge *f*ixe

ſeverall playes, viz: one playe called a badd begiuininge (*sic*)
makes a good endinge, One other called *th*e Capteyne, One
other the Alcumiſt./ One other Cardenno/ One other *The
Hotſpur*/ And one other called *Benedicte and Betteris*, All
playeḍ within the tyme of this Accompte viz: paid Fortie
powndes, Anḍ by waye of his Majeſties rewarde twentie powndes,
In all lx li.

Rawl. MS., *A.* 239, *leaf* 47 (*in the Bodleian*). *Printed in
New Sh. Soc.'s Transactions*, 1875-6, *Part II, p.* 419.

[Lord Stanhope's accounts give six of Shakespere's plays as acted in
1613 (those printed in italics above). It is believed that *Sir John Falstaffe*
refers to 1 *Henry IV*, or *The Merry Wives of Windsor*; *Cæsars Tragedye* to
Julius Cæsar; *The Hotspur* possibly to 1 *Henry IV*; while *Benedicte and
Betteris* must be *Much Ado About Nothing*. L. T. S.]

BEN JONSON, 1614.

It is alſo agreed, that every man heere, exerciſe his owne Iudgement, and not cenſure by *Contagion*, or upon *truſt*, from anothers voice, or face. * * * Hee that will ſweare *Ieronimo* or *Andronicus* are the beſt playes, yet ſhall paſſe unexcepted at, heere, as a man whoſe Iudgement ſhewes it is conſtant, and hath ſtood ſtill, theſe five and twentie, or thirtie yeeres.

(*fourth page.*)

* * * *

If there bee never a *Servant-monſter* i' the *Fayre*, who can help it? he¹ ſayes; nor a neſt of *Antiques*? Hee is loth to make Nature afraid in his *Playes*, like thoſe that beget *Tales*, *Tempeſts*, and ſuch like *Drolleries*, to mix his head with other mens heeles.

(*fifth page.*)

Bartholomew Fayre. Induction. Workes, 1640 (*the publication of this play being dated* 1631).

¹ "He" is the Author, Ben Jonson.

In the first extract from the *Induction* to *Bartholomew Fair* we have *Titus Andronicus*; in the second the mention of "a servant monster" recals Caliban in Shakespeare's *Tempest:* and the expression "to mix his head with other men's heels" recals a scene in that play where Trinculo takes refuge from the storm under Caliban's gabardine. Antiques means antics, cf. the cavalier Cleveland, 30 years later,

"A jig, a jig, and in this antick dance"
(Mixt Assembly. *Poems.* 1687. p. 34.)

There can be no doubt that Jonson was alluding to the *Tempest*.

[Whalley supposes that some words on the second page of this *Induction*, "and then a substantial watch to have stolen in upon them, & taken them away, with mistaking words, as the fashion is in the stage-practice," are a sneer upon Shakespere alluding to the Watch and their blunders in *Much Ado about Nothing*. But, as Lieut.-Col. Cunningham points out (Jonson's *Works*, 1871, vol. ii. p. 144, note), "the guardians of the night had been proverbial for their blundering simplicity before Shakespere was born," and he does not think this comedy was referred to. Dr. B. Nicholson, however, does, and thinks that the conjunction of the three bits in this *Induction* prove that a sneer against Shakespere was intended by Jonson. L. T. S.]

THOMAS FREEMAN, 1614.

To Master W. Shakespeare.

Shakespeare, that nimble *Mercury* thy braine,
Lulls many hundred *Argus*-eyes asleepe,
So fit, for all thou fashionest thy vaine,
At th' *horse-foote* fountaine thou hast drunk full deepe,
Vertues or vices theame to thee all one is:
Who loves chaste life, there's *Lucrece* for a Teacher:
Who list read lust there's *Venus* and *Adonis,*
True modell of a most lascivious leatcher.
Besides in plaies thy wit windes like *Meander:*
When needy new-composers borrow more   [Whence]
Thence *Terence* doth from *Plautus* or *Menander.*   Than]
But to praise thee aright I want thy store:
   Then let thine owne works thine owne worth upraise,
   And help t' adorne thee with deserved Baies.

Runne, and a Great Cast. The Second Bowle. (Being the second part of Rubbe, and a Great Cast, 1614.) Epigram 92, sign. K 2, back. [4to.]

ROBERT TAILOR, 1614.

And if it prove fo happy as to pleafe,
Weele fay 'tis fortunate like *Pericles*.

> *The Hogge hath lost his Pearle.* **1614.** [4*to.*] *Last two lines of Prologue.* [*Bodleian Lib. Malone* 169.]

As to date, &c., of *Pericles*, see before, p. 82, *note.*

EDMUND HOWES, 1614.

Our moderne, and prefent excellent Poets which worthely florifh in their owne workes, and all of them in my owne knowledge lived togeather in this Queenes raigne, according to their priorities as neere as I could, I have orderly fet downe (viz) *George Gafcoigne* Efquire, *Thomas Churchyard* Efquire, Sir *Edward Dyer* Knight, *Edmond Spencer* Efquire, Sir *Philip Sidney* Knight, Sir *John Harrington* Knight, Sir *Thomas Challoner* Knight, Sir *Frauncis Bacon* Knight, & Sir *John Davie* Knight, Mafter *Iohn Lillie* gentleman, Maifter *George Chapman* gentleman, M. *W. Warner* gentleman, M. *Willi. Shakefpeare* gentleman, *Samuell Daniell* Efquire, *Michaell Draiton* Efquire, of the bath, M. *Chriftopher Marlo* gen., M. *Benjamine Johnfon* gentleman, *Iohn Marfton* Efquier, M. *Abraham Frauncis* gen., mafter *Frauncis Meers* gentle. mafter *Jofua Siluefter* gentle. mafter *Thomas Deckers* gentleman, M. John Flecher gentle., M. *John Webfter* gentleman, M. *Thomas Heywood* gentleman, M. *Thomas Middleton* gentleman, M. *George Withers*.

John Stow's Annales, or generall Chronicle of England ; continued to the end of 1614 *by Edmond Howes.* 1615. *p.* 811. [*Reign of Queen Elizabeth.*]

Deckers became Decker in the 1631 edition of Stow's *Annals;* no other alteration was then made in this list.

C[HRISTOPHER] B[ROOKE], 1614.

My tongue in firie dragons' fpleene I fteepe,
That acts, with accents, cruelty may found;
(Part 1. St. viii.)
To him that impt my fame with Clio's quill,
Whofe magick raif'd me from oblivion's den;
That writ my ftorie on the Mufes hill,
And with my actions dignifi'd his pen:
He that from Helicon fends many a rill,
Whofe nectared veines, are drunke by thirftie men;
   Crown'd be his ftile with fame, his head with bayes;
   And none detract, but gratulate his praife.

Yet if his fcænes have not engroft all grace,
The much-fam'd action could extend on ftage;
(Part 2. Stanzas i, ii.)
My working head (my counfell's confiftory)
Debates how I might raigne, the princes living:
(Ibid. St. xxvi.)
The devlifh fury in my breft entends,
In fpite of danger and all oppofite barrs;
   To cut this knot the miftick fates conteyne,
   And fet my life and kingdome on this mayne. [caſt]
(Part 3. St. xxxviii.)

The Ghost of Richard the Third. Expressing himselfe in these three Parts. 1. *His Character* 2. *His Legend* 3. *His Tragedie Containing more of him than hath been heretofore shewed: either in Chronicles, Playes, or Poems.* 1614. [*Unique copy in Bodleian.*] *Reprinted by Rev. A. B. Grosart in the Fuller Worthies' Library, Complete Poems of Christopher Brooke,* 1872, *in which see pp.* 62, 79, 88, 134. — *Also for the Shakspere Society, by Mr. J. P. Collier,* 1844.

C[HRISTOPHER] B[ROOKE], 1614.

Besides the direct allusion to the play of *Richard III*, in Christopher Brooke's poem, there are several lines caught from Shakespeare's work. The three most striking are here given. The first refers to these lines in Act V. Sc. iii:

> "Our ancient word of courage, fair St. George
> Inspire us with the spleen of fiery dragons!"

The third refers to a line in Act II. Sc. ii:

> "My other self, my counsel's consistory."

The fourth refers to these lines in Act V. Sc. iv:

> "Slave, I have set my life upon a cast,
> And I will stand the hazard of the die."

[The second quotation is pointed out by Mr. Collier and Dr. Grosart as a "clear allusion to Shakespere and to his play on the history of *Richard III*." (Grosart's reprint, p. 150.) It is Richard's "Ghost" himself who speaks. L. T. S.]

SIR WILLIAM DRUMMOND, 1614.

The authors I have feen on the Subject of Love, are the Earl of *Surrey*, Sir *Thomas Wyat* (whom, becaufe of their Antiquity, I will not match with our better Times) *Sidney, Daniel, Drayton,* and *Spenfer*, * * The laft we have are Sir *William Alexander* and *Shakefpear*, who have lately publifhed their Works.

Works : Fo : 1711. *p.* 226.

This note of Drummond's must belong to the period of 1614-1616 ; for Alexander was not knighted till 1614, and Shakespeare, who died in 1616, is here spoken of as a living author. The word "lately" induces us to give the earliest date possible to the note. See *Drummond of Hawthornden; the Story of his Life and Writings*. By David Masson, 1873, p. 81, *note*.

RICHARD BRATHWAITE, 1615.

Ile be thy *Venus*, pretty Ducke I will,
And though leſſe faire, yet I have farre more ſkill,
In Loves affaires : for if I *Adon* had,
As *Venus* had : I could have taught the lad
To have beene farre more forward then he was,
And not have dallied with to apt a laſſe.
(The Civill Devill, pp. 44, 45.)

If I had liv'd but in King Richards dayes,
Who in his heat of paſſion, midſt the force
Of his Aſſailants troubled many waies
Crying *A horſe, a Kingdome for a horſe.*
O then my horſe which now at Livery ſtayes,
" Had beene ſet free, where now hee's forc't to ſtand
" And like to fall into the Oſtler's hand.
(Upon a Poets Palfrey, p. 154.)

No cure he finds to heale this maladie,
But makes a vertue of neceſſity.
(The Wooer, p. 95.)

A Strappado for the Divell. Epigrams and Satyres alluding to the time, with divers measures of no lesse Delight. 1615. [8vo.]
Reprinted by R. Roberts, Boston, 1878.

[Brathwaite's *Strappado* thus gives us recollections of four of Shakespere's works, *Venus and Adonis, Richard III* (Act V, sc. iv, l. 8), *Two Gentlemen of Verona* (Act IV, sc. i, l. 62), and in the extract next following, to a part of *Pericles*, although that part is not Shakespere's. A verse on p. 82 of the reprint may refer to the "park" of l. 231 of *Venus and Adonis*. L. T. S.]

RICHARD BRATHWAITE, 1615.

A cage of uncleane birds, which is poſſeſſt,
Of none ſave ſuch as will defile their neſt.
Where fires of Hell hounds never come abroade,
But in that earthly Tophet make aboade.
Where bankrupt Factors to maintaine a ſtate,
Forlorne (heaven knows) and wholy deſperate,
Turne valiant *Boults, Pimps,* Haxtars, roaring boyes,
Till fleſht in bloud, counting but murders toyes,
Are forc't in th' end a dolefull Pſalme to ſing,
Going to Heaven by *Derick* in a ſtring.

Strappado for the Diuell (The Conyburrow), 1615, *p.* 151.

[Rev. J. W. Ebsworth on p. xxv of his Introduction to a Reprint of the above by R. Roberts, Boston, 1878, says, "In a Satyre, called 'The Coniborrowe,' we find a palpable allusion to one of the characters in Shakespeare's *Pericles*, [but not in Shakespere's part of the play] the damned doorkeeper" Boult. The public hangman is mentioned in the proverbial saying of "going to Heaven by *Derick* in a string:" there was a tune known about that time, with a burden "Take 'im, Derrick!" *Bagford Ballads,* printed for the Ballad Society (p. 778). F. J. F.]

Anonymous, 1615.

A Purveiour of Tobacco.

Call him a Broker of Tobacco, he ſcornes the title, hee had rather be tearmed a cogging Merchant. Sir *John Falſtaffe* robb'd with a bottle of Sacke; ſo doth hee take mens purſes, with a wicked roule of Tobacco at his girdle.

> *New and choiſe Characters: of seveiall Authors, with the Wife, written by Syr Thomas Overburie.* 1615. *Sign. M* 8. [*Bodleian Lib. Bliss* 2. 2140.]

This curious passage is taken from the Edition of 1615, a copy of which has been recently acquired by the British Museum, [but is unfortunately now, 9 October, 1878, inaccessible. L. T. S.] The "Characters" were added to Sir Thomas Overbury's *Wife*, in the second edition of 1614 (in which year there were five editions): by 1664 *The Wife & Characters* appear to have run to seventeen editions, of which thirteen are in the British Museum; but the "Purveiour of Tobacco" does not occur in any, except in that of 1615.

ROBERT ANTON, 1616.

Or why are *women* rather growne so mad,
That their *immodeſt feete* like *planets* gad
With ſuch *irregular motion* to baſe *Playes*,
Where all the *deadly ſinnes* keepe *hollidaies*
There ſhall they ſee the *vices* of the *times*,
Oreſtes inceſt, *Cleopatres* crimes.

    *   *   *   *

Sooner may ſhameleſſe wives hate *Braindford feaſts*,
Albertus Magnus, or the *pilfred Jeſts*
Of ſome ſpruce *Skipjack Citizen* from *Playes*,
A *Coach*, the ſecret *Baudihouſe* for *waies*,
And *riotous waſte* of ſome new *Freeman* made,
That in one *yeere* to *peices* breakes his *trade*,
Then waſh the toad-like ſpeckles of *defame*,
That ſwell the *world* with *poyſon* of their *ſhame*:
What *Comedies* of errors ſwell the *ſtage*
With your moſt *publike vices*, when the *age*
Dares perſonate in *action*, for, your *eies*
Ranke *Sceanes* of your *luſt*-ſweating *qualities*.

      The Philosopher's Satyrs. 1616. [4*to.*] *Pp.* 46 & 51
      Fifth Satyr. Of Venus.

SIR WILLIAM DRUMMOND, 1616.

Ah *Napkin*, ominous Prefent of my Deare,
Gift miferable, which doth now remaine
The only Guerdon of my helpleffe Paine,
   *   *   *
  *   deare *Naphin* doe not grieve
That I this Tribute pay thee from mine Eine
And that (thefe pofting Houres I am to live)
I laundre thy faire Figures in this Brine.

Poems by William Drummond of Hawthorne-denne.
Second Impression. Edinburgh,</i> 1616, <i>sign. H</i> 3,
back (eleventh Sonnet in the Second Part).

[Drummond in this sonnet made use of an idea which appears in the second and third lines of the 3rd Stanza of Shakespere's *Lover's Complaint*, first printed in 1609.

  "Oft did she heave her Napkin to her eyne,
   Which on it had conceited characters:
  Laundring the silken figures in the brine,
   That seasoned woe had pelleted in teares."
    (Shakespere's Sonnets, 1609, sign. K, back.) L. T. S.]

BEAUMONT AND FLETCHER, 1611, 1616.
[B. died 16$\frac{15}{16}$. F. died 1625.]

Welford. . But fhall wee fee thefe Gentleweomen to-night?

Sir Roger. Have patience Sir, untill our fellowe *Nicholas* bee deceaft, that is, a fleepe; for fo the word is taken; to fleepe to die, to die to fleepe: a very Figure Sir.

Wel. Cannot you caft another for the Gentleweomen?

Ro. Not till the man bee in his bed, his grave; his grave, his bed; the very fame againe Sir. Our Comick Poet gives the reafon fweetly; *Plenus rimarum eft*, he is full of loopeholes.

The Scornful Ladie, Act II. Sc. i. [4to.] 1616, *sign. C* 4.

> By heaven me thinkes it were an eafie leape
> To plucke bright honour from the pale-fac'd Moone,
> Or dive into the bottome of the fea,
> Where never fathome line touch't any ground,
> And plucke up drowned honor from the lake of hell.

Knight of the Burning Pestle. Prologue. 1613. [4to.] *Sign. B* 2.

[The date when the *Scornful Ladie* was written is uncertain, it was firſt printed in 1616. Hamlet's Soliloquy (Act III. i.) seems to have given rise to some merriment here, not dreamt of perhaps by "our Comick Poet."

The *Knight of the Burning Pestle* was probably written in 1611, though not printed till 1613. Ralph, the 'Prentice, being called in to "speak a huffing part" to show his powers, spouts Hotspur's lines (First Part *Henry IV*, Act I. sc. iii. l. 201). Steevens infers that this or a similar passage was "used as a common burlesque phrase for attempting impossibilities," and quotes W. Cartwright's satirical poem on Mr. [William] Stokes' Book on the Art of Vaulting.

> "Then go thy ways, Brave *Will*, for one,
>   By *Jove* 'tis thou must Leap or none,
>   To pull bright honour from the Moon" (*Poems*, 1651, p. 212).

See another quotation from *The Knight*, before, p. 78. L. T. S.]

BEN JONSON, 1616.

[The author will not]
    purchaſe your delight at ſuch a rate
As, for it, he himſelf muſt juſtly hate :
To make a child, now ſwadled, to proceede
Man, and then ſhoote up, in one beard, and weede,
Paſt threeſcore years : or, with three ruſtie ſwords,
And helpe of ſome few foot-and-halfe-foote words,
Fight over *Yorke*, and *Lancaſter's* long jarres :
And in the tyring-houſe bring wounds, to ſcarres.
He rather prayes, you will be pleaſ'd to ſee
One ſuch, to-day as other playes ſhould be ;
Where neither *Chorus* wafts you ore the ſeas ;
Nor creaking throne comes downe, the boys to pleaſe.

    Every Man in his Humour. Prologue. 1616. *p.* 3. [*fol.*]

    In this Prologue, according to Hunter, Jonson censured Shakespere, pointing especially at several of his plays : (1) Infancy and maturity in the same character,—*Winter's Tale;* (2) the Wars of York and Lancaster with their duels and battles,—*Henry VI;* (3) the shifting the scene from one country to another,—*Henry V;* (4) the descent of a creaking throne,—the masques in the *Tempest* and in *Cymbeline.* The final line of the prologue in which Jonson assures his audience that, if they laugh at popular errors,

    "You that have so graced monsters, may like men,"

is supposed to refer to Caliban.
    (Hunter's *New Illustrations of Shakespere,* 1845, I. 136. Stokes' *Chronological order of Shakespere's Plays,* 1878, p 177.) L. T. S.]
    [The first or Italian version of *Every Man in his Humour* was published in 1601 without a prologue. The second or English version in 1616 with the prologue. This states that the *play* (not this second version) was acted by the Lord Chamberlain's servants in 1598.
    Gifford would make out that the 1601 edition was edited, not by B. Jonson, but from the copy used at Henslowe's theatre in 1596, and hence that the prologue was really existent in that year. To his assertions may be

opposed these facts. 1. There may be a possibility, but not a shadow of proof, that "The Humours" or "The Comedy of Humours" had anything to do with Jonson or with his play. The word "Humours" was then fashionable cant. 2. The 1601 4to. bears on its title-page,—"as it hath been . . acted by . . the Lord Chamberlaine his servants." Are we to believe without proof that there was here printed a direct lie? 3. And can we believe that Jonson, an irascible man, would in the same year, 1601, give his *Fountaine of Self Love* to the publisher who had just brought out *Every Man in his H.*, against his interests, and with a lying title-page, for Henslowe who had quarrelled with him? 4. The 1601 edition also bears on its title-page " Written by Ben Johnson," asserted by Gifford to be a mis-spelling. It is so spelt in three plays, and he never spelt it Jonson till 1604, when he printed with a Latin title-page his part of the celebration of James' entry into London. 5. The 1601 4to. has none of the blunders of a spurious edition, but like all by Jonson, is very carefully punctuated. 6. That "this play" on the title-page of the 1616 folio does not mean "this new version" is shown by the parallel case of *Sejanus*. Before it Jonson says " this play was first acted in 1603," while shortly after he tells us it was a different version. 7. Lastly, this second or now known version cannot, by internal evidence, have been written before 1605 or 1606. For, 1. Bobadil in the 1601 4to. speaks of the taking of Ghibelletto some ten years back, and of that of Tortosa ; but in the later version he alters the names to " Strigonium " and " what do you call it." Now Strigonium (Graan) was taken from the Turks in 1596, which makes the date of speaking 1606 ; while, unable to find a parallel for Tortosa, he makes Bobadil pretend to forget the name he would say. 2. In the 1616 version Act I. sc. ii. is introduced for the first time—" Our Turkey Company never sent the like [present] to the Grand Seignor,"—clearly an allusion to a recent event. But the only occasions when they sent such a present were, one too early in Elizabeth's reign to be alluded to in a familiar letter, and one of the value of £5,322 given them by James for a present to the Porte, in December, 1605, soon after the re-constitution of the Company.

If these facts be correct there can be no reason for assigning the prologue to a date earlier than 1606, as shown by internal evidence to be that of the version with which it first appears. B. N.]

[Another passage was quoted from Jonson (*Sejanus*) in the first edition of the *Centurie* (p. 330), which, though believed by some critics upon merely supposititious grounds to refer to Shakespere, I now omit in the text, Dr. Brinsley Nicholson having pointed out in the *Academy*, Nov. 14, 1874, that the "second Pen" was in all probability that of Samuel Sheppard. Jonson says in the Preface to *Sejanus* (1605),—

"Lastly I would informe you, that this Booke, in all numbers, is not the same with that which was acted on the publike Stage, wherein a second Pen had good share : in place of which I have rather chosen, to put weaker (and no doubt lesse pleasing) of mine own, then to defraud so happy a *Genius* of his right, by my lothed usurpation."

In 1646 Samuel Sheppard published *The Times Displayed in Six Sestyads* (see after, under date). The sixth sestyad is a series of verses in praise of the greater poets, Daniel, Drayton, Shakespere, Jonson, and others. The eleventh encomium runs thus :—

> "So His that Divine PLAUTUS equalled,   Ben Johnston
> Whose Commick vain MENANDER nere could hit,
> Whose tragick sceans shal be with wonder Read
> By after ages for unto his wit
> My selfe gave personal ayd *I* dictated
> To him when as *Sejanus* fall he writ,
> And yet on earth some foolish sots there bee
> That dare make Randolf his Rival in degree."

On these Dr. Nicholson remarks, "As Sheppard is not a master of English verse or style, so his 'dictate' is not happily chosen, but the meaning and intent of it and its context are clear. Read by the light of Jonson's words, they are not only clear, but distinct, and we see Sheppard's disappointment, and the strugglings of his self-conceit to record the fact that he had been a part-author in *Sejanus*—strugglings which are shown in his 'And yet,' and 'for,' and which destroy his encomium by making it ridiculous." Dr. Ingleby, however, asks me to add that he regards Sheppard's authorship in *Sejanus* as impossible, and that, with Mr. Fleay, he is now disposed to assign the "second pen" to Chapman. L. T. S.]

April 25, 1616.

Good frend for Iesvs sake forbeare,
To digg the dvst encloased heare:
Bleste be ye man y^t spares thes stones,
And cvrst be he y^t moves my bones.

Inscription on the Tablet over Shakespeare's Grave, given in Halliwell's Life of Shakespere, **1848,** *p.* **286.**

The inscription on Shakespeare's grave-stone is feebly parodied in the Apology prefixed to Graves' *Spiritual Quixote.* (Ed. 1773. Vol. i. p. vii.)

SHAKESPEARE'S
CENTURIE OF PRAYSE.

SECOND PERIOD.

1617—1642.

1617—1622.

Ivdicio Pylivm, genio Socratem, arte Maronem,
Terra tegit, popvlvs mæret, Olympvs habet.

Stay Passenger, why goest thov by so fast?
read if thov canst, whom enviovs Death hath plast,
with in this monvment Shakspeare with whome
qvick natvre dide : whose name doth deck ẙ Tombe
far more then cost: sieh all, ẙ He hath writt, [sith]
Leaves living art, bvt page, to serve his witt.
obiit ano doⁱ 1616
Ætatis, 53. die 23 ap.

Inscriptions upon the Tablet under Shakespere's Bust, in the Chancel-north-wall of Stratford Church; heliotyped in Shakespere's Home and Rural Life, by Major James Walter, 1874, p. 17. See also Halliwell's Life of Shakespere, p. 289.

Steevens conjectured that the scribe wrote *Sophoclem*, not *Socratem*. Assuredly one who had scholarship enough to compose the verses could hardly have believed that the o in the latter word had a common quantity. Besides, the comparison of Shakespere to Sophocles is significant : to Socrates trifling : Ben Jonson and Samuel Sheppard compare Shakespere to Sophocles. (See pp. 148, 261, 285.) If Sheppard wrote *Sophocles* in an English verse, that would be irrelevant ; for he would not have written it in a Latin one.

The converse misprint occurs in *The Playhouse Pocket Companion*, 1779, p. 47, in the first line of the Catalogue of which "Sophocles" is an error for *Socrates*. (See *Biog. Dram.* 1812. Int. lxxiii.)

[Admitting Dr. Ingleby's criticism to be correct, I can but endorse the remark of a friend that the likening of Shakespere to Socrates, one of the wisest of men, seems the right reading in the first line. The comparison to Virgil, the representative poet, next following, renders the allusion to Sophocles unnecessary, whereas Nestor, Socrates, and Virgil, make a grand trio of ideal men. The bust (by G. Johnson, see after, Dugdale, 1653) was set up before 1623, as we know from the mention of it by Leonard Digges. (See after, p. 154.) L. T. S.]

JOHN TAYLOR, THE WATER POET, 1617.

[Defcription of the hang-man at Hamburgh] His poft-like legges were anfwerable to the reft of the great frame which they fupported, and to conclude, fir *Bevis, Afcapart, Gog-magog,* or our Englifh fir *John Falftaff*, were but fhrimpes to this bezzeling Bombards longitude, latitude, altitude, and craffitude, for hee paffes, and furpaffes the whole Germane multitude.

※   ※   ✻

Three Weekes, **three daies,** *and three houres obfervations and travel, from London to Hamburgh.* London, 1617. [4to.] *Sign. C.*

NATHANIEL FIELD, 1618.

I doe heare
Your Lordſhip this faire morning is to fight,
And for your honor: Did you never ſee
The Play where the fat Knight, hight *Old-caſtle*,
Did tell you truly what this honor was?

Amends for Ladies. 1618. [4*to.*] *Sign.* G.

Nathaniel Field (like Alexander Brome, in his *Epistle* to the *Five new Plays* of Richard Brome, 1653, in a passage quoted in the *Third Period*) here refers to the speech of Falstaff, which concludes the first scene of 1 *Henry IV*, Act V. See as to Oldcastle and Falstaff, after, *note* on George Daniel, 1647.

RICHARD CORBET, 1618—1621.

Mine hoſt was full of ale and hiſtory;
  * * * * * *
      Why, he could tell
The inch where Richmond ſtood, where Richard fell:
Beſides what of his knowledge he could ſay,
He had authenticke notice from the Play;
Which I might gueſſe, by's muſtring up the ghoſts,
And policyes, not incident to hoſts;
But cheifly by that one perſpicuous thing,
Where he miſtooke a player for a King.
For when he would have ſayd, King Richard dyed,
And call'd—A horſe! a horſe!—he, Burbidge cry'de.

    Iter Boreale. pp. 193, 194 (*see also p.* 170). *Poems of Richard Corbet, Bishop of Oxford & of Norwich. Edited by Octavius Gilchrist.* 1807.

[Gilchrist remarks that "from this passage we learn that Richard Burbage was the original representative of Shakespeare's *Richard the Third.*" L. T. S.]

BEN JONSON, 1619.

His cenſure of the Engliſh Poets was this

* * * * * *

That Shakſpeer wanted arte.

* * * *

Sheakſpear, in a play, brought in a number of men ſaying they had ſuffered ſhip-wrack in Bohemia, wher yͬ is no ſea neer by ſome 100 miles.

> *Notes by William Drummond of Conversations with Ben Jonson, at Hawthornden, January, 1619. Extracts from the Hawthornden MSS. by David Laing, Archæologia Scotica, vol. iv. Edinburgh, 1831-32, pp. 81, 89. Also edited by the same for the Shakespeare Society, 1842, pp. 3, 16.*
> *(First published, incorrectly, in Drummond's Works, 1711.)*

Sir William Drummond was evidently a weak-minded man, whose memory had the knack of retaining only what was trivial or worthless. We may be quite sure that Jonson's assertions were not given in this naked form. No one understood Shakespeare's *art* better than Jonson ; and he could hardly have based the charge of wanting art on geographical or on chronological errors, which Shakespeare took, not ignorantly, but as he found them in the current stories. [Ben probably meant that Shakespeare did not observe those Rules of Art in dramatic writing to which he himself rigidly adhered. The word *wanted* here means *lacked*, rather than the modern sense, which would imply " that Shakespere *ought to have had* art " (see Dryden's use of the word in the same sense, after, p. 351). The word *censure* too should not be taken as necessarily meaning condemnation, it meant *opinion* or judgment, cf.—

> " Madam, and you, my mother, will you go
> To give your *censures* in this weighty business ? "
>
> *Richard III*, Act II. sc. iii.

The remark was made of Shakespere's work by others. L. T. S.] Fuller asserts that "*Nature* itself was all the *Art* which was used upon him" (see under date 1643): which Cartwright echoes in 1647: "Nature was all his art." Milton has—

> "Sweetest Shakespere, Fancy's child,
> Warble his native wood-notes wild" (after, p. 184);

and forty-two years after its utterance we meet it once more in the *Diary* of the Rev. John Ward, who had "heard that Shakspeare was a natural wit without any art at all" (date 1661). But Ben Jonson and L. Digges allow Shakespeare a sort of art. The former writes:

> "Yet must I not give Nature all: Thy Art,
> My gentle *Shakespeare*, must enjoy a part" (p. 149).

And Digges assigns him:

> " Art without Art unparaleld as yet " (date 1640).

[So also the Epitaph before, p. 125, and John Taylor, after, p. 133, credit him with art. The report of Jonson's sayings relating to Shakespere, as found in Drummond's Works of 1711, is shown in its true form in Mr. Laing's print of the MS. As regards the accusation against Shakespere's geography, it may be worth noting that in 1262 Ottocar II was king of Bohemia and Austria, "and soon obtains possession of Styria, Carinthia, and Istria, when his dominions extend from the Baltic to the Adriatic" (*Manual of Dates*). Bohemia then at one time had a sea-board, and no date being necessary to the play, it may be said that "the shipwreck in the *Winter's Tale* is no breach of geography" (see the *Monthly Magazine*, Jan. 1, 1811, vol. xxx. p. 538). But that it was understood as an error in Shakespere's time, and that others besides Jonson laughed at him for it, seem to be shown by the quotation from Taylor the Water Poet, after, p. 178. L. T. S.]

H. About 1618-19.

On ye Death of ye famous Actor R. Burbadge. H.

12 Hees gon' & wth him w^t a world are dead.

Oft haue I feene him leape into a Graue
Suiting ye perfon, (wch he us'd to haue)
Of a mad Louer, wth fo true an Eye
That there I would haue fworne hee meant to dye
Oft haue I feene him play his part in Jeft,
So liuely, y^t fpectators, & ye reft
Of his Crewes, whilft hee did but feeme to bleed
Amazed, thought hee had bene deade indeed.

Octavo MS. in the library of the late Mr. Henry Huth, p. 174. Printed by Mr. Joseph Haslewood in the Gentleman's Magazine, June 1825, Vol. XCV, Part I, p. 498.

A Funerall Ellegye on ye Death of the famous Actor Richard Burbedg who dyed on saturday in Lent the 13 of March 1618.

12 hee's gone & wth him what A world are dead.
which he reniu'd, to be reuiued foe,
no more young Hamlett, ould Heironymoe
kind Leer, the Greued Moore, and more befide,
16 that liued in him; haue now for euer dy'de,
oft haue I feene him, leap into the Graue
fmiting the perfon wch he feem'd to haue
of A fadd Louer with foe true an Eye
20 that theer I would haue fworne, he meant to dye,
oft haue I feene him, play this part in ieaft,
foe liuely, that Spectators, and the reft
of his fad Crew, whilft he but feem'd to bleed,
24 amazed, thought euen then hee dyed in deed.

Folio MS. in the library of the late Mr. Henry Huth, pp. 99, 100. Printed by Mr. J. P. Collier, Annals of the Stage, 1831, Vol. I, p. 430, note.

[A controversy in the *Academy*, in January, 1879, as to the meaning of lines 17 to 24 of this elegy led to the discovery of two original MSS. of it in the library of the late Mr. Henry Huth, which was pointed out by Mr. Alfred H. Huth in the *Academy* of April 3, 1879. As in the first edition of the *Centurie* Dr. Ingleby declared his belief that lines 13-16, printed by Mr. Collier, were spurious, an opinion at first shared by Mr. Furnivall, it is satisfactory now to find that both MSS. of the poem are undoubtedly genuine, and acknowledged to be so by those critics (see Mr. Furnivall in *Academy* of 19 April, 1879). By the kindness of Mr. Alfred H. Huth, and of Mr. F. S. Ellis, who is preparing the Catalogue of the library, I have carefully collated both versions with the MSS., and give the dozen lines which relate to Shakespere, the rest of the poem—consisting in all of 82 lines in the octavo and 86 lines in the folio—being a eulogy upon the excellence of the acting of Burbage in general. The only sign of authorship is the letter H affixed to the title in the Octavo copy. Both MSS. belonged to Mr. Haslewood, and the discrepancies between Mr. Collier's print and l. 15 ("King Lear," "creuel Moore") may be owing to the copy which an autograph note in one of them says that he sent Mr. Collier.

In his *New Particulars*, 1836, and *Memoirs of Actors*, 1846, Mr. Collier quotes other MSS. by which the poem is extended to 124 lines. These have not yet come to light.

It was pointed out by Mr. Moy Thomas (*Academy*, Jan. 4, 1879) that the imperfect quarto *Hamlet* of 1603 is the only authority for making Hamlet leap into Ophelia's grave to out-face Laertes (Act V. sc. i. l. 281); the above lines, however, show that Burbage was in the habit of doing so. Kemble in his acting edition of Shakespere, and Mr. Irving in his present representation of Hamlet, omit the leap into the grave. The rest of the lines seem to allude to the close of the last scene in the play.

While treating on the acting of Burbage, I may recall a reminiscence (though a late one) of the comparative merits of Shakespere as Actor and Poet. James Wright, in his interesting little tract *Historia Histrionica*, 1699, which is a "Dialogue of Plays and Players," thus speaks through his personages :—

"*Lovewit.* Pray Sir, what Master Parts can you remember the Old *Black-friers* men to Act, in *Johnson, Shakespear*, and *Fletcher's* Plays.

Truman. What I can at present recollect I'll tell you; *Shakespear* (who as I have heard, was a much better Poet, than Player) *Burbadge, Hemmings*, and others of the Older sort, were Dead before I knew the Town." (p. 4. Reprinted in Hazlitt's edition of *Dodsley*, 1876, vol. 15, p. 400.) L. T. S.]

JOHN TAYLOR, THE WATER POET, 1620.

In paper, many a Poet now furvives
Or elfe their lines had perifh'd with their lives.
Old *Chaucer, Gower,* and Sir *Thomas More,*
Sir *Philip Sidney,* who the Lawrell wore,
Spencer, and *Shakefpeare* did in Art excell,
Sir *Edward Dyer, Greene, Nafh, Daniell.*
Silvefter, Beumont, Sir *John Harrington,*
Forgetfulneffe their workes would over run,
But that in paper they immortally
Doe live in fpight of death, and cannot die.

The Praise of Hemp-seed. 1620. [*4to.*] *p.* 26 :
Works, 1630, *iii. p.* 72. [*Fo.*]

Farmer says it is " impossible to give the original dates " of many of John Taylor's pieces. "He may be traced as an author for more than half a century" (*Essay on the Learning of Shakspeare,* 1821, p. 101, *note*).

Anonymous, 1620—36.

On the Time-Poets.

One night, the great *Apollo*, pleaf'd with *Ben*,
Made the odde number of the Mufes ten ;
The fluent *Fletcher*, *Beaumont* rich in fenfe,
In complement and courtfhips quinteffence ;
Ingenious *Shakefpeare* ; *Maffinger*, that knowes
The ftrength of plot to write in verfe and profe,
Whofe eafie Pegaffus will amble ore
Some threefcore miles of fancy in an houre ;
Cloud-grapling *Chapman*, whofe Aerial minde
Soares at Philofophy, and ftrikes it blinde ; &c.

Choyce Drollery, Songs, and Sonnets, being a collection of divers excellent pieces of poetry of several eminent authors, never before printed. Anon. 1656. *The piece is reprinted in the Shakespeare Society's Papers*, Vol. III., 1847, p. 172.

The lines 5—8 are quoted by Gerard Langbaine in his *Account of the English Dramatick Poets*, 1691 (p. 353), where they are merely assigned to "an old poet"; and Rev. J. W. Ebsworth, in his reprint of *Choyce Drollery*, 1876, says, "we must confess that nothing is yet learnt as to the authorship," though as to the date he believes "it was certainly written between 1620 and 1636" (pp. 270, 271). Langbaine's version has "ramble" for *amble ;* an error which we conjecturally set right, before we had collated it with the text reprinted in the *Shakespeare Society's Papers*. It is in this piece that we meet with a couplet on Ben Jonson's servant and amanuensis, Richard Brome, or Broom, which in another form did duty for W. Broome, Pope's assistant. Here we have,

"Sent by Ben Johnson, as some authors say,
Broom went before, and kindly swept the way ;"

which a century later assumed this form :

"Pope came off clean with Homer ; but they say,
Broome went before, and kindly swept the way."

(See Johnson's *Lives of the Poets*, William Broome, in which the couplet is attributed to Henley.) Isaac D'Israeli supposed that epigram to be borrowed from a line in Randolph's Ode, "Ben, do not leave the stage," &c., st. 4, l. 4. *Curiosities of Literature*, 1839, p. 139.

JOHN FLETCHER, 1621.

Oriana. Are all my hopes come to this? Is there no faith
No troth, nor modefty, in men?

Wild Goose Chace, 1652 [*fol.*], *p.* 16.

[This passage recals the words of the Nurse in *Romeo and Juliet* (Act III. ii.)—imitated earlier by Barrey, see before, p. 95:

"There's no trust
No faith, no honesty in men."

Fletcher's *Wild Goose Chace* is placed under date 1621, on the authority of Malone, who says "it appears from Sir Henry Herbert's manuscript" (see after, p. 157) that this play is "found among the court exhibitions of the year 1621" (*Variorum*, vol. iii. p. 225). But the play was lost in 1647, and was first printed in folio, separately, in 1652. L. T. S.]

[In another play Fletcher has evidently imitated *Hamlet* (I. v):

"Hic et ubique? then we'll shift our ground
Once more remove good friends;"—

viz. in *The Woman's Prize, or the Tamer tam'd* (Act V. iii). Rowland, having received a statement on oath from his friend Tranio, makes him swear to it again:

"Let's remove our places. Sweare it again."

This play was first printed in the Works of Beaumont and Fletcher, folio, 1647, its date is uncertain. It is said to have been written in ridicule of *The Taming of the Shrew*, but there is not in it a single line or word that can by any kind of ingenuity be so interpreted. It is, as Steevens remarks, a sequel to it, in which the plot is reversed, and Petruchio tamed by a second wife; but the notion of *ridicule* is quite unfounded. P. A. Daniel.]

WILLIAM BASSE, 1622.

[1] *On Mr. Wm. Shakespeare. he dyed in Aprill 1616.*

Renowned Spencer lye a thought more nye
2 To learned Chaucer, and rare Beaumont lye
A little neerer Spenser, to make roome
4 For Shakespeare in your threefold, fowerfold Tombe.
To lodge all fowre in one bed make a shift
6 Vntill Doomesdaye, for hardly will a fift
Betwixt *this* day and *that* by Fate be flayne,
8 For whom your Curtaines may be drawn againe.
If your precedency in death doth barre
10 A fourth place in your sacred sepulcher,
Vnder this carued marble of thine owne,
12 Sleepe, rare Tragœdian, Shakespeare, sleep alone :
Thy vnmolested peace, vnshared Caue,
14 Possesse as Lord, not Tenant, of thy Graue,
That vnto us & others it may be
16 Honor hereafter to be layde by thee.
            Wm. Basse.

Brit. Mus. MS. Lansdowne 777, *fo*. 67 *b.*

[2] *On Mr. William Shakespeare.*

Renowned Spencer lie a thought more nigh
To learned Beaumont, and rare Beaumont ly
A little nearer Chaucer, to make roome
For Shakespeare in your threfold, fourfold tombe.
To lodge all foure in one bed make a shifte
Until Domes day, for hardly will (a) fifte
Betwixt this day and that by fate bee slaine,
For whom the curtains shal bee drawne againe.
But if Precedencie in death doe barre
A fourth place in your sacred Sepulcher,
In this uncarved marble of thy owne,
Sleepe, brave Tragedian, Shakespeare, sleepe alone ;
Thy unmolested rest, unshared cave,
Possesse as lord, not tenant, to thy grave,
That unto others it may counted bee
Honour hereafter to bee layed by thee

Fennell's Shakespere Repository, 1853, *p.* 10, *printed from a MS. temp. Charles I.*

These lines, which are usually attributed to the elder W. Basse, have come down to us in so many discrepant versions, manuscript as well as printed, that it is difficult to determine their original or their finished form. The version [no. 2] selected for this work is derived, at second-hand, from a manuscript which, unfortunately, the compiler has not had an opportunity of inspecting. But the choice was made for cogent reasons. The original was certainly a sonnet, of the usual number of lines; to which two lines (now standing as the 13th and 14th) were subsequently added. The addition, probably, occasioned changes in other lines; and some of the manuscript and printed versions we possess are merely experimental ways of making the augmented elegy hold together. The couplet

$$\left.\begin{matrix}\text{Thy}\\or\text{ Thine}\end{matrix}\right\} \text{unmolested rest,} \left\{\begin{matrix}\text{unshared}\\or\text{ thy unshar'd}\\or\text{ in an unshar'd}\end{matrix}\right\} \text{cave,}$$
$$\text{Possess as lord, not tenant, to} \left\{\begin{matrix}\text{thy}\\or\text{ the}\end{matrix}\right\} \text{grave,}$$

introduced an absurdity, which the lines in Donne's Poems do not contain: for, first, Shakespeare's peace would not be unmolested simply because his grave was unshared; and secondly, it would not be unmolested at all, if others were in after time to be laid by him. Why not, then, adopt the version in Donne's Poems? Because it is evident that at least one line in it was altered from one in a version which had the additional couplet: viz. line 11. The Ashmole copyist had written *curved* for *carved*, as the word stands in the Brander copy, and in both the Rawlinson copies: and it was evidently from a version like that or the Ashmole copy, which read *curved*, that the Donne copyist obtained his singular blunder of *curled*. We believe that the Fennell version (adopted as our text), "In this uncarved marble," is an earlier, as it is unquestionably a much finer, reading than either "Under this *carved* marble," or "Under this *sable* marble," which last occurs in the Sloane copy. As much might be said in defence of the other portions of the Fennell version. Yet it is quite certain that it is not the *original*, but the *finished* form of the elegy.

None of the versions comport with the *status quo* in Westminster Abbey, where Chaucer's tomb is pretty central between Spencer's and Beaumont's: whereas, in the Fennell copy, Donne's version, and the Harleian and Phillipps MSS. Beaumont is the central figure; in all the rest Spencer lies between Beaumont and Chaucer.

In the original draft it is most likely that lines 9-12 ran (as in the Sloane copy, with one exception) thus:

"If your precedencie in death doeth barre
A fourth to have place in your sepulchre,
Under this sacred marble of thy owne   [sable, *Sloane*]
Sleep, rare Tragedian, Shakespeare, sleepe alone,
That unto others," &c.

Perhaps Donne or Basse improved upon them, thus :

> "*But* if precedencie in death doe } barre
> *or* doth }
> A fourth place in your *sacred* sepulchre,
> Under this [   ] marble of thy owne
> Sleep, rare Tragedian, Shakespeare, sleep alone," &c.

and further it seems not improbable that the third of these lines became,

> "*In* this *unsharéd* marble of thy owne,"

before the additional couplet was added, when *unshared* was supplanted by *uncarved*.

[Not quite agreeing with Dr. Ingleby in his view of this Epitaph, I have left his remarks, as they stood, and append a few of my own ; I print the version from Lansdowne 777, because it is an early MS., probably of the end of James I, and because it closely agrees with the two other earliest copies, viz. that given by Malone, and Mr. Halliwell's fac-simile. We therefore are likely here, as I think, to get the nearest approach to the original. An argument in favour of this is, that the names of the poets in the first three lines of these, as in nearly all the versions (Nos. 3, 4, 5, 6, 7, 9, II, III, IV), are placed in chronological order,—Spencer is to go nearer Chaucer, and is to be followed by Beaumont ; thus, besides avoiding the repetition of Beaumont in line 2, giving more force to the allusion in line 9. This is confirmed by the quotation from the epitaph given by Jonson (after, p. 145). The variations in the different versions are considerable, but are generally such as would arise from the lines having been written down from memory, rather than errors of a copyist ; the verses evidently were popular, on a popular subject, and hence are found in common-place-books and miscellaneous collections. Two only of our fifteen copies omit lines 13, 14 (those in Donne's Poems, and Harl. 1749), they therefore probably were in the poem as first written, with the rest of which they seem to me quite consistent. Perhaps the most curious variation falls upon line 11 ; besides the two texts above we find "In an uncarued", "curved" (badly written for carved in the Ashmole copy), "curled" (Donne), "cabled" (which I think badly written for "curled," Harl. 1749), this copy closely follows Donne's ; "sacred," and "sable," instead of "carved." It seems to me that "Under this carved marble" has more sense, either figuratively, or positively, with a possible reference to Shakespere's tomb at Stratford, than to suppose him buried *in* marble, carved or uncarved. L. T. S.]

The following is a list of all the manuscript copies that are known to us.

* (1.) Brit. Mus. MS. Lansdowne 777, fo. 67 *b*.

† (2.) A collection of Miscellaneous Poems in a handwriting of the early part of the reign of Charles I ; from which these verses are printed in Fennell's *Shakespeare Repository*, p. 10.

* (3.) A MS. copy inserted in the Halliwell Collection of printed Proclamations and Broad-sides, in the Chetham Library, Manchester. See fac-simile of it in the catalogue (London, 1851, privately printed), No. 2757.

* (4.) A collection of manuscript poems, formerly in the possession of Gustavus Brander, Esq., containing these verses. Cited by Malone, who says "the MS. appears to have been written soon after the year 1621." *Shakespere's Works*, 1821, vol. i. pp. 470—472.

* (5.) A volume of manuscript poems composed by W. Herrick and others, and *inter alia* Basse's lines ; in the Rawlinson Collection, Bodleian Library, Oxford. (Cited by Malone, but a diligent search has failed to discover it.)

* (6.) A volume of manuscripts, containing poems by Bishop Corbet, and *inter alia* Basse's lines ; also in the Rawlinson Collection. MS. Poet. Vol. 117, p. 40 (resembles Lans. 777).

* (7.) British Museum MS. Sloane 1792 (not 1702 as Malone quotes it), fo. 114.

† (8.) Phillipps MSS. at Cheltenham (formerly Middlehill), No. 9569 : printed at the end of *The Marriage of Wit and Wisdom*, edited by J. O. Halliwell for the Shakespere Society, 1846 ; p. 92 (written about 1638).

" (9.) A volume of manuscripts, containing six poems by W. Herrick, and also Basse's lines. Vol. 38, No. 421, in the Ashmole Collection : Bodleian Library, Oxford.

† (10.) Harl. MS. 1749, fo. 289 *b* (a corrupt version : it wants lines 13, 14). To these may be added the following five early printed versions.

† I. Donne's Poems. 1633. [4to.] p. 149. (Sign. Y 3 ; the paging is wrong, it should be 165.)

* II. Verses appended to Shakespeare's Poems. 1640. [12mo.] Sign. K 8, back.

* III. Witt's Recreations : selected, &c. 1640 [12mo.], where Basse's lines are numbered Epitaph 5, sign. AA 2.

† IV. Witt's Recreations Augmented, &c. 1641 [12mo.], where Basse's lines are numbered 144 of the Epitaphs.

* V. Poems : by Francis Beaumont [with additions by various writers]. 1652. [sm. 8vo.] Sign. M. The Epitaph is not in the edition of these Poems of 1640, it is among the additions of 1652.

Of these, II, III, and IV are substantially the same, and follow in the main, No. (1). The * and † show the type to which each copy belongs

As to the evidence of authorship : In (1) the lines are subscribed, "Wm. Basse," (2) headed "Mr. Basse," and (3) "Mr. Willm. Basse" : (4) "Basse his elegie one Poett Shakespeare, who died in April, 1616" : (5) "Shakespeare's Epitaph," without author's name. (6) "Basse his elegye on Shakespeare" : (7) Headed "vpon shackpeare" ; no author's name. (8) Headed "On Shakespeare, Basse." (9) Subscribed "finis, Dr. Doone." (10) Nothing. In I. they are assigned to Dr. Donne ; but they are omitted from the next edition of his *Poems*. In II. they are subscribed W. B. : in III, IV, and V, they are anonymous. They are not included in "The Pastorals and other Workes of William Basse," printed in 1653.

THOMAS ROBINSON, 1622.

And when he is merrily difpofed (as that is not feldom) then muft his dearling *Kate Knightley* play him a merry fit, and fifter *Mary Brooke*, or fome other of his laft-come Wags, muft fing him one bawdy fong or other to digeft his meat. Then after fupper it is ufuall for him to reade a little of *Venus* and *Adonis*, the iefts of *George Peele*, or fome fuch fcurrilous booke: for there are few idle Pamphlets printed in *England* which he hath not in the houfe.

> *The Anatomy of the English Nunnery at Lisbon in Portugall: Dissected and laid open by one that was sometime a yonger Brother of the Covent.* 1622. *p.* 17. [4*to.*]

By the use of the expression "idle pamphlets" Brother Robinson did not necessarily intend (as Mr. Collier supposes, *Bibliog. and Crit. Account*, ii. 274) to depreciate Shakespeare's poem. An "idle pamphlet," at that time of day, meant one which afforded diversion rather than edification. Surely "scurrilous booke" (to which Mr. Collier takes no exception) implies a much graver charge.

B[EN] J[ONSON], 1623.

To the Reader.

This Figure, that thou here feeſt put,
It was for gentle Shakeſpeare cut;
Wherein the Graver had a ſtrife
With Nature, to out-doo the life:
O, could he but have drawne his Wit
As well in Braſſe, as he hath hit
His Face; the Print would then ſurpaſſe
All, that was ever writ in Braſſe.
But, ſince he cannot, Reader, looke
Not on his Picture, but his Booke.

B. I.

*Facing Droeshout's portrait of Shakespeare prefixed
to the First Folio Edition of his Works.*

[Jonson here contrives to pay both Engraver and Poet the highest compliment; if the former could have drawn the wit of the latter as well as he has drawn his face, the print from his drawing would be the finest thing ever done. It seems to be the engraver's brass to which Digges refers on p. 154. L. T. S.] Mr. Grosart (Ed. of Sir John Beaumont's *Poems*, pp. 194 & xxv) hears in Ben's lines "an echo" of some in Beaumont's *Elegiac Memorials of Worthies*:

"Or had it err'd, or made some strokes amisse,
——For who can pourtray Vertue as it is?——
Art might with Nature have maintain'd her strife,
By curious lines to imitate true life.
But now those pictures want their lively grace
As after death none can well draw the face:"

Mr. Hain Friswell notices the resemblance "with a certain back twist" (as he writes it) of Ben's lines to the elegiac couplet under an old portrait (1588) of Sir Thomas More, in the *Tres Thomæ* of Stapleton:

> "Corporis effigiem dedit ænea lamina. At ô si
> Effigiem mentis sic daret iste liber."

And in *Venus and Adonis*, we read,

> "Look when a painter would surpass the life,
> His art with nature's workmanship at strife" (ll. 289, 291);

which Dryden echoes in his *Epistle to Sir Godfrey Kneller:*

> "Such are thy pieces, imitating life
> So near, they almost conquered in the strife."

We need not, however, go out of Shakespeare's "Booke" to find an instance of this common conceit :

> "the cutter
> Was as another Nature, dumb, outwent her,
> Motion and breath left out."
> *Cymbeline,* ii. 4.

Mat. Smalwood, in his commendatory verses prefixed to some copies of Wm. Cartwright's *Works*, 1651, thus comments on the wretched print of Cartwright's face, which serves as frontispiece to the volume :—

> "Then, do not blame his serious Brow and Look,
> 'Twill be thy Picture if thou read his Book."

[Jonson not improbably took the conceit in his last lines from the verses appended to the portrait of Du Bartas in Sylvester's eds. of 1621, &c., a work to which Jonson himself had contributed a commendatory poem. They run thus :—

> "Ces traits au front, marquez de *Scavoir* & d'*Esprit*
> Ne sont que du BARTAS un ombre *exterieur*.
> Le Pinçeau n'en peut plus : Mais, de sa propre Plume
> Il s'est peint le *Dedans,* dans son divin *Volume.*"

Englished thus :-

> "This Map of *Vertues* in a *Muse*-full Face ;
> Are but a blush of BARTAS *outward* part.
> The Pencil could no more : but his owne Pen
> Limns him, *with-in,* the Miracle of Men."

> (*Du Bartas his Diuine Wickes and Workes : translated by Josuah Sylvester.* [*fo.*] 1633. *Verses placed under the portrait of Du Bartas, A* 5, *back.*)

L. T. S.]

JOHN HEMINGE, HENRY CONDELL, } 1623.

Right Honourable,

Whilſt we ſtudie to be thankful in our particular, for the many favors we have received from your L. L. we are falne upon the ill fortune, to mingle two the moſt diverſe things that can bee, feare, and raſhneſſe; raſhneſſe in the enterprize, and feare of the ſucceſſe. For, when we valew the places your H. H. ſuſtaine, we cannot but know their dignity greater, then to deſcend to the reading of theſe trifles: and, while we name them trifles, we have depriv'd our ſelves of the defence of our Dedication. But ſince your L. L. have beene pleaſ'd to thinke theſe trifles ſome-thing, heeretofore; and have proſequuted both them, and their Authour living, with ſo much favour: we hope, that (they out-living him, and he not having the fate, common with ſome, to be exequutor to his owne writings) you will uſe the like indulgence toward them, you have done unto their parent. There is a great difference, whether any Booke chooſe his Patrones, or finde them: This hath done both. For, ſo much were your L L. likings of the ſeverall parts, when they were acted, as before they were publiſhed, the Volume aſk'd to be yours. We have but collected them, and done an office to the dead, to procure his Orphanes, Guardians; without ambition either of ſelfe-profit, or fame: onely to keepe the memory of ſo worthy a Friend, & Fellow alive, as was our SHAKESPEARE, by humble offer of his playes, to your moſt noble patronage. Wherein, as we have juſtly obſerved, no man to come neere your L. L. but with a kind of religious addreſſe; it hath bin the height of our care, who are the Preſenters, to make the preſent worthy of your H. H. by the perfection. But, there we muſt alſo crave our abilities to be confiderd, my Lords. We cannot go beyond our owne powers. Country hands reach foorth milke, creame, fruites, or what they have: and many Nations (we have heard) that had not gummes & incenſe, obtained their requeſts with a leavened Cake. It was no fault to approch their Gods, by what meanes they could: And the moſt, though meaneſt, of things are made more precious, when they are dedicated to Temples. In that name therefore, we moſt humbly confecrate to your H. H. theſe remaines of your fervant *Shakeſpeare*; that what delight is in them, may be ever your L. L. the reputation his, & the faults ours, if any be committed, by a payre ſo carefull to ſhew their gratitude both to the living, and the dead, as is

Your Lordſhippes moſt bounden,
John Heminge.
Henry Condell.

Dedication to William, Earl of Pembroke, and Philip, Earl of Montgomery. (Prefixed to the First Folio Edition of Shakeſpeare's Works, 1623.)

The first part of the peroration of this address is so good as to evoke the suspicion that it is not original. Malone quotes from Morley's Dedication of a Book of Songs[1] to Sir Robert Cecil, 1595, a very similar passage. But in truth the beginning of the peroration is literally translated from Pliny's dedicatory epistle to Vespasian, prefixed to his *Natural History* (§ 11, ed. Sillig), which runs thus :—

"dis lacte rustici multæque gentes supplicant, et mola tantum salsa litant qui non habent tura ; nec ulli fuit vitio deos colere quoquo modo posset."

That is,

"country people and many nations offer milk to their gods; and they who have not incense obtain their requests with only meal and salt; nor was it imputed to any as a fault to worship the gods in whatever way they could."

The writer of the address of 1623 added "cream and fruits" in one place, and "gummes" in another: and for *mola salsa* appears to have, not unskilfully, caught up Horace's "farre pio" (*Odes* III, 23, ll. 17-20). He adds, too, very gracefully, that "the meanest things are made more precious when they are dedicated to temples." If he employed Philemon Holland's translation of Pliny (1635) he did not reproduce its words.

---

[1] "Cantvs. Of Thomas Morley the first booke of ballets to five voyces" is the real title. [L. T. S.]

JOHN HEMINGE, } 1623.
HENRIE CONDELL,

To the great Variety of Readers.

From the moſt able, to him that can but ſpell: There you are number'd. We had rather you were weighd. Eſpecially, when the fate of all Bookes depends upon your capacities: and not of your heads alone, but of your purſes. Well! It is now publique, & you wil ſtand for your priviledges wee know: to read, and cenſure. Do ſo, but buy it firſt. That doth beſt commend a Booke, the Stationer ſaies. Then, how odde ſoever your braines be, or your wiſedomes, make your licence the ſame, and ſpare not. Judge your ſixe-pen'orth, your ſhillings worth, your five ſhillings worth at a time, or higher, ſo you riſe to the juſt rates, and welcome. But, what ever you do, Buy. Cenſure will not drive a Trade, or make the Jacke go. And though you be a Magiſtrate of wit, and ſit on the Stage at *Black-Friers*, or the *Cock-pit*, to arraigne Playes dailie, know, theſe Playes have had their triall alreadie, and ſtood out all Appeales; and do now come forth quitted rather by a Decree of Court, then any purchaſ'd Letters of commendation.

It had bene a thing, we confeſſe, worthie to have bene wiſhed, that the Author himſelfe had liv'd to have ſet forth, and overſeen his owne writings; But ſince it hath bin ordain'd otherwiſe, and he by death departed from that right, we pray you do not envie his Friends, the office of their care, and paine, to have collected & publiſh'd them; and ſo to have publiſh'd them, as where (before) you were abuſ'd with diverſe ſtolne, and ſurreptitious copies, maimed, and deformed by the frauds and ſtealthes of injurious impoſtors, that expoſ'd them: even thoſe, are now offer'd to your view cur'd, and perfect of their limbes; and all the reſt, abſolute in their numbers, as he conceived thē. Who, as he was a happie imitator of Nature, was a moſt gentle expreſſer of it. His mind and hand went together: And what he thought, he uttered with that eaſineſſe, that wee have ſcarſe received from him a blot in his papers. But it is not our province, who onely gather his works, and give them you, to praiſe him. It is yours that reade him. And there we hope, to your divers capacities, you will finde enough, both to draw, and hold you: for his wit can no more lie hid, then it could be loſt. Reade him, therefore; and againe, and againe: And if then you doe not like him, ſurely you are in ſome manifeſt danger, not to underſtand him. And ſo we leave you to other of his Friends, whom if you need, can bee your guides: if you neede them not, you can leade your ſelves, and others. And ſuch Readers we wiſh him.

John Heminge.
Henrie Condell.

Address prefixed to the First Folio Edition of Shakespeare's Works.

The statement of these editors "that what he [Shakespeare] thought, he uttered with that easiness, that wee have scarce received from him a blot [*litura*] in his papers," is seemingly confirmed by Ben Jonson (p. 174). [But if by this they intended to convey to the reader the notion that the text of the folio 1623 was printed from the author's own manuscript, they must stand convicted of a *suggestio falsi* ; for five at least of the plays included in that volume are little more than reprints of the previous quarto editions, characterised by them as "surreptitious copies," &c.; others of these quartos must also have been used in preparing the folio for press, and for the remainder, with perhaps a few exceptions, the corrupted stage-copies were probably used. See Prefaces and Notes of Cambridge Editors, of Dyce, Staunton, and others. P. A. D.]

[In all probability, say the Cambridge editors, not one of Shakespere's works was corrected by himself, "nor, with few exceptions, were they printed from the author's manuscript" (*Works*, vol. ix, preface, p. xxi). L. T. S.]

BEN JONSON, 1623.

To the memory of my beloved, the AUTHOR
Mr. WILLIAM SHAKESPEARE:
and what he hath left us.

To draw no envy (*Shakespeare*) on thy name,
    Am I thus ample to thy Booke, and Fame:
While I confeffe thy writings to be fuch,
    As neither *Man*, nor *Mufe*, can praife too much.
'Tis true, and all mens fuffrage. But thefe wayes
    Were not the paths I meant unto thy praife:
For feelieft Ignorance on thefe may light,
    Which, when it founds at beft, but eccho's right;
Or blinde Affection, which doth ne're advance
    The truth, but gropes, and urgeth all by chance;
Or crafty Malice, might pretend this praife,
    And thinke to ruine, where it feem'd to raife.
Thefe are, as fome infamous Baud, or Whore,
    Should praife a Matron. What could hurt her more?
But thou art proofe againft them, and indeed
    Above th' ill fortune of them, or the need.

I, therefore will begin. Soule of the Age!
  The applaufe! delight! the wonder of our Stage!
My *Shakefpeare*, rife; I will not lodge thee by
  Chaucer, or *Spenfer*, or bid *Beaumont* lye
A little further, to make thee a roome:
  Thou art a Moniment, without a tombe,
And art alive ftill, while thy Booke doth live,
  And we have wits to read, and praife to give.
That I not mixe thee fo, my braine excufes;
  I meane with great, but difproportion'd *Mufes*:
For, if I thought my judgement were of yeeres,
  I fhould commit thee furely with thy peeres,
And tell, how farre thou didftft[1] our *Lily* out-fhine,
  Or fporting *Kid*, or *Marlowes* mighty line.
And though thou hadft fmall *Latine*, and leffe *Greeke*,
  From thence to honour thee, I would not feeke
For names; but call forth thund'ring *Æfchilus*,
  Euripides, and *Sophocles* to us,
Paccuvius, *Accius*, him of *Cordova* dead,
  To life againe, to heare thy Bufkin tread,
And fhake a Stage: Or, when thy Sockes were on,
  Leave thee alone, for the comparifon
Of all, that infolent *Greece*, or haughtie *Rome*
  fent forth, or fince did from their afhes come.

  · *Sic* in original.

Triúmph, my *Britaine*, thou haſt one to ſhowe,
  To whom all Scenes of *Europe* homage owe.
He was not of an age, but for all time !
  And all the *Muſes* ſtill were in their prime,
When like *Apollo* he came forth to warme
  Our eares, or like a *Mercury* to charme !
Nature her ſelfe was proud of his deſignes,
  And joy'd to weare the dreſſing of his lines !
Which were ſo richly ſpun, and woven ſo fit,
  As, ſince, ſhe will vouchſafe no other Wit.
The merry *Greeke*, tart *Ariſtophanes*,
  Neat *Terence*, witty *Plautus*, now not pleaſe ;
But antiquated and deſerted lye
  As they were not of Natures family.
Yet muſt I not give Nature all : Thy Art,
  My gentle *Shakeſpeare*, muſt enjoy a part.
For though the *Poets* matter, Nature be,
  His Art doth give the faſhion. And, that he,
Who caſts to write a living line, muſt ſweat,
  (ſuch as thine are) and ſtrike the ſecond heat
Upon the *Muſes* anvile : turne the ſame,
  (And himſelfe with it) that he thinkes to frame ;
Or for the lawrell, he may gaine a ſcorne,
  For a good *Poet's* made, as well as borne.

And fuch wert thou. Looke how the fathers face
   Lives in his iffue, even fo, the race
Of *Shakefpeares* minde and manners brightly fhines
   In his well torned, and true-filed lines :
In each of which, he feemes to fhake a Lance,
   As brandifh't at the eyes of Ignorance.
Sweet Swan of *Avon !* what a fight it were
   To fee thee in our waters yet appeare,
And make thofe flights upon the bankes of *Thames,*
   That fo did take *Eliza,* and our *James !*
But ftay, I fee thee in the *Hemifphere*
   Advanc'd, and made a Conftellation there !
Shine forth, thou Starre of *Poets,* and with rage,
   Or influence, chide, or cheere the drooping Stage ;
Which, fince thy flight frō hence, hath mourn'd like night,
   And defpaires day, but for thy Volumes light.
                            Ben : Jonfon.

Prefixed to the First Folio Edition of Shakespeare's Works.

It has not, hitherto, been observed, that Ben Jonson's forty couplets have a regular structure. The compiler has ventured upon an innovation to indicate this. Fortunately the three marks of division, to which he has had recourse, fall on the top of each page, so that they serve indifferently as paginal decorations, or as the headings of the second, third, and fourth divisions. By virtue of the latter function, they indicate the following constituent parts of the poem.

(1.) An Introduction } each of eight couplets.
(4.) A Peroration
(2.) An Address to Shakespeare } each of twelve couplets.
(3.) An Address to Britain

In the third, however, is a passing deviation, viz. "*Thy* Art, my Shakespeare," &c. A few obscurities in the course of this piece may be noted. "*To draw no envy,*" &c., certainly does not mean what the editor of Brome's *Five New Plays*, 1659 (To the Reader, p. 4), imputes to it; as if Ben thought to lower Shakespeare by extravagantly praising him. He meant to say, that while Ignorance, Affection, or Malice, by excessive, indiscriminate or unjust praise, would be sure to provoke the detraction of Envy,

"these ways
Were not the paths I meant unto thy praise;"

for he could with full knowledge and strict impartiality award him the highest praise that could be expressed. One is reminded (especially by the seventh couplet) of what Ben wrote in *Cynthia's Revels*, where Crites is made to say,

"So they be ill men,
If they spake worse, 'twere better: for of such
To be dispraised, is the most perfect praise." (Act III. sc. iii.)

"*I will not lodge thee,*" &c., refers to Basse's lines, and means that he will not class Shakespeare with Chaucer, Spenser, and Beaumont, because he is out of all proportion greater than they—men "of yeeres" or "for an age." Nor will he praise him by declaring how far he excelled Lily, Kid, and Marlow. Shakespeare, indeed, like them (yet beyond them) was, for the age in which he flourished; but he was also for all time, and not *of* an age. It is worth remarking, that on the occasion of the Tercentenary Celebration, in London, when "blinde Affection" worshipped the gigantic bust of Shakespeare, at the Agricultural Hall, "seeliest Ignorance" had surmounted the proscenium with the abominable travestie, HE WAS NOT FOR AN AGE, BUT FOR ALL TIME; and the same evil genius presided over Mr. John Leighton's "Official Seal for the National Shakespeare Committee," when he engraved on the scroll at the base of the device the same discreditable perversion, NOT FOR AN AGE, BUT FOR ALL TIME. Mr. Frederick Brett Russell is to be congratulated on his fidelity and sense in surrounding his memorial salver with the actual line of Jonson.

"*Leave thee alone for the comparison,*" &c., is almost repeated *verbatim* in Jonson's *Timber*, where he points to Bacon as

"he who hath fill'd up all numbers, and perform'd that in our tongue, which may be compar'd, or preferr'd, either to insolent *Greece*, or haughty *Rome*." (Jonson's *Works*, fol. 1640, p. 102.)

It is indeed as applicable to Bacon's prose as to Shakespeare's verse. Mr. W. H. Smith endeavours to make capital out of the coincidence, in his *Bacon and Shakespeare*. 1857. pp. 35-36.

"*For though thou had'st,*" &c. Here *hadst* is the subjunctive. The passage may be thus paraphrased :

"Even if thou hadst little scholarship, I would not seek to honour thee by calling thee, as others have done, Ovid, Plautus, Terence, &c., *i.e.*, by the names of the classical poets, but would rather invite them to witness how far thou dost outshine them."

Ben does not assert that Shakspeare had "little Latine and less Greek," as several understand him, though doubtless, compared with Ben's finished scholarship, Shakespeare's was small : but, that the lack of that accomplishment could only redound to Shakespeare's honour, who could be Greek or Roman, according to the requirements of the play and the situation.

One could wish that Ben had said all this in Shakespeare's lifetime ; and one is reminded of what Horace says of the great Poet (Epist. II, i. 13-14).

"Urit enim fulgore suo, qui prægravat artes
 Infra se positas : extinctus amabitur idem."

In the verses prefixed to Cartwright's *Works*, 1651, signed W. Towers, it is said,

"Thy skill in Wit was not so poorely meek
 As theirs whose little *Latin* and no *Greek*
 Confin'd their whole Discourse to a Street phrase,
 Such Dialect as their next Neighbour's was."

This was in allusion to Jonson's critique on Shakespeare.

HUGH HOLLAND, 1623.

Upon the Lines and Life of the Famous Scenicke Poet,

Master WILLIAM SHAKESPEARE.

Thofe hands, which you fo clapt, go now, and wring
You *Britaines* brave ; for done are *Shakefpeares* dayes :
His dayes are done, that made the dainty Playes,
Which make the Globe of heav'n and earth to ring.
Dry'de is that veine, dry'd is the *Thefpian* Spring,
Turn'd all to teares, and *Phœbus* clouds his rayes :
That corp's, that coffin now befticke thofe bayes,
Which crown'd him *Poet* firft, then *Poets* King.
If *Tragedies* might any *Prologue* have,
All thofe he made, would fcarfe make one to this :
Where *Fame*, now that he gone is to the grave
(Deaths publique tyring-houfe) the *Nuncius* is.
  For though his line of life went foone about,
  The life yet of his lines fhall never out.

Hugh Holland.

Prefixed to the First Folio Edition of Shakespeare's Works.

LEONARD DIGGES, 1623.

To the Memorie
of the deceafed Authour Maifter
W. Shakespeare.

Shake-fpeare, at length thy pious fellowes give
The world thy Workes : thy Workes, by which, out-live
Thy Tombe, thy name muft : when that ftone is rent,
And Time diffolves thy *Stratford* Moniment,
Here we alive fhall view thee ftill. This Booke,
When Braffe and Marble fade, fhall make thee looke
Frefh to all Ages : when Pofteritie
Shall loath what's new, thinke all is prodegie
That is not *Shake-fpeares*; ev'ry Line, each Verfe,
Here fhall revive, redeeme thee from thy Herfe.
Nor Fire, nor cankring Age, as *Nafo* faid,
Of his, thy wit-fraught Booke fhall once invade.
Nor fhall I e're beleeve, or thinke thee dead
(Though mift) untill our bankrout Stage be fped
(Impoffible) with fome new ftrain t' out-do
Paffions of *Juliet*, and her *Romeo* ;
Or till I heare a Scene more nobly take,
Then when thy half-Sword parlying *Romans* fpake,
Till thefe, till any of thy Volumes reft
Shall with more fire, more feeling be expreft,
Be fure, our *Shake-fpeare*, thou canft never dye,
But crown'd with Lawrell, live eternally.

L. Digges.

Prefixed to the First Folio Edition of Shakespeare's Works.

I. M., 1623.

To the memorie of M. W. Shake-fpeare.

Wee wondred (*Shake-fpeare*) that thou went'ſt ſo ſoone
From the Worlds-Stage, to the Graves-Tyring-roome.
Wee thought thee dead, but this thy printed worth,
Tels thy Spectators, that thou went'ſt but forth
To enter with applauſe. An Actors Art,
Can dye, and live, to acte a ſecond part.
That's but an *Exit* of Mortalitie;
This, a Re-entrance to a Plaudite.

Prefixed to the First Folio Edition of Shakespeare's Works.

These lines have been attributed to John Marston, Jasper Mayne, and James Mabbe. Those who know Marston feel assured they are not his. Mr. Bolton Corney, who first preferred a claim on behalf of Mabbe, supported it by the following extract from Mabbe's translation of *Guzman de Alfarache*, Part I, p. 175; a work published by Edward Blount, 1623, and attributed to Mateo Aleman. (See *Notes and Queries:* 2nd S., XI, 4.)

"It is a miserable thing, and much to be pittied, that such an Idoll as one of these [a proud courtier], should affect particular adoration; not considering, that he is but a man, a representant, a poore kinde of Comedian that *acts his part upon the Stage of this World*, and comes forth with this or that Office, thus and thus attended, or at least resembling such a person, and that when the play is done (which can not be long) he must presently enter into the *Tyring-house of the grave*, and be turned to dust and ashes as one of the sonnes of the Earth, which is the common Mother of us all."

[The simile of the "tyring house" was not uncommon; Holland uses it, before, p. 153, and Davies of Hereford (*Scourge of Folly*, p. 229) says to Robert Armin, "When th' art in the tyring house of earth," and repeats it elsewhere.

It is a question whether such ideas and phrases as those printed in italics in this extract from Mabbe were not the common property of the age (they differ from the "play-scraps" which caught the popular ear and tongue). Here is another from the same writer, p. 13, lecturing women for painting their faces he says, "O affront, above all other affronts! that God having given thee one face, thou shouldst abuse his image, and make thy selfe another," which resembles Hamlet's objurgation of Ophelia (Act III, sc. i), "I have heard of your paintings too, well enough ; God has given you one face, and you make yourselves another"; both evidently follow the biblical arguments of the "stricter sort" against this vice, the strongest expression of which was given by Philip Stubbes in his *Anatomie of Abuses*, 1583. Citing St. Ambrose he has, "For what a dotage is it (saith hee) to chaunge thy naturall face which God hath made thee for a painted face, which thou hast made thyself" (see *Reprint* for the New Sh. Soc., 1877, pp. 64—66).

Compare also the extracts from Law's *Day Tricks*, before, p. 82, and pp. 53, 54.

The last line alludes to the ancient practice of approbation given at the close of a performance or new play. See Ben Jonson, before, p. 31, and in the *Histrio-mastix*, a play of 1610, we have "wher's the *Epilogue* must beg the *plaudite?*" (sign. C 1, back). When Jonson's play *The Silent Woman* was first acted, verses were afterwards found on the stage concluding that it was well named the *Silent* woman, because there was "never one man to say plaudite to it." Drummond's *Works*, 1711, p. 226. L. T. S.]

SIR HENRY HERBERT, 1623—1636.

To the Duchefs of Richmond, in the kings abfence, was given *The Winter's Tale*, by the K. company, the 18 Janu. 1623. Att. Whitehall.

Upon New-years night, the prince only being there, *The Firſt Part of Sir John Falſtaff*, by the king's company. Att Whitehall, 1624 [*Page* 228]

For the king's players. An olde playe called *Winter's Tale*, formerly allowed of by Sir George Bucke, and likewyſe by mee on Mr. Hemmings his worde that there was nothing profane added or reformed, thogh the allowed booke was miſſinge; and therefore I returned it without a fee, this 19 of Auguſt, 1623.

[Received] from Mr. Hemmings, in their company's name, to forbid the playing of Shakeſpeare's plays, to the Red Bull Company, this 11 of April 1627, £5. o. o. [*Page* 229]

On Saterday the 17th of Novemb. [miſtake for 16th] being the Queen's birthday, *Richarde the Thirde* was aɹted by the K. players at St. James, wher the king and queene were preſent, it being the firſt play the queene ſawe ſince her M.^{tys} delivery of the Duke of York. 1633.

On tuſday night at Saint James, the 26 of Novemb. 1633, was aɹted before the King and Queene, *The Taminge of the Shrew*. Likt.

On Wenſday night the firſt of January, 1633, *Cymbeline* was aɹted at Court by the Kings players. Well likte by the Kinge.
[*pages* 233, 234]

The *Winter's Tale* was aɹted on thurſday night at Court, the 16 Janua. 1633, by the K. players, and likt [*page* 236]

Julius Cæsar, at St. James, the 31 Janu. 1636 [*page* 239]

> Sir Henry Herbert's Office Book, manuscript quoted in Malone's Historical Account of the English Stage, Variorum vol. iii, pages as given above.

SIR HENRY HERBERT, 1623—1636.

["The office-book of Sir Henry Herbert contains an account of almost every piece exhibited at any of the theatres from August 1623, to the commencement of the rebellion in 1641" (*Malone*, III, p. 59), but it "does not furnish us with a regular account of the plays exhibited at court every year" (p. 228). The above are all the entries which relate to Shakespere's plays from this manuscript as quoted by Malone (see *note*, after, p. 173); but Sir Henry Herbert left several other papers, from which Malone gives us the following notices of Shakespere's plays. Out of twenty "stock-plays" of the Red Bull actors (afterwards called the King's servants), from 1660 to 1663, three were Shakespere's, viz. *Henry the Fourthe, Merry Wives of Windsor*, and *Othello*. Out of a list of sixty-seven plays entered by Sir H. Herbert from 5 Nov. 1660 to July 23, 1662, only three were Shakespere's, viz. 8 Nov. 1660, *Henry the Fourth*; 9 Nov., *The Merry Wives of Windsor*; 8 Dec., *The Moore of Venise*. In another of his lists dated Nov. 3, 1663, we have *Henry the 5th, Taming the Shrew, Macbeth*, and *K. Henry 8*, the last three marked as "revived" plays. Downes the prompter's list of the stock-plays of the king's servants, from the Restoration to 1682, gives only *Henry IV*, Part I, *Merry Wives of Windsor, Othello*, and *Julius Cæsar*, of Shakespere's. All these particulars seem to belong to the company of Red Bull actors, afterwards called the king's servants (*Malone*, III, pp. 272—276). Sir Wm. Davenant's company acted between about 1660 and 1671, *Pericles, King Lear, Hamlet, King Henry VIII, Romeo and Juliet, Twelfth Night*, and as altered by Davenant, *Macbeth* and *The Tempest* (*ib.* p. 277): after 1671, they acted *King Lear*, as altered by Davenant and Shadwell, *Timon of Athens, Macbeth*, and *The Tempest*. The "United companies" acted between 1682 and 1695, in Lincoln's Inn Fields, *Othello, Midsummer Night's Dream*, and *The Taming of the Shrew*—the two last being altered. "Dryden's *Troilus and Cressida*, however, the two parts of *King Henry IV, Twelfth Night, Macbeth, King Henry VIII, Julius Cæsar*, and *Hamlet*, were without doubt sometimes represented in the same period: and Tate and Durfey furnished the scene with miserable alterations of *Coriolanus, King Richard II, King Lear*, and *Cymbeline*. Otway's *Caius Marius*, which was produced in 1680, usurped the place of our poet's *Romeo and Juliet* for near seventy years. * * * Dryden's *All for Love*, from 1678 to 1759, was performed instead of our author's *Antony and Cleopatra*; and Davenant's alteration of *Macbeth* in like manner was preferred to our author's tragedy, from its first exhibition in 1663, for near eighty years" (*ib.* pp. 287-291).

We thus get official notices of fifteen of Shakespere's plays, that were acted or accustomed to be acted between 1623 and 1663, by the king's players and the Red Bull actors. The notes for the next thirty years show us ten of Shakespere's own (of which five were other than the previous fifteen), and ten of Shakespere's plays altered by various writers, which were performed before the end of our century (1692). L. T. S.]

E. S. (B. of D.) 1624

Thefe ambi-dexter *Gibionites*, are like the *Sea-calfes*, *Crocodiles*, *Otters* & *Sea-colt*, *Aristotle* & *Plinie* fpeake of, which are one while in the water, other-while a land for their greater booties : juftly tearmed *Dubia* by *Ifodore*, in that being *Natatilia* & *Grassabilia*, men know not where to find them : for they are like *Hamlets ghost, hîc & ubique*, here and there, and every where, for their owne occafion.

Anthropophagus : the Man-Eater. London. 1624. p. 14.

[The author is here speaking of time-servers and flatterers; the probability that he had himself seen the play gives the allusion additional interest. Mr. Elliot Browne conjectures from this that the stage business of the ghost "was as prominent a feature of the early representation as it has been in later times" (*Athenæum*, Nov. 13, 1875). L. T. S.]

JOHN GEE, 1624.

The *Jesuites* being or having *Actors* of such dexteritie, I see no reason but that they should set up a company for themselves, which surely will put down The *Fortune, Red-bull, Cock-pit,* & *Globe*. Onely three exceptions some make against them ⁂ ⁂ ⁂ ⁂ The third abatement of the honor and continuance of this Scenicall company is, that *they make their spectators pay to deare for their Income*. Representations and Apparitions from the dead might be seene farre cheaper at other Play-houses. As for example, the *Ghost* in *Hamblet, Don Andreas Ghost* in *Hieronimo*. As for flashes of light, we might see very cheape in the Comedie of *Piramus* and *Thisbe*, where one comes in with a Lanthorne and Acts *Mooneshine*.

New Shreds of the old Snare. Containing The Apparitions of two new female Ghosts, &c. 1624. *pp.* 17, 20.

As to the ghost in *Jeronymo*, see after, Randolph, 1651.

ROBERT BURTON, 1624.

When *Venus* ranne to meet her rofe-cheeked *Adonis*, as an elegant *Poet of ours fets her out,   *Shakespeare.

    ——*the bushes in the way*
Some catch her necke, fome kiffe her face,
Some twine about her legs to make her ftay,
And all did covet her for to embrace.
                 Part 3. Sec. 2. Memb. 2. Subs. 2.

*   *   *   *   *   *

And many times thofe which at the firft fight cannot fancy or affect each other, but are harfh and ready to difagree, offended with each others carriage, [like *Benedict* and *Betteris* in the *Comedy] & in whom they finde many faults, by *Shakespeare. this living together in a houfe, conference, kiffing, colling, & fuch like allurements, begin at laft to dote infenfibly one upon another.
            Part 3. Sec. 2. Memb. 2. Subs. 4. *The words in* [ ]
            appear for the first time in the 3rd Edition, 1628. [*Fo.*]

*   *   *   *   *   *

Who ever heard a ftory of more woe,
Then that of Juliet and her Romeo?
                 Part 3. Sec. 2. Memb. 4.

     The Anatomy of Melancholy. 2nd Edition. 1624. [*Fo.*]
     pp. 371 (*misprinted* 372), 380, 427. *Edition* 1676. [*Fo.*]
     pp. 284, 298, &° 332, *the " Members " differ in this edition.*

For the lines quoted in the first extract Burton trusted to his memory, for in his own copy in the Bodleian Library, [8°. *M. 9. Art. BS.,*] they run thus :

"the bushes in the way,
Some catch her neck, some kisse her face,
Some twine about her thigh to make her stay :
She wildly breaketh from their strict embrace."
Venus and Adonis, 1602. 8vo. st. 146. (Sign. C v.)

The second line, which is exactly as Burton quotes it, has lost the words "by the." In the British Museum copy of the same edition, that line runs thus :

"Some catch her by the neck, some kisse her face." (Sign. C v.)

The omission was probably detected after a few copies had been pulled, and corrected before the edition was worked off. The Edinburgh edition 1627 was evidently printed from one of the uncorrected copies of the edition of 1602, for it reads

"Some catch her neck, and some doe kisse her face " (p. 36),

eking out the line by the addition of "and" and "doe."

In the second extract, the parenthesis, "like Benedict and Betteris in the comedie," was added in the third edition of Burton's book, issued in 1628. We get *Benedicte and Betteris* for *Much ado about nothing, ante*, p. 104. "Betteris" is phonetic spelling: Beatrice was doubtless vulgarly so pronounced. The Duchess of Newcastle, in one of her *Sociable Letters*, printed in the *Third Period*, spells the name *Bettrice ;* so also in *Eastward Hoe*, before, p. 70. D'avenant, too, in *The Man's the Master*, has the name Bettris. Leonard Digges, however (under date 1640), gives her three syllables.

The third extract quotes the concluding couplet of *Romeo and Juliet*. They run thus in the old folio :

"For never was a story of more woe
Than this of Juliet and her Romeo."

The old editions of *The Anatomy of Melancholy* bear the dates, 1621, 1624, 1628, 1632, 1638, 1651-2, 1660 and 1676. The British Museum has copies of all of them. That of 1651-2 was the first published after Burton's death (January, 1639). The first edition (1621) only contains the second of the passages quoted, without the words in [ ].

BEN JONSON, 1625.

Prologue. Wee aſke no favour from you; onely wee would entreate of Madame Expectation——
Expect. What, Mr Prologue?
Pro. That your Ladi-ſhip would expect no more then you underſtand.
Expect. Sir, I can expect enough.
Pro. I feare, too much, Lady, and teach others to do the like
Expect. I can doe that too, if I have cauſe.
Pro. Cry you mercy, *you never did wrong, but with juſt cauſe.*

The Staple of News. Printed 1631. *Induction.* [*In folio edition of Jonson's Works, Vol. II, with title-page, dated* 1640.]

["This is meant as a satire on a line in Shakespeare's *Julius Cæsar*, though it nowhere occurs as it is here represented." Whalley's edition of Ben Jonson's Works, 1756, vol. iv. p. 128. See also Gifford's edition of Jonson's Works, 1816, vol. v. p. 162, note; see also note, after, p. 175. L. T. S.]

RICHARD JAMES, 1625. *circa.*

To my noble friend Sr Henry Bourchier.

Sir Harrie Bourchier, you are defcended of Noble Aunceftrie, and in ye dutie of a good man loue to heare and fee fair reputation preferved from flander and oblivion. Wherefore to you I dedicate this edition of Ocleve, where Sr Iohn Oldcaftel apeeres to have binne a man of valour and vertue, and only loft in his own times becaufe he would not bowe under the foule fuperftition of Papiftrie * *

A young Gentle Lady of your acquaintance, naving read ye works of Shakefpeare, made me this queftion. How Sr John Falftaffe, or Faftolf, as he is written in ye Statute book of Maudlin Colledge in Oxford, where everye day that fociety were bound to make memorie of his foul, could be dead in ye time of Harrie ye Fift and again live in ye time of Harrie ye Sixt to be banifhed for cowardice: Whereto I made anfwear that it was one of thofe humours and miftakes for which Plato banifht all poets out of his commonwealth. That Sr John Falftaffe was in thofe times a noble valiant fouldier, as apeeres by a book in ye Heralds Office dedicated unto him by a Herald who had binne with him, if I well remember, for the fpace of 25 yeeres in ye French wars; that he feems alfo to have binne a man of learning, becaufe, in a Library of Oxford, I find a book of dedicating Churches fent from him for a prefent unto Bifhop Wainflete, and infcribed with his own hand. That in Shakefpeares firft fhew of Harrie the fift,[1] the perfon with which he undertook to playe

---

[1] [The 1st Part of *Henry IV* is here meant. The words "Harrie the fift" are the same in both MSS. L. T. S.]

a buffone was not Falftaffe, but Sir Jhon Oldcaftle, and that offence beinge worthily taken by Perfonages defcended from his title (as peradventure by many others allfo whoe ought[1] to have him in honourable memorie, the poet was[1] putt to make an ignorant fhifte of abufing Sir Jhon Falftophe, a man not inferior of Vertue, though not fo famous in pietie as the other, who gave witneffe unto the truth of our reformation with a conftant and refolute Martyrdom, unto which he was purfued by the Priefts, Bifhops, Moncks, and Friers of thofe days.

> Dedication to Sir Henrye Bourchier, prefixed to The Legend and Defence of the Noble Knight and Martyr Sir Jhon Oldcastle James MS. 34, Bodleian Library, Oxford. Printed by Mr. J. O. Halliwell Phillipps in his work, entitled, On the Character of Sir John Falstaff, as originally exhibited by Shakespeare in the two parts of King Henry IV. 1841. [12mo.] pp. 19, 20.

[1] A line omitted in Grenville MS., to have—was.

Compare this extract with the following:
"One word more, I beseech you; if you be not too much cloid with Fat Meate, our humble Author will continue the Story (with *Sir John* in it) and make you merry, with faire *Katherine of France:* where (for any thing I know) *Falstaffe* shall dye of a sweat, unlesse already he be kill'd with your hard Opinions: For *Old-Castle* dyed a Martyr, and this is not the man."
Epilogue to 2 *Henry IV*.

[John Weever, in the dedication of his *Mirror of Martyrs*, 1601, speaking of his poem, says that it "some two yeares agoe was made fit for the Print; that so long keeping the corner of my studie, wherein I vse to put waste paper: This first trew Oldcastle thought himselfe iniurde, because he might not bee suffered to sustaine the second Martyrdome of the Presse." Mr. Collier sees in this an allusion to "the second false Oldcastle," of Shakespeare's creation. *Bibliographical Account*, vol ii. p. 498. (See note as to Oldcastle and Falstaff, after, George Daniel, 1647.)

Occleve's *Legend & Defence of Sir John Oldcastle* appears never to have been printed, a fate which Richard James' edition of the poem also shared, though he added many notes to its 73 stanzas. The British Museum Grenville MS. XXXV, is another copy, the dedication in it differing slightly in spelling from the Bodleian MS. L. T. S.]

JOHN FLETCHER (*died* 1625).

It was not poyſon, but a ſleeping potion
Which she received, yet of ſufficient ſtrength
So to bind up her ſences, that no ſigne
Of life appeard in her, and thus thought dead
In her beſt habit, as the cuſtome is
You know in Malta, with all ceremonies
She's buried in her families monument,
In the Temple of St. *John*; i'le bring you thither,
Thus, as you are diſguiſd; ſome fix howers hence
The potion will leave working.

*The Knight of Malta, Act IV. sc. i; Beaumont
and Fletcher's Works*, 1647. [*Fol.*]

[The *Knight of Malta* is by Fletcher only, according to Dyce; by Fletcher and Middleton, according to Fleay, who says it was written before 1619. The above passage is certainly in imitation of Friar Lawrence' speech, Act IV. sc. i. of *Romeo and Juliet*. P. A. Daniel.]

*JOHN FLETCHER (*and another*) (*died* 1625)

"the faire dames,
Beauties, that lights the Court, and makes it fhew
Like a faire heaven, in a frofty night:
And mongft thefe mine, not pooreft,———'

*The Noble Gentleman. Act I. sc. i. Beaumont
and Fletcher's Works. Fol.* 1647.

[The date of this play is uncertain, as well as the name of the second writer who had a hand in it. The lines given above seem to be in imitation of the following from *Romeo and Juliet*, Act I. sc. ii.—

"At my poor house, look to behold this night
Earth treading stars, that make dark heaven light:

* * * * *

Such amongst view of many, mine being one," etc.

P. A. Daniel.]

MICHAEL DRAYTON, 1627.

Shakeſpeare thou hadſt as ſmooth a Comicke vaine,
Fitting the ſocke, and in thy natural braine,
As ſtrong conception, and as Cleere a rage,
As any one that trafiqu'd with the ſtage.

> " *To my most dearely-loved friend* HENERY REYNOLDS, *Esquire, of* Poets and Poesie." *Elegies, at the end of the Battaile of Agincourt* [*and other poems*]. 1627. *p.* 206.

Professor David Masson in his admirable *Life of Sir William Drummond*, 1873 (p. 113), appears to refer this epistle to the date 1619-1620. Langbaine and others refer to it as "a Censure of the Poets," but the above is the correct title. There is a copy of the Edition of Drayton's " Poems collected into one volume," with title bearing date 1620, in the Grenville Library, and a copy of the same Edition, with titles bearing date 1619, in the British Museum Library: but the Epistle " on Poets and Poesie " is not in either. We believe it was first printed in this collection of 1627, which contains an entirely different set of poems to that of 1620.

ROBERT GELL, 9 *August*, 1628.

On teufday his Grace was prefent at y° acting of [1] K. Hen. 8 at y° Globe, a play befpoken of purpofe by himfelf; whereat he ftayd till y° Duke of Buckingham was beheaded, & then departed. Some fay, he fhould rather have feen y° fall of Cardinall Woolfey, who was a more lively type of himfelf, having governed this kingdom 18 yeares, as he hath done 14.

Letter from Robert Gell to Sir Martyn Stuteville, Harl. MS. 383, fo. 65. Printed in the Shakespere Society's Papers, 1845, vol. ii. p. 151.

[1] "of" repeated twice in MS.

["His Grace" who bespoke the performance of *Henry VIII.* was the Duke of Buckingham, "Baby Charles'" "Steenie." The "fall of Cardinall Woolsey" is perhaps Chettle's play of *Cardinal Wolsey* mentioned in Henslowe's Diary (Shakespere Society, ed. 1845, pp. 189, 194). Mr. Furnivall, however, thinks that Gell did not mean that Buckingham might have appropriately seen another play, but that he might have staid to see the end of *Henry VIII*, and the fall of Wolsey in it. L. T. S.]

ABRAHAM COWLEY. Between 1628 and 1631.

  Away got I [1]; but e'er I farre did goe
  I flung (the Darts of wounding *Poetrie*)
  Thefe two or three fharpe curfes backe : may hee
  Bee by his Father in his ftudy tooke,
  At *Shakefpeares* playes, inftead of my L. *Cooke*.

  A Poeticall Revenge. Minor poem, in Silva, or Divers copies of Verses made upon sundry Occasions. Added to Poeticall Blossomes. 2nd edition, 1636, sign. E 6, back.

[1] [The point of this is, the pert school-boy Cowley in Westminster Hall flinging his "darts" against the foppish young lawyer who has thrust him from his seat. The poems in " Silva " are among those which Cowley himself says, "I wrote at school from the age of ten years, till after fifteen" (Preface to *Poems*, leaf a. 3, back, ed. 1656), and which he first printed in 1633 and 1636. They are afterwards found in the " Second Parte " of his "Works." L. T. S.]

*PHILIP MASSINGER, 1629.

Paris.   Sir, with your pardon,
I'll offer my advice! I once obſerv'd
In a Tragedie of ours, in which a murther
Was acted to the life, a guiltie hearer
Forc'd by the terror of a wounded conſcience
To make diſcoverie of that, which torture
Could not wring from him. Nor can it appeare
Like an impoſſibilitie, but that,
Your Father looking on a covetous man
Preſented on the Stage as in a mirror
May ſee his owne deformity, and loath it.

The Roman Actor. A Tragedie. 1629, *sign. D* 2.

See *Hamlet,* Act II. scene ii. :
"The play's the thing
Wherein I'll catch the conscience of the king."

[This may or may not be an allusion to *Hamlet:* Massinger may have had in his mind some of the incidents in real life which probably suggested the scene to Shakespere himself, or have remembered the same ideas in the old play, *A Warning to Fair Women,* 1599. See R. Simpson's *School of Shakspere,* 1878, Vol. II, pp. 212—216, 311, where some tales of the kind are narrated. L. T. S.]

BEN JONSON, 1629—1630.

No doubt fome mouldy tale,
   Like *Pericles;* and ftale
As the Shrieve's cruffts, and nafty as his fifh-
   fcraps, out [of] every difh
Throwne forth, and rak't into the common tub,
   May keepe up the *Play-club:*
There, fweepings do as well
   As the beft order'd meale.
For, who the relifh of thefe ghefts will fit,
Needs fet them, but, the almes-bafket of wit.

Ode [first line, *Come leave the lothed stage*] *appended to The New Inn, or The Light Heart.* 1631. [12mo.] *Sign. H* 2.

Ben Jonson's verses were written as a vent for his indignation, after the failure of *The New Inn* in 1629 had left him straitened and discomfited.

Owen Feltham's verses, p. 180, are a clever parody on Jonson's: Jug, Pierce, Peck, and Fly, are characters in Jonson's play. "Discourse so weighed" refers to the third and fourth Acts of *The New Inn.*

T. Randolph, T. Carew, and J. Cleveland all wrote odes to console Ben for his disappointment, and to win him back to his work. What an irritable, self-seeking, praise-loving old genius he was!

[The word ending the third line is usually printed with a dash after it, *scraps* in the next line beginning with a large S. The above is the form of the print of 1631. L. T. S.]

SIR HENRY HERBERT, 1629-31.

1629. The benefitt of the winters day from the kinges company being brought mee by Blagrave, upon the play of *The Moor of Venife*, comes, this 22 of Nov. 1629, unto—9*l*. 16*s*. 0*d*.

1631. Received of Mr. Benfielde, in the name of the kings company, for a gratuity for ther liberty gaind unto them of playinge, upon the ceffation of the plague, this 10 of June, 1631—3*l*. 10*s*. 0*d*.—This was taken upon *Pericles* at the Globe.

1631. Received of Mr. Shanke, in the name of the kings company, for the benefitt of their fummer day, upon ye fecond daye of *Richard ye Seconde*, at the Globe, this 12 of June, 1631—5*l*. 6*s*. 6*d*.

MS. of Sir Henry Herbert, printed by Malone is his Historical Account of the English Stage, 1821. *Variorum, iii.* 177.

[Sir Henry Herbert was Master of the Revels to James I, Charles I, and Charles II. From his Office Book, now lost, Malone printed many interesting details, from which I gather those which refer to the acting of Shakespere's plays during the period over which its entries extend, from 1623 to 1642. Under date 1628, Herbert notes that the king's company "have given mee the benefitt of too dayes in the yeare, the one in summer, thother in winter, to bee taken out of the second daye of a revived playe, att my owne choyse." (Malone, iii. p. 176.) Three of these benefits, as seen above, were taken on plays of Shakespere. See before, pp. 157, 158. L. T. S.]

BEN JONSON, 1630-37.

<small>De Shakespeare nostrat.</small> I *remember*, the Players have often mentioned it as an honour to *Shakespeare*, that in his writing, (whatsoever he penn'd) hee never blotted out line. My answer hath beene, would he had blotted a thousand. Which they thought a malevolent speech. I had not told posterity this, but for their ignorance, who choose that circumstance to commend their friend by, wherein he most faulted. And to justifie mine owne candor, (for I lov'd the man, and doe honour his memory (on this side Idolatry) as much as any.) Hee was (indeed) honest, and of an open, and free nature: had an excellent *Phantsie*; brave notions, and gentle expressions: wherein hee flow'd with that facility, that sometime it was necessary he should be stop'd: *Sufflaminandus erat*; as *Augustus* said of *Haterius*. His wit was in his owne power; would the rule of it had beene so too. Many times hee fell into those things, could not escape laughter: As when hee said in the person of *Cæsar*, one speaking to him; *Cæsar thou dost me wrong*. Hee replyed: *Cæsar did never wrong, but with just cause:* and such like; which were ridiculous. But hee redeemed his vices, with his vertues. There was ever more in him to be prayfed, then to be pardoned.

<small>*Timber: or, Discoveries made upon men and matter; as they have flow'd out of his daily Readings; or had their refluxe to his peculiar Notion of the Times.* Works: 1641. [*Fo.*] *vol. ii. pp.* 97-98.</small>

In the remarks *de Shakespeare nostrati* we have, doubtless, Ben's closet-opinion of his friend, opposed as it seems to be to that in his address to Britain (p. 149), where Ben appears to praise him for that very quality "wherein he most faulted:" for evidently Shakespeare did not dream of conforming to the Horatian precept (Sat. I, x. 72-73):

"Sæpe stylum vertas, iterum quæ digna legi sint Scripturus."

Though Ben regretted and condemned his friend's rapidity of execution, it does not appear that he assumed (like Cowley, in a passage quoted in the *Third Period*) the right "to prune and lop away" what did not square with his canons of criticism.

In his *Timber*, under the head, *De Stylo, et optimo scribendi genere*, Ben expatiates on the duty of self-restraint in composition. He says (*inter alia dicta*), "No matter how slow the style be at first, so it be labour'd and accurate;" and again, "So that the summe of all is, ready writing makes not good writing; but good writing brings on ready writing: yet, when wee thinke wee have got the faculty, it is even then good to resist it;" &c.

Ben's critique on the passage (as it must have originally stood) in *Julius Cæsar* is captious. The justice of the cause is not inconsistent with wrong inflicted on others beside the expiator. Mr. J. O. Halliwell-Phillips rightly observes, "If *wrong* is taken in the sense of *injury* or *harm*, as Shakespeare sometimes uses it, there is no absurdity in this line. [Cf.] 'He shall have wrong.' 2 *Henry VI*, v. 1." (*Life of Shakespeare*, 1848, p. 185.) Again, in *A Winter's Tale*, v. 1, *Paulina*, speaking of the hapless Queen, says,

"Had she such power,
She had just cause.
Leontes. She had, and would incense me
To murther her I married."

That is, she had just cause to incite him to do another a grievous wrong. This is even more amenable to Jonson's censure than the passage which fell under it.

[The line as it stands at present, with the punctuation of the *Globe* edition, is as follows,—

"Know, Cæsar doth not wrong, nor without cause
Will he be satisfied." Act III, Sc. i, l. 47.

There are no words of Metellus answering to those cited by Jonson, "Cæsar thou dost me wrong." If he quoted correctly (he has the words twice over, see before, p. 163), the folio contains an alteration (the folio of 1623 being the first authority we have for *Julius Cæsar*). Whatever the exact words, it seems to me highly probable that Shakespere in putting this sentiment on Cæsar's lips, had in his mind the well known maxim, "the King can do no wrong," a phrase which means that the king is but the mouthpiece of the law; and it is consistent with this that Cæsar founds his refusal to pardon Cimber upon the law,—"Thy brother by decree is banished." L. T. S.]

JOHN MILTON, 1630.

An Epitaph on the admirable Dramaticke Poet,
W. SHAKESPEARE.

What neede [1] my *Shakeſpeare* for his honour'd bones,
The labour of an Age, in piled ſtones
Or that his hallow'd Reliques ſhould be hid
4 Under a ſtarre-ypointing Pyramid?
Dear Sonne of Memory, great Heire of *Fame,*
What needſt thou ſuch dull [2] witneſſe of thy Name?
Thou in our wonder and aſtoniſhment
8 Haſt built thy ſelfe a laſting [3] Monument:
For whil'ſt to th' ſhame of ſlow-endevouring Art
Thy eaſie numbers flow, and that each part, [4]
Hath from the leaves of thy unvalued Booke,
12 Thoſe Delphicke Lines with deepe Impreſſion tooke
Then thou our fancy of her [5] ſelfe bereaving,
Doſt make us Marble with too much conceiving,
And ſo Sepulcher'd in ſuch pompe doſt lie
16 That Kings for ſuch a Tombe would wiſh to die.

Prefixed to the Second Folio Edition of Shakespeare's Works, 1632: *appended to Shakespeare's Poems,* 1640, *sign. K* 8, *and republished in Milton's Poems,* 1645, *p.* 27.

[In the edition of Milton's Poems, 1645, these lines are headed, "On Shakespear, 1630," this is our only authority for giving them that date.

The following variations are found in the three editions: Shakespere's Poems, 1640, is referred to as A; Milton's Poems, 1645, as B.

[1] *needs* for *need,* B.   [2] *weake* for *dull,* A, B.
[3] *live-long* for *lasting,* A, B.   [4] *heart* for *part,* A, B.
[5] *our selfe* A, *it self* B, for *her selfe.*

L. T. S.]

JOHN MILTON, 1630.

We have the choice of three early printed versions of Milton's lines:
1. The commendatory verses prefixed to the Folio Edition of Shakespeare, 1632. 2. Those appended to the unauthorised edition of Shakespeare's Poems, published in 1640. 3. The edition of Milton's poems published in 1645. We have preferred the first and least pleasing of the three, as being, unquestionably, Milton's first draft of the lines: allowing, of course, that *part* is a press-error for "hart" (*i. e.* heart).

The expression "star-ypointing pyramid" was doubtless intended to signify, *pointing to the stars:* and the prefix y is similarly used by Sackville, in his legend, entitled, *The Complaint of Henry Duke of Buckingham* (Sackville-West's Ed., 1859, p. 140).

"Sans earthly guilt ycausing both be slain."

(See *Notes and Queries*, 4th S., iv, p. 331.) Had the line in Milton run

"Under a star-ypointed pyramid,"

the sense would have been, under a pyramid surmounted with a star. (See Marsh's *Lectures*, edited by Dr. Wm. Smith, 1862, Lecture xv, p. 232, note.) One is reminded of some lines attributed to Shakespeare, quoted by many editors and biographers of Shakespeare.

"Not monumentall stone preserves our fame,
Nor skye-aspiring piramids our name,"

and the assertion, that each heart hath

"Those delphic lines with deep impression took,"

recals a passage in Shakespeare's *Lucrece*, where he speaks of

"The face, that map which deep impression bears,
Of hard misfortune carved in it with tears."

Coleridge wrote lines 7, 8, 15, 16, on the margin of one of Donne's letters to the Lady G., opposite the following passage:

"No prince would be loath to die that were assured of so fair a tomb to preserve his memory." (Notes Theological, Political, and Misc., 1853, p. 258.)

Milton's meaning, however, is this. Every heart, by the plastic power of fancy, takes deep impression of Shakespeare's lines. Then, by deprivation of fancy, we are turned to marble; and we thus become an *inscribed monument* to Shakespeare. But the conceit is affected, and the conjugate use of "whilst" and "then" in these verses is, to say the least, very unusual.

*JOHN TAYLOR, THE WATER POET, 1630.

I am no fooner eafed of him, but *Gregory Gandergoofe*, an Alderman of *Gotham*, catches me by the goll, demanding if *Bohemia* be a great Towne, and whether there bee any meate in it, and whether the laft fleet of fhips be arrived there.

Taylor's Travels to Prague in Bohemia. Works, 1630, iii. p. 90.

[This seems to be a good-humoured laugh at Shakespere's blunder in the *Winter's Tale*, in placing Bohemia near the sea, in which he followed Greene's *Pandosto*, the story on which he founded his play. See before, p. 130. L. T. S.]

JOHN TAYLOR, THE WATER POET, 1630.

And laſt he laughed in the Cambrian tongue, & began to declare in the Utopian ſpeech, what I have here with moſt diligent negligence Tranſlated into the Engliſh Language, in which if the Printer hath placed any line, letter or ſillable, whereby this large volume may be made guilty to be underſtood by any man, I would have the Reader not to impute the fault to the Author, for it was farre from his purpoſe to write to any purpoſe, ſo ending at the beginning, I ſay as it is applawſefully written and commended to poſterity in the Midſummer nights dreame. If we offend, it is with our good will, we came with no intent, but to offend, and ſhew our ſimple ſkill.

> *To Nobody. Epistle prefixed to Sir Gregory Nonsense; his news from no place. Works (collected by himself), 1630. [Fol.] [First piece in the Second Part.]*

OWEN FELTHAM, 1630?

Jug, Pierce, Peck, Fly, and all
    Your Jefts fo nominal,
Are things fo far beneath an able Brain,
    As they do throw a ftain
Through all th' unlikely plot, and do difpleafe
    As deep as *Pericles,*
    Where yet there is not laid
    Before a Chamber-maid
Difcourfe fo weigh'd, as might have ferv'd of old
For Schools, when they of Love & Valour told.

Lusoria or, Occasional Pieces, first printed as an addition to the eighth edition of Feltham's Resolves, 1661, *folio. No. xx. An answer to the Ode,* Come leave the loathed Stage, *&c. (See extract and note* on p. **172.**)

"*Anonimos*," 1630.

One travelling through *Stratford* upon *Avon*, a Towne moſt remarkeable for the birth of famous *William Shakeſpeare*, and walking in the Church to doe his devotion, eſpyed a thing there worthy obſervation, which was a tombeſtone laid more then three hundred years agoe, on which was ingraven an Epitaph to this purpoſe, I *Thomas* ſuch a one, and *Elizabeth* my wife here under lye buried, and know Reader *I. R. C.* and *I. Chryſtoph. Q.* are alive at this houre to witneſſe it.

A Banquet of Jeasts or Change of Cheare. 1630. *No.* 259. *Bodleian Lib.*, 8° *L.* 78, *Art.*, *and* 8° *M.* 27. *Med. Se Collier's Bibliog. and Crit. Account*, *ii. pp.* 335-6.

*JOHN SPENCER, 1631.

Likewife wee doe order that Mr. Wilfon becaufe hee was a fpeciall plotter and Contriver of this bufines and did in fuch a brutifhe Manner act the fame with an Affes head, therefore hee fhall vppon Tuifday next from 6 of the Clocke in the Morning till fixe of the Clocke at night fitt in the Porters Lodge at my Lord Bifhopps houfe with his feete in the ftockes and Attyred with his Affe head and a bottle of haye fett before him and this fuperfcripcion on his breaft;

> Good people I have played the beaft
> And brought ill things to paffe
> I was a man, but thus have made
> Myfelfe a Silly Affe.

Lambeth MS. 1030, *art.* 5, *p.* 3.

[Among the MSS. at Lambeth Palace is an Order made by the Commissary-General, John Spencer, against John Williams, Bishop of Lincoln, for having had "a playe or Tragidie" acted in his house on Sunday, 27 September, 1631. The Order includes censure of several other persons who appear to have been present, the last one being as above. A letter from Spencer, censuring one of the ladies present, occupies the other leaf of the same sheet, in which he notices that she went "to heare such excellent Musicke, such rare Conceits, and to see such Curious Actours." I give this doubtful "allusion" because several, following Collier's *Annals of the Stage*, Vol. II, p. 27, have taken for granted that it refers to the *Midsummer Night's Dream*. Beyond these notices, however, there is nothing to tell with certainty what the play was. Near the bottom of page 3, in the margin have been written the words "the play M Night Dr," but these are evidently the work of a later hand and have been written over an erasure: they are not in the hand of either Laud, Lincoln, or Spencer, or of the endorser of the paper, but look like a bad imitation of old writing. No reliance can therefore be placed upon them.

Elsewhere Spencer speaks of the play as a *comedy*; if Wilson were not the author, at least he had a large share in the arrangement of it. In a *Discourse of Divers Petitions*, 1641, p. 19, speaking of Bp. Lincoln and this presentment, Spencer says, "one Mr. Wilson a cunning Musition having contrived a curious Comodie, and plotted it so, that he must needs have it acted upon the Sunday night, for he was to go the next day toward the Court; the Bishop put it off till nine of the clock at night." L. T. S.]

JOHN MILTON, 1632—1638.

Then to the well-trod ſtage anon,
If *Jonson's* learned ſock be on,
Or ſweeteſt *Shakeſpeare*, Fancy's child,
Warble his native wood-notes wild.

> *L'Allegro, ll.* 131—134. *Poetical Works of John Milton, by David Masson. Vol. II, pp.* 205, 422. *Milton's Poems.* 1645 [12 *mo.*], *p.* 36.

*PHILIP MASSINGER, 1632.

Livio. To dye the beggers death with hunger, made
Anatomies while we live, cannot but cracke
Our heart-ftrings with vexation.
Ferdinand. Would they would breake,
Breake altogether, how willingly like *Cato*
Could I teare out my bowells, rather then
Looke on the conquerors infulting face,
But that religion, and the horrid dreame
To be fuffer'd in the other world denyes it.

The Maid of Honour. 1632. [4*to.*] *Sign. E* 3.

[See *Hamlet*, Act III. scene i. ll. 78—80.
Part of the two last lines seem to be a reminiscence of Hamlet's famous words,—

"But that the dread of something after death,
The undiscover'd country from whose bourn
No traveller returns, puzzles the will
And makes us rather bear those ills we have
Than fly to others that we know not of."

L. T. S.]

George Chapman and James Shirley, 1632.

    Lady Lucina. I did propound a bufineſſe to you fir.
    Coronell. And I came prepar'd to anſwer you.
    Luc. Tis very well, Ile call one to be a witneſſe.
    Co. That was not I remember in our Covenant,
You ſhannot neede. *Luc.* Ile fetch you a booke to ſware by.
    Co. Let it be *Venus* and *Adonis* then,
Or *Ovids* wanton Elegies, Ariſtotles
Problemes, Guy of Warwicke, or Sr. Beavis,
Or if there be a Play Booke you love better,
Ile take my oath upon your Epilogue.

                    The Ball, a Comedy. 1639, *sign. H.*

[This play, according to Gifford, was licensed in 1632, and first printed in 1639 (*Works of James Shirley, with notes by Gifford and Dyce*, 1833, vol. iii. p. 3). L. T. S.]

*THOMAS RANDOLPH 1632.

Asotus [addressing the Poets skull]

I scorn thy Lyrick and Heroick strain,
Thy tart Iambick, and Satyrick vein.
Where be thy querks and tricks? show me again
The strange conundrums of thy frisking brain,
Thou Poets skull, and say, What's rime to chimney?
(p. 60.)

* * * * *

Sexton. It had been a mighty favour once, to have kiss'd these lips that grin so. * * Oh! if that Lady now could but behold this physnomie of hers in a looking-glasse, what a monster would she imagine herself? Will all her perrukes, tyres and dresses, with her chargeable teeth, with her ceruffe and pomatum, and the benefit of her painter & doctor, make this idol up again?
Paint Ladies while you live, and plaister fair,
But when the house is fallne 'tis past repair.
(p. 61.)

* * * * * *

Asotus. Phœbus whip
Thy lazy team, run headlong to the West,
I long to taste the banquet of the night.
(p. 19.)

Simo. That I should have so ravishing a face,
And never know it!—Miser that I was!

188   THOMAS RANDOLPH, 1632.

  I will go home & buy a looking glaſſe
  To be acquainted with my parts hereafter.
               (p. 46.)

   Tyndarus.   Pamphilus, welcome : Shake thy ſorrows off,
  Why in this age of freedome doſt thou ſit
  A captiv'd wretch?   I do not feel the weight
  Of clay about me.   Am I not all aire?
  Or of ſome quicker element?   I have purg'd out
  All that was earth about me, and walk now
  As free a ſoul as in the ſeparation.
               (p. 24.)

      The Jealous Lovers. A Comedie. 1632.

[The whole scene (sc. iii. Act IV.) from which the two first of these extracts are taken recalls strongly the grave-digger's scene in *Hamlet*, and is worth reading with it; though the expressions are not absolutely repeated, the author must have had Shakespere in his mind when he wrote. The third extract is another use of the idea expressed in the first three lines of Juliet's speech, *Rom. & Jul.*, Act III. sc. ii. The fourth may recall the last part of Gloucester's soliloquy, *Rich. III*, Act I. sc. ii.

The fifth resembles the sentiment in Cleopatra's ecstatic words at her death (*Ant. and Cleop.*, Act V. sc. ii. l. 292), but need not necessarily have been borrowed from Shakespere. See notes before, pp. 53, 155. There is some interest, as Prof. Dowden remarks, in noting the involuntary tribute to Shakespere from Randolph, a professed pupil of Jonson, who would probably look on him as the dramatist by art, and who talked of Shakespere as having written for money. See extracts from his *Hey for Honesty*, 1651. L. T. S.]

Anonymous, 1632.

Upon the Effigies of my worthy Friend,
the Author
Mafter William Shakefpeare,
and his Workes.

Spectator, this Life's Shaddow is ; To fee
The truer image and a livelier he
Turne Reader. But, obferve his Comicke vaine,
Laugh, and proceed next to a Tragicke ftraine,
Then weepe ; So when thou find'ft two contraries,
Two different paffions from thy rapt foule rife,
Say, (who alone effect fuch wonders could)
Rare *Shake-fpeare* to the life thou doft behold.

Prefixed to the Second Folio Edition of Shakespeare's
Works ; 1632.

I. M. S., 1632.

*On Worthy Master Shakespeare
and his Poems*

  A Mind reflecting ages paſt, whoſe cleere
  And equall ſurface can make things appeare
  Diſtant a Thouſand yeares, and repreſent
  Them in their lively colours juſt extent.
5 To outrun haſty time, retrive the fates,
  Rowle backe the heavens, blow ope the iron gates
  Of death and Lethe, where (confuſed) lye
  Great heapes of ruinous mortalitie.
  In that deepe duſkie dungeon to diſcerne
10 A royall Ghoſt from Churles; By art to learne
  The Phyſiognomie of ſhades, and give
  Them ſuddaine birth, wondring how oft they live.
  What ſtory coldly tells, what *Poets* faine
  At ſecond hand, and picture without braine
15 Senſeleſſe and ſoulleſſe ſhowes. To give a Stage
  (Ample and true with life) voyce, action, age,
  As *Plato's* yeare and new Scene of the world
  Them unto us, or us to them had hurld.
  To raiſe our auncient Soveraignes from their herſe
20 Make Kings his ſubjects, by exchanging verſe
  Enlive their pale trunkes, that the preſent age
  Joyes in their joy, and trembles at their rage:
  Yet ſo to temper paſſion, that our eares
  Take pleaſure in their paine; And eyes in teares
25 Both weepe and ſmile; fearefull at plots ſo ſad,
  Then, laughing at our feare; abuſ'd, and glad

To be abuſ'd, affected with that truth
Which we perceive is falſe ; pleaſ'd in that ruth
At which we ſtart; and by elaborate play
30 Tortur'd and tickled ; by a crablike way
Time paſt made paſtime, and in ugly ſort
Diſgorging up his ravaine for our ſport——
——While the *Plebeian* Impe, from lofty throne,
Creates and rules a world, and workes upon
35 Mankind by ſecret engines ; Now to move
A chilling pitty, then a rigorous love :
To ſtrike up and ſtroake down, both joy and ire ;
To ſteere th' affections ; and by heavenly fire
Mould us anew. Stolne from ourſelves——
40   This, and much more which cannot be expreſt,
But by himſelfe, his tongue and his owne breſt,
Was *Shakeſpeares* freehold, which his cunning braine
Improv'd by favour of the ninefold traine.
The buſkind Muſe, the Commicke Queene, the graund
45 And lowder tone of *Clio ;* nimble hand,
And nimbler foote of the melodious paire,
The Silver voyced Lady ; the moſt faire
Calliope, whoſe ſpeaking ſilence daunts.
And ſhe whoſe prayſe the heavenly body chants.
50   Theſe joyntly woo'd him, envying one another
(Obey'd by all as Spouſe, but lov'd as brother)
And wrought a curious robe of ſable grave
Freſh greene, and pleaſant yellow, red moſt brave,
And conſtant blew, rich purple, guiltleſſe white
55 The lowly Ruſſet, and the Scarlet bright;
Branch'd and embroydred like the painted Spring
Each leafe match'd with a flower, and each ſtring
Of golden wire, each line of ſilke ; there run
Italian workes whoſe thred the Siſters ſpun ;

60 And there did fing, or feeme to fing, the choyce
   Birdes of a forraine note and various voyce.
   Here hangs a moffey rocke ; there playes a faire
   But chiding fountaine purled : Not the ayre,
   Nor cloudes nor thunder, but were living drawne,
65 Not out of common Tiffany or Lawne.
   But fine materialls, which the Mufes know
   And onely know the countries where they grow.
      Now, when they could no longer him enjoy
   In mortall garments pent ; death may deftroy
70 They fay his body, but his verfe fhall live
   And more then nature takes, our hands fhall give.
   In a leffe volumne, but more ftrongly bound
   Shakefpeare fhall breath and fpeake, with Laurell crown'd
   Which never fades. Fed with Ambrofian meate
75 In a well-lyned vefture rich and neate.
      So with this robe they cloath him, bid him weare it
   For time fhall never ftaine, nor envy teare it.
            The friendly admirer of his
                 Endowments.
                         I. M. S.

Prefixed to the Second Folio Edition of Shakespeare's Works.

The compiler has followed the example of all his predecessors in treating the letters I. M. S. as the initials of the author's name : so he has placed them at the head of this noble composition. But it has not been without compunction that he has made this concession : for he is inclined to believe that those letters fignify the words *In Memoriam Scriptoris.* The fact is—what has been often recognised—that this magnificent tribute to Shakespeare's worth is a sort of rival to that of Ben Jonson, thus ennobling the second folio, as Jonson's had graced the first. Now Jonson declared his poem to be *In Memory of the (deceased) Author,* &c. ; so it is natural to look for some echo of this description in the rival poem : and these words might be precisely rendered by *In Memoriam Scriptoris (decessi),* the last word being quite unimportant. This reading leaves the field clear for conjecture on the identity of the Friendly Admirer. Apart from all attempt to fit the initials on a poet's name, only one conjecture has been made ; viz. that of Boaden, in his *Inquiry*, 1824, pp. 106, 119. After dismissing the view that I. M. S. meant Jasper Mayne (Student), John Marston (Student, or Satirist), or John Milton (Senior), he advocates the claims of George Chapman, and makes out a plausible case for that admirable poet. A correspondent in *Notes and Queries* (2nd S., VII. 123) suggests J. M. (Scotus), identifying I. M. S. with the person who presented Chapman with the plate prefixed to his *Iliad*, and the probable author of the subscribed couplet, signed " Scotiæ Nobilis." Some time back the editor privately proposed to father this poem on Dr. John Donne. There are similarities of diction which countenance this view, and surely Donne was equal to the effort.[1] On the other hand, it is impossible to extract from Donne's poems a piece of equal length which is not disfigured by some lines of amazing harshness ; while in the poem of the Friendly Admirer there is little or no interruption to the majestic flow and delicious smoothness of the verse. Its reigning fault is a certain looseness of metaphor. It might serve to lament and praise *any* great dramatic poet ; nothing is accurately significant of Shakespeare's peculiar genius : in this view the "curious robe" woven by the muses is an *eye-sore:* but the description of it is so exquisitely beautiful, that it provides the compensating *eye-salve*. William Godwin (*Life of E. & J. Phillips*, 1815, p. 171, *note*) suggested that I. M. S. meant *John Milton Senior :* Mr. Collier (*Shakespere's Works*, 1858, i. p. [257, *note*) attributed the poem to *John Milton, Student.* The latter view has found an able advocate in Professor Henry Morley. But it is easily shown that the structure of the verse belongs to an earlier period than that of Milton.

The late Mr. Dyce (Ed. of Shakespeare, 1864, vol. i. p. 169) appears to favour the claim preferred for Jasper Mayne : but such an opinion only serves to show how little reliance can be placed upon Mr. Dyce's critical deliverances. The best of Mayne's verses, such as those pointed out by Mr. Dyce, and those praised by the late Mr. Bolton Corney (*Notes and Queries*, 4th S., II. 147) are merely respectable. His worst verses make us wonder what could have been the vanity that prompted them, and the flattery that praised them ! Mayne might just as well have composed a poem comparable to *Paradise Lost*, as have written the elegy of the Friendly Admirer. But Mr. Dyce had as little sensibility to the higher graces of poetry as Samuel Johnson. Mr. Hunter's idea, adopted by Singer, and arrived at independently by Watkiss Lloyd, was that I. M. S. were the consonants of the surname of Richard James. If such a poet were to be discovered, the conjecture would still be out of court, for it is not a poet

---

[1] [Dr. B. Nicholson has read Donne carefully and often, and can affirm that these lines cannot be by him. This poem seems in some degree to have followed Donne's style, he had various imitators ; there is a slight imitation of his pauses and cadence, and in the first part of the poem of his roughness of wording. L. T. S.]

that we require, but *a very great* poet. Besides, in the editor's judgment, "*The Friendly* Admirer" implies that the author was an eminent rival of Shakespere's who bore him no envy.

A few notes on the text of this poem may be helpful. (It should be remarked that the punctuation of the original print, though somewhat defective, is followed.) The first nineteen couplets consist of six substantive clauses (neither governed by nor governing any verb), terminated by full points, or signs of aposiopesis. These serve to convey the finest possible description of the dramatic function.

Line 20. Read :

"Make Kings his subjects by exchanging verse : "

i. e., by verse which effects the exchange. Lines 40, 41, are echoed by Digges :

"Some second *Shakespeare* must of *Shakespeare* write."

Line 43. Though "the ninefold train" is mentioned, only eight Muses seem to be specified : unless, indeed, "the melodious *pair*" be intended to designate Euterpe, Erato and Terpsichore. A pack of cards used to be called "a *pair* of cards" ; and we still say "a *pair* of stairs" : *pair* being a *set of matched things*.

Line 63. "Purléd" : not *purfled* (*i. e., embroidered*, as Boaden understood by it), but *rippled ;* the poet could not say of a picture *purling*. But *purled* seems to have had also the sense of *embroidered*.

Line 64. "Living drawne"—*i. e.*, drawn as if they were substantial things.

It may be safely asserted that no English encomiastic poem has ever come near this for graceful melodious verse and mastery of language. It is, besides, so free and unstudied, that one might well believe it was written "without blot."

WILLIAM PRYNNE, 1632.

[*] Ben Johnsons, Shackspeers, and others.

* Some Play-books fince I firſt undertooke this ſubject, are growne from *Quarto* into *Folio;* which yet beare ſo good a price and ſale, that I cannot

† Shackspeers Plaies are printed in the best Crowne paper, far better than moſt Bibles.

but with griefe relate it, they are now † new-printed in farre better paper than moſt Octavo or Quarto *Bibles,* which hardly finde ſuch vent as they: And can then one *Quarto* Tractate againſt Stage-playes be thought too large, when as it muſt aſſault ſuch ample Play-houſe *Volumes?* Beſides, our *Quarto*-Play-bookes ſince the firſt ſheetes of this my Treatiſe came unto the Preſſe, have come

‡ Above forty thousand Play-bookes have been printed and vented within these two yeares.

forth in ſuch ‡ abundance, and found ſo many cuſtomers, that they almoſt exceede all number, one ſtudie being ſcarce able to holde them, and two yeares time too little to peruſe them all.

Histrio-Mastix. The Players Scourge or Actors Tragædie. 1633. [4*to.*] (*Address* " *To the Christian Reader."* fo. 1, *back.*)

[In 1648-9 was printed *Mr. William Prynn, his defence of Stage plays, or a Retractation of a former Book of his called Histrio-Mastix,* which he indignantly declared to be "a meere forgery and impoſture," and, notwithstanding the ſufferings he had undergone for the book, declared his adheſion to *Histrio-Mastix,* in a broad-side sheet, dated 10 Jan. 1648, headed: *The Vindication of William Prynne Esquire, From some Scandalous Papers and Imputations newly Printed and Published,* &c. (Brit. Museum, Press-mark 669 f. 13/67.). The "forgery" bears testimony to the custom in acting women's parts, — "men or boyes do wear the apparel of women, being expressly forbidden in the Text. To this I answer, first, that if this be all, it is a fault may be easily amended; and we may do in England, as they do in *France, Italy, Spain,* and other places, where those which play womens parts, are women indeed." (p. 7.) L. T. S.]

SIR ASTON COKAINE, 1632.

Thou more then Poet, our *Mercurie* (that art
Apollo's Meſſenger, and do'ſt impart
His beſt expreſſions to our eares) live long
To purifie the ſlighted Engliſh tongue,
That both the *Nymphes* of *Tagus,* and of *Poe,*
May not henceforth deſpiſe our language ſo.
Nor could they doe it, if they ere had ſeene
The matchleſſe features of the faerie Queene;
Read *Johnſon, Shakeſpeare, Beaumont, Fletcher,* or
Thy neat-limnd peeces, ſkilfull *Maſſinger.*

Commendatory Verses prefixed to Massinger's Emperour of the East. 1632. [4to.]

*WILLIAM ROWLEY, 1633.

Alexander. Good fir, be fatisfied, the Widdow and my fifter fung both one fong, and what was't, but *Crabbed age and youth cannot live together.*

A Match at Midnight. Act v. sc. 1. 1633. [4*to.*]
Sign. I 2, *back.*

[This is the first line of the twelfth song in the *Passionate Pilgrim* (*Globe* edition of Works), which is one of those in that collection perhaps written by Shakespere. The song is included in Percy's *Reliques*, Gilfillan's edition, 1858, vol. i., Book ii. 16.

The star * is appended to this extract, not because there is any doubt about the allusion by Rowley, but because it is not only now doubtful whether Shakespere wrote the song, but after Heywood's printed protest (see before, p. 99) it may not have been generally attributed to Shakespere in 1633, though published under his name. L. T. S.]

JOHN HALES, OF ETON. Before 1633.

In a Converſation between Sir *John Suckling*, Sir William *D'Avenant, Endymion Porter*, Mr. *Hales of Eaton*, and *Ben Johnſon*, Sir *John Suckling*, who was a profeſſ'd admirer of *Shakeſpear*, had undertaken his Defence againſt *Ben. Johnſon* with ſome warmth; Mr. *Hales*, who had ſat ſtill for ſome time, hearing *Ben* frequently reproaching him with the want of Learning, and Ignorance of the Antients, told him at laſt, "That if Mr. *Shakeſpear* had not read the Antients, he had likewiſe not ſtollen any thing from 'em; [a fault the other made no Conſcience of] and that if he would produce any one Topick finely treated by any of them, he would undertake to ſhew ſomething upon the ſame Subject at leaſt as well written by *Shakeſpear.*"

Some Account of the Life of Mr. William Shakespear, prefixed to the edition of his Works by Nicholas Rowe. 1709. *Vol. I, p. xiv.*

[Rowe gives no authority for this anecdote, but we find another version of it given as from the mouth of Dryden by Charles Gildon in an essay addressed to Dryden in 1694.

"To give the World some Satisfaction, that *Shakespear* has had as great a Veneration paid his Excellence by men of unqueſtion'd parts, as this I now express for him, I shall give some Account of what I have heard from your Mouth, Sir, about the noble Triumph he gain'd over all the Ancients by the Judgment of the ableſt Critics of that time.

"The Matter of Fact (if my Memory fail me not) was this, Mr. *Hales*, of *Eaton*, affirm'd that he wou'd shew all the Poets of Antiquity, outdone by *Shakespear*, in all the Topics, and common places made use of in Poetry.

JOHN HALES, OF ETON. Before, 1633.

The Enemies of *Shakespear* wou'd by no means yield him so much Excellence: so that it came to a Resolution of a trial of skill upon that Subject; the place agreed on for the Dispute, was Mr. *Hales's* Chamber at *Eaton*; a great many Books were sent down by the Enemies of this Poet, and on the appointed day, my Lord *Falkland*, Sir *John Suckling*, and all the Persons of Quality that had Wit and Learning, and interested themselves in the Quarrel, met there, and upon a thorough Disquisition of the point, the Judges chose by agreement out of this Learned and Ingenious Assembly, unanimously gave the Preference to *Shakespear*. And the Greek & Roman Poets were adjudg'd to Vail at least their Glory in that to the English Hero. I cou'd wish, Sir, you wou'd give the Public a juster Account of this Affair, in Vindication of that Poet I know you extreamly esteem, and whom none but you excels." (Some Reflections on Mr. Rymer's 'Short View of Tragedy' and an Attempt at a Vindication of Shakespear. *Miscellaneous Letters and Essays*, 1694, pp. 85, 86.)

The anecdote seems to have had some foundation in truth, for Dryden himself reports Hales's saying, "That there was no subject of which any poet ever writ but he would produce it much better done in Shakespeare." (*Essay of Dramatic Poesie*, 1668, Scott's ed. of Dryden, 1821, Vol. 15, p. 351.) And Nahum Tate, in the Dedication to his *Loyal General*, 1680, addressed to Edw. Tayler, says, "I cannot forget the strong desire I have heard you express to see the Common Places of our *Shakespear* compar'd with the most famous of the Ancients. * * Our Learned *Hales* was wont to assert 'That since the time of *Orpheus* and the Oldest Poets, no Common Place has been touch'd upon, where our Authour has not perform'd as well.'" P. Des Maizeaux, who collects three of these versions together, in his *Life of the Ever-memorable Mr. John Hales*, 1719 (p. 61, note), adds: "But neither of them [Dryden nor Tate] take notice of the conversation above mention'd, nor do they tell us how that saying came to their knowledge." If the conversation or "disquisition" did take place, as seems highly probable, it must have been before 1633, the year in which Falkland died; all the other partakers in it survived him. Hales was born in 1584, he died in 1656. L. T. S.]

WILLIAM HABINGTON, 1634.

To a Friend,
Inviting him to a meeting upon promiſe.

May you drinke beare, or that adult'rate wine
Which makes the zeale of *Amſterdam* divine;
If you make breach of promiſe. I have now
So rich a ſacke, that even your ſelfe will bow
T' adore my *Genius*. Of this wine ſhould *Prynne*
Drinke but a plenteous glaſſe, he would beginne
A health to *Shakeſpeare's* ghoſt.

Castara. 1634. *The Second Part.* [4*to.*] 8*th Poem, p.* 52.

Habington refers to William Prynne, the author of the *Histrio-Mastix* of 1633, from which we have given an extract. He supposes Prynne, under the genial stimulus of his rich sack, to put off the Puritan, and to toast the prince of playwrights. This Prynne is probably the second saint described in *Hudibras*, Part III. C. ii. ll. 421-4 & ll. 1065-6.

There was a former *Histrio-Mastix*, published in 1610, which is said to contain an allusion to Shakespeare's *Troilus and Cressida*, I. iii. l. 73 : but there is evidence to prove that it had, by some years, precedence of Shakespeare's play. Some critics have seen in the expression "mastick jaws" an allusion by Shakespeare to the *Histrio-Mastix* of 1610 : others an allusion to Decker's *Satyro-Mastix*. Such fancies are wholly without foundation. The word "mastick" in *Troilus and Cressida* means either slimy, or gnashing, in either case conveying a singularly forcible and offensive image of Thersites' jaws. "Mastick" is either from the Greek μαστίχη, the gum of the lentisk tree, or from the Latin *mastico*, the equivalent of the Greek μαστιχάω, from μάσταξ, the jaws : certainly not from *mastix*, which means a *whip* or *scourge*.

[See on this subject Mr. R. Simpson's arguments in his *School of Shakspere*, 1878, Vol. I. p. 9.]

JAMES SHIRLEY, 1634.

[Jacintha, after listening to her several suitors who mutually dispraise each other to her, exclaims],—

> Falſtaffe, I will beleeve thee,
> There is noe faith in vilanous man.
>
> *The Example*, 1637, Act II, Sc. i, sign. C 4, back.

Shirley's play, *The Example*, was licensed in 1634, though not printed till later. Jacintha here refers to Falstaff's answer to Prince Hal, 1 Part *Henry IV*, Act II. sc. iv.

"You rogue, here's lime in this sack too: there is nothing but roguery to be found in villanous man." Compare the same sentiment in *Romeo and Juliet*, III. ii, where the nurse says,

> "There is no trust
> No faith, no honesty in men."

(See before, p. 135.)

THOMAS HEYWOOD, 1635.

   Our moderne Poets to that paffe are driven,
   Thofe names are curtal'd which they firft had given;
   And, as we wifht to have their memories drown'd,
   We fcarcely can afford them halfe their found.
Rob. G...ne. Greene, who had in both Academies ta'ne
   Degree of Mafter, yet could never gaine
   To be call'd more than *Robin :* who had he
   Profeft ought fave the *Mufe,* Serv'd, and been
    Free
   After a feven yeares Prentifefhip; might have
   (With credit too) gone *Robert* to his grave
Chrift. Marlo. *Marlo,* renown'd for his rare art and wit,
   Could ne're attaine beyond the name of *Kit ;*
   Although his *Hero* and *Leander* did
Thomas Kid. Merit addition rather. Famous *Kid*
Thom. Watson. Was call'd but *Tom.* *Tom Watfon,* though he wrote
   Able to make *Apollo's* felfe to dote
   Upon his Mufe; for all that he could ftrive,
   Yet never could to his full name arrive.
Thomas Nash. *Tom Nafh* (in his time of no fmall efteeme)
   Could not a fecond fyllable redeeme.
Francis Bew-mont. Excellent *Bewmont,* in the formoft ranke
   Of the rar'ft Wits, was never more than *Franck.*
William Shakespeare. Mellifluous *Shake-fpeare,* whofe inchanting Quill
   Commanded Mirth or Paffion, was but *Will.*

> ^{Benjam.} And famous *Johnſon*, though his learned Pen
> ^{Johnson.}
>   Be dipt in *Caſtaly*, is ſtill but *Ben*.
> ^{John Fletcher.} *Fletcher* and *Webſter*, of that learned packe
> ^{John Webster,}
> ^{&c.}   None of the mean'ſt, yet neither was but *Jacke*.
>   *Deckers* but *Tom ;* nor *May*, nor *Middleton*.   ^{1 Sic.}
>   And hee's now but *Jacke Foord*, that once were[1] *John*.
>
>   *The Hierarchie of the Blessed Angells. Lib.* 4. 1635.
>   *p.* 206. [*Fo.*]

[In the affectionate familiarity of his friends Shakespere "was but Will" or "good Will" (see John Davies of Hereford, before, p. 94), though they did not often express his "curtal'd" name in print. He himself made delicate and skilful use of this common abbreviation in his Sonnets 135 and 136. L. T. S.]

THOMAS CRANLEY, 1635.

[The defcription of Amanda's room]
And then a heape of bookes of thy devotion
Lying upon a fhelfe clofe underneath,
Which thou more think'ft upon then on thy death.
 They are not prayers of a grieved foule,
 That with repentance doth his finnes condole.
But amorous Pamphlets, that beft likes thine eyes,
And Songs of love, and Sonets exquifit.
Among thefe *Venus,* and *Adonis* lies,
With *Salmacis,* and her Hermaphrodite :
Pigmalion's there, with his transform'd delight.
 And many merry Comedies, with this,
 Where the *Athenian Phryne* acted is.

The Converted Courtezan. . . . shadowed under the **name** *of Amanda.* 1639. *p.* 32. [4*to.*]

[The reference to *Venus and Adonis* in the description of Amanda's room and its contents is a proof of the popularity of that poem among ladies of the day. See also other examples, after, pp. 224, 238. Cranley's book was licensed by Dr. William Hayward, chaplain to Archbishop Laud, in 1635. L. T. S.]

SIR JOHN SUCKLING, *about* 1636—1641.

*A Supplement of an imperfect Copy of Verses
of Mr. Wil. Shakespears.*

1

One of her hands, one of her cheeks lay under,
  Cozening the pillow of a lawful kisse,
Which therefore swel'd and seem'd to part asunder,
  As angry to be rob'd of such a blisse:
    The one lookt pale, and for revenge did long,
    Whilst t'other blush't, cause it had done the wrong.

2

Out of the bed the other fair hand was
  On a green sattin quilt, whose perfect white
Lookt like a Dazie in a field of grasse,
[1] And shew'd like unmelt snow unto the sight,   [1] Thus far Shake-spear.
    There lay this pretty perdue, safe to keep
    The rest o th' body that lay fast asleep.

3

Her eyes (and therefore it was night) close laid,
  Strove to imprison beauty till the morn,
But yet the doors were of such fine stuffe made,
  That it broke through, and shew'd itself in scorn.
    Throwing a kind of light about the place,
    which turnd to smiles stil as 't came near her face.

4

Her beams (which fome dul men call'd hair) divided
Part with her cheeks, part with her lips did fport,
But thefe, as rude, her breath put by ftill ; fome
Wifelyer downwards fought, but falling fhort,
Curl'd back in rings, and feem'd to turn agen
To bite the part fo unkindly held them in.

Fragmenta Aurea. A Collection of all the Incomparable Peeces, written by Sir John Suckling. And published by a Friend to perpetuate his memory. Printed by his owne Copies. 1646. *p.* 29-30. [8*vo.*]

The first nine lines are from the *Rape of Lucrece*, ll. 386—396. Suckling would appear to have employed a version of Shakespeare's poem which materially differs from that known to us. Each stanza of *The Rape of Lucrece*, in all the old copies, has seven lines : the complete one given by Suckling has but six. But it is more likely that he curtailed and otherwise altered Shakespeare's lines. The relative stanzas run thus in *England's Parnassus*, 1600, p. 396 : as they do in the Quarto of *Lucrece*, 1594,—except that the latter has "cheeke lies" in the first line, and slight differences of spelling and punctuation.

"Her Lilly hand her rosie cheekes lie under,
Coosning the pillow of a lawful kisse,
Who therefore angry, seemes to part in sunder,
Swelling on eyther side to want his blisse,
Betweene whose hills her head entombed is ;
Where, like a vertuous monument she lyes,
To be admirde of lewd unhallowed eyes.

Without the bed her other fayre hand was
On the greene Coverlet, whose perfect white
Shewd like an Aprill daisie on the grasse,
with pearlie sweat, resembling dew of night."

It is almost impossible to date many of Suckling's pieces. He died on 7 May, 1641, having lived but thirty-two years.

[It may be doubted whether Suckling "curtalled and otherwise altered Shakespeare's lines." The verses are entituled, "*A Supplement of an Imperfect Copy of Verses of Mr. Wil Shakespeares*," and at the commencement of the tenth line is an asterisk with the note, "Thus far Shake-spear." Not only too are the stanzas in a different form from those of our present *Lucrece*—six lines instead of seven—but lines 5 and 6 of the first stanza differ from lines 5-7 of the present version, not merely in wording but wholly in thought. Neither if the verses were originally in seven-line stanzas would they be imperfect, being merely a different version of lines long before completed in *Lucrece* (*Lucrece* published 1594, Suckling 1636-41). It is more probable, as appears to me, that Shakespere at first thought of composing his *Lucrece* in the stanza of *Venus and Adonis*, and for a trial commenced not at the beginning but at the central point of importance and interest, namely, at Tarquin's view of *Lucrece* after forcing her door, but that he, for some unknown reason, after writing about a stanza and a half, threw it aside and took to the seven-line stanza. B. N.]

SIR JOHN SUCKLING, *about* 1636—1641.

>The fweat of learned *Johnſon's* brain,
>And gentle *Shakeſpear's* eaſ'er ſtrain,
>A hackney-coach conveys you to,
>In ſpite of all that rain can do :
>And for your eighteen pence you fit
>The Lord and Judge of all freſh wit.

Fragmenta Aurea: &c. 1646. *p.* 35. [8*vo.*]

[This is part of a letter in verse addressed to Mr. John **Hales of Eton,** "Sir John invites him to come to Town, and enjoy the company of his friends." (*Life of Mr. John Hales*, by P. Des Maizeaux, 1719, p. 58.) L. T. S.]

SIR JOHN SUCKLING, *about* 1636—1641.

I muſt confeſſe it is a juſt ſubject for our ſorrow, to hear of any that does quit his ſtation without his leave that placed him there; and yet as ill a Mine as this Act has, 'twas *a-la-Romanſci*, as you may ſee by a Line of Mr. *Shakeſpears*, who bringing in *Titinius* after a loſt battel, ſpeaking to his ſword, and bidding it find out his heart, adds

By your leave, Gods, this [is] *a Romanes Part.*

Fragmenta Aurea: Letters, 1646. *p.* 61.

*   *   *   *

We are at length arriv'd at that River, about the uneven running of which, my Friend Mr. *William Shakeſpear* makes *Henry Hotſpur* quarrel ſo highly with his fellow Rebels; and for his Sake I have been ſomething curious to conſider the Scantlet of Ground that angry Monſieur wou'd have had in, but can not find it cou'd deſerve his Choler, nor any of the other Side ours, did not the King think it did.

Letters; printed in Works. Dublin, 1766. *p.* 142.

[Both the above passages occur in Suckling's *Letters*, a part only of which were printed in the *Fragmenta Aurea* of 1646; the letter containing the second extract is among the additions made to them in 1766.

The line quoted by Suckling occurs in *Julius Cæsar*, Act V, Sc. iii, l. 89. Hotspur's objection to the winding of the Trent comes in 1 *Henry IV*, Act III, Sc. i :—

> "See how this river comes me cranking in
> And cuts me from the best of all my land
> A huge half-moon, a monstrous cantle out," &c., &c.

L. T. S.]

SIR JOHN SUCKLING, *about* 1636—1641.

Wit in a Prologue, Poets juftly may
Stile a new impofition on a Play.
When *Shakefpeare, Beamont, Fletcher,* rul'd the Stage,
There fcarce were ten good pallats in the age,
More curious Cooks then guefts ; for men would eat
Moft hartily of any kind of meat :
And then what ftrange variety each Play,
A Feaft for Epicures, and that each day.
But marke how odly it is come about,
And how unluckily it now fals out :
The pallats are growne higher,[1] number increaf'd,
And there wants that which fhould make up the Feaft ;
And yet y'are fo unconfcionable. You'd have
Forfooth of late, that which they never gave,
Banquets before ; and after.
(Prologue to *The Goblins.*)

Th[ief] *1.* We have had fuch fport;
Yonder's the rareft Poet without,
Has made all his confeffion in blanke verfe ;
Nor left a God, nor a Goddeffe in Heaven,
But fetch't them all downe for witneffes ;
Has made fuch a defcription of Stix,
And the Ferry,
And verily thinks has paft them.
Enquires for the bleft fhades

---

[1] growne, higher *in original*

And afkes much after certaine Brittifh blades,
One *Shakefpeare* and *Fletcher*:
And grew fo peremptory at laft,
He would be carried, where they were. (p. 35.)

*The Goblins. A Comedy. Printed with
Fragmenta Aurea.* 1646.

[*The Goblins* contains one or two other allusions (see *Fragmenta*, pp. 26, 45), but enough is given from Suckling's works to show the close acquaintance he had with "my friend Mr. William Shakespear." Dryden considers (Preface to *The Tempest, or the Enchanted Island*, 1676) that Sir John Suckling, "a profess'd admirer of our author" (Shakespere), has follow'd his footsteps in the *Goblins;* that his *Reginella* is an open imitation of Shakespear's *Miranda;* and that his spirits, though counterfeit, are copied from *Ariel*. But, though Warburton echoes this idea, the student must judge for himself how feeble an imitator Suckling was. L. T. S.]

JASPER MAYNE, 1637.

Elſe, (though wee all conſpir'd to make thy *Herſe*
Our *Workes*) ſo that 't had beene but one great *Verſe*,
Though the *Prieſt* had tranſlated for that time
The *Liturgy*, and buried *thee* in *Rime*,
So that in *Meeter* wee had heard it ſaid,
Poetique duſt is to *Poetique* laid:
And though that *duſt* being *Shakſpears*, thou might'ſt have
Not his *roome*, but the *Poet* for *thy grave;*
So that, as *thou* didſt *Prince* of *Numbers* dye
And live, ſo now *thou* mightſt in *Numbers* lie,
'Twere fraile *ſolemnitie; Verſes* on *Thee*
And not like *thine*, would but kind *Libels* be;

  * * * * * *

Who without *Latine helps* had'ſt beene as *rare*
As *Beaumont, Fletcher,* or as *Shakeſpeare* were:
 And like *them*, from thy *native Stock* could'ſt ſay,
 Poets and *Kings* are not borne every day.

  Jonſonus Virbius: or, The Memorie of Ben. Johnson revived by the Friends of the Muses. 1638. *pp.* 29, 33. [4*to.*]

[There are two copies of this little book in the British Museum, professing to be of the same impression and apparently agreeing in all particulars, save that in only one of them is the signature I. Mayne found to the verses whence the above extract is taken. The book was entered on the Stationers' Register, 3 Feb. 1637. L. T. S.]

It is the author of this finger-counting doggrel who is credited by some with the splendid elegy on Shakespeare, which we have given on pages 120-3. We had some compunction in reproducing Mayne's trashy verses at all: and the italics in these extracts from Jonsonus Virbius could have had no possible meaning: it was a fantastical trick of the time. See, for instances, Sir Roger L'Estrange's lines prefixed to Beaumont and Fletcher's *Works*, 1647: those of Alexander Brome on Richard Brome, in the *Five New Plays*, 1653: and the first edition, 1682, of Dryden's *Religio Laici*.

OWEN FELTHAM, 1637.

So in our *Halcyon* dayes, we have had now
Wits, to which, all that after come, muſt bow.
And ſhould the Stage compoſe her ſelfe a Crowne
Of all thoſe *wits*, which hitherto ſh'as knowne:
Though there be many that about her brow
Like ſparkling ſtones, might a quick luſtre throw:
Yet *Shakeſpeare, Beaumont, Johnſon*, theſe three ſhall
Make up the Jem in the point Verticall.
And now ſince JOHNSONS gone, we well may ſay,
The Stage hath ſeene her glory and decay

Jonsonus Virbius. 1638. *pp*. 42, 43. [4to.]

RICHARD WEST, 1637.

Shakefpeare may make *griefe* merry, *Beaumonts* ftile
Ravifh and melt anger into a fmile;
In winter *nights*, or after *meales* they be,
I muft confeffe very good companie:
But *thou* exact'ft our beft houres induftrie; [Jonson]
Wee may read *them;* we ought to ftudie *thee.*

Jonsonus Virbius. 1638. p. 56. [4to.]

West was probably thinking of *A Winter's Tale:* "A sad tale's best for winter," ii. 1, and "Upon a barren mountain, and still winter," iii. 2.

H. RAMSAY, 1637.

What are his fauls (O Envy !) that you ſpeaĸe [Jonson's faults]
Engliſh at Court, the learned Stage acts Greeke.
That Latine Hee reduc'd, and could command
That which your *Shakeſpeare* ſcarce could underſtand ?

Jonsonus Virbius. 1638. *p.* 60. [4*to*]

"Faul," for *fault,* occurs in *The Merry Wives of Windsor,* i. 1,—" the faul is in the 'ort dissolutely." [Dyce's Shakspere, 1866, Vol. I, p. 351. The Cambridge edition and the folio of 1623 have "fall."] In the mention of Jonson's command of Latin, Ramsay is probably thinking of his reflection on Shakespeare's "small Latin and less Greek."

SIR WILLIAM D'AVENANT, 1637.

In Remembrance of
Mafter *William Shakefpeare*.
ODE.

1.

Beware (delighted Poets!) when you fing
To welcome Nature in the early Spring;
   Your num'rous Feet not tread
The Banks of Avon; for each Flowre
(As it nere knew a Sunne or Showre)
   Hangs there, the penfive head.

2.

Each Tree, whofe thick, and fpreading growth hath made,
Rather a Night beneath the Boughs, than Shade,
   (Unwilling now to grow)
Lookes like the Plume a Captive weares,
Whofe rifled *Falls* are fteept i' th teares
   Which from his laft rage flow.

3.

The piteous River wept it felfe away
Long fince (Alas!) to fuch a fwift decay;
   That reach the Map; and looke
If you a River there can fpie;
And for a River your mock'd Eie,
   Will finde a fhallow Brooke.

      Madagascar, with other Poems. 1638. *p.* 37. [12mo.]
        (*Imprimatur Feb.* 26, 1637.)

In the last line of the first verse, D'Avenant seems to be recalling a line in Milton's *Lycidas*:

"And cowslips wan that hang the pensive head."

The third verse is sufficient to prove that D'Avenant had an ear.

The late Mr. George Jabet (Eden Warwick) believed that here 'delighted' meant 'deprived of light,' and employed this instance to enforce his interpretation of 'the delighted Spirit,' in *Measure for Measure*. Dr. Brinsley Nicholson takes the same view of the latter (see *N. & Q.*, 3rd S., I., Ap. 5, 1862, & 5th S., X., 1878, pp. 83, 182, 303). But though, doubtless, 'delighted' means the same in these two passages, it is, in Davenant, very plainly opposed to 'pensive.' He is checking the poets in their delight, and bidding them shun the banks of Avon as being a region of sorrow which even dimmed

"The radiant looks of unbewailing flowers."

In connection with Davenant we must not omit to notice the tradition of a letter written by the King to Shakespeare.

In the Advertisement to Lintott's edition of Shakespeare's *Poems*, 1709 [8vo.], we read:

"That most learn'd Prince, and great Patron of Learning, King *James* the First, was pleas'd with his own Hand to write an amicable letter to Mr. *Shakespeare;* which Letter, tho now lost, remain'd long in the Hands of Sir William D'Avenant, as a credible Person now living can testify."

T. TERRENT, 1637.

Haud aliter noftri præmiffa in principis ortum
Ludicra *Chauceri*, claffifq; incompta fequentum;
Nafcenti apta parum divina hæc machina regno,
In noftrum fervanda fuit tantæq; decebat
Prælufiffe Deos ævi certamina famæ;
Nec geminos vates, nec Te *Shakfpeare* filebo,
Aut quicquid facri noftros conjecit in annos
Confilium Fati.
Jonsonus Virbius. 1638. *p.* 64. [4*to.*]

[Terrent was educated at Christ Church Oxford, where he took the degree of Master of Arts, and was tutor of the College, according to Gilchrist (see Cunningham's edition of *Gifford's Works of Jonson.* 1872. Vol. iii. p. 521). L. T. S.]

This obscure but excellent poet writes that

"the tales of Chaucer heralded the rise of our Chief (Jonson), as did also the unpolished band (of poets) who succeeded him. This god-like device (the Jonsonian comedy), but little suited to (the taste of) an early age, was to be reserved for ours; and it was fitting that the gods should rehearse the contests of that age, as a preparation for so great a genius; nor will I pass over in silence the twin-bards (Beaumont and Fletcher) nor Thee *Shakespeare,* or whatever (other) sacred (name) the plan of Fate has cast upon our times."

It was in Comedy that Jonson professed to have introduced new laws, that is, he brought back the rigid use of the old classic laws of unity in time and place. He compliments Richard Brome, in verses prefixed to *The Northern Lasse,* 1632, on the applause he had gained

"By observation of those Comick Lawes
Which I, your Master, first did teach the Age."

Some years later Sir John Suckling (*Sessions of the Poets, Fragmenta Aurea,* 1646, p. 7) represents Ben asserting that

"he had purg'd the stage
Of errors that had lasted many an age."

ABRAHAM WRIGHT, *about* 1637 (*or earlier*).

Othello by Shakſpeare.

A very good play, both for lines and plot, but eſpecially the plot. Jago for a rogue, and Othello for a jealous huſband, two parts well penned. Act 3, the ſcene between Jago and Othello, and the firſt ſcene of the fourth act, between the ſame, ſhew admirably the villanous humour of Jago when he perſuades Othello to his jealouſy.

> *Manuscript Common-place book of Abraham Wright, Vicar of Okeham, in Rutlandshire. Quoted in Historical Papers, Part I, edited for the Roxburghe Club by Bliss and Bandinel. 1846. Introduction, p. vi.*

Anonymous. About 1637.

*An Elegie on the death of that famous Writer
and Actor, M.* William Shakſpeare.

I dare not doe thy Memory that wrong,
Unto our larger griefes to give a tongue;
Ile onely ſigh in earneſt, and let fall
My ſolemne teares at thy great Funerall;
For every eye that raines a ſhowre for thee,
Laments thy loſſe in a ſad Elegie.
Nor is it fit each humble Muſe ſhould have,
Thy worth his ſubject, now th' art laid in grave;
No its a flight beyond the pitch of thoſe,
Whoſe worthles Pamphlets are not fence in Proſe.
Let learned *Johnſon* ſing a Dirge for thee,
And fill our Orbe with mournefull harmony:
But we neede no Remembrancer, thy Fame
Shall ſtill accompany thy honoured Name,
To all poſterity; and make us be,
Senſible of what we loſt in loſing thee:
Being the Ages wonder whoſe ſmooth Rhimes
Did more reforme than laſh the looſer Times.
Nature her ſelfe did her owne ſelfe admire,
As oft as thou wert pleaſed to attire
Her in her native luſture, and confeſſe,
Thy dreſſing was her chiefeſt comlineſſe.
How can we then forget thee, when the age
Her chiefeſt Tutor, and the widdowed Stage

Her onely favorite in thee hath loſt,
And Natures ſelfe what ſhe did bragge of moſt.
Sleepe then rich ſoule of numbers, whilſt poore we,
Enjoy the profits of thy Legacie ;
And thinke it happineſſe enough we have,
So much of thee redeemed from the grave,
As may ſuffice to enlighten future times,
With the bright luſtre of thy matchleſſe Rhimes.

Appended to Shakespeare's Poems. 1640.
Sign. L. [12mo.]

This is a creditable copy of verses, reminding one of Ben Jonson. The line

"Let learned *Johnson* sing a Dirge for thee,"

proved that they were written in Jonson's lifetime: and he died 1637. The best lines in it, "Nature herself," &c., closely resemble a couplet in Ben's elegy :

"Nature herself was proud of his designs,
And joy'd to weare the dressing of his lines."

JAMES MERVYN, 1638.

There are fome men doe hold, there is a place
Cal'd *Limbus Patrum*, if fuch have the grace
To wave that Schifme, and Poëtarum faid [vice *Patrum*]
They of that faith had me a member made,
That *Limbus* I could have beleev'd thy braine
Where *Beamont, Fletcher, Shakefpeare*, & a traine
Of glorious Poets in their active heate
Move in that Orbe, as in their former feate.
When thou began'ft to give thy Mafter life,
Me thought I faw them all, with friendly ftrife
Each cafting in his dofe, *Beamont* his weight,
Shakefpeare his mirth, and *Fletcher* his conceit,
With many more ingredients, with thy fkill
So fweetely tempered, that the envious quill
And tongue of Criticks muft both write and fay,
They never yet beheld a fmoother Play.

*Lines prefixed to The Royall Mafter, a play by
James Shirley.* 1638. *Sign. B 2.* [4*to.*]

WILLIAM CHILLINGWORTH, 1638.

So that as a foolifh fellow who gave a Knight the Lye, defiring withall leave of him to fet his Knighthood afide, was anfwered by him, that he would not fuffer any thing to be fet afide that belonged unto him : So might we juftly take it amiffe, that conceiving as you doe ignorance and repentance fuch neceffary things for us, you are not more willing to confider us with them, then without them.

The Religion of Protestants a Safe Way to Salvation, &c. Chap. I. *Part* 1. § 5. *p.* 33. 1638. [*Fo.*]

Chillingworth refers to 2 *Henry IV*, i, 2, where the Chief Justice's attendant says,

"I pray you Sir, then set your knighthood and your soldiership aside ; and give me leave to tell you, you lie in your throat," &c., to which Falstaff replies, "I give thee leave to tell me so ! I lay aside that which grows to me! " &c.

T[HOMAS] R[ANDOLPH?] 1638.

Corn. *Venerem* etiam & *Adonidem,* petulantem fatis Librum
In finu portat, eoque multò peritior evafit
Quàm probæ neceffe eft : fed ifta parum movent,
Eduxi, nec vanâ lactavi fpe, ut fpero.
Eludere difcat, aut pereat.

Cornelianum Dolium, 1638. [12mo.] *Act I, sc. v, p.* 22.

[Douce has ingeniously conjectured that T. R. is Thomas Randolph, and the initials and the words on the title-page "*Auctore,* T. R. ingeniosissimo hujus ævi HELICONIO." support his conjecture. But there are some things against it. Cornelius is here speaking of one of his illegitimate daughters, of whose tendencies and tastes he does not give a very favourable account. B. N.]
[Cornelius here says,

"She carries in her bosom too a rather wanton book (called) *Venus and Adonis,* and through it has become much more knowing than is meet for an honest girl ! But these things move me little ; I have brought her up, and not deluded her, I hope, w th vain expectations. Let her learn to behave better, or perish."

This is a particular instance of what John Johnson, *Academy of Love,* 1641 (see after, p. 238), says was the general practice. C. M. I.]

[Mr. Roberts points out another reference to the habit in *The English Gentleman,* by Richard Brathwait, 1630 (4to, p. 28) :—

"But alas ; to what height of licentious libertie are these corrupte timer growne ? When that *Sex,* where Modesty should claime a native preroga tive, gives way to foments of exposed loosenesse ; by not only attending to the wanton discourse of immodest Lovers, but carrying about them (even in their naked Bosomes, where chastest desires should only lodge) the amorous toyes of *Venus* and *Adonis:* which Poem, with others of like nature, they heare with such attention, peruse with such devotion, and retaine with such delectation, as no subject can equally relish their unseasoned palate, like those lighter discourses." L. T. S.]

RICHARD BROME, 1638.

Thefe lads can act the Emperors lives all over,
And Shakefpeares Chronicled hiftories, to boot,
And were that *Cæfar*, or that Englifh Earle
That lov'd a Play and Player fo well now living,
I would not be out-vyed in my delights.

Antipodes. 1640. *Sign. C* 2. [4*to.*]
(" *Acted in the yeare* 1638.")

R[OBERT] C[HAMBERLAIN], 1639.

One aſked another what Shakeſpeares works were worth, all being bound together. He anſwered, not a farthing. Not worth a farthing! ſaid he; why ſo? He anſwered that his plays were worth a great deale of mony, but he never heard, that his works were worth any thing at all.

> *Conceits, Clinches, Flashes, and Whimzies. Newly studied, with some Collections, but those never published before in this kinde.* 1639. [*Reprinted by J. O. Halliwell,* 1860, *p.* 30; *also in Hazlitt's Shakespeare Jest-Books; Third volume, last article* 1864. *p.* 49.]

[Since Mr. Hazlitt reprinted the "Conceits," he has found that there was a second edition printed under the title of "Jocabella, or a Cabinet of Conceits, whereunto are added Epigrams and other Poems" in 1640, and has accordingly placed the two books together under the name of Robert Chamberlaine in his "Hand-book," 1867.

The "conceit" recalls that which Sir John Suckling puts into the mouth of "good old Ben" Jonson (see note, after, p. 233). L. T. S.]

THOMAS BANCROFT, 1639.

To *Shakefpeare*.

Thy Mufes fugred dainties feeme to us
Like the fam'd Apples of old *Tantalus*:
For we (admiring) fee and heare thy ftraines,
But none I fee or heare, thofe fweets attaines.

To *the fame*.

Thou haft fo uf'd thy *Pen*, (or *fhocke thy Speare*)
That Poets ftartle, nor thy wit come neare.

Two Bookes of Epigrammes, and Epitaphs.
1639. [4*to.*] *Nos.* 118 *and* 119.

Anonymous, 1639.

To Mr. William Shake-ſpear.

Shake-ſpeare, we muſt be ſilent in thy praiſe,
'Cauſe our encomion's will but blaſt thy Bayes,
Which envy could not, that thou didſt ſo well;
Let thine own hiſtories prove thy Chronicle.

Witts Recreations Selected from the finest Fancies of Moderne Muses. With A Thousand out-Landish Proverbs. Epigram 25. 1640.
(*Imprimatur*, 1639.)

JOHN BENSON, 1640.

To the Reader.

I here prefume (under favour) to prefent to your view, fome excellent and fweetely compofed Poems, of Mafter *William Shakefpeare*, Which in themfelves appeare of the fame purity, the Authour himfelfe then living avouched; they had not the fortune by reafon of their Infancie in his death, to have the due accommodatiō of proportionable glory, with the reft of his ever-living Workes, yet the lines of themfelves will afford you a more authentick approbation than my affurance any way can, to invite your allowance, in your perufall you fhall finde them *Seren*, cleere and eligantly plaine, fuch gentle ftraines as fhall recreate and not perplexe your braine, no intricate or cloudy ftuffe to puzzell intellect, but perfect eloquence; fuch as will raife your admiration to his praife: this affurance I know will not differ from your acknowledgement. And certaine I am, my opinion will be feconded by the fufficiency of thefe enfuing Lines; I have beene fome what folicitus to bring this forth to the perfect view of all men; and in fo doing, glad to be ferviceable for the continuance of glory to the deferved Author in thefe his Poems.

The Publisher's address, prefixed to Shakespeare's Poems. 1640. [12mo.]

LEWIS SHARPE, 1640.

Pupillus.   Oh for the book of *Venus* and *Adonis,* to court my Miſtris by.

The Noble Stranger.   1640.   G 4.

[Pupillus makes this exclamation after having swallowed one of Mercutio's paper pills, containing " a wanton lovers rapture." In this amusing scene Mercutio undertakes to furnish Pupillus " with as much wit as shall serve for a Country Justice, or an Alderman's heire," by means of "certaine Collections out of learned and witty Authors, for all humours in an accomplished wit. Now sir, you must eate every one of hem one by one." Surely Lewis Sharpe fore-saw the " cramming" of modern days! L. T. S.]

LEONARD DIGGES, 1640.

Upon Mafter WILLIAM SHAKESPEARE, *the Deceafed Authour, and his* POEMS.

Poets are borne not made, when I would prove
This truth, the glad rememberance I muft love
Of never dying *Shakefpeare*, who alone,
Is argument enough to make that one.
Firft, that he was a Poet none would doubt,
That heard th' applaufe of what he fees fet out
Imprinted; where thou haft (I will not fay [1]
Reader his Workes for to contrive a Play:
To him twas none) the patterne of all wit,
Art without Art unparaleld as yet.
Next Nature onely helpt him, for looke thorow
This whole Booke, thou fhalt find he doth not borrow,
One phrafe from Greekes, nor Latines imitate,
Nor once from vulgar Languages Tranflate,
Nor Plagiari-like from others gleane,
Nor begges he from each witty friend a Scene
To peece his Acts with, all that he doth write,
Is pure his owne, plot, language exquifite,
But oh! what praife more powerfull can we give
The dead, then that by him the Kings men live,
His Players, which fhould they but have fhar'd the Fate,
All elfe expir'd within the fhort Termes date;

[1] say) in the original, but it is a misprint.

How could the Globe have profpered, fince through want
Of change, the Plaies and Poems had growne fcant.
But happy Verfe thou fhalt be fung and heard,
When hungry quills fhall be fuch honour bard. [barr'd]
Then vanifh upftart Writers to each Stage,
You needy Poetafters of this Age,
Where *Shakefpeare* liv'd or fpake, Vermine forbeare,
Leaft with your froth you fpot them, come not neere;
But if you needs muft write, if poverty
So pinch, that otherwife you ftarve and die
On Gods name may the Bull or Cockpit have
Your lame blancke Verfe, to keepe you from the grave:
Or let new Fortunes younger brethren fee,
What they can picke from your leane induftry.
I doe not wonder when you offer at
Blacke-Friers, that you fuffer: tis the fate
Of richer veines, prime judgements that have far'd
The worfe, with this deceafed man compar'd.
So have I feene, when Cefar would appeare,
And on the Stage at halfe-fword parley were,
Brutus and *Caffius:* oh how the Audience
Were ravifh'd, with what wonder they went thence,
When fome new day they would not brooke a line,
Of tedious (though well laboured) *Catiline*[1];
Sejanus too was irkefome, they priz'de more
Honeft *Iago*, or the jealous Moore.
And though the Fox and fubtill Alchimift,
Long intermitted could not quite be mift,
Though thefe have fham'd all the Ancients, and might raife,
Their Authours merit with a crowne of Bayes.
Yet thefe fometimes, even at a friends defire
Acted, have fcarce defrai'd the Seacoale fire

[1] Catalines *in the original*.

And doore-keepers: when let but *Falſtaffe* come,
Hall, Poines, the reſt you ſcarce ſhall have a roome
All is ſo peſter'd: let but *Beatrice*
And *Benedicke* be ſeene, loe in a trice
The Cockpit Galleries, Boxes, all are full
To hear *Malvoglio,* that croſſe garter'd Gull.
Briefe, there is nothing in his wit fraught Booke,
Whoſe ſound we would not heare, on whoſe worth looke
Like old coynd gold, whoſe lines in every page,
Shall paſſe true currant to ſucceeding age.
But why doe I dead *Sheakſpeares* praiſe recite,
Some ſecond *Shakeſpeare* muſt of *Shakeſpeare* write;
For me tis needleſſe, ſince an hoſt of men,
Will pay to clap his praiſe, to free my Pen.

Prefixed to Shakespeare's Poems. 1640. [12mo.]

In his verses of 1623 (before, p. 154) Leonard Digges speaks twice of Shakespeare's *Works.* In the above lines he refuses that term to the plays, because it was to Shakespeare no work "to contrive a play." H. Fitzgeoffrey thus writes in his *Certaine Elegies,* 1618 (Book i, Sat. i. sign. A 8):

"Bookes, made of Ballades: Workes, of Playes,"

and Sir John Suckling, in his *Sessions of the Poets (Fragmenta Aurea,* 1646, p. 7), writes,

"The first that broke silence was good old *Ben,*
Prepar'd before with Canary wine,
And he told them plainly he deserv'd the Bays,
For his were call'd Works, where others were but Plaies."

The fact is that Jonson had in 1616 issued his Plays under the title of *Workes.* Perhaps the joke at page 226, in the extract from *Conceits, Clinches,* &c., had no reference to this; the *works* there referred to seem to be Shakespenre's *good works:* still there is the same opposition to plays and books. In 1633 Wm. Sheares published John Marston's plays; and prefixed an "Epistle Dedicatory," in which he asks, Why are "Playes in generall" "so vehemently inveighed against"? "Is it because they are Playes? The name it seemes somewhat offends them, whereas if they were styled Workes, they might have their Approbation also." Whalley, in his *Life* prefixed to his edition of Jonson's Works, 1756 (p. xlv), records that some one addressed to him this Epigram,—

> "Pray tell me, Ben, where does the myst'ry lurk?
> What others call a Play, you call a work"?

to which the following answer was returned,—

> "The author's friend thus for the author says;
> Ben's plays are works, when others works are plays."

When Digges writes

> "Vermine forbeare,
> Least with your froth you spot them, come not neere;
> But if you needs must write, if poverty
> So pinch, that otherwise you starve and die," &c.

he is specially referring to Ben Jonson's "apologeticall dialogue" at the end of the *Poetaster*, where Ben says of the Marston faction,

> "If it gave 'em Meat,
> Or got 'em Clothes, 'tis well" (*Works*, 1616, p. 351).

And there is also a remembrance of *A Midsummer Night's Dream*, and in particular of the words

> "Newts and blindworms do no wrong,
> Come not near our fairy queen."

Digges' verses are curious and valuable, as a testimony to the supreme popularity of *Julius Cæsar*, *Othello*, *Henry IV*, *Much Ado About Nothing*, and *Twelfth Night*. They also show that Ben Jonson had reason for viewing Shakespeare's success with jealousy. We know that his *New Inn* was a complete failure, as it deserved to be. We learn from Digges, that even *Catiline* and *Sejanus* were found tedious and irksome.

JOHN WARREN, 1640.

Of Mr. William Shakefpeare.

What, lofty *Shakefpeare*, art againe reviv'd?
And *Virbius* like now fhow'ft thy felfe twife liv'd,
Tis [Benfon's] love that thus to thee is fhowne,
The labours his, the glory ftill thine owne.
Thefe learned Poems amongft thine after-birth,
That makes thy name immortall on the earth,
Will make the learned ftill admire to fee,
The Mufes gifts fo fully infus'd on thee.
Let Carping *Momus* barke and bite his fill,
And ignorant *Davus* flight thy learned fkill :
Yet thofe who know the worth of thy defert,
And with true judgement can difcerne thy Art,
Will be admirers of thy high tun'd ftraine,
Amongft whofe number let me ftill remaine.

Prefixed to Shakespeare's Poems. 1640. [12mo.]

And VIRBIUS *like : Virbius* is the name borne by Hippolytus, after his revival. See Virgil's *Æneid*, lib. vii. Conington (1867, p. 251) thus renders the relative passage :

"But Trivia kind her favourite hides,
And to Egeria's care confides,
To live in woods obscure and lone,
And lose in Virbius' name his own."

There may be an allusion to the little volume called *Jonsonus Virbius* (Jonson Revived), a collection of verses in praise of Ben Jonson, published in the next year after his death, and two years before the publication of Warren's verses (see before, p. 212). The title, *Jonsonus Virbius*, was, according to Aubrey, given to this little work by Lord Falkland. Cf. the couplet,

"Whose Pious *Cœmetery* shall still keep
Thy *Virbius* waking, though thy *Ashes* sleep."

which occurs in a copy of verses by Robert Gardiner prefixed to Cartwright's works, ed. 1651.

'*Tis* [*Benson's*] *love,* &c. The publisher's name has been conjecturally added, to eke out the verse, and complete the sense.

JAMES SHIRLEY, September, October, 1640.

Does this look like a Term? I cannot tell,
Our Poet thinks the whole Town is not well,
Has took fome Phyfick lately, and for fear
Of catching cold dares not falute this Ayr.
But ther's another reafon, I hear fay
London is gone to *York*, 'tis a great way;
Pox o' the Proverb, and of him fay I,
That look'd ore *Lincoln*, caufe that *was*, muft we
Be now tranflated North? I could rail to [too]
On Gammar *Shiptons* Ghoft, but 't wo' not doe,
The Town will ftill be *flecking*, and a Play
Though ne'r fo new, will ftarve the fecond day:
Upon thefe very hard conditions,
Our Poet will not purchafe many Towns;
And if you leave us too, we cannot thrive,
I'l promife neither Play nor Poet live
Till ye come back, think what you do, you fee
What audience we have, what Company
" *To* Shakefpear *comes, whofe mirth did once beguile*
" *Dull hours, and bufkind, made even forrow fmile,*
" *So lovely were the wounds, that men would fay*
" *They could endure the bleeding a whole day:*
He has but few friends lately, think o' that,
Hee'l come no more, and others have his fate.
" Fletcher *the Mufes darling, and choice love*
" *Of* Phœbus, *the delight of every Grove;*

" *Upon whose head the Laurel grew, whose wit*
" *Was the Times wonder, and example yet,*
'Tis within memory, Trees did not throng,
As once the Story said to *Orpheus* song.
" *Johnson, t' whose name, wise Art did bow, and Wit*
" *Is only justified by honouring it:*
" *To hear whose touch, how would the learned Quire*
" *With silence stoop?* and when he took his *Lyre,*
" Apollo *dropt his Lute, asham'd to see*
" *A Rival to the God of Harmonie.*
You do forsake *him* too, we must deplore
This fate, for we do know it by our *door.*
How must this Author fear then, with his guilt
Of weakness to thrive here, where late was spilt
The *Muses* own blood, if being but a few,
You not conspire, and meet more frequent too?
There are not now *nine Muses,* and you may
Be kind to ours, if not, he bad me say,
    Though while you careless kill the rest, and laugh,
    Yet he may live to write your *Epitaph.*

The Sisters. 1652. [8vo.] *Prologue at the Black-Fryers.*

[It is suggested by Genest (*Account of English Stage*, iii, p. 143) that the words "London is gone to York" indicate a date when the King and Court were at York, in 1640, and that *The Sisters* was probably acted then, at Blackfriars. L. T. S.]

JOHN JOHNSON, 1641.

In ſpeaking of this we entred Loves Library, which was very ſpacious, and compleatly filled with great variety of Bookes of all faculties, and in all kindes of Volumes.

*   *   *   *   *

There was alſo *Shakeſpeere*, who (as *Cupid* informed me) creepes into the womens cloſets about bed time, and if it were not for ſome of the old out-of-date Grandames (who are ſet over the reſt as their tutoreſſes) the young ſparkiſh Girles would read in *Shakeſpeere* day and night, ſo that they would open the Booke or Tome, and the men with a Feſcue in their hands ſhould point to the Verſe.

The Academy of Love, deſcribing ye folly of younge men & ye fallacy of women. 1641, pp. 96, 99 (mis-paged, pages 97, 98 are left out). [4to.]

MARTINE PARKER, 1641.

All Poets (as adition to their fames)
Have by their Works eternized their names,
As Chaucer, Spencer, and that noble earle,
Of Surrie thought it the moſt precious pearle,
That dick'd his honour, to Subſcribe to what
His high engenue ever amed at [,]
Sydney and *Shakſpire, Drayton, Withers* and
Renowned *Jonſon* glory of our Land :
Deker, Learn'd *Chapman, Haywood* al thought good,
To have their names in publike underſtood,
And that ſweet Seraph of our Nation, *Quarles*
(In ſpight of each planatick cur that ſnarles)
Subſcribes to his Celeſtiall harmony,
While Angels chant his Dulcid melodie.
And honeſt *John* from the water to the land
Makes us all know and honour him by's hand;

*The Poets blind mans Bough, or, Have among you
my blind Harpers.* 1641, *sign. A* 4. [4*to.*]

SHAKESPEARE'S
CENTURIE OF PRAYSE.

THIRD PERIOD.
1642—1660

CHARLES BUTLER, VICAR OF WOTTON, 1642.

Rhythmi genera partim fyllabarum fuarum numero, partim variâ fonorum refonantium difpofitione diftingui poffunt: fed ea (4) optimorum poetarum obfervatio optime docebit.

* * * * *

(4) Quales sunt apud nos Homero, Maroni, Ovidio, cœterisque melioris notæ priscis æquiparandi, D. PHILIPPUS SIDNEY, EDMUNDUS SPENCER, SAMUEL DANIEL, MICHAEL DRAYTON, JOSUAH SYLVESTER, &, quem cum honore memoro, Divinus ille Vates GEORGIUS WITHER, aliique ingenio & arte florentes, quorum hæc ætas uberrima est: atque inprimis horum omnium magister, unicum caligantis sui seculi lumen, D. GALFRIDUS CHAUCER.
(*Edition, London*, 1629, *sign. E* 3.)

(4) Quales sunt apud nos Homero, Maroni, Ovidio, cœterisque melioris notæ priscis æquiparandi, *D. Philippus Sidney, Edmundus Spencer, Samuel Daniel, Michael Drayton, Josuah Sylvester*, ingeniose pius *Franciscus Quarles*, & quem cum honore memoro, Divinus ille vates *Georgius Wither*, aliique ingenio & arte florentes, quorum hæc ætas uberrima est. Quibus accedat ex Poetis scenicis, Senecæ, Plauto, Terentio neutiquam inferior, tragicus comicus historicus *Guilielmus Shakespeare*: aliique singularis illius artificii æmulatores non pauci.
(*Editions, London*, 1642, *p.* 41; *and Leyden*, 1642, *pp.* 38, 39.)

Rhetorica Libri Duo. Quorum Prior de Tropis & Figuris, Posterior de Voce & Gestu præcipit: in usum scholarum postremo recogniti. Quibus recens accesserunt de oratoria Libri duo. Lib. I. cap. 13.

[Edmund Bolton (before, pp. 91, 92) cites Shakespere for a model of English, as does Charles Butler for a model of rhythm. Butler says,—

"The kinds of rhythm may be distinguished, partly by the number of their syllables, partly by the different arrangement of the echoing sounds; but observation of the best poets * teaches these things best.

* Such among us, fit to be compared to Homer, Virgil, Ovid and others of the better ancient fame, are Sir *Philip Sidney, Edmund Spencer, Samuel Daniel, Michael Drayton, Josuah Sylvester*, the naturally serious *Francis Quarles*, and he whom I name with honour, that Divine poet *George Wither*, and others now eminent in genius and in skill of whom this age is most fruitful. To whom is added of the dramatic poets, in no whit inferior to Seneca, Plautus, Terence, the tragi-comic-historic *William Shakespeare:* and not a few others professing that special art." L. T. S.]

* *Anonymous*, 1643.

[addreſſing the Parliament]
We will not dare at your ſtrange Votes to Jear,
Nor perſonate King *Pym* with his State-flear
Aſpiring *Cataline* ſhall be forgot,
Bloody *Sejanus*, or who e're would Plot
Confuſion to a State; the Warrs betwixt
The Parliament, and juſt *Henry* the ſixt,
Shall have no thought or mention, cauſe their power,
Not only plac'd, but left him in the *Tower*;
Nor yet the Grave advice of learned Pym
Make a Malignant, and then Plunder him.

  * * * *

Methinks there ſhould not ſuch a difference be
'Twixt our profeſſion and your quality,
You meet, plot, talk, conſult, with minds immenſe,
The like with us, but only we ſpeak ſenſe
Inferiour unto you; we can tell how
To depoſe Kings, there we are more than you,
Although not more then what you would.

> *Rump. An Exact Collection of the choycest Poems and Songs relating to the late Times, from Anno* 1639 *to Anno* 1661. *The Players Petition to the Parliament.* 1662. *Part I. p.* 33. [8*vo.*]

[The *Players Petition* was not included in the first edition of this collection, which came out in 1660, nor is it contained in the reprint of the work published in 1731. It, however, appears to have been written in 1643, from the following lines near the beginning :—

> " O wise mysterious Synod, what shall we
> Do for such men as you e're forty three
> Be half expir'd, and an unlucky season
> Shall set a period to *Triennial Treason ;—*"

and the numerous allusions in it to "King Pym," who died 8 Dec., 1643. The Long Parliament made an Order for closing the theatres, 2 Sept. 1642 (see after, p. 253), and this poem seems to have been a protest against such severity. The writer may have alluded to Shakespere's *Henry VI.* and *Richard II.* in the lines quoted above.

Mr. Hazlitt (Roxburghe Library, *English Drama and Stage*, 1869, p. 273) prints the last word in the second line *State-Bear*, which conveys no sense; the fl is slightly blurred, but it is plainly flear = fleer, a scornful look. L. T. S.]

THOMAS FULLER, 1643—1662.

WILLIAM SHAKESPEARE was born at *Stratford* on *Avon* in this County, in whom three eminent Poets may feem in fome fort to be compounded.

1. *Martial,* in the *Warlike* found of his Sur-name (whence fome may conjecture him of a *Military extraction*) *Hafti-vibrans,* or *Shake-fpeare.*

2. *Ovid,* the moft *naturall* and *witty* of all Poets; and hence it was that Queen *Elizabeth,* coming into a Grammar-School, made this extemporary verfe,

'*Perfius* a **Crab-ftaffe**, Bawdy *Martial,*
Ovid a fine Wag.'

3. *Plautus,* who was an exact Comœdian, yet never any Scholar, as our *Shake-fpeare* (if alive) would confeffe himfelf. Adde to all thefe, that though his Genius generally was *jocular* and inclining him to *feftivity,* yet he could (when fo difpofed) be *folemn* and *ferious,* as appears by his Tragedies; fo that *Heraclitus* himfelf (I mean if fecret and unfeen) might afford to fmile at his Comedies, they were fo *merry;* and *Democritus* fcarce forbear to figh at his Tragedies, they were fo *mournfull.*

He was an eminent inftance of the truth of that Rule, *Poeta not fit, fed nafcitur;* one is not *made,* but *born* a Poet. Indeed his Learning was very little, fo that, as *Cornish diamonds* are not polifhed by any Lapidary, but are pointed and fmoothed even as they are taken out of the Earth, fo *nature* it felf was all the *art* which was ufed upon him.

Many were the *wit-combates* betwixt him and *Ben Johnſon;* which two I behold like a *Spaniſh great Gallion* and an *Engliſh man of War*: Maſter *Johnſon* (like the former) was built far higher in Learning; *Solid*, but *Slow* in his performances. *Shake-ſpear*, with the *Engliſh man of War*, leſſer in *bulk*, but lighter in *ſailing*, could turn with all tides, tack about, and take advantage of all winds, by the quickneſs of his Wit and Invention. He died Anno Domini 16 . . , and was buried at *Stratford* upon *Avon*, the Town of his Nativity.

The History of the Worthies of England: Warwickshire.
1662. [*Fo*.] *p*. 126.

[Fuller was collecting the materials for his "Worthies" in 1643, but the work was not published till after his death, by his son in 1662. See *Biog. Brit*. ed. 1750, p. 2055, and *Memorials of Thos. Fuller*, by Rev. A. T. Russell, 1844, p. 152. L. T. S.]

We find Shakespeare treated as a name of "high qualitie" (*i. e.* a heroic name) in a work called *Polydoron*, mentioned by C. B. Carew in *Notes and Queries*, 3rd Ser., vol. i. p. 266. [*Polydoron* is perhaps the secondary title, no work appears to be known under that name. L. T. S.]

"Names were first questionlesse given for distinction, facultie, consanguinitie, desert, qualitie: for Smith, Taylor, Joyner, Sadler, &c., were doubtlesse of the trades; Johnson, Robinson, Williamson, of the blood: Sackville, Saville, names of honorable desert; Armestrong, Shakespeare of high qualitie:"

And R. Verstegan, in the chapter "Of the Sirnames of our ancient Families" in his *Restitution of Decayed Intelligence*, 1634, p. 294, says:—

"*Breakspear, Shakspear*, and the like, have beene sirnames imposed upon the first bearers of them for *valour, and featcs of armes*."

Shakespeare, as Fuller says, is *Hastivibrans* in Latin. In Greek it is Δορίπαλτος and ʼΕγχεσπάλος. Cf. Spenser's *Faery Queen*, b. iv, c. iii, st. 10:

"He, all enrag'd, his shivering speare did shake,
And charging him afresh thus felly him bespake."

[Mr. Ruskin's remark (*Fors Clavigera*: Letter 15, p. 12) of the coincidence, "that the name of the chief poet of passionate Italy [was] 'the bearer of the wing,' and that of the chief poet of practical England, the bearer or shaker of the spear," fails as regards Dante, whose family name *Alighieri*, with its softened form *Aldighieri*, is Germanic, reappearing in the French form *Audigier*.¹ Two other instances of our phrase are as follow,—

"They laught to scorne the shaking of the Speare."

(Davies of Hereford, *Triumph of Death*, p. 47, of *Humours Heaven on Earth*, Grosart's Chertsey Worthies Library, 1876.)

"And he laugheth at the shaking of the speare."
(Job xli. 21, *Genevan Version*, 1560: v. 29 *Authorized Version*.)

See also before, p. 223, Thomas Bancroft's Epigrams. L. T. S.]

As we have given an example of the heroic employment of the phrase *to shake a spear*, we add one of the mock-heroic, from *Histrio-mastix, or the Player Whipt*, 4to, 1610, the work mentioned before, page 200.

"*Enter Troylus and Cressida.*
Troy. Come *Cressida* my Cresset light,
Thy face doth shine both day and night,
Behold, behold, thy garter blue,
Thy knight his valiant elboe weares,
That when he shakes his furious Speare,
The foe in shivering fearfull sort,
May lay him downe in death to snort.
Cres. O knight with vallour in thy face,
Here take my skreene weare it for grace,
Within thy Helmet put the same,
Therewith to make thine enemies lame.
Landulpho. Lame stuffe indeed the like was never heard."
(Sign. C. 4.)

In *Post-haste, the Poet*, who accompanies the Players of the mock-play "Troylus and Cressida," Mr. Richard Simpson sees a caricature of Shakespeare. (*School of Shakspere*, vol. ii. pp. 11—14.) The first four lines here spoken by Troylus contain the supposed allusion to an incident in Shakespeare's *Troilus and Cressida*, Act IV. Sc. iv. ll. 72, 73, which we believe to be rebutted by the dates.

See also, Edmund Gayton on Sancho Panza, under date 1654.

---

¹ Mr. Ruskin probably had in view the fact that the Alighieri family, on their removal to Verona, changed their arms to *azure*, a wing *or*. See H. Clark Barlow's *Contributions to the Study of the Divina Commedia*, 1864, p. 9; and K. Witte, *Dante Forschungen* (1879), p. 25.

THOMAS FULLER, 1643—1662.

John Faſtolfe, Knight * * the Stage hath been overbold with his memory, making him a *Thraſonical Puff*, & emblem of *Mock-valour*.

True it is, *Sir John Oldcaſtle* did firſt bear the brunt of the one, being made the *make-ſport* in all plays for a *coward*. It is eaſily known out of what *purſe* this black *peny* came. The *Papiſts* railing on him for a *Heretick*, and therefore he muſt alſo be a *coward*, though indeed he was a *man* of *arms, every inch of him*, and as valiant as any in his age

Now as I am glad that *Sir John Oldcastle* is *put out*, ſo I am ſorry that *Sir John Fastolfe* is *put in*, to relieve his memory in this baſe ſervice, to be the *anvil* for every *dull wit* to ſtrike upon. Nor is our Comedian excuſable, by ſome alteration of his name, writing him *Sir John Falſtaſe* (and making him the *property of pleaſure* for King *Henry* the fifth to abuſe) ſeeing the *vicinity* of ſounds intrench on the memory of *that worthy Knight*, and few do heed the *inconſiderable difference* in ſpelling of their name.

The Worthies of England. 1662. *Norfolk, p.* 253.

[Worthy old Fuller was determined to vindicate the two heroes who had been apparently vilified by Shakespere's fun. Mr. W. G. Stone kindly points out what he says on this behalf in his *Church History*:—

"*Stage-poets* have themselves been very *bold* with, and others very *merry* at, the Memory of Sʳ John Oldcastle, whom they have fancied a *boon Companion*, a *jovial Royster*, and yet a *Coward* to boot, contrary to the credit of all Chronicles, owning him a *Martial man* of merit. The best is, Sʳ *John Falstaffe*, hath relieved the memory of Sʳ *John Oldcastle*, and of late is substituted *Buffoone* in his place; but it matters as little what *petulant Poets*, as what *malicious Papists* have written against him."

(Thos. Fuller, *Church History*, fol. 1655, bk IV. cent. XV. p. 168.) See further on this subject, after, p. 268. L. T. S.]

SIR RICHARD BAKER, 1643.

Men of Note in her time [Elizabeth].

After fuch men[1], it might be thought ridiculous to fpeak of Stage-players; but feeing excellency in the meaneft things deferve remembring, and *Rofcius*[2] the Comedian is recorded in Hiftory with fuch commendation, it may be allowed us to do the like with fome of our Nation. *Richard Bourbidge* and *Edward Allen*, two fuch Actors, as no age muft ever look to fee the like: and, to make their Comedies compleat, *Richard Tarleton*, who for the Part called the Clowns Part, never had his match, never will have. For Writers of Playes, and fuch as had been Players themfelves, *William Shakefpeare*, and *Benjamin Johnfon*, have fpecially left their Names recommended to pofterity. (p. 120.)

William Shakefpeare an excellent writer of Comedies.

(*Index, referring to the above passage.*)
Sir Richard Bakers Chronicle. 1643. [*fo.*] *The Raigne of Queen Elizabeth.*

---

[1] Statesmen, Writers and Divines.
[2] Misprinted Boscius.

Anonymous, 1644.

Although he came with confidence to the fcaffold, and the blood wrought lively in his cheeks, yet when he did lye down upon the block he trembled every joint of him; the fenfe of fomething after death, and the undifcovered country unto which his foul was wandering ftartling his refolution, and poffeffing every joint of him with an univerfal palfey of fear.

London Post, January, 1644. (On the Execution of Archbishop Laud.)

[This forcible passage contains an evident reference to *Hamlet*, ii. 2 :—

"But that the dread of something after death,
The undiscovered Country, from whose Borne
No Traveller returnes, Puzels the will," &c.

(Fo. 1623.)

It is quoted in the *Academy*, January 31, 1874, p. 121. L. T. S.]

Anonymous, 1644.

Aulicus keeps to the old way of devotion, and that is the offering up the incenſe of ſo many *lies and intelligence* every *Sonday morning:* one would thinke that the Judgements which have been writ from heaven againſt the prophanation of that day, recorded by our protomartyr, Maſter *Burton*, ſhould be able to deterre a *Diurnall maker*, a paper-intelligencer, a penny worth of newes, but the Creature hath writ himſelfe into a *reprobate ſenſe*, and you may ſee how it thrives with him, for his braines have been wonderfully blaſted of late, and plannet-ſtrucke, and he is not now able to provoke the meaneſt Chriſtian to laughter, but lies in a paire of *foule ſheets*, a wofull ſpectacle and object of dullneſſe, and tribulation, not to be recovered by the Proteſtant or *Catholique liquour*, either *Ale* or ſtrong beer, or Sack, or Claret, or Hippocras, or Muſcadine, or Roſaſolis, which hath been reputed formerly by his Grandfather *Ben Johnſon* and his Uncle *Shakeſpeare*, and his Couzen Germains *Fletcher*, and *Beaumont*, and noſe-leſſe *Davenant*, and Frier *Sherley* the Poets, the onely bloſſoms for the brain, the reſtoratives for the wit, the [¹ sic] bathing for the wine[1] muſes, but none of theſe are now able either to warme him into a quibble, or to inflame him into a ſparkle of invention, and all this becauſe he hath prophaned the *Sabbath* by his pen.

Mercurius Britanicus: Numb. 20 *(January* 4-11, 1644). *Communicating the affaires of Great Britaine: For the better Information of the People.*

ANONYMOUS, 1644.

This curious extract from one of the *Mercuries*, or Newspapers, of the Rebellion is a Puritanical attack on "the old way of devotion," viz., the publication of a Sunday Newspaper. It must be borne in mind that the Theatres were now closed by order of the Parliament, though in point of fact the prohibition had not succeeded in wholly putting down theatrical performances. The Theatres had been partially closed in June, 1600, and again, on account of the plague, in May $\frac{1}{1}\frac{0}{6}$, 1636. Civil war broke out in August, 1642; the first battle being fought on September 22 in that year. The first order of Parliament for closing the Theatres was dated September 2, 1642; and this being found ineffectual to suppress stage-plays, a more stringent order was promulgated in 1647, bearing date Oct. 22. The theatre was thus practically in abeyance till the performance of Davenant's *Siege of Rhodes* in 1656. Our *Third Period*, however, is continued till the Restoration, 1660: when the floodgates of pleasure were once more opened, and the stage was deluged with theatrical licentiousness.

The "Master Burton" here referred to was the Rev. Henry Burton, the Puritan author, who suffered (with Prynne and Dr Bastwicke) in 1637, for publishing a tract entitled "For God and the King." See *A New Discovery of the Prelates Tyranny*. 1641. [4to.] Restored to liberty in 1640, he wrote his life, published in 1643. He died in 1648.

The extract was quoted by Mr. G. Bullen in the *Athenæum* of Aug. 13, 1870.

JOHN CLEVELAND, *about* 1644. (DIED 1658.)

Strange Scarlet Doctors thefe; they'll pafs in Story
For Sinners half refin'd in Purgatory;
Or parboyl'd Lobfters, where there joyntly rules
The fading Sables, and the coming Gules.
The Flea that *Falſtaff* damn'd thus lewdly ſhows
Tormented in the Flames of *Bardolph's* Nofe;
The Mixt Assembly (*p.* 33).

The terror of whofe [Rupert's] Name can out of feven
Like *Falſtaf's* Buckram-men, make fly eleven.
Rupertismus (*p.* 53); *To Prince Rupert* (*p.* 275).

The Works of Mr. John Cleveland, 1687. *Edition* 1677, *pp.* 43, 67, 101.

[Cleveland warmly espoused the king's side, and was evidently well acquainted with Shakespere's works. The first extract is from *The Mixt Assembly*, a sharp satire upon the Westminster Assembly of Divines, one of the great objections to which by the episcopal party was that "there was a mixture of laity with the clergy." The Assembly first met on 1 July 1643, and continued till Feb. 22, 1648-9; we may presume that Cleveland wrote his satire in the early days of their meeting, and assign 1644 as a probable date for it. "The character of a Diurnal maker," in which he says that "a Diurnal-maker is the sub-almoner of History, Queen *Mab's* Register" (*Works*, 1687, p. 78), belongs to the same time (see Nichols' *History and Antiquities of Leicester*, Vol. III, Part II, pp. 913—916). Cleveland may have had Mercutio's famous speech in mind when he spoke of Queen Mab, or he may have thought of Hotspur's speech in 1 *Henry IV* when he wrote—

"He that the noble *Piercie's* Blood inherits
Will he strike up a Hot-Spur of the Spirits?"
(*Mixt Assembly*, *p.* 34.)

But there is nothing to show that he alluded to Shakespere in naming these well-known mythological and historic personages.

The Elegies upon Ben Jonson at pp. 310—314, and p. 330, of the 1687 edition of Cleveland's Works, falsely attributed to him, are by Jaspar Mayne and Richard West. Extracts from both are given before, pp. 212, 214.

Sir John Fastolf (died 1459) bequeathed estates to Magdalene College, Oxford, part of which were appropriated to buy liveries for some of the senior scholars. But this, in time, yielding but a penny a week, the scholars "were called, by way of contempt, Falstaff's Buckram-men." (See 1 *Henry IV*, Act II. sc. iv.) Warton, *Hist. of English Poetry*, ed. 1840, vol. ii. p. 17. L. T. S.]

THOMAS PRUJEAN, 1644.

The Argument of *Romeos* and *Juliets*:

Romeo and *Juliet*, iſſues of two enimies, *Mountegue* and *Capulet*, Citizens of *Verona*, fell in love one with the other: hee going to give her a viſit meetes *Tybalt* her kinſman, who urging a fight was ſlaine by him: for this Romeo was baniſhed and reſided at *Mantua*, where he received an Epiſtle from *Juliet*.

> *Aurorata,* [*having as a second part*] *Loves Looking Glasse Divine and Humane. The Divine one in Christs Birth and Passion faithfully showne: The Humane one in foure Epistles of Juliets, Romeos, Lisanders, Calistas.* (*Argument to Epistles from Juliet to Romeo, and from Romeo to Juliet.*) *Sign. E.* 1644. [12mo.]

[The above extract is the *Argument* to two poems entitled *Juliet to Romeo* and *Romeo to Juliet,* of 100 lines each. There is nothing in them specially referring to or drawn from Shakespere, but the recent popularity of his great love-play makes it more likely that Prujean referred to the remembrance of Shakespere in the minds of his readers, than of Arthur Brooke's earlier version of the story. Neither, however, made epistles pass between the lovers. Mr. P. A. Daniel, editor of Brooke's poem and Shakespere's play for the New Sh. Society, who has kindly examined Prujean's work for me, concurs in these remarks. L. T. S.]

VINDEX ANGLICUS, 1644.

There is no ſort of verſe either ancient, or modern, which we are not able to equal by imitation; we have our Engliſh Virgil, Ovid, Seneca, Lucan, Juvenal, Martial, and Catullus : in the Earl of Surry, Daniel, Johnſon, Spencer, Don, Shakeſpear, and the glory of the reſt, Sandys and Sydney.

> *Vindex Anglicus; or the Perfections of the English language defended and asserted.* Oxford, 1644.
> Reprinted in the *Harleian Miscellany*, 8vo. edition, Vol. v. p. 431.

[No author's name is given for this tract in the reprint,[1] nor in Hazlitt or Lowndes. None of these seem to be aware that it is an ingenious re-cast of Richard Carew's essay on "The Excellencie of the English Tongue," printed in the 1614 and subsequent editions of Camden's *Remaines concerning Britain*, into which the writer has also worked passages from Camden's chapter on "Languages" which precedes Carew's essay. He even has stolen thoughts if not expressions from Sidney's *Apologie for Poetrie*. We have here a clear case of literary theft, for Carew died in 1620, and Camden in 1623, and 1644 must be about the true date when *Vindex Anglicus* was written, from the author's exclamation "What matchless and incomparable pieces of eloquence hath this time of civil war afforded? Came there ever from a prince's pen such exact pieces as are his majesty's declarations?" and his reference to Digby's speeches (p. 431). The passage above is copied and altered from the passage quoted from Carew, before, p. 20.   L. T. S.]

---

[1] I owe the reference to Mr. F. J. Furnivall.

PAUL AYLWARD, 1645.

To his deere friend Mr. Henry Burkhead, upon his Tragedy of Cola's fury.

You I preferre. *Johnſon* for all his wit
Could never paint out times as you have hit
The manners of our age : The fame declines
Of ne're enough prayſ'd *Shakeſpeare* if thy lines
Come to be publiſht : *Beaumont* and *Fletcher's* ſkill
Submitts to yours, and your more learned quill.

DANIELL BREEDY, 1645.

[To the ſame]

Deere friend ſince then this peece ſo well limn'd
As moſt would thinke 'twas by *Ben. Johnſon* trimm'd,
That *Shakeſpeare*, *Fletcher*, and all did combine
To make *Lirenda* through the Clouds to ſhine.

Commendatory lines prefixed to A Tragedy of Cola's Furie
or Lirendas Miſerie. Kilkenny, 1645.

GEORGE WITHERS?, 1645.

John Taylour, then the Courts ſhrill *Chanticleere*
Did ſummon all the *Jurours* to appeare :
Hee had the Cryers place : an office fit,
For him that hath a better voyce, then wit.
Hee, who was called firſt in all the Liſt,
George Withers hight, entitled Satyriſt ;
Then *Cary, May,* and *Davenant* were call'd forth ;
Renowned Poets all, and men of worth,
If wit may paſſe for worth. Then *Sylveſier,*
Sands, Drayton, Beaumont, Fletcher, Maſſinger,
Shakeſpeare, and *Heywood,* Poets good and free ;
Dramatick writers all, but the firſt three :
Theſe were empanell'd all.
(p. 9.)

* * * * * *

Theſe were the crimes, whereof he[1] was accuſ'd
To which he pleads not guilty, but refuſ'd
[ſic] By Hiſtriomicke Poëts to be try'd,
'Gainſt whom, he thus maliciouſly enveigh'd
Juſtice (ſayd he) and no ſiniſter fury,
Diſwades me from a tryall by a jury,
That of worſe miſdemeanours guilty bee,
Then thoſe which are objected againſt mee :
Theſe mercinary pen-men of the Stage,
That foſter the grand vices of this age,

[1] The *Intelligencer.*

Should in this Common-wealth no office beare,
But rather ftand with vs Delinquents here:
Shakefpear's a Mimicke, *Maſſinger* a Sot,
Heywood for *Aganippe* takes a plot:
Beaumount and *Fletcher* make one poët, they
Single, dare not adventure on a Play.
Thefe things are all but th' errour of the Mufes,
Abortive witts, foul fountains of abufes.
Reptiles, which are equivocally bred,
Under fome hedge, not in that geniall bed
Where lovely art with a brave wit conjoyn'd,
Engenders Poëts of the nobleft kind.
Plato refuf'd fuch creatures to admit
Into his Common-wealth, and is it fit
Parnaſſus fhould the exiles entertaine
   Of Plato?'

   * * * *

Thus fpake the Prif'ner.
[*Plautus, Terence, Menander, Aristophanes* mutter among the crowd.]
And while 'mongft thefe the murmure did encreafe,
The Cryer warn'd them all to hold their peace.
 The Court was filent, then *Apollo* fpake:
If thou (faid He) chiefly for vertues fake,
Or true affection to the Common-weale,
Didft our Dramatick Poëts thus appeale,
We fhould to thy exception give confent,
But fince we are affur'd, 'tis thy intent,
By this refufall, onely to deferre
That cenfure, which our juftice muft conferre
Upon thy merits; we muft needs decline
From approbation of thefe pleas of thine,
And are refolv'd that at this time, and place,

They ſhall as Jurours, on thy tryall paſſe,
But if our *Cenſour* ſhall hereafter find,
They have deſerved ill, we have deſign'd
That they likewiſe ſhall be to judgement brought,
To ſuffer for thoſe crimes, which they have wrought,
Thus ſpake the Soveraign of the two-topp'd Mount.

The Great Assises Holden in Parnassus. London. 1645.
pp. 9, 31—33.

[The title of this curious Satire on the newsletters and newspapers of the day runs as follows ;—" The Great Assises holden in Parnassvs by Apollo and his Assessovrs : At which Sessions are Arraigned *Mercurius Britanicus, Mercurius Aulicus, Mercurius Civicus, The Scout, The writer of Diurnalls, The Intelligencer*" and six others. The constitution of the court is set out on the second page, Apollo is president, the judges, Lord Verulam, Sidney, Erasmus, &c., follow, then two lists, one of "The Malefactours" (the same as those given on the title-page), the other of "The Jurours," whose names are *George Wither, Thomas Cary, Thomas May, William Davenant, Josuah Sylvester, Georges Sandes, Michael Drayton, Francis Beaumont, John Fletcher, Thomas Haywood, William Shakespeere, Philip Massinger.* The other officers of the court are, "*Joseph Scaliger,* the Censour of manners in *Parnassus, Ben. Johnson,* Keeper of the Trophonian Denne, *John Taylour,* Cryer of the Court, *Edmund Spencer,* Clerk of the Assises."

The jurors are successively hit at by the challenging of the prisoners. In Apollo's defence of the "Dramatick Poets" given above, Withers gives a cautious opinion.

This book does not bear Withers' name, but it was ascribed to him on the authority of Dalrymple and Hearne by Bliss in his edition of Wood's *Athenæ Oxoniensis,* vol. iii. p. 773. But the Rev. Mr. Ebsworth is of a contrary opinion, not believing that any man would describe himself so insultingly as some lines in this poem do Withers. See "Choyce Drollery," Boston, 1876, pp. 405, 406. L. T. S.]

SAMUEL SHEPPARD, 1646.

See him whofe Tragic Sceans EURIPIDES
Doth equal, and with SOPHOCLES we may
Compare great SHAKESPEAR ARISTOPHANES
Never like him, his Fancy could difplay,
Witnefs the Prince of *Tyre*, his Pericles,
His fweet and his to be admired lay
He wrote of luftful *Tarquins* rape fhews he
Did underftand the depth of Poefie.

The Times Displayed in Six Sestyads, 1646. *The sixth
Sestyad: St.* 9, *p.* 22. !4to.

Anonymous, 1647.

But directed by the example of some, who once steered in our qualitie, and so fortunately aspired to choose your *Honour*, joyned with your (now glorified) *Brother, Patrons* to the flowing compositions of the then expired sweet *Swan* of *Avon* SHAKESPEARE; * * we have presumed to offer to your *Selfe*, what before was never printed of these *Authours*.

> *The dedicatory epistle of ten Players "to Philip Earle of Pembroke and Mountgomery." Prefixed to the first edition of Beaumont and Fletcher's Works:* 1647. [*Fo.*]

The writer here adopts Ben Jonson's graceful *sobriquet* for Shakespeare : " Sweet Swan of Avon" (p. 150).

[Prefixed to the first folio of Beaumont and Fletcher there is, besides this Epistle of the ten players, whose names are subscribed to it, an address "To the Reader" signed *Ja. Shirley*, and one by "The Stationer to the Reader," signed *Humphrey Moseley*. There is nothing to show who wrote the ten Players' epistle. L. T. S.]

SIR JOHN DENHAM, 1647.

Then was wits Empire at the fatall height,
When labouring and finking with its weight,
From thence a thoufand leffer Poets fprong,
Like petty Princes from the Fall of *Rome*,
When JOHNSON, SHAKESPEARE, and thy felfe did fit,
And fway'd in the Triumvirate of wit—
Yet what from JOHNSONS oyle and fweat did flow,
Or what more eafie nature did beftow
On SHAKESPEARES gentler Mufe, in thee full growne
Their Graces both appeare, yet fo, that none
Can fay here Nature ends, and Art begins
But mixt like th' Elements, and borne like twins,
So interweav'd, fo like, fo much the fame,
None this meere Nature, that meere Art can name:
'Twas this the Ancients meant, Nature & Skill
Are the two topps of their Pernaffus Hill.

Commendatory Verses on John Fletcher, prefixed to the first edition of Beaumont and Fletcher's Works.

[On the contrast between the nature and art of Shakespere and of Jonson see before, p. 130, and after, Winstanley, 1684. On "the elements so mix'd" see before, p. 53. L. T. S.]

JAMES HOWELL, 1647.

Had now grim Ben bin breathing, with what rage
And high-fwolne fury had Hee lafh'd this age,
SHAKESPEARE with CHAPMAN had grown madd, and torn
Their gentle *Sock*, and lofty *Bufkins* worne,
To make their Mufe welter up to the chin
In blood;

> *Commendatory Verses " upon Master Fletcher's Dramaticall Workes." Prefixed to the first edition of Beaumont and Fletcher's Works.*

GEORGE DANIEL OF BESWICK, 1647.

The Sweeteſt Swan of Avon, to ye faire
And Cruel Delia, paſſionatelie Sings;
Other mens weakeneſſes and follies are
Honour and witt in him; each Accent brings
    A Sprig to Crowne him Poet; and Contrive
    A Monument, in his owne worke, to live.
Draiton is ſweet and Smooth; though not exaƈt
Perhaps, to ſtriƈter Eyes; yet he ſhall live
Beyond their Malice. To the Sceane, and Aƈt,
Read Comicke Shakeſpeare; or if you would give
    Praiſe to a Juſt Deſert, crowning the Stage
    See Beaumont, once the honour of his Age.

Poems. Vindication of Poesie. Add. MS. 19,255, p. 17 (*British Museum*). *Privately printed by Dr. Grosart,* 1878, 4 *vols.* [4*to.*] *Vol. 1, pp.* 28, 29.

[By the "sweetest Swan of Avon" is intended Samuel Daniel the Royalist poet (no relation to George. Upon the " Swan of Avon " see Jonson and the ten Players, before, pp. 150, 262; and Appendix A). George Daniel rated Jonson above all, saying of him,

"Hee was of English Drammatickes, the Prince."

Dr. Grosart says that "he idolized Ben Jonson, and set himself resolutely against the supremacy of Shakespere," and he finds a consciousness of this in the lines,

"I am not tyed to any general ffame,
Nor fixed by the Approbation
Of great ones." (*Vindication of Poesie,* p. 30.)

                                                                  L. T. S.]

GEORGE DANIEL OF BESWICK, 1647.

47.

The worthy Sʳ whom Falftaffe's ill-vs'd name
Perfonates, on the Stage, left fcandall might
Creep backward, & blott Martyr, were a shame,
Though Shakefpeare, Story, & Fox, legend write;
 That Manual, where dearth of Story brought
 Such Sᵗˢ worthy this Age, to make it out.

50.

Another Knight but of noe great Account
(Soe fay his freinds) was one of thefe new Saints
A Prieft! but the fatt Mault-Man! (if yoᵘ don't
Remember him, Sʳ Iohn has let his rants [1]
 Flye backward), the firft Knight to be made
 And golden Spurres, hee, in his Bofome had.

(*MS.*, *pp.* 464, 465; *reprint*, *pp.* 112, 113.)

136.

Here, to Evince the Scandall, has bene throwne
Vpon a Name of Honour, (Charactred
From a wrong Person, Coward, and Buffoone;)
Call in your eafie faiths, from what y 'ave read
 To laugh at Falftaffe, as an humor fram'd
 To grace the Stage, to pleafe the Age, misnam'd.

137.

But thinke, how farre vnfit? how much below
Our Harrie's Choice, had fuch a Perfon bene?

---

[1] The MS. has the) after "rants," but the sense requires it after "backward."

To fuch a Truft? the Town's a Taverne now
And plumpe Sr Iohn, is but the Bufh far-feene;
  As all the Toyle of Princes had beene Spent
  To force a Lattice, or Subdue a Pinte.¹   [1 Pent—roof.]

138.
Such Stage-mirth, have they made Him; Harry faw
Meritt; and Scandall but purfues the Steps
Of Honour, with ranke Mouth, if Truth may draw
Opinion, wee are paid; how ere the heapes
  Who crowd to See, in Expectation fall
  To the Sweet Nugilogues, of Jacke, and Hall.

139.
Noe longer pleafe your felves to iniure Names
Who liv'd to Honour; if (as who dare breath
A Syllable from Harrie's Choice) the fames
Conferr'd by Princes, may redeeme from Death?
  Live Falftaffe then : whofe Truft, and Courage once
  Merited the firft Government in France;

140.
This may Suffice, to right him; let the Guilt
Fall where it may; unqueftion'd Harrie Stands
From the foure Points of vertue, equall built,
Judgment Secur'd, the Glorie, of his Hands:
  And from his bountie, blot out what may rife
  Of Comicke Mirth, to Falftaff's præjudice.

            (*MS.*, *pp.* 477, 478; *reprint*, *pp.* 135-6.)

Poems, 1616—1657. *Privately printed from the MS.* (*Add.* 19,255) *in the British Museum by Dr. Grosart*, 1878. *Trinachordia, The Raigne of Henrie the Fifth, vol. iv.*

[Doubtless the popularity of the Plays [*I. and II. King Henry IV.* and *Merry Wives of Windsor*], and so the universal acceptance of Falstaff, stung the Royalist Poet thus to reprimand Shakespere. See end of note, p. 269.
  In stanza **138**, *Nugilogues*=triflings or banter, *i.e. nugæ*, trifles. Jacke and Hall are of course Falstaff and Prince Hal. A. B. Grosart.]

[In stanza 50, the Priest probably refers to Sir John of Wrotham, and the fatt Mault-Man to William Murley the Malt-man of Dunstable, the would-be knight, both in the play called *The First Part of Sir John Oldcastle*, 1600, sign. F 4, D 1, bk, G 2.

From stanza 47 it is evident that George Daniel was aware that Falstaffe was formerly called Oldcastle on the stage, and that this "ill-used name" had been suppressed and changed "lest scandall might" "blott Martyr." He, however, like Thomas Fuller (see before, p. 249), speaks out in vindication of the fair fame of Fastolf, the Norfolk knight to whose "trust and courage," as distinguished captain and governor in France in the 15th century, he alludes in stanza 139.

The prologue of the *First Part of the Life of Sir John Oldcastle*, two editions of which came out in 1600, contained the following lines:—

> "It is no pamper'd Glutton we present,
> Nor aged Councellour to youthfull sinne,
> But one, whose vertue shone above the rest,
> A valiant Martyr, and a vertuous Peere ;
> In whose true faith and loyalty exprest
> Unto his soveraigne and his Countries weale :
> We strive to pay that tribute of our love
> Your favours merit. Let faire Truth be grac'd,
> Since forg'd invention former time defac'd."

which seem clearly to point to the popular misapprehension of Oldcastle under the character of Falstaff, and the desire of the author of this play to clear Oldcastle's memory. (The name of Shakespere was affixed by the bookseller to one of the two 1600 editions of the play. See Chas. Knight's *Studies of Shakespere*, 1849, p. 270–272.) L. T. S.]

[In justice to Shakespere I would add a word on an error begun ignorantly in his own day, and continued—spite of Theobald and others—by literate names in this nineteenth century, namely, that Shakespere's plump Jack and the historical Sir John Fastolf were one.

When Shakespere substituted Falstaff for Oldcastle he perhaps chose the name because it was existent at the time of his plays, but in Elizabeth's day extinct, and because he thought he could not further vilify the name of one who had, as he believed (see 1 *Henry VI.*), proved himself a coward. But fat Sir Apple-John was an old man in the latter days of Henry IV, and died just before Henry V. embarked for France. The Falstaff [Fastolf] of history had a government in France under Henry V, and was accused of cowardice in the next reign, as shown in 1 *Henry VI.* It matters not to this question whether 1 *Henry VI.* be Shakespere's or not. The play was at least known to him, and was acted before the change was made from Oldcastle to Falstaff in *Henry IV.* Shakespere therefore not only knew the difference between the two Falstaffs, but intended it to be known. Hence perhaps the reason why he in 1s *Henry V.* never even alludes to the historical Sir John, thus allowing a long break between the death of one and the appearance of the other. B. N.]

[The case seems to be this : in 1 *Henry IV*, as acted at first, the jovial boon companion and coward (a lollard) bore the name of Sir John Oldcastle, who had suffered martyrdom as a Lollard in the days of Henry V ; this giving offence to the family of Oldcastle (see Dr. James, before, p. 164), Shakespere changed the name before the play was printed to Falstaff (*Stationers' Registers*, Feb. 25, 1597-8).[1] Falstaff was but a modification of the name of Sir John Fastolf, who was a noted warrior and brave commander under Henry V. and Henry VI. ; he was also a lollard, and having passed under the imputation of cowardice (though afterwards triumphantly cleared, see Mr. Jas. Gairdner's article in *Fortnightly Review*, March 1873, Vol. 13, p. 343), and being a somewhat unpopular man in his own day, Shakespere found that he fitted the character for whom he wanted a name. He disguised the name slightly by the common change of letters (see what Fuller says, before, p. 249), yet the confusion crept into the common mind, so that the fat jovial coward was remembered by the name of Oldcastle as late as 1618 (see Field's *Amends to fair Ladies*, before, p. 127), perhaps even down to 1651. (See after, T. Randolph's *Hey for Honesty*, p. 293.) The testimony of Dr. Richard James, George Daniel, and Fuller, taken together, show clearly that the distinction between Sir John Oldcastle, Sir John Fastolf, and Falstaff in their historical and poetical characters was well understood certainly by some. (See authorities cited in Dyce's *Shakespere*, 1866, Vol. iv. p. 204, and Mr. Gairdner's article as above.) L. T. S.]

[1] The *Epilogue* to 2 *Henry IV*, in which Falstaff is to die of a sweat, "for Oldcastle died a martyr, and this is not the man," shows that Shakespere was disclaiming the identity in the Second play (1597-8) about the same time that the First was being printed.

"That Falstaff was first calld Oldcastle in the play, we know also from *Old* having been printed at the head of the speech, ' Very well, my lord, very well,' in the quarto 1600, of 2 *Henry IV*, Act I, sc. ii, and from Prince Hal calling Falstaff in 1 *Henry IV*, Act I, sc. ii, ' My old lord of the castle,' " &c.—Furnivall's Introduction to *Leopold Shakspere*, p. 1, *note*. Dyce and Prof. Dowden point out that Shakespere borrowed the name of Oldcastle in the first instance from *The Famous Victories of Henry V*, a popular play acted before 1588, in which one of the Prince's wild companions is a Sir John Oldcastle.

As this sheet goes to press, Dr. Grosart sends me the following from John Trapp, M.A., to the same effect as Fuller and Daniel :—" If dirt will stick to a mudwal, yet to marble it will not * * N. D., Author of the three conversions, hath made Sr. *John Oldcastle* the Martyr, a Ruffian, a Robber, and a Rebel. His authority is taken from the Stage-players, of like conscience for lyes as all men know." *Commentary upon Nehemiah*, 1657. Chap. VI., v. 6.

WILLIAM CARTWRIGHT, 1647.

Twixt *Johnſons* grave, and *Shakeſpeare's* lighter found
His muſe ſo ſteer'd that ſomething ſtill was found,
Nor this, nor that, nor both, but ſo his owne,
That 'twas his marke, and he was by it knowne.

* * * * *

Shakeſpeare to thee was dull, whoſe beſt juſt lyes
I' th Ladies queſtions, and the Fooles replyes;
Old faſhion'd wit, which walkt from town to town
In turn'd Hoſe, which our fathers call'd the Clown,
Whoſe wit our nice times would obſceanneſs call,
And which made Bawdry paſs for Comicall:
Nature was all his Art, thy veine was free
As his, but without his ſcurility;

> *Upon the Dramatick Poems of Mr. John Fletcher; prefixed to the first edition of Beaumont and Fletcher's Works, and included (under that title) in Cartwright's Comedies, Tragi-comedies, and Poems,* 1651 [*sm.* 8vo.], *pp.* 270 *and* 273.

Canon Kingsley calls Cartwright a "wondrous youth." (*Essays*, 1873, p. 58.) The fact is, he was not a good poet; but for his manifold and precocious accomplishments he might have been nicknamed *Drusus*. Like Jasper Mayne, he was a dramatist in Holy Orders; but he wrote twice as many plays as Mayne: viz., four.

J. BERKENHEAD, 1647.

Shakefpear was early up, and went fo dreft
As for thofe *dawning* houres he knew was beft;
But when the Sun fhone forth, *You Two* thought fit
To weare juft Robes, and leave off Trunk-hofe-Wit.

                *   *

Brave *Shakefpeare* flow'd, yet had his Ebbings too,
Often above Himfelfe, fometimes below,
Thou Alwayes Beft; if ought feem'd to decline,
Twas the unjudging Rout's miftake, not Thine.

*Prefixed to the First Folio Edition of Beaumont and
Fletcher's Works,* 1647.

SIR GEORGE BUCK, 1647.

Let *Shakeſpeare*, *Chapman*, and applauded *Ben*,
Weare the Eternall merit of their Pen,
Here I am love-ficke: and were I to chufe,
A Miſtris corrivall 'tis *Fletcher's* Muſe.

*Prefixed to the first edition of Beaumont
and Fletcher's Works.* 1647.

T. PALMER, 1647.

I could prayſe *Heywood* now: or tell how long,
Falſtaffe from cracking Nuts hath kept the throng:
But for a *Fletcher*, I muſt take an Age
And ſcarce invent the Title for one Page.

*Prefixed to the first edition of Beaumont
and Fletcher's Works.* 1647.

Anonymous, 1648.

Wedneſday the 27 of December.

From Windſor came to White-Hall this day thus. That the King is pretty merry, and ſpends much time in reading of Sermon Books, and ſometimes *Shakſpeare* and *Ben: Johnſons* Playes.

> *Perfect Occurences of Every Daies iournall in Parliament, Proceedings with His Majesty, and other moderate intelligence.* No. 104. *Fryday Dec.* 22 *to Fryday Dec.* 30 1648.

[It is well known that the cultivated taste of Charles I. delighted in Shakespere; we here see how he could thus find distraction from his troubles within a month of his death. See also after, J. Cook, p. 276. L. T. S.]

JOHN MILTON, 1649.

From Stories of this nature both Ancient and Modern which abound, the Poets alſo, and ſome Engliſh, have been in this Point ſo mindful of *Decorum*, as to put never more pious Words in the Mouth of any Perſon, then of a Tyrant. I ſhall not inſtance an abſtruſe Author, wherein the King might be leſs converſant, but one whom we well know was the Cloſet Companion of theſe his Solitudes, *William Shakeſpeare:* who introduces the Perſon of *Richard* the Third, ſpeaking in as high a ſtrain of Piety, and mortification, as is uttered in any paſſage of this Book [Εικὼν Βασιλικὴ]; and ſometimes to the ſame ſenſe and purpoſe with ſome words in this Place, *I intended,* ſaith he, *not only to oblige my Friends, but mine Enemies.* The like ſaith *Richard, Act* 2, *Scen.* 1.

> "*I do not know that Engliſh Man alive,*
> *With whom my Soul is any jot at odds,*
> *More then the Infant that is born to night;*
> *I thank my God for my Humility.*"

Other ſtuff of this ſort may be read throughout the whole Tragedy, wherein the Poet uſ'd not much Licence in departing from the Truth of Hiſtory, which delivers him a deep Diſſembler, not of his affections only, but of Religion.

> ¹ Εικονοκλάστης, *in Answer to a Book intitul'd* Εικὼν βασιλικη 1690 [8*vo*], §1, *pp.* 9-10.

In the compiler's judgment Malone was in error in taking these remarks to imply a rebuke to Charles I for making Shakespeare his closet-companion. Milton merely takes a book which he knew was a favourite with the king, and out of it reads him a lesson. Apart from the single word "stuff," there is nothing like disparagement of Shakespeare in his remarks; and the contemptuous use of that word is the growth of a later age. Milton uses it also in the Introduction to *Samson Agonistes*, 1671. Having alluded to a tragedy named *Christ Suffering*, attributed to St. Gregory Nazianzen, Milton writes,

"This is mention'd to vindicate Tragedy from the small esteem, or rather infamy, which in the account of many it undergoes at this day with other common Interludes; hap'ning through the Poets error of intermixing Comic stuff with Tragic sadness and gravity; or introducing trivial and vulgar persons, which by all judicious hath bin counted absurd; and brought in without discretion, corruptly to gratifie the people."—*Of that sort of Dramatic Poem which is call'd Tragedy.*

J. COOK, 1649.

Had he [King Charles] but ſtudied Scripture half ſo much as Ben: Johnſon or Shakeſpear, he might have learnt, That when Amaziah [&c.] [Cf. 2 Kings xiv. and 2 Chron. xxv.—C. M. I.]

King Charls his Case: or, an Appeal to all Rational Men, concerning his Tryal. 1649. *p.* 13. [4*to.*]

[Sam. Butler, the author of *Hudibras*, wrote an answer to Cook's pamphlet, entitled *The Plagiary exposed: or an Old answer to a Newly revived Calumny against the memory of King Charles I* (published 1691, but written "above forty years since"), in which he retorts upon Cook for the affectation of his language, "therefore you do ill to accuse him of reading *Johnsons* and *Shakespears* Plays, which should seem you have been more in yourself to much worse purpose, else you had never hit so right upon the very Dialect of their railing Advocates, in which (believe me) you have really outacted all that they could fansie of passionate and ridiculous Outrage" (p. 2). L. T. S.]

Anonymous, 1650.

Mr Ben: Johnſon and Mr Wm: Shake-ſpeare Being Merrye att a Tavern Mr Jonſon haveing begune this for his Epitaph

  Here lies Ben Johnſon that was once one   [one's son.

he gives ytt to Mr Shakſpear to make upp who preſently wrightes

    Who while hee liv'de was a floe thing
    and now being dead is Nothinge.

Manuscript. Ashmolean Collection, vol. 38, *p.* 181.
Printed in Halliwell's Life of Shakespeare, p. 186.

[I print "sloe thing" as my own reading of the MS., and that of Dr. Neubauer, the accomplished vice-librarian at the Bodleian, who has kindly looked at it for me. That he was slow was a common accusation against Jonson (see *e. g.* before, p. 247). Dr. Ingleby would read "shoe"; I accordingly leave his note as it stands. L. T. S.]

Mr. Halliwell misprints "slow thing" for "shoe thing": *shoe* is the early orthography of *show* (see *ante,* p. 10). "A shoe thing" meant a player (q. d. a poor thing that lives by show). According to this view, "shoe thing" (show-thing), like "Shake-scene," is a neologism, and a term of reproach and contempt. Both coinages, then, bear witness to the low estate of the actor before the Restoration. John Davies' *Microcosmos* (from which we have given an extract on p. 58) was published in the same year as the first quarto edition of *Hamlet,* when, one may suppose, the player was at his lowest. Davies thus comments on the mixture of pride and baseness exhibited in such an one—

  "Good *God!* that ever *pride* should stoope so low,
  That is by nature so exceeding hie:
  Base *pride,* didst thou thy selfe, or others know,
  Wouldst thou in *harts* of Apish *Actors* lie,
  That for a *Cue* wil sel their *Qualitie?*
  Yet they through thy perswasion (being strong)
  Doe weene they merit *immortality,*
  Onely because (forsooth) they use their *Tongue,*
  To speake as they are taught, or right or *wronge.*

If *pride* ascende the *stage* (ô base ascent)
Al men may see her, for nought comes thereon
But to be seene, and where *Vice* should be shent,
Yea, made most odious to ev'ry one,
In blazing her by demonstration
Then *pride* that is more then most vicious,
Should there endure open damnation,
And so shee doth, for shee's most odious
In *Men* most base, that are ambitious."

Microcosmos, &c. 1603. [4to.] Sig. Ff 3. pp. 214-15.

Mr. Halliwell writes,

"The conclusion of the first line of the epitaph should probably be 'that was *one's son*,' for in an early MS. common-place book I have seen the following lines:—

B. Johnson in seipsum,—
Heere lies Johnson,
Who was ones sonne:
Hee had a little hayre on his chin,
His name was Benjamin!"

Life of Shakespeare. 1848. p. 186.

ROBERT BARON, 1650.
PARALLEL PASSAGES.

Fortune's Tennis-Ball.	*Venus and Adonis.*
Like him that toar from Love-sick Love her Love.	And now the happy season once more fits
This fate (Woods mutter) he deserv'd, hunting there,	That love-sick Love by pleading may be blest (*l.* 328).
When *Venus* would be's Parke, if he her Deere (*St.* 6).	I'll be a park, and thou shalt be my deer (*ll.* 231, 239).
Finding their balefull foe so grim and curst,	Finding their enemy to be so curst
They all strain court'sie which should cope him first (*St.* 17).	They all strain courtesy who shall cope him first (*l.* 888).
The airy Queen (sounds child) each yell replies	Then do they spend their mouths: Echo replies,
As if another chase were in the skies (*St.* 18).	As if another chase were in the skies (*l.* 695).
* * * The Hounds are at a Bay (*St.* 20).	By this, she hears the hounds are at a bay (*l.* 877).
Shaking their eares, tatter'd and torne with scratches,	Clapping their proud tails to the ground below,
Their stiff tailes 'gainst the grasse they clap and beat (*St.* 21).	Shaking their scratch'd ears, bleeding as they go (*l.* 923).

	Lucrece.
A mantle of green Velvet (wrought to wonder)	Without the bed her other fair hand was
Her maidens o'r her curious limbes did cast,	On the green coverlet; whose perfect white
It over her shoulder went, and under	Show'd like an April daisy on the grass,
Her right Arm; on her breast it was made fast	With pearly sweat, resembling dew of night (*l.* 393).
With claspes of radient Diamons, now as	
A Dazie shew'd she, in a field of grasse (*St.* 175).	

So *Falstaffe* triumph'd o'r *Hotspur's* stiffe clay ;
But, what cannot resist is Asses prey.
Fortune's Tennis-Ball, St. 232.

To Sir *Iohn Falstaffe*
Thou think'st Sack makes men fat, faith't makes them leane
If they drink much of 't, 'gainst the wall I mean.
Epigrams, 21, p. 129

Pocula Castalia : [*containing*] *The Authors Motto ; Fortune's Tennis-Ball ; Eliza ; Poems ; Epigrams. By R. B. Gen.* 1650.

[Baron's *Fortune's Tennis-Ball* is founded on the story of the Emperor and the Forester's Son in the *Gesta Romanorum* (Sir F. Madden's edition for the Roxburghe Club, 1838, p. 164) ; which also may have been in Shakespere's mind when he made the King compass Hamlet's death by sending him to England with treacherous letters (Act III, sc. iii ; Act IV, sc. iii). Baron owed much to Shakespere's influence, for, besides what may be the coincidence of his having taken the motto from Ovid to *Venus and Adonis* for his collection called *Pocula Castalia, Fortune's Tennis-Ball* is full of words and phrases caught from the remembrance of *Venus and Adonis* and *Lucrece*, in the earlier portion of the poem which relates the boar-hunt. In the description of the marriage he has followed another master, Ben Jonson. Dr. Brinsley Nicholson has taken some pains to seek out the numerous parallels of which we here give specimens. L. T. S.]

ANTHONY DAVENPORT, 1650.

See how the Learned fhades do meet,
And like Æriall fhadowes fleet,
More in number then were fpide
To flock 'bout the *Dulichian* Guide.
The first, *Mufeus*, then *Catullus*,
Then *Nafo*, *Flaccus*, and *Tibullus* ;
Then *Petra*[r]*ch*, *Sydney*, none can move
Shakefpeare out of *Adonis* Grove,
There fullenly he fits ; but thefe
Admire thy novell Rhapfodies.
Dear Friend, which ever fhall fubfift,
Spight of *Oblivion's* hiding-mift.

Verses prefixed to the Loves of Amandus and Sophronia.
By Samuel Sheppard. 1650. [8vo.]

[Davenport here intends the highest praise to the *Venus and Adonis;* Shakespere sits alone, none can come near him in the grove of Adonis. Other amatory poets show their admiration for Sheppard, but Shakespere, the chief of all, sole in that grove, holds aloof. *Sullenly* is here used in its older meaning, drawn from the Fr. *solein*, i. e. sole, alone. Compare Sheppard's own use of "sole," after, third line of p. 287. Mr. Bullen of the British Museum, and Dr. Richard Morris, concur in this interpretation. L. T. S.]

SIR NICHOLAS L'ESTRANGE, 1650-55.

Shake-ſpeare was Godfather to one of Ben : Johnſons children, and after the chriſtning being in a deepe ſtudy, Johnſon came to cheere him up, and aſkt him why he was ſo Melancholy? no faith Ben : (ſayes he) not I, but I have beene confidering a great while what ſhould be the fitteſt gift for me to beſtow upon my God-child, and I have reſolv'd at laſt; I pry'the what, ſayes he? I faith Ben : I'le e'en give him a douzen good Lattin Spoones, and thou ſhalt tranſlate them.

Merry Passages and Jeasts. No. **11.** *Harleian Manuscript* 6395, *leaf* 2. *First printed in Capell's Notes on Shakespeare, Vol. I, Part II, pp.* 93, 94.

It has been inferred from L'Estrange's authority for this anecdote that he had derived it from Dr. John Donne. At the end of the MS. (fos. 89—91) is a list of authorities for 603 of the anecdotes (there being a few additional ones for whom no names are given). In this we find that No. 4 is referred to "Mr. Dunn," Nos. 11 and 12 to "Mr. Dun:" (where the : is doubtless —as in all other cases—a sign of abbreviation); Nos. 26, 56, and others to "Mr. Donne." One of the authorities is Captain Duncomb: whence it would appear that "Dun:" may be an abbreviation of *Duncomb*. Dr. John Donne is not mentioned at all.

[Sir Nicholas was the elder brother of the famous Sir Roger L'Estrange. (See notices of the family prefixed to *Anecdotes and Traditions*, edited for the Camden Society by W. J. Thoms, 1839.) L. T. S.]

SAMUEL SHEPPARD, 1651.

To Mr. Davenport *on his Play called the Pirate.*

Make all the cloth you can, hafte, hafte away,   [Set all the canvass.]
The Pirate will o'retake you if you ftay :
Nay, we will yeeld our felves, and this confeffe,
Thou Rival'ft *Shakefpeare*, though thy glory's leffe

> *Epigrams Theological, Philosophical, and Romantick.*
> *Six Books, &c., with other Select Poems.* 1651.
> [*sm.* 8*vo.*] *Book* 2. *Epig.* 19. *p.* 27.

SAMUEL SHEPPARD, 1651.

On Mr. Davenants *moſt excellent Tragedy of*
    Albovine k[ing] *of* [the] Lombards.

Shakeſpeares Othello, Johnſons Cataline,
Would loſe the their luſter, were thy *Albovine*
Placed betwixt them, and as when the Sunne,
Doth whirling in his fiery Chariot runne,
All other lights burn dim, ſo this thy play,
Shall be accepted as the Sun-ſhine day :
While other witts (like Tapers) onely ſeems
Good in the want of thy Refulgent beames.
This Tragedy (let who liſt dare diſſent)
Shall be thy everlaſting Monument.

Epigrams Theological, Philoſophical, and Romantick.
Six Books, &c., with other Select Poems. 1651
[*ſm.* 8*vo.*] *Book* 4. *Epig.* 30 *p.* 98

SAMUEL SHEPPARD, 1651.

In Memory of our Famous Shakeſpeare.

1.

Sacred Spirit, whiles thy *Lyre*
Ecchoed o're the *Arcadian* Plaines,
Even *Apollo* did admire,
Orpheus wondered at thy Straines.

2.

Plautus Sigh'd, *Sophocles* wept
Teares of anger, for to heare
After they ſo long had ſlept,
So bright a *Genius* ſhould appeare :

3.

Who wrote his Lines with a Sunne-beame,
More durable then Time or Fate,
Others boldly do Blaſpheme,
Like thoſe that ſeeme to Preach, but prate.

4.

Thou wert truely Prieſt Elect,
Choſen darling to the Nine,
Such a Trophey to erect
(By thy wit and ſkill Divine)

5.

That were all their other Glories
(Thine excepted) torn away,
By thy admirable Stories,
Their garments ever ſhall be gay.

6.

Where thy honoured bones do lie
(As *Statius* once to *Maro's* Urne)
Thither every year will I
Slowly tread, and ſadly mourn.

Epigrams Theological, Philosophical, and Romantick. Six Books, &c., with other Select Poems. 1651. [sm. 8vo.] *Book* 6, *Epig.* 17, *pp.* 150, 152, *and* 154. [*Should be pp.* 154, 155, 156, *but there is some mis-paging.*]

The first line of the second verse almost requires us to read " Sophócles." The lyric, as a whole, is very weak : but it has one good line—the last.

SAMUEL SHEPHARD, 1651.

With him * contemporary then   [* Ben Jonson.]
(As *Naso*, and fam'd *Maro*, when
Our fole Redeemer took his birth)
Shakefpeare trod on *Englifh* earth,
His Mufe doth merit more rewards
Then all the *Greek* or *Latine* Bards,
What flowd from him, was purely rare,
As born to bleffe the *Theater*:
He firft refin'd the *Commick Lyre*,
His Wit all do, and fhall admire,
The chiefeft glory of the Stage,
Or when he fung of war and *ftrage*,[1]
Melpomene foon viewd the globe,
Invelop'd in her fanguine Robe,
He that his worth would truely fing,
Muft quaffe the whole *Pierian* fpring.

   *   *   *

Two happy wits, late brightly fhone,
The true fonnes of *Hyperion*,
Fletcher, and *Beaumont*, who fo wrot,
Johnfons Fame was foon forgot,
Shakefpeare no glory was alow'd,
His Sun quite fhrunk beneath a Cloud.

Epigrams Theological, &c., with other Select Poems, 1651.
Third Pastoral, pp. 249, 250, 251.

---

[1] [Strage, *i.e.* slaughter. Compare,—
"I have not dreaded famine, fire, nor strage."
    Webster's *Appius and Virginia*, Act V. sc. iii.
    Dyce's edition, p. 179. P. A. Daniel.]

WILLIAM BELL, 1651.

To the Memory of Mr. William Cartwright.

How had we loſt both Mint, and Coyn too, were
That ſalvage love ſtill faſhionable here,
To ſacrifice upon the Funerall Wood
All, the deceaſ'd had er held deer and good!
We would bring all our ſpeed, to ranſome thine
With *Don's* rich Gold, and *Johnſon's* ſilver Mine;
Then to the pile add all that *Fletcher* writ,
Stamp'd by thy Character a currant Wit:
Suckling's Ore, with *Sherley's* ſmall mony, by
Heywoods old Iron, and *Shakeſpear's* Alchemy.

Prefixed to Wm. Cartwright's Comedies, Tragi-comedies, and Poems. 1651. [*sm. 8vo.*]

JASPER MAYNE, 1651.

To the deceased Author of these Poems.

For thou to Nature had'st joyn'd Art and skill,
In Thee *Ben Johnson* still held *Shakespear's* Quill:
A Quill, rul'd by sharp Judgement, and such Laws,
As a well studied Mind, and Reason draws.

Prefixed to Wm. Cartwright's Comedies, Tragi-comedies, and Poems. 1651. [*sm. 8vo.*]

Anonymous, 1651.

Poeta is her *Minion*, to whom fhe [Eloquentia] refignes the whole government of her Family. * * *Ovid* fhe makes *Major-domo*. *Homer* becaufe a merry Greek, Mafter of the Wine-Cellars. *Aretine* (for his fkill in Poftures) growing old, is made Pander. *Shack-Spear*, Butler. *Ben Johnfon*, Clark of the Kitchin, *Fenner* his Turn-fpit, And *Taylor* his Scullion.

A Hermeticall Banquet, drest by a Spagiricall Cook : for the better Preservation of the Microcosme. 1652. [12mo.] *p.* 35.

[This little book was dedicated by its author as an offering for the New Year, 1652, to Sir Isaac Wake, English ambassador to Savoy and Piedmont, to whom he was physician. L. T. S.]

Here are associated, Shakespeare, Ben Jonson, Fennor, and John Taylor. In *Certaine Elegies, &c.*, by H. Fitzgeoffrey, 1620 [sign. A 8, back], we have

"Taylor the Ferriman.
Fennor with his Unisounding Eare word;"

whatever that may mean. (Collier's *Hist. of Dramat. Poetry*, iii. 388.) The association of Taylor and Fennor was due to their wit-combats in 1615. See, *Taylor's Revenge* against *Fennor*, and *A cast over the Water to William Fennor*. Taylor's *Works*. 1630. pp. 142, 155. [Fo.]

J. S., 1651.

The true and primary intent of the Tragedians and Commedians of old, was to magnifie Virtue, and to depreſs Vice; And you may obſerve throughout the *Works* of incomparable *Johnſon*, excellent *Shakeſpear*, and elegant *Fletcher*, &c., they (however vituperated by ſome ſtreight-laced brethren not capable of their ſublimity,) aim at no other end.

> *An excellent Comedy, called, the Prince of Priggs revels: or, the Practices of that grand Thief Captain James Hind, relating Divers of his Pranks and Exploits, never heretofore published by any. Repleat with various Conceits, and Tarltonian Mirth, suitable to the Subject.* 1651. [4*to*.] Address " *To the Reader.*"

This mention of Shakespeare was communicated to the *Athenæum* (September 19, 1874) by its discoverer, Mr. George Bullen, the courteous Keeper of Printed Books at the British Museum, to whom we are indebted for valuable aid in our search for extracts. From the *Athenæum* notice we take the following remarks :—

"This being a comedy, so called, and by J. S., one is at first inclined to think that it was most likely written by James Shirley; but upon examination, it will be seen not to bear any traces of Shirley's style. It is, in fact, more in the nature of a *droll*, such as those published by Kirkman in 1673, —'The Wits or sport upon sport,'—as specimens of the mutilated sort of stage-plays that were exhibited by stealth during the time (1642-60) in which stage-plays were prohibited by ordinance of the Lords and Commons Although in five acts, the play is very brief, containing only fourteen pages altogether. The hero of it, Capt. Hinde, a famous highwayman, was said, at the time when it was published, to have accompanied Charles the Second in his wanderings after the Battle of Worcester, and to have actually escorted the Prince and Wilmot to London itself. At least, so it was put forth, but with no ground of truth, in the newspapers of the time. In accordance with this belief, Charles the Second is introduced as one of the characters in the play, under the title of the 'King of Scots.' This is almost conclusive against the supposition that Shirley, who was a devoted Cavalier, was the author of the piece, as he would scarcely have deemed it respectful to his sovereign to introduce him as the companion of a notorious highwayman. Moreover, Dyce, in his edition of Shirley, takes no notice of this piece, although he took pains to collect everything that might fairly be attributed to his author. Hinde was afterwards hung, drawn, and quartered, not for his highway robberies, but for his high treason, and there are some verses upon him, 'by a poet of his own time,' inserted in Johnson's 'Lives of the Highwaymen,' which remind one strongly of Wordsworth's lines on Rob Roy."

THOMAS RANDOLPH, 1651.

Carion. Without thee (*Plutus*) the Lawyer would not go to *London* on any Terms

* * * * * *

Chremylus. Did not *Will Summers* break his wind for thee?
And *Shakefpeare* therefore writ his Comedy?
All things acknowledge thy vaft power divine,
(Great God of Money) whofe moft powerful fhine
Gives motion, life.

Act I. Sc. ii. p. 6.

Blepfidemus. What creature is this with the Red-oker face? She looks as if fhe were begot by Marking-ftones.

Chr. By ftones fure: 'tis fome *Erynnis* that is broke loofe from the Tragedy.

Blep. By *Jeronymo*, her looks are as terrible as *Don Andrea* or the Ghoft in *Hamlet*.

Act II. Sc. iv. p. 14.

Caron. To be rich is the daintieft pleafure in the world; efpecially to grow rich without ventring the danger of *Tiburn* or Whipping. Every Cupbord is full of Cuftards, the Hogfheads replenifhed with fparkling Sacks * * The Kitchen and Buttery is entire Ivory, the very purity of the Elephants tooth. The Sinke is paved with the rich Rubies, and incomparable Carbuncles of *Sir John Oldcaftle's* Nose.

Act IV. Sc. 1. p. 28.

A pleasant Comedie, Hey for Honesty, Down with Knavery. Translated out of Aristophanes his Plutus. Augmented and Published by F. J. 1651.

[Randolph died in March 1634, at the age of twenty-nine; *Hey for Honesty*, however, does not appear to have seen the light till some years later, in 1651, when it was "augmented and published by F. J." I therefore place it under the later date; though what share F. J. had in the play beyond "the setting forth of" it does not appear.

In Randolph's opinion it was by his comedies that Shakespere prospered and grew rich.

Jeronymo, the First Part; with the Wars of Portugal and the Life and Death of Don Andrea, was an anonymous tragedy first printed in 1605, but supposed to have been acted about 1588: Thomas Kyd wrote *The Spanish Tragedy, or Hieronymo is mad again*, which came out in 1603; in both the Ghost of Don Andrea appears, referred to above by Randolph, and by John Gee, before, p. 160. Professor Dowden, who kindly pointed out these passages in *Hey for Honesty*, thinks from his coupling the "Ghost in Hamlet" with the Jeronymo-Ghost, "and from the fact of there being some other somewhat antiquated references" in the play, that Randolph means the old Hamlet-ghost, in the old pre-Shakesperean play to which Lodge refers in *Wit's Miserie and the World's Madnesse*, 1596, p. 56, where he speaks of "the Visard of ye ghost which cried so miserably at ye Theator, like an oister wife, 'Hamlet, revenge.'"

In the third extract, it is noticeable that the name of Oldcastle should have lingered so long, Falstaff being apparently intended. See before, p. 269. (It was, however, Bardolph who had the red nose.)

Mr. Daniel suggests that "Whipping" is a misprint for *Wapping*, that place having been "the usual Place of Execution for hanging of Pirates and Sea-Rovers", and frequently referred to in the old drama, he thinks the coupling of Tyburn and Wapping most probable here. See W. C. Hazlitt's edition of *Dodsley*, 1875, vol. xi. p. 188. L. T. S.]

JO. TATHAM, 1652.

There is a Faction (Friend) in Town, that cries,
Down with the *Dagon-Poet, Johnſon* dies.
His Works were too elaborate, not fit
To come within the Verge, or face of *Wit*.
Beaumont and *Fletcher* (they ſay) perhaps, might
Paſſe (well) for currant Coin, in a dark night:
But *Shakeſpeare* the *Plebean* Driller, was
Founder'd in 's *Pericles*, and muſt not paſs.
And ſo, at all men flie, that have but been
Thought worthy of Applauſe; therefore, their ſpleen.
Ingratefull *Negro-kinde*, dart you your Rage
Againſt the Beams that warm'd you, and the Stage!

Commendatory verſes prefixed to A Joviall Crew: or The
Merry Beggars, by Richard Brome. Preſented &c. in
the yeer 1641. 1652. [4to.]

Of courſe it is the faction oppoſed to Tatham who thus denounces Jonson, Beaumont, Fletcher, and Shakespeare. As to Shakespeare being "founder'd in 's *Pericles*," the libel is disproved by the extract from *Pimlyco* and that from *The Hog hath lost his Pearl* (pp. 89 and 107). But Owen **Feltham's** testimony (p. 180) may be taken for the fact that the Gower interlude and the brothel-scenes in *Pericles* had scandalised, and caused "deep displeasure" to, the friends of public morality.

ALEXANDER BROME, 1653.

But in Epiftles of this nature, fomething is ufually begg'd; and I would do fo too, but, I vow, am puzzled, *what*. Tis not *acceptance*, for then youle expect I fhould *give* it; 'tis not *Money*, for then I fhou'd loofe my *labour*; 'tis not *praife*, for the *Author* bid me tell you, that, now he is dead, he is of *Falftaff's* minde, and cares not for *Honour*; 'tis not *pardon*, for that fuppofes a fault, which (I beleeve) you cannot finde.

Five New Plays by Richard Brome. 1653. [4*to.*] (*To the Readers.*)

[On Falstaff's honour see note, before, p. 127. That Falstaff's name continued as a household word through this century we have another proof in 1684, when, at Lady Ivy's trial, in answer to the Solicitor General's request for leave to question a witness whom he thought mistaken, Lord C. J. Jefferies exclaimed "Mistaken! yes I assure you very grossly. Ask him what questions you will; but if he should swear as long as Sir John Falstaff fought, I would never believe a word he says." (Cobbett's *State Trials*, Vol. 10, p. 570.) L. T. S.]

SIR ASTON COKAIN, 1653.

Judicious *Beaumont*, and th' Ingenious Soule
Of *Fletcher* too may move without controule.
Shakefpeare (moft rich in *Humours*) entertaine
The crowded *Theaters* with his happy veine.
Davenant and *Maffinger*, and *Sherley*, then
Shall be cry'd up againe for Famous men.

> *Five New Playes, by* RICHARD BROME, 1655 [4*to*]
> (*A Præludium to Mr.* RICHARD BROME'S *Playes*).
> *Also included in Cokain's Small Poems,* 1658. [12*mo.*]
> *Pp.* 108-9.

SIR WILLIAM DUGDALE, 1653.

Shakefpeares and John Combes Monum[ts], at Stratford fup Avon, made by one Gerard Johnfon.

> *Sir Wm. Dugdale's Diary. The first entry in 1653. Printed in The Life, Diary, and Correspondence of Sir Wm. Dugdale, edited by Wm. Hamper. 1827. p. 99.*

For an account of Shakespeare's monument and tombstone, with plates, see Dugdale's *Antiquities of Warwickshire*.

In an Appendix, Hamper printed "Certificates returned in Aprill and May 1593, of all the Strangers Forreiners abiding in London," among which is one for Garratt Johnson, whence it appears that he was "a Hollander, born at Amsterdam, a Tombe maker," 26 years resident in London (pp. 510, 512).

EDMUND GAYTON, 1654.

So when our Don at his long home is anchor'd,
His memory in a *Manchegan* Tankard:
By the old Wives will be kept up, that's all,
Counted the merrieſt, toſſeth up the fame.
(*John Falſtaffs Windſor* Dames memoriall)
A Goddard or an Anniverſary ſpice-Bowle,
(Drank off by th' Goſſips, e'r you can have thrice told)
And a God reſt his ſoule. (p. 195.)

* * * * * *

[Note upon Don Quixotes ſword]
The Whineard of the houſe of *Shrewſberry* is not like it, nor the two-handed Fox of *John Falſtaffe*, which hewed in ſunder fourteen out of ſeven principall aſſaylants, and left eighth and twentie equally divided bodies in the Field, all ſlain while *Shrewſberrie* clock could ſtricke ſeven ; (of the men you muſt take in). (p. 87.)

* * * *

The Knight that fought byth' clock at *Shrewſberry*. (p. 183.)

* * * *

Sir John of famous memory ; not he of the *Boares-Head in Eaſtcheap*. (p. 277.)

* * * *

Let Engliſh men write of their owne wits, fancies, ſubjects, diſputes, ſermons, Hiſtories, Romancees are as good, vigorous, laſting, and as well worthy the reading, as any in the world. Our *Fairy Queen*, the *Arcadia, Drayton, Beaumont* and *Fletcher, Shakeſpeare, Johnſon, Rondolph,* and laſtly, *Gondibert*, are of eternall fame. (p. 21.)

* * * * * *

[Addreffing Sancho Panza]
"What makes thee fhake, what makes thy teeth to chatter?
Art thou afraight or frighted? what's the matter?
Thou mak'ft me tremble at thy flefh-quake, *Pancha*,
Look on thy *Don*, the *Shake-fpeare* of the *Mancha*,
Whofe chiefe defence I am : The undertaker
Of all Heroick Actions, though a fhaker." (p. 95.)

* * *

"Our nation alfo hath had its Poets, and they their wives: To paffe the bards: Sir *Jeffery Chaucer* liv'd very honeftly at Woodftock, with his Lady, (the houfe yet remaining), and wrote againft the vice moft wittily, which Wedlocke reftraines. My Father *Ben* begate fonnes and daughters; fo did *Spencer*, *Drayton*, *Shakefpeare*, and more might be reckoned, who doe not only word it, and end in aiery *Sylvia's*, *Galatæa's*, *Aglaura's*:—

"—— fed de virtute locuti,
Clunem agitant . . . ." (p. 150.)

* * * * * * *

His fabulous ftories fhe adores,
As *Defdemona* did the *Moors*. (p. 280.)

* * * * *

Sancho had been *Fluellin* in this fcuffle, (the pillage of fuch battels, alwaies belonging to him) &c. (p. 284.)

Pleasant Notes upon Don Quixot. By Edmund Gayton, Esq., 1654.

[Mr. Eliott Browne has pointed out several of these allusions to Shakespere (*Notes and Queries*, 5 Series, III, 161), and Mr. Roberts of Boston has kindly called my attention to some others. Besides thofe above, see p. 16, where "the trance of the Cobler (drunk into the beliefe) that he was a Lord," may refer to Sly (*Taming of the Shrew*, Induction); pp. 48-9, a dissertation upon Noses, in which Bardolph and Sir John Oldcastle are named; and p. 78, "A Tragicke-Comedie of Errors." For other examples of the play upon the word Shake-spear, see before, p. 247. The last extract above seems to refer to *Henry V*, Act IV, scenes vii and viii. L. T. S.]

Anonymous, 1655.

Know-well. Upon a rainy day, or when you have nought elſe to do, you may read Sir *Walter Raleigh*, Lord *Bacons* Natural Hiſtory, the Holy Warre, and *Browns* Vulgar Errors. You may find too ſome ſtories in the Engliſh *Euſebius*, and the Book of Martyrs, to hold diſcourſe with the Parſon on a Sunday dinner.

Mrs. Love-wit. Sometimes to your wife you may read a piece of *Shak-ſpeare, Suckling,* and *Ben. Johnſon* too, if you can underſtand him.

Know. You may read the *Scout,* and *Weekly Intelligence,* and talk politickly after it. And if you get ſome ſmattering in the Mathematicks, it would not be amiſſe, the Art of dyalling, or to ſet your clock by the quadrant, and Geography enough to meaſure your own land.

The Hectors; or, the Falſe Challenge. [*A comedy.*] *Written in the year MDCLV.* 1656. *p.* 50. (*Notes and Queries:* 5*th S. Vol. I.* 304.)

SAMUEL HOLLAND, 1656.

The fire of Emulation burnt fiercely in every angle of this Paradife; the Brittifh Bards (forfooth) were alfo ingaged in quarrel for Superiority; and who think you, threw the Apple of Difcord amongft them, but *Ben Johnfon*, who had openly vaunted himfelf the firft and beft of Englifh Poets; this Brave was refented by all with the higheft indignation, for *Chaucer* (by moft there) was efteemed the Father of Englifh Poefie, whofe onely unhappines it was, that he was made for the time he lived in, but the time not for him: *Chapman* was wondroufly exafperated at *Bens* boldnefs, and fcarce refrained to tell (his own *Tale of a Tub*) that his *Isabel* and *Mortimer* was now compleated by a Knighted Poet, whofe foul remained in Flefh; hereupon *Spencer* (who was very bufie in finifhing his *Fairy Queen*) thruft himfelf amid the throng, and was received with a fhowt by *Chapman, Harrington, Owen, Conftable, Daniel*, and *Drayton*, fo that fome thought the matter already decided; but behold *Shakefpear* and *Fletcher* (bringing with them a ftrong party) appeared, as if they meant to water their Bayes with blood, rather then part with their proper Right, which indeed *Apollo* and the Mufes (had with much juftice) conferr'd upon them, fo that now there is like to be a trouble in Triplex; *Skelton, Gower* and the Monk of *Bury* were at Daggers-drawing for *Chawcer: Spencer* waited upon by a numerous Troop of the beft Book-men in the World: *Shakefpear* and *Fletcher* furrounded with their Life-Guard viz. *Goffe, Maffinger, Decker, Webfter, Sucklin, Carturight, Careu*, &c.

Don Zara del Fogo. A Mock-Romance. London. 1656. [8vv.] *Book II, chapter iv, pp.* 101, 102.

The scene of this part of this strange romance is laid in Elysium, where the poets take sides with Chaucer, Spenser, Shakespeare and Fletcher against the arrogant self-assertion of Ben Jonson.

ABRAHAM COWLEY, 1656.

At my return lately into England, I met by great accident * * a *Book* entituled, *The Iron Age*, and publifhed under *my name*, during the time of my abfence * * * I efteem myfelf lefs prejudiced by it, then by that which has been done to me, fince almoft in the fame kinde, which is, the publication of fome things of mine without my confent or knowledge, and thofe fo mangled & imperfect, that I could neither with honor acknowledge, nor with honefty quite difavow them. * * * From this which had hapned to my felf, I began to reflect upon the fortune of almoft all *Writers*, and efpecially *Poets*, whofe *Works* (commonly printed after their deaths) we finde ftuffed out, either with *counterfeit pieces*, like *falfe money* put in to fill up the *Bag*, though it adde nothing to the *fum;* or with fuch, which though of their own *Coyn*, they would have called in themfelves, for the bafenefs of the *Allay :* whether this proceed from the indifcretion of their *Friends*, who think a vaft *heap* of Stones or Rubbifh a better *Monument*, then a little *Tomb* of *Marble*, or by the unworthy avarice of fome *Stationers*, who are content to diminifh the value of the *Author*, fo they may encreafe the price of the *Book;* and like *Vintners* with fophifticate mixtures, fpoil the whole veffel of wine, to make it yield more *profit*. This has been the cafe with *Shakefpear*, *Fletcher*, *Johnfon*, and many others; part of whofe *Poems* I fhould take the boldnefs to prune and lop away, if the care of replanting them in print did belong to me; neither would I make any fcruple to cut off from fome the unneceffary yong *Suckars*, and from others the old withered *Branches;* for *a great Wit* is no more tyed to live in a *Vaft Volume*, then in a *Gigantic Body;* on the contrary, it is commonly more vigorous, the lefs fpace it animates.

Poems. 1656. [*fol.*] *Author's Preface, first leaf.*

RICHARD LIGON, 1657.

Dinner being neere halfe done * * in comes an old fellow, * * and plaide us for a Noveltie, The *Paſſame ſares guliard ;* a tune in great efteeme, in Harry the fourths dayes; for when Sir *John Falſtaff* makes his Amours to Miſtreſſe *Doll Tear-ſheet,* *Sneake* and his Companie, the admired fidlers of that age, playes this tune, which put a thought into my head, that if time and tune be the Compoſits of Muſicke, what a long time this tune had in ſayling from *England* to this place.

A true and exact History of the Island of Barbados. By Richard Ligon Gent. 1657. p. 12.

[The place where Ligon and his friends were thus entertained at dinner was St. Iago, one of the Cape Verd Isles. The *galliard* he heard was a favourite dance tune, the galliard being a dance, answering somewhat to the Minuet de la Cour of later times, stately and slow in its movements, suited to the stiff farthingales and wired ruffs of the reign of the Maiden Queen; it had its day between about 1565 and 1603, being essentially an Elizabethan, not a Jacobean dance. The special tune recognized by Ligon is not now easy to identify; Mr. Ebsworth suggests that it may have been the *Passan Pavon* galliard (from pavo, a peacock, the strutting or jetting motions of which were sometimes imitated. Had not the old tune-maker some sly satire in thus christening his tune?). This Galliard was well known before 1602. *Sares* seems to be a mistake for *fares*,—it was a common error to confuse the long s and the f,—fare=fayre=fair, a lady. The whole title then may read, "The Peacock Ladies Galliard," just as we now might say "The Lancers' Quadrilles"; and Ligon, who must have seen the Second Part of *Hen. IV.* performed, and thus incidentally informs us what tune was performed on the stage by "Sneak's noise" (Act II. sc. iv.)—before the civil wars—was not careful to remember to what period the music really belonged. In his mind it was connected with Harry the Fourth. Two galliard tunes are given in *National English Airs*, by W. Chappell, 1840; see vol. ii., pp. 50, 194.

"Noise" was the technical term for a quartette band which would play dance tunes; hence Ligon's "admired fidlers." Compare Thomas Decker's description of "those terrible noises (with thrid bare cloakes) that live by red lattises and Ivy-bushes, having authoritie to thrust into any mans roome, onely speaking but this, 'Will you have any musique?'" (*The Belman of London*, 1608, sign. C.) L. T. S.]

SIR ASTON COKAIN, 1658.

To my worthy, and learned Friend Mr. *William Dugdale*, upon his *Warwickſhire Illuſtrated*.

      *   *   *   *

Now *Stratford* upon *Avon*, we would chooſe
Thy gentle and ingenuous *Shakeſpeare* Muſe,
(Were he among the living yet) to raiſe
T' our Antiquaries merit ſome juſt praiſe:
And ſweet-tongu'd *Drayton* (that hath given renown
Unto a poor (before) and obſcure town,
Harſull) were he not fal'n into his tombe,
Would crown this work with an Encomium.
Our *Warwick-ſhire* the Heart of *England* is,
As you moſt evidently have prov'd by this;
Having it with more ſpirit dignifi'd,
Then all our *Engliſh* Counties are beside.

Small Poems of Divers Sorts. 1658. [*ſm.* 8*vo.*] *p.* 111-112.

[Michael Drayton was born at Harshull or Hartshill, a rural hamlet near Atherstone in Warwickshire, in 1563. L. T. S.]

SIR ASTON COKAIN, 1658.

To Mr. John Honyman.

On hopefull youth, and let thy happy ſtrain
Redeem the Glory of the Stage again:
Leſſen the Loſs of *Shakeſpeares* death by thy
Succeſsful Pen, and fortunate phantaſie.
He did not onely write but act; And ſo
Thou doſt not onely act, but writeſt too:
Between you there no difference appears
But what may be made up with equal years.
This is my Suffrage, and I ſcorn my Pen
Should crown the heads of undeſerving men.

Small Poems of Divers Sorts. 1658. [*m. 8vo.*] *Epigrams,
Book I, Epig.* 10, *p.* 140-141.

SIR ASTON COKAIN, 1658.

To Mr. Clement Fisher *of* Wincotl.

Shakspeare your *Wincot*-Ale hath much renownd,
That fo'xd a Beggar fo (by chance was found
Sleeping) that there needed not many a word
To make him to believe he was a Lord:
But you affirm (and in it feem moft eager)
'Twill make a Lord as drunk as any Beggar.
Bid *Norton* brew fuch Ale as *Shakfpeare* fancies
Did put *Kit Sly* into fuch Lordly trances:
And let us meet there (for a fit of Gladnefs)
And drink our felves merry in fober fadnefs.

Small Poems of Divers Sorts. 1658. [*sm.* 8*vo.*] *Book*
II, Epig. 69, *p.* 224 [*mispaged* 124].

Cokain alludes, of course, to the *Induction* of *The Taming of the Shrew*: naturally so, if, as appears, the scene of that is Wincot, or Wilnecote. See Sly's third speech, Induction : sc. 2.

Anonymous, 1658.

There are a sort who think they lessen this *Author's* worth when they speak the relation he had to *Ben. Johnson*. We very thankfully embrace the Objection, and desire they would name any other Master that could better teach a man to write a good Play * * * we have here prefixt *Ben Johnson's* own testimony to his Servant our *Author ;* we grant it is (according to *Ben's* own nature and custome) magisterial enough; and who looks for other, since he said to *Shakespear——I shall draw envy on thy name* (by writing in his praise) and threw in his face— *small Latine and less Greek ;*

Five New Playes, by *Richard Brome*. (*To the Readers*.) 1658-9. [8vo.]

[The Stationers, in this address *To the Readers*, call attention to Jonson's verses on Brome, which begin "To my old Faithful Servant, and (by his continu'd vertue) my loving Friend, the Author of this work, Mr. Rich. Brome" L. T. S.]

See our remarks on p. 151. Perhaps, however, this writer takes Jonson to mean, as regards Shakespere,

"I am so ample to your book and fame, that I may make others envious of you, for the honour of my encomium, who am usually so sparing of praise : but I do not write with that object."

SAMUEL AUSTIN, 1658.

If I may guefs at Poets in our Land,
Thou beat'ft them all *above*, and *under hand ;*
  *   *   *   *
To thee compar'd, our Englifh Poets all ftop,
An vail their Bonnets, even *Shakefpear's Falftop.**
Chaucer the firft of all was'nt worth a farthing,
Lidgate, and *Huntingdon,* with Gaffer *Harding.*

* It should have been *Falstaff,* if the rhyme had permitted it.

Naps upon Parnassus. A sleepy Muse nipt and pincht, though not awakened. 1658. *Sign. B* 4, *back.*

[The poet here addresses himself in a commendatory "Carmen Jocoserium," under the initials S. W., W. C. C. Oxon. L. T. S.]

SHAKESPEARE'S
CENTURIE OF PRAYSE.

FOURTH PERIOD.
1660—1693.

Anonymous Elegy on R. Lovelace, 1660.

I now concieve the ſcope of their deſigne,
Which is with one conſent to bring, and burn
Contributory Incence on his Urn,
Where each mans Love and Fancy ſhall be try'd,
As when great *Johnſon,* or brave *Shakeſpear* dy'd.

> Elegies Sacred to the Memory of the Author: By several of his Friends. Collected and Published by D[udley] P[osthumus] L[ovelace]. 1660, p. 9. (Printed at the end of " Lucasta. Posthume Poems of Richard Lovelace." 1659.)

RICHARD FLECKNOE, 1660. *Circa.*

In this time were Poets and Actors in their greatest flourish, *Johnson*, *Shakespear*, with *Beaumont* and *Fletcher*, their Poets, and *Field* and *Burbidge* their Actors.

For Playes, *Shakespear* was one of the first, who inverted the Dramatick Stile, from dull History to quick Comedy, upon whom *Johnson* refin'd; as *Beaumont* and *Fletcher* first writ in the Heroick way, upon whom *Suckling* and others endeavoured to refine agen; one saying wittily of his *Aglaura*, that 'twas full of fine flowers, but they seem'd rather stuck, then growing there; as another of *Shakespear's* writings, that 'twas a fine Garden, but it wanted weeding.

* * * * * *

To compare our English Dramatick Poets together (without taxing them) *Shakespear* excelled in a natural Vein, *Fletcher* in Wit, and *Johnson* in Gravity and ponderousness of Style; whose onely fault was, he was too elaborate; and had he mixt less erudition with his Playes, they had been more pleasant and delightful then they are. Comparing him with *Shakespear*, you shall see the difference betwixt Nature and Art; and with *Fletcher*, the difference between Wit and Judgement: Wit being an exuberant thing, like *Nilus*, never more commendable then when it overflowes; but Judgement a stayed and reposed thing, alwayes containing it self within its bounds and limits.

A Short Discourse of the English Stage, by Richard Flecknoe. Printed at the end of Love's Kingdom, a Pastoral Trage-Comedy. 1664. Sign. G 5, 6. [Sm. 8vo.]

SIR RICHARD BAKER, 1660.

Of Men of Note in his Time [Charles I].

Poetry was never more Refplendent, nor never more Graced; wherein *Johnfon, Silvefter, Shakfpere, Beaumont, Fletcher, Shirley, Broom, Maffinger, Cartwrite, Randolph, Cleaveland, Quarles, Carew, Davenant,* and *Sucklin,* not only far excelled their own Countrymen, but the whole World besides.

> *Sir Richard Baker's Chronicle of England.* " *Whereunto is now added in this Third Edition the reign of King Charles I.*" 1660. *Bodleian Lib., Douce B.* 146. *Paris, Bibl. Nationale, Réserve Nº* 36 *A. London, Sion College. P.* 503; *but should be p.* 603, *the printer after the true page* 504 *having counted* 405 *by mistake and continued.*

[The above passage was quite altered in subsequent editions of the chronicle, and many of the names of poets were struck out, among which was Shakespere's.

The first edition of Baker's Chronicle (for an extract from which see before, p. 250) was published in 1643, the second in 1653 with additions by Phillips. It is singular that this third edition of 1660, in which the above passage first occurs, should be rare. After a somewhat extensive search in the libraries of Cambridge, Oxford, London, Dublin, Paris and elsewhere, the copies quoted are the only three that have been found. My thanks are due to my friend Prof. Paul Meyer for his kind assistance herein and collation of the passage. L. T. S.]

SAMUEL PEPYS, 1660—1669.

1660.

October 11.—Here, in the Park, we met with Mr. Salifbury, who took Mr. Creed and me to the Cockpitt to fee "The Moore of Venice," which was well done. Burt acted the Moore; by the fame token, a very pretty lady that fat by me, called out, to fee Defdemona fmothered. (Vol. I. p. 198.)

December 5.—After dinner I went to the New Theatre and there I faw "The Merry Wives of Windfor" acted, the humours of the country gentleman and the French doctor very well done, but the reft but very poorly, and Sir J. Falftaffe as bad as any. (p. 226.)

December 31.—In Paul's Church-yard I bought the play of "Henry the Fourth," and fo went to the new Theatre and faw it acted; but my expectation being too great, it did not pleafe me, as otherwife I believe it would; and my having a book, I believe did fpoil it a little. (p. 234.)

1661.

June 4.—From thence [my Lord Crew's] to the Theatre and faw "Harry the 4th," a good play. (p. 311.)

Auguft 24.—To the Opera, and there faw "Hamlet, Prince of Denmarke," done with fcenes very well, but above all, Betterton did the Prince's parts beyond imagination. (p. 342.)

September 11.—Walking through Lincoln's Inn Fields obferved at the Opera a new play "Twelfth Night," was acted there, and the King there; so I, againft my own mind and refolution, could not forbear to go in, which did make the play feem a burthen to me, and I took no pleafure at all in it. (p. 352.)

September 25.—To the Theatre, and faw " The Merry Wives of Windfor," ill done. (p. 358.)

November 28.—After an hour or two's talk in divinity with my Lady, Captain Ferrers and Mr. Moore and I to the Theatre, and there faw " Hamlet " very well done. (p. 382.)

1661-2.

March 1.—To the Opera, and there faw " Romeo and Juliet," the firft time it was ever acted, but it is a play of itfelf the worft that ever I heard in my life, and the worft acted that ever I faw thefe people do, and I am refolved to go no more to fee the firft time of acting, for they were all of them out more or lefs. (p. 419.)

1662.

September 29.—To the King's Theatre, where we faw " Midfummer's Night's Dream," which I had never feen before, nor fhall ever again, for it is the moft infipid ridiculous play that ever I faw in my life. (Vol. II. p. 51.)

1662-3.

January 6.—After dinner to the Duke's Houfe, and there faw "Twelfth-Night" acted well, though it be but a filly play, and not related at all to the name or day. (p. 121.)

1663.

May 28.—By water to the Royall Theatre; but that was fo full they told us we could have no room. And fo to the Duke's houfe; and there faw " Hamlett " done, giving us frefh reafon never to think enough of Betterton. (p. 224.)

December 10.—To St. Paul's Church Yard, to my bookfeller s, * * I could not tell whether to lay out my money for books of pleafure, as plays, which my nature was moft earneft in ; but at laft, after feeing Chaucer, Dugdale's Hiftory of Pauls, Stow's London, Gefner, Hiftory of Trent, befides Shakefpeare, Jonfon, and Beaumont's plays, I at laft chofe Dr. Fuller's Worthys, the Cabbala or Collections of Letters of State, and a little book, Delices de Hollande, with another little book or two, all of good ufe or ferious pleafure; and Hudibras, both parts, the book now in greateft fafhion for drollery, though I cannot, I confefs, fee enough where the wit lies. (p. 377.)

December 22.—After dinner abroad with my wife by coach to Weftminfter, and I perceive the King and Duke and all the Court was going to the Duke's playhoufe to fee " Henry VIII " acted, which is faid to be an admirable play. * * I did not go. (p. 388.)

December 26.—By and by comes in Captain Ferrers to fee us, and, among other talke, tells us of the goodnefs of the new play of " Henry VIII ", which makes me think it long till my time is out. (p. 390.)

1663-4.

January 1.—Went to the Duke's houfe, the firft play I have been at thefe fix months, according to my laft vowe, and here faw the fo much cried-up play of " Henry the Eighth ; " which, though I went with refolution to like it, is fo fimple a thing made up of a great many patches, that, befides the fhows and proceffions in it, there is nothing in the world good or well done. (p. 394.)

1664.

July 7.—Home, calling by the way for my new bookes, viz Sir H. Spillman's " Whole Gloffary," " Scapula's Lexicon," and Shakefpeare's plays. (Vol III. p. 5.)

November 5.—To the Duke's houfe to a play, " Macbeth," a pretty good play, but admirably acted. (p. 69.)

1666.

Auguſt 20.—To Deptford by water, reading "Othello, Moore of Venice," which I ever heretofore eſteemed a mighty good play, but having to lately read "The Adventures of Five Houres," it ſeems a mean thing. (Vol. IV. p. 56.)

Auguſt 29.—To St. James's, and there Sir W. Coventry took Sir W. Pen and me apart, and read to us his anſwer to the Generall's letter to the King, that he read laſt night; * * * And then, ſpeaking of the ſupplies which have been made to this fleete, more than ever in all kinds to any, even that wherein the Duke of York himſelf was, "Well," ſays he, "if this will not do, I will ſay, as Sir J. Falſtaffe did to the Prince, 'Tell your father, that if he do not like this let him kill the next Piercy himſelf.'" (p. 64.)

December 28.—To the Duke's houſe, and there ſaw "Macbeth" moſt excellently acted, and a moſt excellent play for variety. I had ſent for my wife to meet me there, who did come, and after the play was done, I out ſo ſoon to meet her at the other door that I left my cloake in the play-houſe, and while I returned to get it, ſhe was gone out and miſſed me. I not ſorry for it much did go to White Hall, and got my Lord Bellaſſis to get me into the playhouſe; and there, after all ſtaying above an hour for the players, the King and all waiting, which was abſurd, ſaw "Henry the Fifth" well done by the Duke's people, and in moſt excellent habits, all new veſts, being put on but this night. But I ſat ſo high and far off, that I miſſed moſt of the words, and ſat with a wind coming into my back and neck, which did much trouble me. The play continued till twelve at night; and then up, and a moſt horrid cold night it was, and froſty, and moonſhine. (p. 195.)

1666-7.

January 7.—To the Duke's houſe, and ſaw "Macbeth," which though I ſaw it lately, yet appears a moſt excellent play in all respects, but especially in divertisement, though it be a deep tragedy; which is a strange perfection in a tragedy, it being most proper here, and suitable. (p. 202.)

1667.
April 9.—To the King's house, and there saw " The Tameing of a Shrew," which hath some very good pieces in it, but generally is but a mean play; and the best part " Sawny ", done by Lacy; and hath not half its life, by reason of the words, I suppose, not being understood, at least by me. (p. 298.)

April 19.—To the play-house, where we saw " Macbeth", which, though I have seen it often, yet is it one of the best plays for a stage, and variety of dancing and musique, that ever I saw. (p. 306.)

August 15.—Sir W. Pen and I to the Duke's house, where a new play. The King and Court there: the house full, and an act begun. And so went to the King's, and there saw "The Merry Wives of Windsor: " which did not please me at all, in no part of it. (p. 468.)

October 16.—To the Duke of York's house; * * and I was vexed to see Young who is but a bad actor at best act Macbeth in the room of Betterton, who, poor man! is sick: but Lord! what a prejudice it wrought in me against the whole play, and every body else agreed in disliking this fellow. Thence home, and there find my wife gone home; because of this fellow's acting of the part, she went out of the house again. (Vol. V. p. 57.)

November 1.—My wife and I to the King's playhouse, and there saw a silly play and an old one, "The Taming of a Shrew." (p. 83.)

November 2.—To the King's playhouse, and there saw " Henry the Fourth; " and, contrary to expectation, was pleased in nothing more than in Cartwright's speaking of Falstaffe's speech about "What is Honour?" (p. 83.)

November 6.—With my wife to a play, and the girl—" Macbeth," which we ftill like mightily, though mighty ſhort of the content we uſed to have when Betterton acted, who is ftill fick. (p. 86.)

November 7.—At noon refolved with Sir W. Pen to go to fee "The Tempeft," an old play of Shakeſpeare's, acted, I hear, the firft day. * * The houſe mighty full; the King and Court there: and the moſt innocent play that ever I ſaw; and a curious piece of muſick in an echo of half ſentences, the echo repeating the former half, while the man goes on to the latter; which is mighty pretty. The play has no great wit, but yet good, above ordinary plays. (p. 86.)

November 13.—To the Duke of York's houſe, and there ſaw the Tempeſt again, which is very pleaſant, and full of ſo good variety that I cannot be more pleaſed almoſt in a comedy, only the ſeamen's part a little too tedious. (p. 90.)

December 12.—After dinner all alone to the Duke of York's houſe, and ſaw "The Tempeſt," which as often as I have ſeen it, I do like very well, and the houſe very full. (p. 122.)

1667-8.
January 6.—Away to the Duke of York's houſe, in the pit, and ſo left my wife; * * * Thence, after the play, ſtayed till Harris was undreſſed, there being acted " The Tempeſt," and ſo he withal, all by coach, home. (p. 150.)

February 3. To the Duke of York's houſe, to the play "The Tempeſt," which we have often ſeen, but yet I was pleaſed again, and ſhall be again to ſee it, it is ſo full of variety, and particularly this day I took pleaſure to learn the tune of the ſeaman's dance. (p. 176.)

1668.
Auguſt 12.—After dinner, I, and wife, and Mercer, and Deb., to the Duke of York's houſe, and ſaw "Macbeth," to our great content, and then home. (p. 333.)

August 31.—To the Duke of York's playhouſe, and ſaw "Hamlet," which we have not ſeen this year before, or more; and mightily pleaſed with it, but above all with Betterton, the beſt part, I believe, that ever man acted. (p. 347.)

September 18.—To the King's houſe, and ſaw a piece of "Henry the Fourth." (p. 358.)

December 21.—Went into Holborne, and there ſaw the woman that is to be ſeen with a beard. * * * Thence to the Duke's playhouſe, and ſaw "Macbeth." (p. 425.)

1668-9.

December 30.—After dinner, my wife and I to the Duke's play-houſe, and there did ſee "King Harry the Eighth"; and was mightily pleaſed, better than I ever expected, with the hiſtory and ſhows of it. (p. 430.)

January 15.—With my wife at my cozen Turner's, where I ſtaid, and ſat a while, and carried The. and my wife to the Duke of York's houſe, to "Macbeth." (p. 440.)

January 20.—To the Duke of York's houſe, and ſaw "Twelfth Night," as it is now revived; but, I think, one of the weakeſt plays that ever I ſaw on the ſtage. (p. 445.)

January 21.—Home, where I find Madam Turner, Dyke, and The.; and had a good dinner for them, & merry; and ſo carried them to the Duke of York's houſe, * * and there ſaw "The Tempeſt"; but it is but ill done by Goſnell, in lieu of Moll Davis. (p. 446.)

February 6.—To the King's playhouſe, and there in an upper box * * * did ſee "The Moor of Venice:" but ill acted in moſt parts; Mohun which did a little ſurprize me not acting Iago's part by much ſo well as Clun uſed to do: nor another Hart's, which was Caſſio's; nor, indeed, Burt doing the Moor's ſo well as I once thought he did. (p. 459.)

Diary and Correſpondence of Samuel Pepys, Esq., F.R.S. Deciphered from his MS. by Rev. Mynors Bright. 1875 —1877.

The following tabular summary of the above extracts may be useful: it has been made with the help of Mr. H. B. Wheatley's Index to Rev. M. Bright's edition of *Pepys*. I am indebted to the same gentleman for one or two notes on the plays here recorded.

Play seen by Pepys.	Where Acted.	Date.
Hamlet.	The Opera.	1661, Aug. 24.
,,	The Theatre.	1661, Nov. 28.
,,	The Duke's House.	1663, May 28: 1668, Aug. 31.
Henry IV.	The Theatre.	1660, Dec. 31: 1661, Jun. 4.
,,	The King's House.	1668, Sept. 18.
Henry V.	Acted by the Duke's people at Court.	1666, Dec. 28.
Henry VIII.	Duke's Playhouse.	1663, Dec. 22, 26: Jan. 1; 1668, Dec. 30.
Macbeth.	The Duke of York's house.	1664, Nov. 5: 1666, Dec. 28: 1667, Jan. 7; April 19; Oct. 16; Nov. 6: 1668, Aug. 12; Dec. 21; Jan. 15.
Merry Wives of W.	Lincoln's Inn Fields playhouse.	1660, Dec. 5.
,,	The Theatre.	1661, Sept. 25.
,,	The King's house.	1667, Aug. 15.
Midsr. Night's D.	Kings Theatre.	1662, Sept. 29.
Othello.	Cockpit.	1660, Oct. 11.
,,	King's house.	1668-9, Feb. 6.
Romeo and Juliet.	The Opera.	1662, Mar. 1.
Tempest.	The Duke of York's house.	1667, Nov. 7, 13; Dec. 12: 1668, Jan. 6; Feb. 3: 1669, Jan. 21.
Twelfth Night.	The Opera.	1661, Sept. 11.
,,	The Duke's house.	1663, Jan. 6: 1669, Jan. 20.
Taming of a Shrew. (? the Shrew.)	The King's house.	1667, April 9; Nov. 1.

Besides these, the eager play-goer thrice mentions Shakespere's plays in the form of books.

"The Opera" was a name which the house in Lincoln's Inn Fields, where Davenant's company acted from 1662 to 1671, gained from the nature of the new pieces produced there. Davenant was introducing operatic entertainments into England, and when Pepys speaks of "the opera" in September, 1661, he must refer to an earlier building there, as Downes, who was Davenant's book-keeper and prompter, informs us that the new Theatre in Lincoln's Inn Fields was opened in 1662 (*Roscius Anglicanus*, 1708, reprint, 1789, "*To the Reader*"). Downes nowhere calls this house by the name of Opera, but he mentions that several plays were turned into operas, of which the *Tempest* was one ; to his account of the altered *Macbeth*, "being in the nature of an opera," he adds a "*Note*, that it was acted in Lincoln's Inn Fields" (p. 43). Pepys saw *Macbeth* at the Duke of York's House, and five editions, from 1673 to 1710, give it as "acted at the Duke's Theatre" (see after, p. 356). Here also Pepys saw Davenant's *Henry VIII*. Davenant's company, then, seem to have continued acting in two houses, as Downes says they did from 1660 to 1663.

Of *Twelfth Night* Downes remarks that "It was got up on purpose to be acted on Twelfth Night" (p. 32), which explains Pepys' grumble on 6 Jan. 1662-3.

It must not be thought that all the plays thus seen by Pepys were Shakespere pure and simple. Of the above, *Macbeth* and the *Tempest* were probably those altered by Davenant (but see after, p. 356) ; the latter came out in 1667, as shown by its Epilogue (see after, p. 339), and Pepys says he saw it "the first day." *Henry VIII*. has been thought to be Davenant's; Pepys notes on 10 Dec. 1663 : "a rare play * * of Sir W. Davenant's, the story of Henry the Eighth with all his wives," and as above, on 26 Dec., calls it a "new play." Putting together, however, what Pepys says of it with Downes' record, and Des Maizeaux' note in 1682 (see after, p. 396), it is likely that it was Shakespere's play, put upon the stage in so entirely new a manner as regards dresses and scenery, &c., that it was known as "Davenant's Henry VIII," just as we now talk of "Irving's Hamlet." Downes says, "King *Henry* the 8th. This Play, by order of *Sir William Davenant*, was all new cloathed in proper habits : The King's was new, and all the Lords, the Cardinals, the Bishops, the Doctors, Proctors, Lawyers, Tipstaves, new scenes : The Part of the King was so right and justly done by Mr. *Betterton*, he being instructed in it by Sir William, who had it from old Mr. *Lowen*, that had his instructions from Mr. *Shakespear* himself, that I dare and will aver, none can, or ever will come near him." (p. 34.) As regards *The Taming of a Shrew*, Lord Braybrooke and Dr. Ingleby consider that this was the older play (before Shakespere) ; Sir H. Herbert shows (see before, p. 158) that Shakespere's play had been revived in 1663, and Pepys (Nov. 1, 1667) calls the one he saw "an old one" : but (on April 9, 1667) he mentions "the best part 'Sawny,' done by Lacy" ; the conjunction of these names leads to the conclusion that Lacy's play called *Sawney the Scot*, an adaptation of Shakespere's *Taming of the Shrew*, though only published in 1698, was acted many years earlier under the original title, and that this was the play that Pepys saw.

Strictly speaking, therefore, the entries referring to some of these plays do not belong to this work, but as tending to show the extent to which Shakespere's power was acknowledged even by a degenerate taste, they are included with the rest. L. T. S.]

Anonymous, 1661.

Wilt thou be Fatt, Ile tell thee how,
Thou ſhalt quickly do the Feat;
And that ſo plump a thing as thou
Was never yet made up of meat:
Drink off thy Sack, 'twas onely that
Made *Bacchus* and *Jack Falſtafe* Fatt, Fatt.

A Catch: (Stanza 1.) occurring on p. 72 of An Antidote against Melancholy: Made up in Pills. Compounded of Witty Ballads, Jovial Songs, and Merry Catches. 1661. [4to.] (*See Collier's Bibliog. Account. Vol. I. p.* 25.

This little book contains the song from which Shakespere, in *The Winter's Tale*, makes Antolycus sing the first four lines, beginning:—
"Jog on, jog on, the foot-path way."

JOHN EVELYN, 1661.

November 26.—I saw Hamlet Prince of Denmark played, but now the old plays began to disguſt this refined age, since his Majeſties being so long abroad.

Memoirs and Diary. Edited by William Bray.
1819.   *Vol.* I, *p.* 342.

JOHN WARD, 1661—1663.

Shakefpear had but 2 daughters, one whereof M. Hall, yᵉ phyfitian, married, and by her had one daughter, to wit, yᵉ Lady Bernard of Abbingdon. (43ʳᵈ *leaf from end of the volume.*)

I have heard yᵗ Mʳ. Shakefpeare was a natural wit, without any art at all; hee frequented yᵉ plays all his younger time, but in his elder days lived at Stratford: and fupplied yᵉ ftage with 2 plays every year, and for yᵗ had an allowance fo large, yᵗ hee fpent att yᵉ Rate of a 1,000*l.* a year, as I have heard.

Remember to perufe Shakefpears plays, and bee verfd in *them*, yᵗ I may not bee ignorant in yᵗ matter. (41ˢᵗ *leaf from end.*)

Shakefpear, Drayton, and Ben Jhonfon, had a merry meeting, and itt feems drank too hard, for Shakefpear died of a feavour there contracted. (30ᵗʰ *leaf from end.*)

Whether Dr. Heylin does well, in reckoning up the dramatick poets which have been famous in England, to omit Shakefpeare.

A letter to my brother, to fee Mrs. Queeny, to fend for Tom Smith for the acknowledgment.

MSS. of the Rev. John Ward, in the possession of the Medical Society of London. Printed in the "Diary of the Rev. John Ward, A.M., Vicar of Stratford-upon-Avon, extending from 1648 *to* 1679," *edited by C. Severn, M.D.* 1839. *p.* 183-4.

This "Mrs. Queeny" is Judith Quiney, Shakespeare's daughter. She died in 1662. [The fourth edition of Heylyn's cosmography came out in 1652. He gives but a poor list of men famous "for Poetrie" in England, in the division devoted to Britain.

The manuscripts from which Dr. Severn's book is a selection are fifteen duodecimo volumes filled with notes from various readings, medical receipts, heads of sermons, and observations of all sorts; they are, in fact, common-place books, to which the word diary does not correctly apply. The volumes are not numbered, nor are the leaves paged; but on the fly-leaf at the end of that in which the first four of the paragraphs above given are found is written: "This Booke was begunne Feb. 14, 1661, and finished April ye 25 1663 att Mr. Brooks his hous in Stratford uppon Avon in Warwicke-shire." Dr. Severn gives no reference by which to find the originals of his print; and put these paragraphs together as one whole, whereas they are scattered entries. I am sorry that I have not succeeded in finding in the MS. the last two of the above paragraphs, they are probably in one of the other fourteen volumes, as a careful search through that dated 1661—1663 does not reveal them. (In his Preface (p. viii) Dr. Severn speaks of *seventeen* duodecimo volumes; I saw fifteen only, besides a long note-book apparently belonging to the same collection.) I am indebted to the courtesy of W. E. Poole, Esq., Registrar of the Medical Society of London, for the opportunity of examining these manuscripts. L. T. S.]

Anonymous, 1663.

——— On they ride
*   *   *
unto Town, famous for Hogs,
Butchers, and their like, Maſtiffe-dogs;
And for a Witch that once liv'd there,
Not unlike *Falſtaffe* in *Shakeſpeare*.

Hudibras   Second [Spurious] Part, 1663. *p.* 46.

THOMAS JORDAN, 1660—1664.

 We have been fo perplex't with Gun and Drum,
  Look to your Hats and Cloaks; the Redcoats come.
 D'Amlois is routed, Hotfpur quits the Field,
 Falftaff's out-filch'd, all in confufion yield ;
 Even Auditor and Actor, what before
 Did make the Red-Bull laugh, now makes it roar:

     (*A Prologue to the King, August* 16, 1660.
      Poems, p. 15, *reprint, p.* 18.)

 A Prologue to introduce the firft Woman that came to Act on the Stage in the Tragedy, call'd *The Moor of Venice*.

  I come, unknown to any of the reft
  To tell you news, I faw the Lady dreft;
  The Woman playes to day, miftake me not.

   * *   *

    In this reforming age
  We have intents to civilize the Stage.
  Our women are defective, and fo fiz'd
  You'd think they were fome of the Guard difguiz'd;
  For (to fpeak truth) men act, that are between
  Forty and fifty, Wenches of fifteen ;
  With bone fo large, and nerve fo incomplyant,
  When you call *Desdemona*, enter Giant.

      (*Poems, p.* 22 : *reprint, p.* 24.)

Then quoth the Duke, you muſt perform my command
  Take ſhipping ſtrait,
And bear this Brat into a forreign Land;
Leave it in any wilderneſs you can finde,
  And let it there be nouriſhed
Onely by the rain and winde.

> (*The jealous Duke, and the injur'd Dutchess: a story.
> Songs, p.* 48, *reprint, p.* 124.)
> *A Royal Arbor of Loyal Poesie, consisting of Poems and
> Songs, n. d.* ? 1664. [4to.] (*Bodleian Lib. Malone
> 451.) Reprint edited by J. P. Collier, in Illustrations
> of Old English Literature,* 1866, *Vol. III.*

The ballad from which the third extract is taken is founded on the plot of the *Winter's Tale;* two other ballads of Thomas Jordan, both in the *Royal Arbor,* are also founded on stories used by Shakespeare : viz., *The Forfeiture : a Romance,* and *The Revolution : a Love-story ;* the former like *The Merchant of Venice,* the latter like *Much Ado about Nothing.*

[Two copies of this rare book are in the Malone collection, one of which (No. 432) bears the title "A Rosary of Rarities planted in a Garden of Poetry." Both are without date, but a MS. note on No. 451 says : "Mr. Heber's copy bears date 1664." Some of the contents are variously dated from 1660 to 1662. L. T. S.]

MARGARET CAVENDISH, 1664.

I wonder how that perfon you mention in your letter, could either have the confcience, or confidence to difpraife *Shakefpear's* playes, as to fay they were made up onely with clowns, fools, watchmen, and the like ; but to anfwer that perfon, though *Shakefpear's* wit will anfwer for himfelf, I fay, that it feems by his judging, or cenfuring, he underftands not playes, or wit; for to exprefs properly, rightly, ufually, and naturally, a clown's, or fool's humour, expreffions, phrafes, garbs, manners, actions, words, and courfe of life, is as witty, wife, judicious, ingenious, and obferving, as to write and exprefs the expreffions, phrafes, garbs, manners, actions, words, and courfe of life, of kings and princes; and to exprefs naturally, to the life, a mean country wench, as a great lady, a courtefan, as a chaft woman, a mad man, as a man in his right reafon and fenfes, a drunkard, as a fober man, a knave, as an honeft man, and fo a clown, as a well-bred man, and a fool, as a wife man; nay, it expreffes and declares a greater wit, to exprefs, and deliver to pofterity, the extravagancies of madnefs, the fubtilty of knaves, the ignorance of clowns, and the fimplicity of naturals, or the craft of feigned fools, than to exprefs regularities, plain honefty, courtly garbs, or fenfible difcourfes, for 'tis harder to exprefs nonfenfe than fenfe, and ordinary converfations, than that which is unufual; and 'tis harder, and requires more wit to exprefs a jefter, than a grave ftatefman; yet *Shakefpear* did not want wit, to exprefs to the life all forts of perfons, of what quality, profeffion, degree, breeding,

or birth foever; nor did he want wit to exprefs the divers and
different humours, or natures, or feveral paffions in mankind;
and fo well he hath expreff'd in his playes all forts of perfons, as
one would think he had been tranfformed into every one of thofe
perfons he hath defcribed; and as fometimes one would think he
was really himfelf the clown or jefter he feigns, fo one would
think, he was alfo the king, and privy-councillor; alfo as one would
think he were really the coward he feigns, fo one would
think he were the moft valiant and experienced fouldier; Who
would not think he had been fuch a man as his Sir *John Falftaff*?
and who would not think he had been *Harry* the Fifth? &
certainly *Julius Cæfar*, *Auguftus Cæfar*, and *Antonius*, did [Octavius]
never really act their parts better, if fo well, as he hath
defcribed them, and I believe that *Antonius* and *Brutus* did not
fpeak better to the people, than he hath feign'd them; nay, one
would think that he had been metamorphofed from a man to a
woman, for who could defcribe *Cleopatra* better than he hath
done, and many other females of his own creating, as *Nan Page*,
Mrs. *Page*, Mrs. *Ford*, the doctors maid, *Bettrice*, Mrs. *Quickly*,
Doll Tearfheet, and others, too many to relate? and in his tragick
vein, he prefents paffions fo naturally, and misfortunes fo probably,
as he peirces the fouls of his readers with fuch a true fenfe and
feeling thereof, that it forces tears through their eyes, and almoft
perfwades them, they are really actors, or at leaft prefent at thofe
tragedies. Who could not fwear he had been a noble lover, that
could woo fo well? and there is not any perfon he hath defcribed
in his book, but his readers might think they were well acquainted
with them; indeed *Shakefpear* had a clear judgment, a quick
wit, a fpreading fancy, a fubtil obfervation, a deep apprehenfion,
and a moft eloquent elocution; truly, he was a natural orator, as
well as a natural poet, and he was not an orator to fpeak well
only on fome fubjects, as lawyers, who can make eloquent orations
at the bar, and plead fubtilly and wittily in law-cafes, or divines,
that can preach eloquent fermons, or difpute fubtilly and wittily

in theology, but take them from that, and put them to other subjects, and they will be to seek; but *Shakespear's* wit and eloquence was general, for and upon all subjects, he rather wanted subjects for his wit and eloquence to work on, for which he was forced to take some of his plots out of history, where he only took the bare designs, the wit and language being all his own; &c.

* * * * * *

Remember, when we were very young maids, one day we were discoursing about lovers, and we did injoyn each other to confess who profess'd to love us, and whom we loved, and I confess'd I only was in Love with three dead men, which were dead long before my time, the one was *Cæsar*, for his valour, the second *Ovid*, for his wit, and the third was our countryman *Shakespear*, for his comical and tragical humour; but soon after we both married two worthy men, and I will leave you to your own husband, for you best know what he is; As for my husband, I know him to have the valour of *Cæsar*, the fancy, and wit of *Ovid*, and the tragical, especially comical art of *Shakespear*; in truth he is as far beyond *Shakespear* for comical humour, as *Shakespear* beyond an ordinary poet in that way; &c.

CCXI Sociable Letters written by the Lady Marchioness of Newcastle. 1664. [*Fo.*]
Letters CXXIII and CLXII.

The writer of the *Sociable Letters* was the second wife of William, Marquess of Newcastle, the patron of Ben Jonson. In the preface she writes:

"I have endeavoured under the cover of letters to express the humors of mankind, and the actions of man's life by the correspondence of two ladies living at some short distance from each other."

Margaret Cavendish was a woman of sense and accomplishment; but, while her thoughts are usually common-place, she conveys them by an apparatus of phraseology which is clear rather than forcible, and disproportionately diffuse. Her summary of Shakespeare's virtues is little more than an inventory, and is tautologically particular. Yet we must allow that the occasion called for the critique; and at that day it was not superfluous to insist upon the identity of the poet with each and every of his great

characters. The paradox, "'tis harder to express nonsense than sense," is
a great truth, singularly applicable to Shakespeare's art. What she says as
to the effect of his tragedy on *readers* is also felicitous: and her remark on
the Roman plays—"that *Antonius* and *Brutus* did not speak better to the
people than he hath feigned them"—is reiterated with excellent effect by
Archbishop Trench, in his *Lectures on Plutarch*. That she imitated
Shakespeare, in her poems, is countenanced by similarities of diction; *e. g.*,
in 1653 she writes:

"Had sinews room fancy therein to breed,
Copies of verses might from the heel proceed."

Which appears to be imitated from *King Lear*, where the fool says:

"If a man's brains were in his heels, were't not in danger of kibes?"

[But in her "General Prologue to all my Playes" (prefixed to her *Playes*,
published in 1662) she modestly disclaims any comparison with former
masters:—

"As for *Ben. Johnsons* brain, it was so strong,
He could conceive, or judge, what's right, what's wrong:
His Language plain, significant, and free,
And in the English Tongue, the Masterie:
Yet Gentle *Shakespear* had a fluent Wit,
Although less Learning, yet full well he writ;
For all his Playes were writ by Natures light,
Which gives his Readers, and Spectators sight.
But Noble Readers, do not think my Playes
Are such as have been writ in former daies;
As *Johnson, Shakespear, Beamont, Fletcher* writ;
Mine want their Learning, Reading, Language, Wit." L. T. S.]

Some account of this admirable woman is given in Pepys' *Diary*, vol. iv.
pp. 284, *note*, 302, 315 (Rev. M. Bright's edition, 1877), and in Evelyn's
Diary and Correspondence, vol. ii. pp. 25, 26 (Ed. 1859, in 4 vols.).

CHARLES COTTON, 1665.

"Ah, Sifter, sifter! had'ſt not thou,
Play'd Miſtreſs *Quicklies* office ſo,
And ſooth'd me up till I grew jolly,
I never had committed Folly:

* * * * * *

But 'twas ſo dark, as well it might,
Being 'twixt twelve and one at night;
That had the nimble Currier
In kindneſs ſtaid his leiſure there,
Though clad in *Falſtaff's Kendal Green*,
He could not poſſibly be ſeen.

Scarronides: or Virgil Travestie. A Mock-Poem. In imitation of the Fourth Book of Virgil's Æneis in English Burlesque. 1665, *pp.* 118, 123. (*Works, ed.* 1771, *pp.* 127, 129.)

[These allusions have been kindly pointed out by Mr. R. Roberts of Boston. L. T. S.]

Anonymous, 1667.

In our Old Plays, the humor Love and Paſſion
Like Doublet, Hoſe, and Cloak, are out of faſhion:
That which the World call'd Wit in *Shakeſpears* age,
Is laught at, as improper for our Stage.

*Love Tricks: or the School of Complements,
by James Shirley. Prologue.* 1667.

[This is a different Prologue to that prefixed to the play when it first came out in 1631, in Shirley's life-time, under the title of *The School of Compliment*. James Shirley died in 1666. L. T. S.]

JOHN DRYDEN, 1667.

As when a Tree's cut down, the secret Root
Lives under ground, and thence new Branches shoot;
So, from old *Shakespear's* honour'd dust, this day
Springs up and buds a new reviving Play.
Shakespear, who (taught by none) did first impart
To *Fletcher* wit, to labouring *Johnson* Art.
He, Monarch-like, gave those his Subjects Law,
And is that Nature which they paint and draw.
Fletcher reach'd that which on his heights did grow,
Whilst *Johnson* crept and gather'd all below.
This did his Love, and this his Mirth digest:
One imitates him most. the other best.
If they have since out-writ all other Men,
'Tis with the drops which fell from *Shakespear's* pen.
The Storm which vanish'd on the neighb'ring shore,
Was taught by *Shakespear's* Tempest first to roar.
That Innocence and Beauty which did smile
In *Fletcher*, grew on this *Enchanted Isle*.
But *Shakespear's* Magick could not copy'd be,
Within that Circle none durst walk but he.
I must confess 'twas bold, nor would you now
That liberty to vulgar Wits allow,
Which works by Magick supernatural things:
But *Shakespear's* pow'r is Sacred as a King's.
Those Legends from old Priesthood were receiv'd,
And he then writ, as people then believ'd.

Prologue to The Tempest or The Enchanted Island, **by Sir**
William D'Avenant and John Dryden. 1676.

There is no doubt D'Avenant, whatever may have been his parentage or his morals, had very considerable poetical abilities. Remembering the tradition recorded by Aubrey (page 383), it is interesting to read the testimony of Dryden to his dramatic excellence. It is prefixed to the play written by them jointly upon the suggestion of Shakespeare's *Tempest*, and runs thus:

"In the time I writ with him, I had the opportunity to observe somewhat more nearly of him than I had formerly done, when I had only a bare acquaintance with him : I found him then of so quick a fancy, that nothing was propos'd to him on which he could not suddenly produce a thought extreamly pleasant and surprising : and those first thoughts of his, contrary to the old Latin Proverb, were not always the least happy. And as his fancy was quick, so likewise were the products of it remote and new. He borrowed not of any other ; and his imaginations were such as could not easily enter into any other man. His Corrections were sober and judicious : and he corrected his own writings much more severely than those of another man, bestowing twice the time and labour in polishing, which he us'd in invention."

Preface to The Tempest or The Enchanted Island. 1669.

[This play was first printed in 1670 (which edition I have not been able to see, and therefore take the extracts from that of 1676), Dryden's *Preface* is dated 1669, and the Epilogue points to its first acting in 1667. The Prologue given above is not signed by Dryden, but we take it to have been written by him. The first and third stanzas of the Epilogue run as follows,—

"Gallants, by all good signs it does appear,
That Sixty seven's a very damning year,
For Knaves abroad, and for ill Poets here.
*   .   *   *   *

The Ghosts of Poets walk within this place,
And haunt us Actors wheresoe'r we pass,
In visions bloudier then King *Richard's* was." L. T. S.]

ROBERT WILD, 1668.

Upon some Bottles of Sack *and* Claret, *laid in Sand, and covered with a Sheet.*

Enter, and see this Tomb (Sirs) do not fear,
No Spirits, but of Wine, will fright you here:
Weep o're this Tomb, your Sorrows here may have
Wine for their sweet Companions in the grave.
A dozen *Shakespears* here interr'd do lie;
Two dozen *Johnsons* full of Poetry.

Iter Boreale. With large Additions of several other Poems. 1668. *p.* 63.

JOHN DRYDEN, 1668.

To begin, then, with *Shakefpeare*: he was the man who of all Modern, and perhaps Ancient Poets, had the largeft and moft comprehenfive foul. All the Images of Nature were ftill prefent to him, and he drew them not laborioufly, but luckily: when he defcribes any thing, you more than fee it, you feel it too. Thofe who accufe him to have wanted learning, give him the greater commendation: he was naturally learn'd; he needed not the fpectacles of Books to read Nature; he look'd inwards, and found her there. I cannot fay he is everywhere alike; were he fo, I fhould do him injury to compare him with the greateft of Mankind. He is many times flat, infipid; his Comick wit degenerating into clenches, his ferious fwelling into Bombaft. But he is alwayes great, when fome great occafion is prefented to him: no man can fay he ever had a fit fubject for his wit, and did not then raife himfelf as high above the reft of [the] Poets

Quantum lenta folent, inter viberna cupreffi.

The confideration of this made Mr. *Hales* of *Eton* fay, That there was no fubject of which any Poet ever writ, but he would produce it much better treated of in *Shakefpeare*; and however others are now generally prefer'd before him, yet the Age wherein he liv'd, which had contemporaries with him, *Fletcher* and *Johnfon* never equall'd them to him, in their efteem: And in the laft Kings Court, when Ben's reputation was at higheft, Sir *John Suckling*, and with him the greater part of the courtiers, fet our *Shakefpeare* far above him.

Beaumont and *Fletcher*, of whom I am next to fpeak, had with the advantage of *Shakefpeare's* wit, which was their precedent, great natural gifts, improv'd by ftudy.

Of Dramatick Poesie, an Essay. 1668. [4*to.*] *p.* 47.

JOHN DRYDEN, 1668.

[The following passage from Daniel George Morhoff, fourteen years after Dryden's Essay, which is referred to by Ulrici (*Shakspeare's Dramatische Kunst*, 1874, Part 3, p. 183) as the first mention of Shakespere by a German writer, is interesting in connection with the above extract.

"Der *John Dryden* hat gar woll und gelahrt von der *Dramaticâ Poesi* geschrieben. Die Engelländer die er hierin anführt sein *Shakespeare, Fletcher, Beaumont* von welchen ich nichts gesehen habe. *Ben. Johnson* hat gar viel geschrieben, welcher meines erachtens kein geringes Lob verdienet."

Unterricht von der Teutschen Sprache und Poesie, deren Uhrsprung, Fortgang und Lehrsätzen. Kiel, 1682. *Cap. IV, Von der Engelländer Poeterey, p.* 250.

("John Dryden has well and learnedly written of Dramatic Poesie. The English whom he quotes therein are Shakespeare, Fletcher, Beaumont, of whom I have seen nothing. Ben Johnson has written a great deal which in my judgment deserves no small praise.")

Shakespere was early known abroad; three of his plays, now in Zurich library, were brought over by the Swiss, J. R. Hess, who was in England in 1614; and *Hamlet, King Lear*, and *Romeo & Juliet* were acted at Dresden by the English comedians in 1626, as appears by a list of plays performed by them in that year. Much curious and interesting information on the companies of English Actors in Germany and the Netherlands, in the 16th and 17th centuries, is given in Albert Cohn's *Shakespeare in Germany*, 1865 (see the foregoing facts on pp. xx, cxv), and since the publication of his work recent discoveries in the Minute books of Cologne shew that English actors appeared in that city in several different years between 1592 and 1612. See Dr. L. Ennen's articles in the *Stadt-Anzeiger der Kölnischen Zeitung*, Nov. 17, 20, 21, and 22, 1877. L. T. S.]

SIR JOHN DENHAM, 1668.

Old *Chaucer*, like tne morning Star,
To us difcovers day from far,
His light thofe Mifts and Clouds diffolv'd,
Which our dark Nation long involv'd;
But he defcending to the fhades,
Darknefs again the Age invades.
Next (like *Aurora*) *Spencer* rofe,
Whofe purple blufh the day forefhows;
*   *   *   *   *
By *Shakefpear's, Johnfon's, Fletcher's* lines,
Our Stages luftre *Rome's* outfhines:
Thefe Poets neer our Princes fleep,
And in one Grave their Manfion keep;
*   *   *   *
Time, which made them their Fame outlive,
To *Cowly* fcarce did ripenefs give.
Old Mother Wit, and Nature gave
Shakefpear and *Fletcher* all they have;
in *Spencer*, and in *Johnfon*, Art
Of flower Nature got the ftart;

Poems and Translations, with The Sophy. 1668. *pp.*
89, 90. *On Mr. Abraham Cowley, his Death and Burial amongst the Ancient Poets.*

[Did Sir John really think that Shakespere was buried in Westminster Abbey, as the above lines would seem to imply? Cowley died in 1667, his friend Denham in 1668. L. T. S.]

EDWARD PHILLIPS, 1669.

Hoc feculo [fc. temporibus Elizabethæ reginæ et Jacobi regis] floruerunt * * * Gulielmus Shacfperius, qui præter opera Dramatica, duo Poemata *Lucretiæ ftuprum à Tarquinio*, et *Amores Veneris in Adonidem*, Lyrica carmina nonnulla compofuit : videtur fuiffe, fiquis alius, re verâ Poeta natus. Samuel Daniel non obfcurus hujus ætatis Poeta, etc.

* * * Ex eis qui dramaticè fcripferunt, Primas fibi vendicant Shacfperus, Jonfonus et Flecherus, quorum hic facundâ et politâ quâdam familiaritate Sermonis, ille erudito judicio et Ufu veterum Authorum, alter nativâ quâdam et Poeticâ fublimitate Ingenii excelluiffe videntur. Ante hos in hoc genere Poefeos apud nos eminuit Nemo. Pauci quidem antea fcripferunt, at parum fœliciter ; hos autem tanquam duces itineris plurimi faltem æmulati funt, inter quos præter Sherleium, (proximum à fupra memorato Triumviratu,) Suclingium, Randolphium, Davenantium et Carturitium * * enumerandi veniunt Ric. Bromeus, Tho. Heivodus, etc.

Tractatulus de Carmine Dramatico Poetarum, et compendiosa Enumeratio Poetarum a Tempore Dantis Aligerii usque ad hanc Ætatem. Added to the seventeenth edition of Thesaurus J. Buchleri of 1669. *Collated from the edition of* 1679, *pp.* 396, 397, 399.

RICHARD FLECKNOE, 1670.

Of the difference
Betwixt the Ancient and Modern Playes.

If any one the difference woud know,
Betwixt the *Ancient Playes* and *Modern* now;
In *Ancient Times* none ever went away,
But with a glowing bofome from a Play,
With fomewhat they had *heard*, or *feen* fo fierd,
They feem to be *Celeftially* infpir'd.
Now you have onely fome few light conceits,
Like Squibs & Crackers, neither warms nor heats;
And *fparks of Wit* as much as you'd defire,
But nothing of a true and folid fire:
So hard 'tis now for any one to write
With *Johnfon's* fire, or *Fletcher's* flame & fpright:
Much lefs inimitable *fhakfpears* way,
Promethian-like to animate a Play.

Epigrams. 1670. *p.* **71.**

GEORGE VILLIERS, 2ND DUKE OF BUCKINGHAM. 1671.

Bayes. Now here's an odd furprife: all thefe dead men you fhall fee rife up prefently, at a certain Note that I have made, in *Effaut flat,* and fall a Dancing. Do you hear, dead men? remember your Note in *Effaut flat.* Play on. [*To the Mufick.*
 Now, now, now.   *The Mufick play his Note, and the dead*
 O Lord, O Lord!   *men rife; but cannot get in order.*
 Out, out, out! Did ever men fpoil a good thing fo? no figure, no ear, no time, no thing? you dance worfe than the Angels in *Harry* the Eight, or the fat Spirits in *The Tempeſt,* I gad.

*   *   *   *   *   *

Bayes. Now, Gentlemen, I will be bold to fay, I'l fhew you the greateſt Scene that ever *England* faw: I mean not for words, for thofe I do not value; but for ſtate, fhew, and magnificence. In fine, I'l juſtifie it to be as grand to the eye every whit, I gad, as that great Scene in *Harry* the Eight, and grander too, I gad; for, inſtead of two Biſhops, I have brought in two other Cardinals.

The Rehearsal, 1672. *Act II. Sc. v.; Act V. Sc. i.*
pp. 19, 42.
(*First acted* 7 *Dec.* 1671; *see Arber's reprint,* 1869.)

ANDREW MARVEL, 1672, 1673.

And then as for extortion; who but fuch an Hebrew Jew as you would, after an honeft man had made fo full and voluntary reftitution, not yet have been fatiffied without fo many pounds of his flefh over into the bargain? Though J. O. be in a defperate condition, yet methinks Mr. B., not 'being paft grace,' fhould not neither ' have been paft mercy.'

I cannot but obferve, Mr. Bayes, this admirable way (like fat *Sir John Falftaffe's* fingular dexterity in finking) that you have of anfwering whole Books or Difcourses, how pithy and knotty foever, in a line or two, nay fometimes with a word.

The Rehearsal Transprosed. First Part.
Reprinted by Rev. A. B. Grosart in Works of Andrew Marvel, Vol. III, pp. 54, 135. 1873.

I remember within our time one *Simons*, who rob'd alwayes upon the *Bricolle,* that is to fay, never interrupted the Paffengers, but ftill fet upon the Thieves themfelves, after, like *Sir John Falftaff*, they were gorged with a booty; and by this way, fo ingenious, that it was fcarce criminal, he lived fecure and unmolefted all his dayes with the reputation of a Judge rather than an High-way man.

The Rehearsall Transpros'd. Second Part. 1673.
pp. 46, 47. *Grosart's Reprint, Works, Vol. III,*
p. 265.

[JOHN DRYDEN], 1672.

In country beauties as we often fee,
Something that takes in their fimplicity.
Yet while they charm, they know not they are fair,
And take without their fpreading of the fnare;
Such Artlefs beauty lies in *Shakefpears* wit,
'Twas well in fpight of him whate're he writ.
His excellencies came, and were not fought,
His words like cafual atoms made a thought:
Drew up themfelves in rank and file, and writ,
He wondring how the devil it were fuch wit.
Thus like the drunken Tinker in his Play,
He grew a Prince, and never knew which way.
He did not know what trope or figure meant,
But to perfwade is to be eloquent,
So in this Cæfar which this day you fee,
Tully ne'r fpoke as he makes *Anthony*.
Thofe then that tax his learning are to blame,
He knew the thing, but did not know the name:
Great *Johnfon* did that ignorance adore,
And though he envi'd much, admir'd him more.
The faultlefs *Johnfon* equally writ well,
Shakefpear made faults; but then did more excel.
One clofe at guard like fome old fencer lay,
Tother more open, but he fhew'd more play.
In imitation *Johnfons* wit was fhown,
Heaven made his men, but *Shakefpear* made his own.

[JOHN DRYDEN], 1672.

Wife Johnson's talent in obferving lay,
But others' follies ftill made up his play.
He drew the like in each elaborate line,
But Shakefpear like a mafter did defign.
Johnson with fkill diffected humane kind,
And fhow'd their faults, that they their faults might find;
But then as all anatomifts muft do,
He to the meaneft of mankind did go.
And took from gibbets fuch as he would fhow.
Both are fo great that he muft boldly dare,
Who both of 'em does judge and both compare.
If amongft poets one more bold there be,
The man that dare attempt in either way, is he.

Covent Garden drolery. 1672. [8vo.] *p.* 9.
Prologue to Julius Cæsar.

This clever Prologue was ascribed to Dryden by Mr. Bolton Corney (*Notes and Queries*, 1st S. ix, 95). Boaden (*Inquiry*, 1824, p. 38) regretted "that Dryden did not let out more of his mighty spirit in the verses" addressed to Kneller. "He might have rendered them the vehicle of a discriminated character of Shakespeare, such as should rival that written by himself in such admirable prose." Boaden did not know that Dryden had done this in his prologue to *Julius Cæsar*.
The line—

"'Twas well in spite of him whate'er he writ,"

reminds us of Pope's assertion that Shakespeare

"grew immortal in his own despite."

[Dryden, in his lines "To my Dear Friend Mr. Congreve, on his Comedy call'd, The Double Dealer," 1694, again shows his sense of Shakespere's native genius :—

"Time, Place, and Action, may with Pains be wrought
But Genius must be born ; and never can be taught.
This is your Portion ; This your Native Store ;
Heav'n, that but once was Prodigal before,
To *Shakespear* gave as much ; she cou'd not give him more."

L. T. S.]

JOHN DRYDEN, 1672.

To begin with *Language*. That an alteration is lately made in ours or since the writers of the last age (in which I comprehend *Shakespear, Fletcher,* and *Jonson,*) is manifest. Any man who reads those excellent Poets, and compares their language with what is now written, will see it almost in every line. But, that this is an *improvement* of the language, or an alteration for the better, will not so easily be granted. (p. 162.) * * * * One testimony of this is undeniable, that we are the first who have observ'd them [their improprieties of language]; and, certainly, to observe errours is a great step to the correcting of them. But, malice and partiality set apart, let any man who understands English, read diligently the works of *Shakespear* and *Fletcher;* and I dare undertake that he will find, in every page either some *solecism* of speech, or some notorious flaw in sence; and yet these men are reverenc'd, when we are not forgiven. That their wit is great and many times their expressions noble, envy itself cannot deny.

Neque ego illis detrahere ausim
Hærentem capiti, multa cum laude, coronam :

but the times were ignorant in which they liv'd. Poetry was then, if not in its infancy among us, at least not arriv'd to its vigor and maturity : witness the lameness of their plots : many of which, especially those which they writ first, (for even that age refin'd itself in some measure,) were made up of some ridiculous, incoherent story, which, in one play many times took up the business of an age. I suppose I need not name *Pericles, Prince of Tyre,* nor the Historical Plays of *Shakespear*. Besides

many of the reft, as the *Winter's Tale, Love's labour loft, Meafure for Meafure,* which were either grounded on impoffibilities, or at leaft, fo meanly written, that the Comedy neither cauſ'd your mirth, nor the ferious part your concernment. (p. 163.) * * * *
In reading fome bombaft fpeeches of *Macbeth,* which are not to be underftood, he [*Ben. Johnfon*] ufed to fay that it was horrour. and I am much afraid that this is fo. (p. 165.)

* * * * *

But I am willing to clofe the book [*Catiline*], partly out of veneration to the author, partly out of wearinefs to purfue an argument which is fo fruitful in fo fmall a compafs. And what correctnefs, after this, can be expected from *Shakefpear* or from *Fletcher,* who wanted that learning and care which *Johnfon* had? I will therefore fpare my own trouble of inquiring into their faults: who had they liv'd now, had doubtlefs written more correctly. (p. 167.)

* * * *

By this graffing, as I may call it, on old words, has our tongue been beautified by the three fore-mentioned poets, *Shakefpear, Fletcher,* and *Johnfon*: whofe excellencies I can never enough admire, and in this, they have been follow'd efpecially by Sir *John Suckling* and Mr. *Waller,* who refin'd upon them. (p. 169.)

* * *

I fhould now fpeak of the refinement of wit: but I have been fo large on the former fubject that I am forc'd to contract myfelf in this. I will therefore onely obferve to you, that the wit of the laft age was yet more incorrect than their language. *Shakefpear,* who many times has written better than any poet, in any language, is yet fo far from writing wit always, or expreffing that wit according to the Dignity of the Subject, that he writes, in many places, below—the dulleft Writer of ours, or of any precedent age. Never did any author precipitate himfelf from fuch heights of thought to fo low expreffions, as he often does. He is the very *Janus* of poets; he wears, almoſt everywhere two faces: and you have ſcarce begun to admire the one, e're you deſpiſe the other. Neither is the Luxuriance of *Fletcher*, (which his friends have tax'd in him,) a leſs fault than the careleſſneſs of *Shakeſpear*. (p. 169.)

* * * * * *

Shakeſpear ſhow'd the beſt of his ſkill in his *Mercutio*, and he ſaid himſelf, that he was forc'd to kill him in the third Act, to prevent being kill'd by him. But, for my part, I cannot find he was ſo dangerous a perſon: I ſee nothing in him but what was ſo exceeding harmleſs, that he might have liv'd to the end of the Play, and dy'd in his bed, without offence to any man. (p 172.)

* * * * * *

Let us therefore admire the beauties and the heights of *Shakeſpear*, without falling after him into a careleſſneſs, and (as I may call it) a Lethargy of thought, for whole ſcenes together. (p. 174.)

* * * * * *

The Conquest of Granada by the Spaniards. By John Dryden. 1672. *Second Part. Defence of the Epilogue.*

[In the Preface to *An Evening's Love, or the Mock Astrologer*, 1671, Dryden thus refers to his intended criticism (given above) and shows how he regarded Shakespere's heroic plays. "I had thought, Reader, in this Preface to have written somewhat concerning the difference betwixt the Playes of our Age, and those of our Predecessors on the *English* stage: to have shewn in what parts of Dramatick Poesie we were excell'd by *Ben Johnson*, I mean, humour, & contrivance of Comedy; and in what we may justly claim precedence of *Shakespear* and *Fletcher*, namely in Heroick Playes: but this design I have wav'd on second considerations, at least deferr'd it till I publish the Conquest of Granada." L. T. S.]

* *Anonymous*, 1673.

And fince in every age the fame *faculties* are employ'd, only the *objects* changed, and the *actions* of thofe faculties not many; it muft need be that our whole life is but *re-acting* the fame thing frequently over upon divers fubjects and occafions. As the Fool perfonates the fame humour, tho' in divers Comedies, and tho fometimes *Lance, Jodelet,* or *Scaramuccio,* yet 'tis all but the fame *Buffoon.*

Of Education. Especially of Young Gentlemen. Second Impression. Oxford, 1673, *p.* 43.

[This appears to be an allusion to Launce in the *Two Gentlemen of Verona*. If so, the passage is interesting as classing him with Scaramouche. H. Littledale.]

FRANCIS KIRKMAN, 1673.

The moſt part of theſe Pieces were written by ſuch Penmen as were known to be the ableſt Artiſts that ever this Nation produced, by Name *Shake-ſpear, Fletcher, Johnſon, Shirley*, and others; and theſe Collections are the very Souls of their writings, if the witty part thereof may be ſo termed : * * When the publique Theatres were ſhut up, and the Actors forbidden to preſent us with any of their Tragedies, becauſe we had enough of that in earneſt, and Comedies, becauſe the Vices of the Age were too lively and ſmartly repreſented; then all that we could divert our ſelves with were theſe humours and pieces of Plays, which paſſing under the Name of a merry conceited Fellow, called *Bottom the Weaver, Simpleton the Smith, John Swabber*, or ſome ſuch Title, were only allowed us, and that but by ſtealth too, and under pretence of Rope-dancing, or the like.

The Wits, or Sport upon Sport. Being a Curious Collection of several Drols and Farces. 1673. *Preface.*

[A collection of the opinion of the century upon our great poet would hardly be complete without this illustration of the involuntary homage paid to Shakespere's spirit of fun, which as this volume shows prevailed even against the Ordinance of the Long Parliament, 2 Sept. 1642, that "stage-plays shall cease & be forborne." The book is in two Parts; Part I, 1672; Part II, with a fresh title-page, dated 1673, and a Preface by Kirkman. The first piece in Part I, is taken from *1 Henry IV*, giving the mirth of Prince Hal and Falstaff, under the title of " The Bouncing Knight, or the Robbers Rob'd "; others are " The Grave-makers " scene from *Hamlet*, and, in Part II, "The merry conceited Humours of Bottom the Weaver " (the last was printed, alone, as " a comedy " in 1661 ; a copy is in the Bodleian). On the frontispiece of some copies is a curious engraving representing a stage with foot-lights, and several figures performing thereon : conspicuously towards the front are " Sʳ I. Falstafe" and the " Hostes," which have been copied for the vignette on the title-page of this edition of the " Centurie." The whole frontispiece is reproduced by Mr. Ebsworth in his "*Merry Drollery*," Boston, 1875 (see *ib.* p. 408, *note*). Mr. Halliwell reprinted these three drolls from Shakespere in two thin duodecimos in 1860; but the early date assigned by him to these compilations is uncertain.

For an interesting sketch of the history of " Drolls " and " Drolleries " see " *Westminster Drolleries*," edited by Rev. J. W. Ebsworth. Boston, 1875. Introduction, pp. xiii, xxii. L. T. S.]

THOMAS ISHAM, 1673.

20 [Auguft]. Ad nos perlatum eft Harrifimum focium fuum hiftrionem in fcena cafu occidiffe. Tragœdia Macbeth appellata erat; in qua Harriffius qui Macduffi perfonam gerebat focium fuum Macbethum debebat interficere.

Inter dimicandum autem accidit ut Macduffus Macbetham[1] pugionem in oculum infigeret quo vulnere exanimatus concidit ut ne potuerit pronunciare ultima verba quæ debuerat, " Farewell vane world & what is worfe ambition."

[1 Sic.]   *MS. Journal among the Isham papers at Lamport Hall, Northamptonshire.*

It is reported that Harris has killed his affociate aétor, in a fcene on the ftage, by accident. It was the tragedy called " Macbeth," in which Harris performed the part of Macduff, and ought to have flain his fellow-aétor, Macbeth; but during the fence it happened that Macduff pierced Macbeth in the eye, by which thruft he fell lifelefs, and could not bring out the laft words of his part.

The Journal of Thomas Isham, from 1 Nov. 1671 to 30 Sept. 1673, translated by Rev. Robert Isham, with an Introduction, &c., by Walter Rye. Norwich. 1875, p. 102. (Privately printed.)

[Thomas Isham, eldest son of Sir Justinian Isham, kept his journal in Latin for two years by desire of his father. At the date of the above entry he was a boy of sixteen. *Macbeth* was being acted at this time at "the Duke's Theatre" by Davenant's company, Betterton taking the part of Macbeth; Mrs. Betterton, Lady Macbeth; and Harris, Macduff. But as Betterton died in his bed in 1710, either the fatal ending to the accident was a mere report, or it may have happened to another actor temporarily substituted for Betterton; we know from Pepys that a man named Young acted for him on one occasion (see before, p. 320).

It is noteworthy that the edition of *Macbeth* brought out in 1673 [4to.] does not contain the words "Farewell vane world," &c.; they appear for the first time in the 4to. edition of 1674. "Macbeth; a Tragedy, acted at the Duke's Theatre" in 1673, was Shakespere's play unaltered, save by the insertion of the words adapted to Lock's music (which was published in 1672). But in 1674 came out "Macbeth, a Tragœdy. With all the alterations, amendments, additions, and new songs. As it's now Acted at the Dukes Theatre," and this version was repeated, with the same list of principal actors, which is also that given for the play of 1673, in 1687, 1695, and 1710.[1] Here Macbeth's last speech, referred to (but not exactly recollected) by Thomas Isham, is to be found: "Farewell vain World, and what's most vain in it, Ambition." Davenant then, it would seem, felt his way to the new *Macbeth*, and it may have been Shakespere's own play after all that Pepys sometimes saw between 1664 and 1668 (see before, p. 324); while, on the other hand, the entry in Isham's journal shows that Davenant's altered play was well known before its publication in 1674.

A curious Travesty of *Macbeth*, ridiculing the machinery, witches, and musical accompaniments lately introduced, was published in 1674, in the Epilogue to the farce *Empress of Morocco*. See *Notes & Queries*, 3rd Series, vol. xii. p. 63.

I am indebted to the kindness of Mr. Walter Rye for a copy of the journal in its English dress, and for procuring the extract from the original Latin MS. at Lamport. L. T. S.]

---

[1] *Macbeth* is not among the sixteen plays contained in Davenant's Works, published in 1674 by his widow; nor is it among Davenant's plays described by Langbaine in his *Account of English Dramatists*, 1691. John Downes, Prompter of Sir W. Davenant's company from 1662 to 1706, is the authority on which the altered play is ascribed to Davenant (none of the editions bear his name). See *Roscius Anglicanus*, by John Downes, 1708. Reprint of 1789, p. 42.

JOHN DRYDEN, 1674.

With joy we bring what our dead Authors writ,
And beg from you the value of their Wit;
That *Shakefpear's*, *Fletcher's*, and great *Johnfon's* claim,
May be Renew'd from thofe who gave them fame.

> *Prologue, to the Univerfity of Oxford,* 1674. *Spoken by Mr. Hart. Written by Mr. Dryden. Mifcellany Poems: By the moſt eminent hands.* 1684. *Part I, p.* 265.

SAMUEL SPEED, 1674.

Hunger hath hundreds brought
To *Dine with him,* and all not worth a Groat.
  * * * * *
The Guefts being met, and all prepar'd to eat,
What next fhould come, but what they want, their meat:
  * * * * *
Each fhrugs his fhoulder, walks from place to place,
Nor could they fcarce forbear to blame *his Grace:*
  * * * * *
Their food was thin; however none knew how
To fhew their ill refentments, but as men
Well-pacifi'd, agreed to come agen,
But ere that happy day was fully grown,
A dreadful Fire confumes the Kitchin down:
  * * * * *
On which the DUKE, to fhun a fcorching doom,
Perambulated to *Ben Johnfon's* Tomb,
Where *Shakefpear, Spencer, Cambden,* and the reft,
Once rifing Suns, are now fet in the Weft;
But ftill their luftres do fo brightly fhine,
That they invite our Worthies there to Dine.
  * * * * *
There our ingenious Train have thought it fit
To change their Dyet, and to Dine in Wit.
  * * * * *
Next day *his Grace,* and all his Guefts fo trim,
Do *Shakefpear* find, and then they feaft on him.

Fragmenta Circeris: or The Kings-Bench Scuffle, &c.
1674. [4to.] *The Legend of Duke Humphrey.*
Sign. F 1, back, F 3, F 3, back, F 4, F 4, back.

EDWARD PHILLIPS, 1675.

Wit, Ingenuity, and Learning in Verſe, even Elegancy it ſelf, though that comes neereſt, are one thing, true Native *Poetry* is another: in which there is a certain Air and Spirit, which perhaps the moſt Learned and judicious in other Arts do not perfectly apprehend, much leſs is it attainable by any Study or Induſtry; nay though all the Laws of *Heroic Poem*, all the Laws of *Tragedy* were exactly obſerved, yet ſtill this *tour entrejeant*,[1] this Poetic *Energie*, if I may ſo call it, would be required to give life to all the reſt, which ſhines through the rougheſt moſt unpoliſh't and antiquated Language, and may happly be wanting, in the moſt polite and reformed: let us obſerve *Spencer*, with all his Ruſtic, obſolete words, with all his rough-hewn clowterly Verſes; yet take him throughout, and we ſhall find in him a gracefull and Poetic Majeſty: in like manner *Shakeſpear*, in ſpight of all his unfiled expreſſions, his rambling and indigeſted Fancys, the laughter of the *Critical*, yet muſt be confeſs't a *Poet* above many that go beyond him in Literature ſome degrees. All this while it would be very unreaſonable that thoſe who have but attempted well, much more thoſe who have been learned, judicious or Ingenuous in Verſe ſhould be forgotten and left out of the circuit of *Poets*, in the larger acceptation. (*Preface, leaf* 14.)

* * * * * *

Benjamin Johnſon, the moſt learned, judicious and correct, generally ſo accounted, of our *Engliſh* Comedians, and the more to be admired for being ſo, for that neither the height of natural

---

[1] [Entrejeant = *entregent*, courtesy, civility, interchange; *tour entrejeant* is bad French, but Phillips seems to mean the force of spirit. L. T. S.]

parts, for he was no *Shakefphear,* nor the coft of Extraordinary Education; for he is reported but a Bricklayers Son, but his own proper Induftry and Addiction to Books advanct him to this perfection: (*The Modern Poets,* p. 19.)

* * * * *

Chriftopher Marlow, a kind of a fecond *Shakefphear* (whofe contemporary he was) not only becaufe like him he rofe from an Actor to be a maker of Plays, though inferiour both in Fame and Merit; but alfo becaufe in his begun Poem of *Hero* and *Leander,* he feems to have a refemblance of that clean and unfophifticated Wit, which is natural to that incomparable Poet; (p. 24.)

* * *

John Fletcher, one of the happy *Triumvirat* (the other two being *Johnfon* and *Shakefpear*) of the Chief Dramatic Poets of our Nation, in the laft foregoing Age, among whom there might be faid to be a fymmetry of perfection, while each excelled in his peculiar way: *Ben. Johnfon* in his elaborate pains and knowledge of Authors, *Shakefpear* in his pure vein of wit, and natural Poetic heighth; *Fletcher* in a courtly Elegance, and gentile familiarity of ftyle, and withal a wit and invention fo overflowing, that the luxuriant branches thereof were frequently thought convenient to be lopt off by his almoft infeparable Companion *Francis Beaumont.* (p. 108.)

* * * *

William Shakefpear, the Glory of the Englifh Stage; whofe nativity at *Stratford* upon *Avon,* is the higheft honour that Town can boaft of: from an Actor of Tragedies and Comedies, he became a *Maker;* and fuch a Maker, that though fome others may perhaps pretend to a more exact *Decorum* and *œconomie,* efpecially in Tragedy, never any exprefs't a more lofty and Tragic heighth; never any represented nature more purely to the life, and where the polifhments of Art are moft wanting, as probably his Learning was not extraordinary, he pleafeth with a certain

wild and native Elegance; and in all his Writings hath an
unvulgar ſtyle, as well in his *Venus and Adonis,* his *Rape of
Lucrece* and other various Poems, as in his Dramatics. (p. 194.)

> *Theatrum Poetarum.* 1675. [12mo.] *Preface.*
> *The Modern Poets.*

We have here *Shakesphear*, twice. It is not a misprint, but a recognised
form of spelling our great bard's name. We find it in some editions of
Camden's *Remaines Concerning Britaine:* e. g., the Ed. of 1614, which has
Shakespheare. (See ante, p. 20.) Again, in the deed under which Shakespeare purchased, for £440, the unexpired term in a moiety of the tithes of
Stratford, Old Stratford, Bishopton, and Welcombe, we find the name
spelt eleven times with the 'ph' and only once without.

JOHN DRYDEN, 1676.

Our Author by experience finds it true,
'Tis much more hard to pleafe himfelf than you:
   *   *   *
But fpite of all his pride a fecret fhame,
Invades his breaft at *Shakefpear's* facred name:
Aw'd when he hears his God-like *Romans* rage,
He, in a juft dafpair, would quit the Stage.

Prologue to Aureng-zebe, **a tragedy, by**
John Dryden. 1676.

SIR CARR SCROPE, 1677-8.

When *Shakefpear, Johnfon, Fletcher,* rul'd the Stage,
They took fo bold a Freedom with the Age,
That there was fcarfe a Knave, or Fool, in Town
Of any Note, but had his Picture fhown.

> *In Defense of Satyr.* (*Quoted by the Earl of Rochester in An Allusion to the Tenth Satyr of the First Book of Horace. See note below.*)
> *Poems on several occasions* [*By John Wilmot, Earl of Rochester*], 1685, *p.* 39.

This baronet was author of some poetical things, principally translations from Ovid (*e. g.*, the Epistle of *Sappho to Phaon*), some of which are printed in *Miscellany Poems*, 1684 (see Wood's *Fasti Oxonienses*, Part II, p. 294). The passage we have given corresponds to the first five lines of Horace's Satire iv of Book I, from which we infer that the *Defence of Satyr* is imitated from that satire. We do not know whether Sir Carr Scrope's entire poem is extant. In the Earl of Rochester's *Works* (Tonson), 1714, p. 87, will be found his *Allusion*, &c. ; and Scrope's verses mentioning Shakespeare are quoted at p. 96 (as well as in Rochester's *Poems on several Occasions*, 1685, p. 39). Rochester's reply at p. 100 ends with these personalities :

> "Half-witty and half-mad, and scarce half-brave,
> Half honest (which is very much a Knave)
> Made up of all these Halfs, thou can'st not pass
> For anything intirely but an *Ass.*"

Scrope died in 1680.

JOHN WILMOT, EARL OF ROCHESTER, 1678.

  A jeaft in fcorn points out, and hits the thing
More home, than the *Morofeſt* Satyrs ſting.
Shake-ſpear and *Johnſon* did herein excell,
And might in this be imitated well.

  * * * * *

But does not *Dryden* find ev'n *Johnſon* dull?
Fletcher and *Beaumont* uncorrect and full,
Of lewd Lines, as he calls 'em? *Shake-ſpear*'s ſtile
Stiff and affected; to his own the while,
Allowing all the juſtneſs, that his Pride
So arrogantly had to theſe deny'd?
And may not I, have leave impartially,
To ſearch and cenſure *Dryden*'s Works, and try,
If thoſe groſs faults his choice Pen does commit,
Proceed from want of Iudgment, or of Wit?
Or if his lumpiſh fancy does refuſe
Spirit and Grace to his looſe flattern Muſe?
Five hundred Verſes every Morning writ,
Prove him no more a Poet, than a Wit.

    *An Alluſion to the Tenth Satyr of the First Book
    of Horace*, [in] *Poems on several Occaſions*. 1685,
    pp. 36, 37. *Also in Works of John Earl of
    Rochester*, 1714, *pp.* 89, 93.

[The name Dryden is filled in from later editions, in that of 1685 it is only indicated by a D—. Rochester died in 1680.

In an *Epilogue* to be found in the edition of Rochester's Poems of 1696, p. 128 (but not in that of 1685), wherein he criticiſes the "awkward Actors" of the day, he says—

  "Through-pac'd ill Actors may, perhaps be cur'd;
  Half Players, like Half Wits, can't be endur'd.
  Yet these are they, who durſt expose the Age
  Of the great Wonder of the *English* Stage.
  Whom Nature seem'd to form for your Delight,
  And bid him speak, as she bid *Shakespear* write."

The side-note "Major Mohun" seems to point out that he was the "great wonder of the English stage" intended.   L. T. S.]

THOS. SHADWELL, 1678.

I am now to prefent your Grace with this Hiftory of *Timon*, which you were pleafed to tell me you liked, and it is the more worthy of you, fince it has the inimitable hand of *Shakefpear* in it, which never made more Mafterly ftrokes than in this.

The History of Timon of Athens, the Man-Hater, made into a Play. By Thos. Shadwell. 1678. [4to.] *Epistle Dedicatory.*

THOMAS RYMER, 1678.

I provided me some of those Master-pieces of Wit, so renown'd everywhere, and so edifying to the *Stage*: I mean the choicest and most applauded English Tragedies of this last age; * * * *Otheilo*, and *Julius Cæsar*, by *Shakespear*; and *Cataline* by Worthy *Ben*. (p. 2.)

he may be a true man, though awkward and unsightly, as the *Monster* in the *Tempest*. (p. 4.)

But I grow weary of this Tragedy: In the former I took *Latorch* by his mouth, and ranting air for a copy of *Cassius* in *Shakespear*: and that you may see *Arbaces* here, is not without his *Cassian* strokes [Beaumont & Fletcher's "King and no King."]

    Thus *Cassius* in *Shakespear*.

  Cass. . . . . Brutus *and* Cæsar! *what should there be in that* Cæsar!
Why should that name be sounded more than yours
Write them together, yours is as fair a name:
Sound them; it doth become the mouth as well:
Weigh them, it is as heavy; conjure with them, man:
Brutus *will start a Spirit as well as* Cæsar.
Now, in the name of all the Gods at once,
Upon what meat doth this our Cæsar *feed.*
That he is grown so great? .
    Thus *Arbaces*.
Arb. *I have liv'd*
To conquer men, and now am overthrown

*Only by words, Brother and Sifter: where
Have thofe words dwelling? I will find 'em out,
And utterly deftroy 'em: but they are
Not to be grafp'd: let 'em be men or beafts,
I will cut 'em from the earth; or Towns,
And I will raze 'em, and then blow 'em up:
Let 'em be Seas, and I will drink 'em off,
And yet have unquench'd fire within my breaft:
Let 'em be any thing but meerly voice.* (pp. 101-3.)

> *The Tragedies of The Last Age consider'd and Examin'd
> by the Practice of the Ancients, and by the Common
> sense of all Ages.* 1678. [*Sm.* 8*vo.*]

[Rymer cursorily mentions *Othello* twice (pp. 5, 141), but says his volume is big enough now: he afterwards wrote upon *Othello* and *Julius Cæsar* in "A Short View of Tragedy; Its Original, Excellency, and Corruption; with some Reflections on *Shakespear*, and other Practitioners for the Stage." 1693. This work was reviewed by Motteux in the *Gentleman's Journal* for December, 1692 (see what he says, quoted, after, p. 415); also by John Dunton in *The Compleat Library*, Dec. 1692, vol. ii. p. 58. "Our Author thinks," says Dunton, "that many of the *Tragical Scenes* in *Shakespear*, cried up so much for the Action, of which he gives some instances, may yet do better without such words as he uses." (p. 59.)

Rymer's criticism (if so it can be called) is entirely adverse to Shakespere. The best he can say of *Othello* is his concluding sentence:—"There is in this Play, some burlesk, some humour, and ramble of Comical Wit, some shew, and some *Mimickry* to divert the spectators: but the tragical part is, plainly none other, than a Bloody Farce, without salt or savour" (*Short View*, p. 146). And the following is a specimen of what he has to say upon *Julius Cæsar*:—"In the former Play, our Poet might be the bolder, the persons being all his own Creatures, and meer fiction. * * He might be familiar with *Othello* and *Iago*, as his own natural acquaintance: but *Cæsar* and *Brutus* were above his conversation. To put them in Fools Coats, and make them Jack-puddens in the *Shakespear* dress, is a *Sacriledge*, beyond anything in *Spelman*. The Truth is, this authors head was full of villanous, unnatural images, and history has only furnish'd him with great names, thereby to recommend them to the World" (p. 148). L. T. S.]

JOHN DRYDEN, 1678.

In my Stile I have profefs'd to imitate the Divine *Shakefpeare*; which that I might perform more freely, I have dis-incumber'd my felf from Rhyme. * * I hope I need not to explain my felf, that I have not Copy'd my Author fervilely : Words and Phrafes muft of neceffity receive a change in fucceeding Ages: but 't is almoft a Miracle that much of his Language remains fo pure ; and that he who began Dramatique Poetry amongft us, untaught by any, and, as *Ben Johnfon* tells us, without Learning, fhould by the force of his own Genius perform fo much, that in a manner he has left no praife for any who come after him.

Preface to All for Love; or, the World well Lost.
A Tragedy. 1678. *Sign. b* 4, *back*. [4*to*.]

JOHN DRYDEN, 1679.

The Poet *Æschylus* was held in the fame veneration by the *Athenians* of after Ages as *Shakefpear* is by us; * * * though the difficulties of altering are greater, and our reverence for *Shakefpear* much more juft, then that of the *Grecians* for *Æschylus*, * * * yet it muft be allow'd to the prefent Age, that the tongue in general is fo much refin'd fince *Shakefpear's* time, that many of his words, and more of his Phrafes, are fcarce intelligible. And of thofe which we underftand fome are ungrammatical, others courfe; and his whole ftile is [coarse] fo pefter'd with Figurative expreffions, that it is as affected as it is obfcure. 'Tis true, that in his later Plays he had worn off fomewhat of the ruft; but the Tragedy which I have undertaken to correct, was, in all probability, one of his firft endeavours on the Stage.

* * * * *

Shakefpeare, (as I hinted) in the Aprenticefhip of his Writing, model'd it into that Play, which is now call'd by the [Chaucer's story] name of *Troilus* and *Creffida;* but fo lamely is it left to us, that it is not divided into Acts: which fault I afcribe to the Actors, who Printed it after *Shakefpear's* death; and that too, fo carelefly, that a more uncorrect Copy I never faw. For the Play it felf, the Author feems to have begun it with fome fire; the Characters of *Pandarus* and *Therfites*, are promifing enough; but as if he grew weary of his tafk, after an Entrance or two, he lets 'em fall: and the later part of the Tragedy is nothing but a confufion of Drums and Trumpets, Excurfions and Alarms.

The chief perſons, who give name to the Tragedy, are left alive: *Creſſida* is falſe, and is not puniſh'd. Yet after all, becauſe the Play was *Shakeſpear's*, and that there appear'd in ſome places of it, the admirable Genius of the Author; I undertook to remove that heap of Rubbiſh, under which many excellent thoughts lay wholly bury'd. (Sign. A 4, back.)

* * * * *

I will not weary my Reader with the Scenes which are added [&c.]: but I cannot omit the laſt Scene in it, which is almoſt half the Act, betwixt *Troilus* and *Hector*. The occaſion of raiſing it was hinted to me by Mr. *Betterton:* the contrivance and working of it was my own. They who think to do me an injury, by ſaying that it is an imitation of the Scene betwixt *Brutus* and *Caſſius*, do me an honour, by ſuppoſing I could imitate the incomparable *Shakeſpear:* but let me add, that if *Shakeſpears* Scene, or that faulty copy of it in *Amintor* and *Melantius* had never been, yet *Euripides* had furniſh'd me with an excellent example in his *Iphigenia*, between *Agamemnon* and *Menelaus:* and from thence indeed, the laſt turn of it is borrow'd. The occaſion which *Shakeſpear*, *Euripides*, and *Fletcher*, have all taken, is the ſame; grounded upon Friendſhip: and the quarrel of two virtuous men, raiſed by natural degrees, to the extremity of paſſion, is conducted in all three, to the declination of the ſame paſſion; and concludes with a warm renewing of their Friendſhip. But the particular ground-work which *Shakeſpear* has taken, is incomparably the beſt: Becauſe he has not only choſen two the greateſt Heroes of their Age; but has likewiſe intereſted the Liberty of *Rome*, and their own honors, who were the redeemers of it, in this debate. And if he has made *Brutus*, who was naturally a patient man, to fly into exceſs at firſt; let it be remembered in his defence, that juſt before, he has receiv'd the news of *Portia's* death, whom the Poet on purpoſe neglecting a little Chronology, ſuppoſes to have dy'd

before *Brutus*, only to give him an occasion of being more easily
exasperated. Add to this, that the injury he had receiv'd from
Cassius, had long been brooding in his mind; and that a melancholy man, upon consideration of an affront, especially from a
Friend, would be more eager in his passion, than he who had
given it, though [the latter be] naturally more cholerick. (Sign. a.)

* * * * *

How defective *Shakespear* and *Fletcher* have been in all their
Plots, Mr. *Rymer* has discover'd in his *Criticisms*: * *

The difference between *Shakespear* and *Fletcher* in their
Plotting seems to be this; that *Shakespear* generally moves more
terror, and *Fletcher* more compassion: For the first had a more
Masculine, a bolder and more fiery Genius; the Second a more
soft and Womanish. In the mechanic beauties of the Plot,
which are the Observation of the three Unities, Time, Place, and
Action, they are both deficient; but *Shakespear* most. *Ben
Johnson* reform'd those errors in his Comedies, yet one of *Shakespear's* was Regular before him: which is, *The Merry Wives of
Windsor*. For what remains concerning the design, you are to
be refer'd to our English Critic. (Sign. a 3.)

* * * * *

A character, or that which distinguishes one man from all
others, cannot be suppos'd to consist of one particular Virtue, or
Vice, or passion only; but 't is a composition of qualities which
are not contrary to one another in the same person: thus the
same man may be liberal and valiant, but not liberal and
covetous; so in a Comical character, or humour, (which is an
inclination to this, or that particular folly) *Falstaff* is a lyar, and
a coward, a Glutton, and a Buffon, because all these qualities
may agree in the same man; (Sign. a 4.) * * * 'Tis one
of the excellencies of *Shakespear*, that the manners of his persons
are generally apparent; and you see their bent and inclinations
* * * Our *Shakespear*, having ascrib'd to *Henry the Fourth*
the character of a King, and of a Father, gives him the perfect

manners of each Relation, when either he tranfacts with his Son, or with his Subjects. (Sign. a 4, back.)

* * * * * *

To return once more to *Shakefpear*; no man ever drew fo many characters, or generally diftinguifhed 'em better from one another, excepting only *Johnfon:* I will inftance but in one, to fhow the copioufnefs of his Invention; 'tis that of *Calyban*, or the Monfter in the *Tempeft*. He feems to have created a perfon which was not in Nature, a boldnefs which at firft fight would appear intolerable: for he makes him a Species of himfelf, begotten by an *Incubus* on a Witch; but this as I have elfewhere prov'd, is not wholly beyond the bounds of credibility, at leaft the vulgar ftile believe it. We have the feparated notions of a fpirit, and of a Witch; (and Spirits according to *Plato*, are vefted with a fubtil body; according to fome of his followers, have different Sexes) therefore as from the diftinct apprehenfions of a Horfe, and of a Man, Imagination has form'd a *Centaur*, fo from thofe of an *Incubus* and a *Sorcerefs*, *Shakefpear* has produc'd his Monfter. Whether or no his Generation can be defended, I leave to Philofophy; but of this I am certain, that the Poet has moft judicioufly furnifhed him with a perfon, a Language, and a character, which will fuit him, both by Fathers and Mothers fide: he has all the difcontents, and malice of a Witch, and of a Devil; befides a convenient proportion of the deadly fins; Gluttony, Sloth, and Luft, are manifeft; the dejectednefs of a flave is likewife given him, and the ignorance of one bred up in a Defart Ifland. His perfon is monftrous, as he is the product of unnatural Luft; and his language is as hobgoblin as his perfon: in all things he is diftinguifhed from other mortals. The characters of *Fletcher* are poor and narrow, in comparifon of *Shakefpears*; I remember not one which is not borrow'd from him; unlefs you will except that ftrange mixture of a man in the *King and no King:* So that in this part *Shakefpear* is generally worth our Imitation; and to imitate *Fletcher* is but to Copy after him who was a Copyer. (Sign. b.)

* * * * * *

If *Shakefpear* be allow'd, as I think he muft, to have made his Characters diftinct, it will eafily be infer'd that he underftood the nature of the Paffions: becaufe it has been prov'd already, that confuf'd paffions make undiftinguifhable Characters: yet I cannot deny that he has his failings; but they are not fo much in the paffions themfelves, as in his manner of expreffion: he often obfcures his meaning by his words, and fometimes makes it unintelligible. I will not fay of fo great a Poet, that he diftinguifh'd not the blown puffy ftile, from true fublimity; but I may venture to maintain that the fury of his fancy often tranfported him, beyond the bounds of Judgment, either in coyning of new words and phrafes, or racking words which were in ufe, into the violence of a Catachrefis: 'Tis not that I would explode the ufe of Metaphors from paffions, for *Longinus* thinks 'em neceffary to raife it; but to ufe 'em at every word, to fay nothing without a Metaphor, a Simile, an Image, or defcription, is I doubt to fmell a little too ftrongly of the Bufkin. I muft be forc'd to give an example of expreffing paffion figuratively; but that I may do it with refpect to *Shakefpear*, it fhall not be taken from anything of his: 'tis an exclamation againft Fortune, quoted in his *Hamlet*, but written by fome other Poet.

[Out, out, thou ftrumpet fortune, &c., down to As low as to the Fiends. Act II. sc. ii. l. 515—519.]

And immediately after, fpeaking of *Hecuba*, when *Priam* was kill'd before her eyes:

[The mobbled Queen, &c., down to And paffion in the Gods. Act II. sc. ii. ll. 524—541.]

What a pudder is here kept in raifing the expreffion of trifling thoughts. (Sign. B 2.)

* * * * * *

But *Shakefpear* does not often thus; for the paffions in his

Scene between *Brutus* and *Caſſius* are extreamly natural, the thoughts are ſuch as ariſe from the matter, and the expreſſion of 'em not vicıouſly figurative. I cannot leave this Subject before I do juſtice to that Divine Poet, by giving you one of his paſſionate deſcriptions : 't is of *Richard* the Second when he was depos'd, and led in Triumph through the Streets of *London* by *Henry* of *Bullingbrook :* the painting of it is ſo lively, and the words ſo moving, that I have ſcarce read any thing comparable to it, in any other language. Suppoſe you have ſeen already the fortunate Uſurper paſſing through the croud, and follow'd by the ſhouts and acclamations of the people; and now behold King *Richard* entring upon the Scene : conſider the wretchedneſs of his condition, and his carriage in it ; and refrain from pitty if you can.

[As in a Theatre, &c., down to have pity'd him. *Rich. II*, Act V. sc. i. ll. 23—36.] (Sign. b 3.)

* * * * * *

If *Shakeſpear* were ſtript of all the Bombaſt in his paſſions, and dreſs'd in the moſt vulgar words, we ſhould find the beauties of his thoughts remaining ; if his embroideries were burnt down, there would ſtill be ſilver at the bottom of the melting-pot : but I fear (at leaſt, let me fear it for my ſelf) that we who Ape his ſounding words, have nothing of his thought, but are all out-ſide ; there is not ſo much as a dwarf within our Giants cloaths. Therefore, let not *Shakeſpear* ſuffer for our ſakes ; 't is our fault, who ſucceed him in an Age which is more refin'd, if we imitate him ſo ill, that we coppy his failings only, and make a virtue of that in our Writings, which in his was an imperfection.

For what remains, the excellency of that Poet was, as I have ſaid, in the more manly paſſions ; *Fletcher*'s in the ſofter : *Shakeſpear* writ better betwixt man and man ; *Fletcher*, betwixt man and woman : conſequently, the one deſcrib'd friendſhip better ; the other love : yet *Shakeſpear* taught *Fletcher* to write love ; and *Juliet*, and *Deſdemona*, are Originals. 'T is true, the

Scholar had the softer soul; but the Master had the kinder.
Friendship is both a virtue, and a Passion essentially; love is a
passion only in its nature, and is not a virtue but by Accident:
good nature makes Friendship; but effeminacy Love. *Shakespeare* had an Universal mind, which comprehended all Characters
and Passions; *Fletcher* a more confin'd, and limited: for though
he treated love in perfection, yet Honour, Ambition, Revenge,
and generally all the stronger Passions, he either touch'd not, or
not Masterly. To conclude all; he was a Limb of *Shakespear*.
(Sign. b 3, back.)

> *Troilus and Cressida, or, Truth found too late. A Tragedy, by
> John Dryden.* 1679. *Preface (The Grounds of Criticism in
> Tragedy).*

JOHN DRYDEN, 1679.

See, my lov'd *Britons*, fee your *Shakefpeare* rife,
An awful ghoft confefs'd to human eyes!
Unnam'd, methinks, diftinguifh'd I had been
From other fhades, by this eternal green,
About whofe wreaths the vulgar Poets ftrive,
And with a touch, their wither'd Bays revive.
Untaught, unpractis'd, in a barbarous Age,
I found not, but created firft the Stage.
And, if I drain'd no Greek or Latin ftore,
'Twas, that my own abundance gave me more.
On foreign trade I needed not rely,
Like fruitful Britain, rich without fupply.
In this my rough-drawn Play, you fhall behold
Some Mafter-ftrokes, fo manly and fo bold,
That h, who meant to alter, found 'em fuch,
He fhook; and thought it Sacrilege to touch.
Now, where are the Succeffors to my name?
What bring they to fill out a Poet's fame?
Weak, fhort-liv'd iffues of a feeble Age;
Scarce living to be Chriften'd on the Stage!

*Troilus and Cressida or **Truth found too late**, by John Dryden. 1679. Prologue, Spoken by Betterton representing the Ghost of Shakespeare.*

As Dryden here calls up the Ghost of Shakespeare, so does Bevill Higgons, a score of years later, call up "The Ghosts of Shakespear and Dryden Crown'd with Lawrel" to speak his prologue to George Granville Lord Lansdowne's adaptation of *the Merchant of Venice*. See "*The Jew of Venice*: a Comedy. As it is acted at the Theatre in Little Lincolns-Inn-Fields. By His Majesty's Servants." 1713 (1st Ed. 1701). This is perhaps the worst of the series of plays adapted from Shakespeare.

JOHN MARTYN,
HENRY HERRINGMAN, } 1679.
RICHARD MARIOT,

If our care and endeavours to do our Authors right (in an incorrupt and genuine Edition of their Works) and thereby to gratifie and oblige the Reader, be but requited with a fuitable entertainment, we fhall be encourag'd to bring *Ben Johnfon*'s two volumes into one, and publifh them in this form; and alfo to reprint Old *Shakefpear* : both which are defigned by

yours,
Ready to ferve you,

The Bookfellers to the Reader. Prefixed to the Second Edition of Beaumont and Fletcher's Works. 1679. [*Fo.*]

JOHN WILMOT, EARL OF ROCHESTER,
? 1679 OR 1680.

[Begins one of his letters to Hon. Henry Savile thus,—]

Harry,

If Sack and Sugar be a Sin, God *help the Wicked;* was the faying of a merry fat Gentleman, who liv'd in Days of *Yore,* lov'd a Glafs of *Wine,* wou'd be merry with a Friend, and fometimes had an unlucky Fancy for a Wench.

Works of John, Earl of Rochester. Familiar Letters, 1714. *p.* 134.

[This letter is not itself dated, but several in the collection of those addressed to Savile are dated either 1679 or 1680. Falstaff's saying is in 1 *Henry IV,* Act II. sc. iv. l. 450. L. T. S.]

NAHUM TATE, 1680.

What I have already afferted concerning the neceffity of Learning to make a compleat Poet, may feem inconfiftent with my Reverence for our *Shakefpear*.

——*Cujus amor femper mihi crefcit in Horas.*

I confefs I cou'd never yet get a true account of his Learning, and am apt to think it more than Common Report allows him. I am fure he never touches on a Roman Story, but the Perfons, the Paffages, the Manners, the Circumftances, the Ceremonies, all are Roman. And what Relifhes yet of a more exact Knowledge, you do not only fee a Roman in his Heroe, but the particular Genius of the Man, without the leaft miftake of his Character, given him by their beft Hiftorians. You find his *Anthony* in all the Defects and Excellencies of his Mind, a Souldier, a Reveller, Amorous, fometimes Rafh, fometimes Confiderate, with all the various Emotions of his Mind. His *Brutus* agen has all the Conftancy, Gravity, Morality, Generofity, Imaginable, without the leaft Mixture of private Intereft or Irregular Paffion. He is true to him, even in the imitation of his Oratory, the famous Speech which he makes him deliver, being exactly agreeable to his manner of expreffing himfelf; of which we have this account, *Facultas ejus erat Militaris & Bellicis accommodata Tumultubus.*

But however it far'd with our Author for Book-Learning, 'tis evident that no man was better ftudied in Men and Things, the moft ufeful Knowledge for a *Dramatic* Writer. He was a moft diligent Spie upon Nature, trac'd her through her darkeft

Receſſes, pictur'd her in her juſt Proportion and Colours; in which Variety 'tis impoſſible that all ſhou'd be equally pleaſant, 'tis ſufficient that all be proper.

Of his abſolute Command of the Paſſions, and Maſtery in diſtinguiſhing of Characters, you have a perfect Account in that moſt excellent Criticiſm before, *Troylus* and *Creſſida:* If any Man be a lover of *Shakeſpear* and covet his Picture, there you have him drawn to the Life; but for the Eternal Plenty of his Wit on the ſame Theam, I will only detain you with a few inſtances of his Reflections on the Perſon, and Cruel Practices of *Richard* the Third. [Several quotations from that play follow.]

The Loyal General, a Tragedy, 1680. *Addreſs to Edward Tayler. Sign. A 4, back.*

[The spirit of Tate's criticism of Shakespere's historical characters is exactly opposite to that of Rymer, noticed before, p. 367.

Tate "new-modelled" several of the plays of Shakespere, for whom he professed such reverence; from two of these, quotations are given on pp. 390—392; another is *The History of King Richard the Second*, which was acted under the name of *The Sicilian Usurper*, and printed 1681; having been prohibited on the stage on the third day, he vindicates himself in the dedication by falling back upon "the immortal spirit of its first-Father." "I fell upon the new-modelling of this Tragedy, (as I had just before done on the *History of King Lear*) charm'd with the many Beauties I discover'd in it, which I knew wou'd become the Stage; with as little design of Satyr on present Transactions, as *Shakespear* himself that wrote this Story before this Age began." He goes on, "Our *Shakespear* in this Tragedy, bated none of his characters an Ace of the Chronicle; he took care to shew 'em no worse Men than They were, but represents them never a jot better." (sign. A), and he proceeds to point out some of his own alterations. L. T. S.]

THOMAS OTWAY, 1680.

Our *Shakefpear* wrote too in an age as bleft,
The happieft poet of his time, and beft,
A gracious Prince's favour chear'd his Mufe,
A conftant Favour he ne'er fear'd to lofe.
Therefore he wrote with Fancy unconfin d,
And Thoughts that were Immortal as his Mind.
And from the Crop of his luxuriant Pen
E'er fince fucceeding Poets humbly glean.
Though much the moft unworthy of the Throng,
Our this day's Poet fears h'has done him wrong.
Like greedy Beggars that fteal Sheaves away,
You'll find h'has rifl'd him of half a Play.
Amidft this bafer Drofs you'll fee it fhine
Moft beautiful, amazing, and Divine.
To fuch low Shifts of late are Poets worn,
Whilft we both Wit's and *Cæfar's* abfence mourn.
Oh! when will He and Poetry return ?
When fhall we there again behold him fit,
Midft fhining Boxes and a Courtly Pit,
The Lord of Hearts and Prefident of Wit?

The History and fall of Caius Marius [altered from
Romeo and Juliet.] 1692. Prologue. [4to.]

SIR WILLIAM TEMPLE, 1680—1690.

I do not wonder * * that fo many fhould cry, and with down right Tears, at fome Tragedies of *Shake-fpear*, and fo many more fhould feel fuch Turns or Curdling of their Blood, upon the reading or hearing fome excellent Pieces of Poetry.

* * * * *

Shakefpear was the firft that opened this Vein [the vein of Humour] upon our Stage, which has run fo freely and fo pleafantly ever fince, that I have often wondered to find it appear fo little upon any others, being a Subject fo proper for them ; fince Humour is but a Picture of particular Life, as Comedy is of general.

Miscellanea, Second Part. Essay IV, On Poetry. 1690. *pp.* 12, 54. [8*vo.*] [3rd *edition*, 1692, *pp.* 314, 356.]

JOHN AUBREY, about 1680.

Mr William Shakefpeare was wont to goe into Warwickfhire once a yeare, and did commonly in his journey lye at this houfe in Oxon. [the Crowne Taverne kept by John Davenant] where he was exceedingly refpected. [I have heard parfon Robert fay that Mr. Wm. Shakefpeare having given him a hundred kiffes][1] Now Sr. Wm. would fometimes, when he was pleafant over a glaffe of wine with his moft intimate friends, —e.g. Sam: Butler, (author of Hudibras) &c.,—fay, that it feemed to him that he writt with the very fpirit that Shakefpear [did], and was[2] contented enough to be thought his Son: he would tell them the ftory as above.

* * * *

Mr. William Shakefpear was borne at Stratford upon Avon, in the County of Warwick; his father was a Butcher, and I have been told heretofore by fome of the neighbours, that when he was a boy he exercifed his father's Trade, but when he kill'd a Calfe he would doe it in a high ftyle, and make a Speech. There was at that time another Butcher's fon in this Towne that was held not at all inferior to him for a naturall witt, his acquaintance and coetanean, but dyed young. This Wm. being inclined naturally to Poetry and acting, came to London, I gueffe, about 18: and was an Actor at one of the Play-houfes, and did act exceedingly well: now B. Johnfon was never a good Actor, but an excellent Inftructor. He began early to make effayes at Dramatique Poetry, wch at that time was very lowe, and his Playes tooke well. He was a handfome well fhap't man; very good

[1] [The words between [ ] are crossed through with the pen in the MS. L. T. S.]
[2] [The word "seemed" is written above the word "was" in the MS. L. T. S.]

company, and of a very readie and pleafant fmooth Witt. The Humour of . . . the Conftable, in *a Midfomer-Night's Dreame*, he happened to take at Grenden,[1] in Bucks, wch is the roade from London to Stratford, and there was living that Conftable about 1642, when I firſt came to Oxon. Mr. Jos. Howe is of y^t parifh, and knew him. Ben Johnfon and he did gather Humours of men dayly wherever they came. One time as he was at the Tavern, at Stratford fup*er* Avon, one Combes, an old rich Ufurer, was to be buryed, he makes there this extemporary Epitaph,

> Ten in the Hundred the Devill allowes,
> But Combes will have twelve, he fweares and vowes:
> If any one afkes who lies in this Tombe,
> 'Hoh!' quoth the Devill, ''Tis my John o Combe.'

He was wont to goe to his native Country once a yeare. I thinke I have been told that he left 2 or 300 ^li *per* annum there and thereabout to a fifter. I have heard S^r Wm. Davenant and Mr. Thomas Shadwell (who is counted the beft Comœdian we have now) fay, that he had a moſt prodigious Witt, and did admire his naturall parts beyond all other Dramaticall writers. He was wont to fay, That he never blotted out a line in his life; fayd Ben Johnfon, 'I wifh he had blotted out a thoufand.' His Comœdies will remaine witt as long as the Englifh tongue is underftood; for that he handles *mores hominu*m : now our prefent writers reflect fo much upon particular perfons, and coxcombeities, that 20 yeares hence they will not be underftood. Though, as Ben Johnfon fayes of him, that he had but little Latine and leffe Greek, He underftood Latine pretty well : for he had been in his yonger yeares a Schoolmafter in the Countrey.[2]

Aubrey Manuscripts: No. 4, pp. 27 & 78, Bodleian Library, Oxford. Printed in "Letters written by Eminent persons." 1813. Vol. II. pp. 303, 537. Fac simile of MS. of the second extract in Halliwells Works of Shakespeare, 1853, [fol.] Vol. I. p. 76.

[1] I thinke it was Midsomer night that he happened to lye there.
[2] From Mr. Beeston.

JOHN AUBREY, about 1680.

We have the testimony of Pope to the prevalence of this story in his day. We read under date 1728-30 in Rev. Joseph Spence's *Anecdotes, Observations, and Characters* (Ed. 1820, p. 23),

"That notion of Sir William Davenant being more than a poetical child only of Shakespeare was common in town, and Sir William himself seemed fond of having it taken for truth."

Again, under date 1742-3, we have the following anecdote attributed to Pope (p. 269):

"Shakspeare, in his frequent journeys between London and his native place, Stratford-upon-Avon, used to lie at Davenant's, the Crown, in Oxford. He was very well acquainted with Mrs. Davenant: and her son, afterwards Sir William, was supposed to be more nearly related to him than as a godson only. One day, when Shakespeare was just arrived, and the boy sent for from school to him, a head of one of the Colleges, (who was pretty well acquainted with the affairs of the family), met the child running home, and asked him, whither he was going in so much haste? the boy said, 'to my Godfather, Shakespeare'—'Fie, child,' (says the old gentleman), 'why are you so superfluous? have you not learned yet that you should not use the name of God in vain?'"

Probably this story is but a renovated version of one recorded by John Taylor (*Workes*, Ed. 1630, ii. 184): where the "godfather" in question was "goodman Digland the gardiner."

Oldys writes:

"If tradition may be trusted, Shakespeare often baited at the Crown Inn or tavern in Oxford, in his journey to and from London. The landlady was a woman of great beauty and sprightly wit; and her husband, Mr. John Davenant (afterwards mayor of that city), a grave, melancholy man; who, as well as his wife, used much to delight in Shakespeare's pleasant company. Their son, young Will. Davenant (afterwards Sir William), was then a little school-boy in the town, of about seven or eight years old, and so fond also of Shakspeare, that, whenever he heard of his arrival, he would fly from school to see him. One day an old townsman observing the boy running homeward almost out of breath, asked him whither he was posting in that heat and hurry. He answered to see his *god*-father Shakspeare. 'There is good boy,' said the other, 'but have a care that you don't take *God's* name in vain.' This story Mr. Pope told me at the Earl of Oxford's table . . . . . . and he quoted Mr. Betterton the player for his authority."
—Memoir of Wm. Oldys, together with his Diary, Choice Notes, &c., reprinted from *Notes and Queries*, 1862. Choice Notes, p. 44.

"A PERSON OF HONOUR," 1681.

I can't, without infinite ingratitude to the Memory of thofe excellent perfons, omit the firft Famous Mafters in't, of our Nation, Venerable *Shakefpear* and the great *Ben Johnfon*: I have had a particular kindnefs always for moft of *Shakefpear's* Tragedies, and for many of his Comedies, and I can't but fay that I can never enough admire his Stile (confidering the time he writ in) and the great alteration that has been in the Refineing of our Language fince) for he has expreffed himfelf fo very well in't that 'tis generally approv'd of ftill; and for maintaining of the Characters of the perfons, defign'd, I think none ever exceeded him.

"*An Essay on Dramatick Poetry*," *appended to Amaryllis to Tityrus. Being the First Heroick Harangue of the excellent pen of Monsieur Scudery. A Witty and Pleasant Novel. Englished by a Person of Honour.* 1681. *pp.* 66, 67. [*Sm: 8vo.*]

Georges de Scudery and his sister were once popular French writers, whose works were translated for the English public. The former wrote a work called *Curia Politiæ*, and many poems and plays, as *Alaric, L'Amour Tyrannique, La Mort de César*, &c. Boileau thus refers to the brother and sister:

"Bien heureux Scudery, dont la fertile plume
Peut tous les mois sans peine enfanter un volume."

[The above quotation is, however, from the Essay on Dramatic Poetry, which is evidently from the pen of the translator, and not written by Scudery. L. T. S.]

BALLAD ON THE DUKE OF MONMOUTH, 1681.

 This Duke. . . . . .
Though now he cuts his Capers high,
He may with *Falſtaff* one day cry,
(When Age hath ſet him in the Stocks)
A Pox of my Gout, a Gout on my Pox.[1]
 [Yet that Fat Knight with all his Guts,
That were not then ſo ſweet as Nuts,
Though oft he boldly fought and winkt,
[F]Led *Harry M[onmouth]*—by Inſtinct[2];
Reveres a Buckram Prince of *Wales*,
His great Heart quops, his Courage fails.]
 The Lyon Rampant is too wiſe,
To touch a Prince, though in Diſguiſe:
Much leſs a Prince ſo kind and civil,
To touch a Kingdom for Kings-Evil.

A Canto on the new Miracle wrought by the D[uke] of M[onmouth], in curing a young Wench of the King's Evil.
Bagford Collection, III. 78; *reprinted for the Ballad Society by Rev. J. W. Ebsworth in the Bagford Ballads, pp.* 803, 804.

[Mr. Ebsworth has restored the six lines in [ ] from a copy of the ballad in "Loyal Poems," 1685, in his own collection.

As to "quops," he says, "it sometimes seems to signify *throbs* or *stirs*, but here perhaps it means the contrary, ceases to throb." The allusions are to the First and Second plays of *Henry Fourth*. 1, Second Part, Act i. sc. 2. 2 and 3, First Part, Act ii. sc. 4.

(This extract is due to Mr. Furnivall.) L. T. S.]

HERACLITUS RIDENS, 1681.

Jest. Then here are a world of Irons in the fire, 'tis well if fome of 'em do not burn, and fome-body do not burn their fingers, but let the Bees look to that, as honeſt Sir *John Falſtaff* fays.

Heraclitus Ridens; a Dialogue between Jeſt and Earnest, concerning the Times. No. 2, Feb. 8, 1681.

[The above conclusion by *Jest* comes at the end of a number of statements (put in the form of Queries) on the political and religious affairs of the day. L. T. S.]

J. CROWN, 1681.

To day we bring old gather'd Herbs, 'tis true,
But fuch as in fweet *Shakefpears* Garden grew.
And all his Plants immortal you efteem,
Your Mouthes are never out of tafte with him.
Howe're to make your Appetites more keen,
Not only oyly Words are fprinkled in;
But what to pleafe you gives us better hope,
A little Vineger againft the Pope.

For by his feeble Skill 'tis built alone,
The Divine *Shakefpear* did not lay one ftone.

Henry the Sixth, by J. Crown. [4to.] 1681. Prologues to Parts I and II.

[Crown was evidently a great admirer of Shakespere. In the Prologue to his *Thyestes*, a *tragedy*, 1681, he says, to spite the critics,—

"You upstart Sectaries of wit cry down
What has for twenty ages had renown.
The world will ask (in scorn of your dispraise)
Where was your wit, Sirs, before *Shakespears* days?
Mo matter where, we'l say y'have excellent sence,
If you will please to let us get your pence.
We like the Pope regard not much your praise,
He tickets sells for Heaven, and we for Plays." L. T. S.]

NAHUM TATE, 1681.

Nothing but the Power of your Perſwaſion, and my Zeal for all the Remains of *Shakeſpear*, cou'd have wrought me to ſo bold an Undertaking. I found that the New-modelling of this Story, wou'd force me ſometimes on the difficult Taſk of making the chiefeſt Perſons ſpeak ſomething like their Character, on Matter whereof I had no Ground in my Author. *Lear's* real and *Edgar's* pretended Madneſs have ſo much of *extravagant Nature* (I know not how elſe to expreſs it) as cou'd never have ſtarted but from our *Shakeſpear's* Creating Fancy. The Images and Language are ſo odd and ſurprizing, and yet ſo agreeable and proper, that whilſt we grant that none but *Shakeſpear* cou'd have form'd ſuch Conceptions; yet we are ſatiſfied that they were the only Things in the World that ought to be ſaid on thoſe Occaſions.

Dedication ("*To my esteemed Friend Tho. Boteler, Esq.*") *of the History of King Lear.* 1681.

NAHUM TATE, 1681.

he that did this Evenings Treat prepare,
Bluntly refolv'd before-hand to declare
Your Entertainment fhould be moſt old Fare.
Yet hopes, fince in rich *Shakefpear's* foil it grew,
'Twill relifh yet, with thofe whofe Taſts are True,
And his Ambition is to pleafe a Few.
If then this Heap of Flow'rs fhall chance to wear
Frefh Beauty in the Order they now bear,
E'en this [is] *Shakefpear's* Praife; each Ruftick knows
'Mongft plenteous Flow'rs a Garland to Compofe,
Which ſtrung by his courfe Hand may fairer Show
But 'twas a Power Divine firſt made 'em Grow.

*Prologue to the History of King Lear,
by N. Tate.* 1681. [4*to.*]

[Charles Knight, in his chapter on *King Lear* (*Studies of Shakspere*, 1849, p. 344), says that notwithstanding the metamorphosis and degradation of that play by Tate, whom he calls an "English word-joiner," that "his 'Lear' was ever the 'Lear' of the playhouse, until Mr. Macready ventured upon a modern heresy in favour of Shakspere." See *note* to p. 380. L. T. S.]

NAHUM TATE, 1682.

I impofe not on your Lordfhip's Protection a work meerly of my own Compiling; having in this Adventure Launcht out in *Shakefpear's* Bottom. Much of what is offered here, is Fruit that grew in the Richnefs of his Soil; and what ever the Superftructure prove, it was my good fortune to build upon a Rock.

> *Ingratitude of a Commonwealth, or the Fall of Caius*
> *Martius Coriolanus.* 1682. [4*to.*]
> *Dedication to Charles, Lord Herbert.* Sign. *A* 2.

SIR GEORGE RAYNSFORD, 1682.

Our Author do's with modefty fubmit
To all the Loyal Criticks of the Pit,
    *   *   *   *   *
Yet he prefumes we may be fafe to Day,
Since *Shakefpear* gave Foundation to the Play:
'Tis alter'd—and his facred Ghoft appeaf'd;
I wifh you All as eafily were pleaf'd:

> *Prologue to the above.*

ALEXANDER RADCLIFFE, 1682.

To *Play-Houſes* thou now ſhalt bid adieu,
Although the Farce be gay enough and new,
Ne're before Acted, brings thee not among
Thoſe that ſell Two and Six-pence for a Song.
No Idle Scenes fit buſie times as theſe,
Inſtead of *Playes* we now converſe with *Pleas*;
And 't's thought the laſt do favour more of Wit,
For thoſe have Plots to ſpend, but theſe to get.
(Give way, Great *Shakeſpear*, and immortal *Ben*,
To *Doe* and *Roe*, *John Den* and *Richard Fen*.)

*The Sword's Farewell, contained in The Ramble: an
Anti-Heroick Poem.* 1682. *pp.* 118, 119.

JOHN SHEFFIELD, EARL OF MULGRAVE, 1682.

Plato and *Lucian* are the beft remains
Of all the wonders which this art contains ;
Yet to our felves we juftice muft allow,
Shakefpear and *Fletcher* are the wonders now :
Confider them, and read them o're and o're,
Go fee them play'd, then read them as before.
For though in many things they grofly fail,
Over our Paffions ftill they fo prevail,
That our own grief by theirs is rockt afleep,
The dull are forc'd to feel, the wife to weep.
Their Beauties Imitate, avoid their faults ;

* * * *

The other way's too common, oft we fee
A fool derided by as bad as he ;
Hawks fly at nobler game, but in his way,
A very *Owl* may prove a Bird of prey ;
Some *Poets* fo will one poor Fop devour ;
But to Collect, like Bees from every flower,
Ingredients to compofe that precious juice,
Which ferves the world for pleafure and for ufe,
In fpite of faction this will favour get,
But *Falftaff* feems unimitable yet.

An Essay upon Poetry. 1682. [4*to.*] *pp.* 14 & 16.

Sheffield was Earl of Mulgrave from 1658 to 1694, and not Duke of Buckinghamshire till 1703.

JOHN BANKS, 1682.

I fay not this to derogate from thofe excellent Perfons, who, I ought to believe, have written more to pleafe their Audiences, than themfelves; but to perfwade them, as *Homer,* and our *Shakefpear* did, to Immortalize the Places where they were born;

*Virtue Betray'd, or Anna Bullen: a Tragedy.
Dedication,* 1682—92.

CHARLES DE ST. DENIS, SIEUR DE ST. EVREMOND, 1682.

J'ai toujours eu fur la confcience d'avoir foupçonné que vos Yeux pouvoient f'ufer à la Baffete. * * vôtre Beauté eft incapable de recevoir aucune altération * * N'apprehendez pas, Madame, de perdre vos charmes à *Newmarket;* montez à cheval dez cinq heures du matin ; galopez dans la foule à toutes les Courfes qui fe feront ; enroüez-vous a crier plus haut que Mylord *Thomond* aux Combats des Coqs ; ufez vos poûmons à pouffer des *Done* à droit et à gauche ; entendez tous les foirs ou la Comédie de Henri VIII * ou celle de la Reine Elizabeth ; † crevez-vous d'Huîtres à fouper, & paffez les nuits entiéres fans dormir ; vôtre Beauté qui eft échapée à la Baffete de Monfieur *Morin,* fe fauvera bien des fatigues de *Newmarket.*

* Composée par le fameux *Shakespear,* mort en 1616.
† Composée par *Thomas Heywood,* qui fleuriffoit fous les Regnes d'*Elisabeth* & de *Jaques* I. Toutes les Piéces de Théatre de ces tems-là font extrêmement longues et fort ennuyeufes.

Lettre a Madame la Duchesse Mazarin, Œuvres Meslées de St. Evremond, Londres, 1705. *Vol. II. pp.* 305, 306. [1st *edition, by Des Maizeaux.*]

[*Bassete* was a game at cards introduced into England by Mons. Morin in 1681, and of which the Duchess of Mazarin was passionately fond. The witty St. Evremond in thus assuring Madame Mazarin that her beauty was proof against all these dissipations, acquaints us with the fact that *Henry VIII* must have been at this time a popular play much resorted to ; even if she ventured there by way of finishing up his imaginary day at Newmarket, she would be none the worse for it.

He uses the word comedy for "play" in a general sense; he applies it
also to Thomas Heywood's historical play of Queen Elizabeth. That it
was Shakespere's *Henry VIII* we are informed by the note appended by
his friend Des Maizeaux, who does not appear to have shared the more
favourable opinion of English drama expressed by St. Evremond in his
Essay on English Comedy. Malone states that King Henry VIII was without
doubt sometimes represented between 1682—1695 (*Historical Account
of the English Stage*, 1821, p. 290), and from a list of Sir H. Herbert's
we learn that it had been a "Revived" play in 1663 (*ib.* p. 276).[1] There
were one or two other pieces on the same or a like subject, *viz.* an Enterlude
of K. Henry 8th, entered on the Stationer's Register, 12 Feb. 1604-5; and
Samuel Rowley's *When you see me you know me, or the famous chronicle
History of Henry VIII*, 1605. Henry Chettle's *Life of Cardinal Wolsey*,
1601, was probably the play mentioned by Robert Gell in 1628 (before, p.
169), and could not be the "comedy" referred to by St. Evremond; and the
"Rising of Cardinal Wolsey," partly written by Anthony Munday, was put
out subsequently as Part I to Chettle's drama. (See Henslowe's *Diary*,
Shakespeare Society's edition, pp. 189, 202, 204.)

In his short essay on English Comedy, written in 1677, St. Evremond
does not refer to Shakespere by name, but Dr. Jules Jusserand suggests that
he may probably have had the *Merchant of Venice* in his mind when he
wrote, after speaking of Jonson's *Bartholomew Fair* and Shadwell's *Epsom
Wells*—"There are some other plays which have in a manner two Arguments, that are brought in so ingeniously the one into the other, that the
mind of the Spectators (which might be offended by too sensible a change
finds nothing but satisfaction in the agreeable variety they produce."
English translation of 1685, p. 17. See also *Œuvres de St. Evremond,
par Des Maizeaux*, Amsterdam, 1726, tom. III. p. 280. L. T. S.]

---

[1] See too Pepys, before, p. 324. It was probably Davenant's re-cast of
the play that still kept the stage in 1682.

JOHN DRYDEN, 1684.

Your *Ben* and *Fletcher* in their firſt young flight
Did no *Volpone*, no *Arbaces* write.
But hopp'd about, and ſhort excurſions made
From Bough to Bough, as if they were afraid,
And each were guilty of ſome *slighted Maid*.
Shakeſpear's own Muſe her *Pericles* firſt bore,
The Prince of *Tyre* was elder than the *Moore :*
'Tis miracle to ſee a firſt good Play,
All Hawthorns do not bloom on *Chriſtmas-day*.
A ſlender Poet muſt have time to grow,
And ſpread and burniſh as his Brothers do.
Who ſtill looks lean, ſure with ſome Pox is curſt,
But no Man can be *Falſtaff* fat at firſt.

*Prologue to Charles Davenant's Circe. Miscellany
Poems,* 1684. *p.* 292. [*In the Bodleian Library.*]

[A Prologue was written by Dryden to C. Davenant's *Circe*, but he afterwards much altered it (Scott's edition of Dryden's Works, Vol. X. 333, 335). The altered Prologue, of which the above are the 11th to 23rd lines, is not found prefixed to either of the three first editions of Charles Davenant's *Circe* (1677, 1685, 1703); though Mr. Christie erroneously states that "both forms of the Prologue were published with the play in 1677" (Globe edition of Dryden's Poetical Works, p. 431). The earliest printed form appears to be that in the "Miscellany Poems" of 1684, where it is not called a Prologue, but "An Epilogue written by Mr. Dryden." L. T. S.]

The Slighted Maid is a comedy by Sir R. Stapylton, first edition [sm. 4to.], 1663. Dryden again mentions it in the Preface to his *Troilus and Cressida*, 1679 : "Of this nature is the *Slighted Maid ;* where there is no scene in the first Act, which might not by as good reason be in the fifth."

KNIGHTLY CHETWOOD, 1684.

Such was the cafe when *Chaucer's early* toyl
Founded the *Mufes* Empire in *our* Soyl.
Spencer improv'd it with his painful hand
But *loft* a *Noble* Mufe in *Fairy-land.*
Shakfpeare fay'd all that *Nature* cou'd impart,
And *Johnfon* added *Induftry* and *Art.*
Cowley, and *Denham* gain'd immortal praife ;
And fome who *merit* as they *wear*, the Bays, [etc.]

*Commendatory Verses prefixed to An Essay on Translated
Verse, by the Earl of Roscommon.* 1684. [4*to.*]

WILLIAM WINSTANLEY, 1684.

The Life of King *Richard* the Third.

* * * * *

But as Honour is always attended on by Envy, so hath this worthy Princes fame been blasted by malicious traducers, who like *Shakespear* in his Play of him, render him dreadfully black in his actions, a monster of nature, rather then a man of admirable parts; (p. 174.)

The Life of Mr. *Wil. Shakespeare*.

This worthy Poet Mr. *Shakespeare*, the glory of the English Stage, [was born at *Stratford* upon *Avon* in *Warwickshire*,] and is the highest honour that Town can boast of; [in whom three eminent Poets may seem in some sort to be compounded. 1. *Martial*, in the warlike sound of his Surname, *Hasti-Vibrans* or *Shakespeare*, whence some have conjectured him of Military extraction. 2. *Ovid*, the most natural and witty of all Poets; and hence it was that Queen *Elizabeth* coming into a Grammar-School made this extemporary Verse.

Persius *a Crab-staff,* Bawdy Martial, Ovid *a fine Wag.*

3. *Plautus*, a very exact Comedian, and yet never any Scholar, as our *Shakespeare* (if alive) would confess himself;] but by his conversing with jocular Wits, whereto he was naturally enclined, he became so famously witty, or wittily famous, as without learning, he attained to an extraordinary height in the Comique strain; [yet was he not so much given to Festivity, but he could (when so disposed) be solemn and serious; so that *Heraclitus* himself might afford to smile at his Comedies they were so merry,

and *Democritus* scarce forbear to sigh at his Tradgedies, they were so mournful.]

From an Actor of Tradgedies and Comedies, he became a *Maker*; and such a Maker, that though some others may perhaps pretend to a more exact Decorum and Oeconomie, especially in Tradgedy, never any exprest a more lofty and Tragick height; never any represented Nature more purely to the life, and where the polishments of Art are most wanting, (for as we said before, his learning was not extraordinary) he pleaseth with a certain wild and native Elegance; and in all his writings hath an unvulgar Style, as well in his *Venus and Adonis*, his *Rape of Lucrece*, and other various Poems, as in his Drammaaticks.

[He was an eminent instance of the truth of that Rule, *Pœta non fit sed nasciter*, one is not *Made* but *Born* a Poet, so that as *Cornish Diamonds* are not Polished by any Lapidary, but are pointed and smoothed even as they are taken out of the Earth, so Nature it self was all the Art which was used on him.]

(To enumerate his Comedies, they are so many, would be too tedious, that of his *Henry* the fourth, though full of sublime Wit, is very much blamed by some, for making Sir *John Falkstaff* the property of pleasure for King *Henry* to abuse, as one that was a *Thrasonical Puff*, and Emblem of mock-valour; though indeed he was a man of Arms, every inch of him, and as Valiant as any in his Age.)

[Many were the Wit Combats betwixt him and *Ben Johnson*, which two we may compare to a *Spanish great Gallion*, and an *English-man of War*, Mr. *Johnson* (like the former) was built far higher in Learning; Solled but slow in his performances; *Shakespeare* with the *English-man of War*, lesser in bulk, but lighter in sailing, could turn with all Tides, tack about and take advantage of all Winds, by the quickness of his Wit and invention. This our famous Comedian died, *Anno Domini* 16 . . . and was buried at *Stratford* upon *Avon*, the Town of his Nativity,] upon whom one hath bestowed this Epitaph.

> *Renowned* Spenser, *lye a thought more nigh* [Wm. Basse.]
> *To learned* Chaucer, *and rare* Beaumont *lye,*
> *A little nearer* Spenser, *to make room*
> *For* Shakespear, *in your threefold, fourfold Tomb,*
> *To lodge all four in one Bed make a shift*
> *Until Dooms-day, for hardly will a fifth*
> *Betwixt this day and that, by Fates be slain,*
> *For whom your Curtains may be drawn again.*
> *If your precedency in death do bar,*
> *A fourth place in your sacred Sepulchar;*
> *Under this sacred Marble of thine own,*
> *Sleep rare Tragedian* Shakespear! *sleep alone,*
> *Thy unmolested peace in an unshar'd Cave.*
> *Possess as Lord not Tenant of thy Grave,*
> *That unto us, and others it may be,*
> *Honour hereafter to be laid by thee.*
>
> *England's Worthies. Select Lives Of the most Eminent Persons of the English Nation.* 1684. *pp.* 345-7. [8vo.]

[The passages above marked between [ ] are, with the alteration of a few words only, taken bodily from Fuller's notice of Shakespere, and the passage between ( ) is ingeniously made up of sentences from Fuller's notice of Fastolf, the Norfolk Knight. See Part III of *The Worthies of England*, 1662; *Warwickshire*, p. 126; *Norfolk*, p. 253. See before, pp. 246, 249.

For Basse's Epitaph, see before, p. 136.

Winstanley places Shakespere the last of four Lives, the others being, Sam. Daniel, Drayton, and Ben Jonson, presenting his readers "with a Quaternion of Poets, such as were of the best rank, endued with parts of admirable perfection, and deservedly coming under the notion of Worthies." In writing of Jonson he thus pays a tribute to Shakespere's genius :

"He was paramount in the Dramatique part of Poetry, and taught the Stage an exact conformity to the Laws of Comedians, being accounted the most learned, judicious, and correct of them all, and the more to be admired for being so, for that neither the height of Natural parts, for he was no *Shakespeare*, nor the cost of extraordinary Education, but his own proper industry and addiction to Books advanced him to this perfection" (p. 343).

Winstanley's feeling as to the traducers of Richard III agrees with a similar sentiment expressed by Sir. W. Cornwallis (see before, p. 41). The Life of Richard III. was in the edition of *England's Worthies* of 1660. The Life of Shakespeare is not in that edition. L. T. S.]

Anonymous, 1685.

Let then thefe *Owls* againſt the *Eagle* preach,
And blame thofe Flights which they want Wing to reach.
Like *Falſiaffe* let 'em conquer Heroes dead,
And praife *Greek* Poets they cou'd never read.

Valentinian : a Tragedy. As 'tis altered by the late Earl of Rochester [from the play by Beaumont & Fletcher of 1647] 1685. [4to.] *Prologue. Spoken by Mrs. Cook the second day.* [*Written after Rochester's death.*]

EDWARD RAVENSCROFT, 1686.

I think it a greater theft to Rob the dead of their Praife, then the Living of their Money. That I may not appear Guilty of fuch a Crime, 'tis neceffary I fhould acquaint you, that there is a Play in Mr. *Shakefpears* Volume under the name of *Titus Andronicus*, from whence I drew part of this. I have been told by fome anciently converfant with the Stage, that it was not Originally his, but brought by a private Author to be Acted, and he only gave fome Mafter-touches to one or two of the Principal Parts or Characters; this I am apt to believe, becaufe 'tis the moft incorrect and indigefted piece in all his Works, It feems rather a heap of Rubbifh then a Structure.

Titus Andronicus, or the Rape of Lavinia.
1687. [4to.] *To the Reader.*
(*Licensed, Dec.* 21, 1686.)

WILLIAM FULMAN, AND [RICHARD DAVIES],
about 1688.

William Shakefpeare was born at Stratford upon Avon in Warwickſhire, about 1563-4. [Much given to all unluckineffe in ftealing venifon and Rabbits particularly from Sr Lucy, who had him oft whipt & fometimes Imprifoned & at laſt made Him fly his Native Country to his great Advancem^t but His reveng was fo great, that he is his Juſtice Clodpate, and calls him a great man & y^t in allufion to his name bore three lowfes rampant for his Arms.]

From an Actor of Playes he became a Compofer. He dyed Apr. 23, 1616, Ætat. 53, probably at Stratford, for there he is buryed and hath a Monument. [on w^{che} He lays a Heavy curfe upon any one who fhal remoove his bones. He dyed a papiſt]

Dugd. p. 500.

Fulman Manuscripts (1670—1688), *vol. xv. No.* 7, *p.* 22. *In the Library of Corpus Christi College, Oxford.* (*The portions here in brackets are those attributed to Davies.*)

This annotator on the *adversaria* of the Rev. William Fulman is believed to have been the Rev. Richard Davies, Rector of Sapperton in Gloucesterſhire: but his name does not appear on the manuscript. It is in five or six different hands; and only two other annotations, both very short, are in Davies' supposed autograph. Little is known of him. He died in 1708. Fulman died in 1688. By "Justice Clodpate" Davies designates Shakespeare's Shallow. We observe that Dowdall, at the end of his letter to Southwell (quoted after, p. 417), applies the same nickname to one of the sitting judges of the Spring Assize at Warwick, in 1693.

THOMAS BROWNE, 1688.

Eugen. Tho you cannot ſay **Mr Bays** with the Heroe in *Shakeſpear*, that the World's your Oyſter, and you have opened it with your Sword; * yet you may ſafely ſay the World's your Sheet of Paper, and you have blotted it with your Ink.

(*p.* 7.)

Crites. But pray **Mr Bays**, what did you ſay to *Shakeſpear*, *Johnſon*, & the reſt of them? Methinks your new-ſettled Monarchy ſhould ſtand in a great deal of danger, as long as theſe Authors continued in any reſpect and authority among the People.

Bays. To prevent, Sir, all ſtorms that might have iſſued from that quarter, I preſently ſet me up an *Index expurgatorius* * * I fulminated *Johnſons* affected Style, his dull way of making Love, his Thefts and mean characters: *Shakeſpears* Ignorance, long Periods, and Barbarous Language: *Fletchers* want of a Gentlemans Education; ſo often, you do obſerve me Mr *Crites*, that ſcarce one in a hundred had the aſſurance to offer one good word in their behalf.

(*p.* 15.)

The Reaſons of Mr. Bays changing his Religion 1688 [4*to*].

---

* [Pistol, in the *Merry Wives of Windsor*, Act II. sc. ii. l. 2.]

JOHN EVELYN, 12 Aug. 1689.

For there were the Pictures of Fisher, Fox, Sr Tho. More, Tho. Lord Cromwell, Dr. Nowel, &c. And what was most agreeable to his Lo^{ps} general humor, Old Chaucer, Shakspere, Beaumont and Fletcher, who were both in one piece, Spencer, Mr. Waller, Cowley, Hudibras, which last he plac'd in the roome where he us'd to eate & dine in publiq, most of which, if not all, are at the present at Cornebery, in Oxfordshire;

Letter " To Mr. Pepys," describing the then late Lord Clarendon's house.
Memoirs: Edited by William Bray. 1819. Vol. 2, p. 242.

GERARD LANGBAINE, 1691.

I am only forry that my Power is not equal to the zeal I have for the memory of thofe Illuftrious Authors, the Claſſicks, as well as thofe later Writers of our own Nation, Mr. *Shakefpear, Fletcher, Johnfon, Cowley* &c. that I might be capable of doing them better Service, in vindicating *Their* Fame, and in expofing our Modern *Plagiaries*, by detecting *Part* of their Thefts, (Preface, fign. a 4.)

* * * *

Mr. *Dryden's* Plays owe their Advantage to his fkill in the French Tongue, or to the Age, rather than his own Conduct, or Performances. Honeft *Shakefpear* was not in thofe days acquainted with thofe great Wits, *Scudery, Calprenede, Scarron, Corneille*, &c. He was as much a Stranger to French as Latine, (in which, if we believe *Ben Johnfon,* he was a very fmall Proficient;) and yet an humble Story of *Doraftus* and *Fawnia* ferv'd him for *A Winter's Tale*, as well as *The Grand Cyrus*, or *The Captive Queen*, could furnifh out a Laureat for a *Conqueft of Granada*. *Shakefpear's Meafure for Meafure*, however defpif'd by Mr. *Dryden*, with his *Much Ado about Nothing*, were believ'd by *Sʳ William Davenant* to have Wit enough in them to make one good play.[1]   (pp. 141-2.)

[1] [Davenant's tragi-comedy called *The Law against Lovers*, 1673, was founded on these two plays. L. T. S.]

WILLIAM SHAKESPEAR.

One of the moſt Eminent Poets of his Time ;   *   *   *
His Natural Genius to *Poetry* was ſo excellent, that like thoſe Diamonds[1], which are found in *Cornwall*, Nature had little, or no occaſion for the Aſſiſtance of Art to poliſh it. The Truth is, 't is agreed on by moſt, that his Learning was not extraordinary ; and I am apt to believe, that his Skill in the *French* and *Italian* Tongues, exceeded his Knowledge in the *Roman* Language :   *   *   * ſo I ſhould think I were guilty of an Injury beyond pardon to his Memory, ſhould I ſo far diſparage it, as to bring his Wit in competition with any of our Age.   *   * I ſhall take the Liberty to ſpeak my Opinion, as my predeceſſors have done, of his Works ; which is this, That I eſteem his Plays beyond any that have ever been publiſhed in our Language : and tho' I extreamly admire *Johnſon*, and *Fletcher ;* yet I muſt ſtill aver, that when in competition with *Shakeſpear*, I muſt apply to them what *Juſtus Lipſius* writ in his Letter to *Andræas Schottus*, concerning *Terence* and *Plautus*, when compar'd ; *Terentium amo, admiror, ſed Plautum magis.* (Pp. 453-4.)

An Account of the Engliſh Dramatick Poets, Oxford.
1691. [8*vo.*]

Two copies of Langbaine's *Account* were annotated by the antiquarian Oldys. The one which received his second annotations is in the British Museum Library. *A propos* of this book, we venture to suggest that it would be a very great convenience if the Chief Librarian of the British Museum would issue a hand-list of printed books which have manuscript annotations ; such as Dr. Thomas Warton's copy of Spenser's works, and Tieck's copy of Ben Jonson's works, with the *marginalia* and other notes in full.

---

[1] Dr. *Fuller* in his Account of *Shakespear*. [See before, p. 246.]

Oldys' notes on Langbaine belong to a period later than our *Centurie* There is, however, a well-known epigram, said to be by Jonson and Shakespeare, which according to George Steevens, Oldys puts forth as if he had derived it from an authentic source of some antiquity. We have not been able to recover the particular manuscript in which he is said to have given it. In Johnson and Steevens' 2nd Edition of Shakespeare 1778, vol. i. pp. 204-5 (see also Malone's Edition, 1790, vol. i. p. 163), the following is given:

"Verses by Ben Jonson and Shakespeare, occasioned by the motto to the Globe Theatre—*Totus mundus agit histrionem.*

  Jonson. If but *stage actors* all the world displays,
    Where shall we find *spectators* of their plays?

  Shakespeare. Little or much of what we see we do;
    We're all both *actors* and *spectators* too."

According to Steevens, Oldys' authority for these verses is "Poetical Characteristicks, 8vo MS., vol. i., some time in the Harleian Library; which volume was returned to its owner."

The whole story is suspicious. The alleged "motto to the Globe Theatre" is altered from the *Fragmenta* of Petronius Arbiter. See ed. Peter Burmann, *Trajecti ad Rhenum*, 1709, p. 673. The original words are "quod fere totus mundus exerceat histrionem."

Then again, on the title page of Oldys' *second* copy of Langbaine, we have evidence that Oldys himself wrote the verses: for there we read

  "Totus mundus agit histrionem.

    If all the world the actor plays,
    Who are *Spectators* of its Plays?"

This is again altered by Oldys into

    "If but Stage-Actors all the World displays,
    Who are allowed *Spectators* of their Plays?

and finally he has written on the left side margin,

    "Little or much of what we see we do,
    We are both Actors and Spectators too."

Not a word of Ben Jonson or Shakespeare. Can it be that these two verses were dished up by George Steevens, and assigned by him to Jonson and Shakespeare, as a hoax on his credulous public.

For a full account of Oldys' annotated Langbaine, see *Notes and Queries*, 3rd S., vol. i. p. 81.

JOHN DRYDEN, 1691.

How's this, you cry? an Actor write? we know it;
But *Shakſpear* was an Actor, and a Poet.
Has not great *Johnſons* learning often fail'd?
But *Shakſpear's* greater Genius ſtill prevail'd.

> *The Mistakes, a Tragi-comedy, by Joseph Harris.* 1691.
> *Prologue writ by Mr. Dryden.*

[Shakespere's genius prevailed, Dryden says, in spite of his having been an Actor. And it must have been this feeling that led the puritan John Howes, formerly Cromwell's chaplain, and (says Dr. Grosart) the most intellectual of nonconformist writers, to pay the following tribute to an author who seems none other than Shakespere. Gloucester's mocking *aside*, (*Richard III*, Act II. sc. ii. l. 109),—

> "Amen; and make me die a good old man!
> That is the butt-end of a mother's blessing,"—

was surely in mind when, answering an objector, Howes remarked by the way, "At length he says, 'The Butt-end of this hypothesis,' &c. I like not *that Phrase* the worse for the *Author's* sake, of whom it seems borrowed, whose Memory greater things will make live, when we are forgot." *A View of that Part of the late Considerations addressed to H. H. about the Trinity*, 1695, 8vo. p. 14. (This tract was written in 1694 or 1695, being the last in a controversy on the Trinity.) See *Representative Nonconformists*, by Rev. A. B. Grosart, 1879, p. 104. L. T. S.]

WILLIAM WALSH, 1691.

Let *Mifogynes* appear, at the Head of his Regiment, that makes a worfe Figure than *Sir John Falfiaffe's*. (p. 166.)

Let [*Mifogynes*] confider the Stories of *Bradamante* in *Ariofto*, of *Aureftilla* in *Confalo de Cepedes*, of *Othello* in *Shakefpeare*, and let him fee how far Jealoufy may feem reafonable, whilft neverthelefs the Perfon of whom they are jealous may be innocent. (p. 205.)

A Dialogue concerning Women, being a Defence of the Sex. 1691.
Printed in *The Works of William Walsh, Esq.* 1736. [8vo.]

[William Walsh was a friend of Dryden and Pope, the former said he was "the best critic of our Nation in his time"; the latter called him

"the Muse's Judge and Friend,
Who justly knew to Blame, or to Commend;
To Failings mild, but zealous for Desert;
The clearest Head, and the sincerest Heart."

(*Elogium*, dated 1708, prefixed to Walsh's Works, 1736.) L. T. S.]

JOHN DRYDEN, 1693.

When I was drawing the Out-Lines of an Art, without any living Mafter to inftruct me in it; an Art which had been better prais'd than ftudy'd here in *England*, wherein *Shakefpear*, who created the Stage among us, had rather written happily, than knowingly and juftly. * * *

And to forgive the many Failings of thofe, who with their wretched Art, cannot arrive to thofe Heights that you poffefs, from a happy, abundant, and native Genius. Which are as inborn to you, as they were to *Shakefpear* * * *

In Tragedy and Satire I offer myfelf to maintain againft fome of our Modern Criticks, that this Age and the laft, particularly in *England*, have excell'd the Ancients in both thofe kinds; and I wou'd inftance in *Shakefpear* of the former, of your Lordfhip in the latter fort.

The Satires of Juvenal and Persius, translated into English verse. Dedication (or Discourse on Satire) to Charles Earl of Dorset and Middlesex, pp. ii., vii. 1693. [*fol.*]

JOHN DRYDEN, 1693.

*Shakespear's Picture drawn by Sir *Godfrey Kneller*, and given to the Author.

Shake*s*pear,* thy Gift, I place before my *s*ight;
With awe, I a*s*k his Ble*ss*ing 'ere I write;
With Reverence look on his Maje*s*tick Face;
Proud to be le*s*s; but of his Godlike Race.
His Soul In*s*pires me, while thy Prai*s*e I write,
And I like *Teucer*, under *Ajax* fight;
Bids thee through me, be bold; with dauntle*s*s brea*s*t
Contemn the bad, and Emulate the be*s*t.
Like his, thy Criticks in th' attempt are lo*s*t;
When mo*s*t they rail, know then, they envy mo*s*t.

To Sir Godfrey Kneller. (*Miscellany Poems.*) 1694. Part IV. *p.* 92.

PETER ANTHONY MOTTEUX, 1692-3.

'The Merry Wives of Windsor,' an old Play, hath been reviv'd, and was play'd the laft day of the year.

* * * * * * *

Mr. *Rhymer's* Book which the Ingenious expected with fo much Impatience, is publifh'd and is call'd, *A Short View of Tragedy, &c.* being dedicated to the Right Honourable the Earl of *Dorfet*. Mr. *Rhymer*, like fome of the *French* that follow *Ariftotle's* Precepts, declares for *Chorus's*, and takes an occafion at examin fome Plays of *Shakefpear's*, principally *Othello*, with the fame feverity and judgment with which he criticifed fome of *Beaumont and Fletcher's* in his Book called, *The Tragedies of the laft Age.* * * The Ingenious are fomewhat divided about fome Remarks in it, though they concur with Mr. *Rhymer* in many things, and generally acknowledge that he difcovers a great deal of Learning through the whole. For thefe Reafons I muft forbear faying any more of it, and refer you to the Book it felf.

* * * * * * *

We are promifed a fecond Part [of *The Impartial Critick*], wherein Mr. *Dennis* defigns to prove, that, tho *Shakefpear* had his faults, yet he was a very great Genius, which Mr. *Rymer* feems unwilling to grant. I am only forry that the time, which the perufal of the many excellencies which are diffuf'd thro *Shakfpear's* Plays, requires, will keep Mr. *Dennis* very long from giving us that Book.

Gentleman's Journal, January 169½. *p.* 36. *December* 1692, *p.* 15. *January*, 169⅔, *p.* 26.

[See Rymer's two books quoted before, pp. 366, 367.

Motteux, who had acquired a remarkable facility in English, was the projector and editor of the *Gentleman's Journal* (forty years before the appearance of the *Gentleman's Magazine*), and was, says Mr. C. Elliot Browne, "probably the first Frenchman who was able to appreciate our great poet" (*Notes and Queries*, 5 Ser., Vol. ix, p. 163). In printing Sir Charles Sedley's Prologue to Higden's *Wary Widdow*, he says,

"you are too great an Admirer of *Shakespear*, not to assent to the Praises given to the Fruits of his rare *Genius*, of which I may say as *Ovid* to *Græcinus*,

>   Quos prior est mirata, sequens mirabitur Ætas,
>   In quorum plausus tota Theatra sonant."
>   (February, 1693, p. 61.)

See also Mr. C. E. Browne in the *New Quarterly Magazine*, Vol. ix, p. 326. (Jan. 1878.)

We have, however, an earlier reference to Shakespere by a Frenchman, namely, by St. Evremond, ten years earlier than Motteux (see before, p. 396); but that his appreciation of Shakespere went so far as is implied by A. Lacroix (*De L'influence de Shakspeare sur le Théatre Français*, p. 3) is hardly shown in his writings on English Tragedy and Comedy. Both Motteux and St. Evremond were refugees in England on account of religion, and lived here many years, but the latter, unlike Motteux, knew little of the language.

Mr. Ward, in his *History of English Dramatic Literature*, Vol. I. p. 301, states that Cyrano de Bergerac "had borrowed thoughts and even phrases from Shakspere in his tragedy of *Agrippine*," which was first published in 1654. But, while Corneille and Molière appropriated from Bergerac (who wrote but two plays), his critics, such as P. Lacroix, A. Vitu, and especially Charles Nodier, have no thought that the independent pen of Bergerac himself stole from Shakespere. I am unable to point out any other passages than slight resemblances to parts of Hamlet in the speeches of Agrippine, Act III. sc. i, and Act IV. sc. ii, in which she addresses the spirit of her murdered husband, promising him revenge (*Œuvres de Cyrano de Bergerac*, ed. P. L. Jacob, *Bib. Gauloise*, Paris, 1858, pp. 376, 392); also perhaps her taunt of Sejanus, "Et cette incertitude où mère le trépas"? (p. 409.) L. T. S.]

MR. DOWDALL. APRIL 10, 1693.

the 1ſt Remarkable place in this County y^t I viſitted was Stratford ſuper avon, where I ſaw the Effigies of our Engliſh tragedian, m^r Shakſpeare, parte of his Epitaph I ſent m^r Lowther, and Deſired he w^{ld} Impart it to you, wch I finde by his Laſt Letter he has Done: but here I ſend you the whole Inſcription.

Juſt und^r his Effigies in the wall of the chancell is this written.

[Here follows the Inſcription, as on page 125 *ante*.]

Neare the wall where his monument is Erected Lyeth a plaine free ſtone, underneath wch his bodie is Buried with this Epitaph, made by himſelfe a little before his Death.

[Here follows the Inſcription, as on page 121 *ante*.]

the clarke that ſhew'd me this Church is above 80 y^{rs} old; he ſays that this *Shakeſpear* was formerly in this towne bound apprenti[c]e to a butcher; but that he Run from his maſter to London, and there was Received Into the playhouſe as a ſerviture, and by this meanes had an oppertunity to be *what* he afterwards prov'd. he was the beſt of his family, but the male Line is extinguiſhed: not one for feare of the Curſe aboveſ^d Dare touch his Grave Stone, tho his wife and Daughters Did Earneſtly Deſire to be Layd in the ſame Grave wth him.

> "*Letter*" *from Mr. Dowdall to Mr. Edw. Southwell, endorsed* "*Description of Severall places in Warwickshire.*" *Halliwell's Life of Shakespere,* 1848, *p.* 87. *Facsimile of the MS. in Halliwell's Works of Shakespeare,* 1853 [*fol.*], *Vol. I. p.* 78

[The original MS. of Dowdall's "Letter" is in Mr. Halliwell-Phillipps' possession. It was first printed in 1838 by Mr. T. Rodd under the title of "Traditionary Anecdotes of Shakespeare collected in Warwickshire in the year 1693;" this print, however, contains several inaccuracies. L. T. S.]

SIR CHARLES SEDLEY. 1693.

But againſt old as well as new to rage,
Is the peculiar Phrenſy of this Age.
Shackſpear muſt down, and you muſt praiſe no more
Soft *Deſdemona*, nor the Jealous *Moor:*
Shackſpear whoſe fruitfull Genius, happy Wit
Was fram'd and finıſht at a lucky hit
The Pride of Nature, and the ſhame of Schools,
Born to Create, and not to Learn from Rules ;
Muſt pleaſe no more, his Baſtards now deride
Their Fathers Nakedneſs they ought to hide,
But when on Spurs their *Pegaſus* they force,
Their Jaded Muſe is diſtanc'd in the Courſe.

The Wary Widdow, or Sir Noisy Parrat, a Comedy by Henry Higden. Prologue by Sir Charles Sydley. 1693.

Song, end of 17th century.

We merry wives of Windsor,
　Whereof you make your play;
And act us on your stages,
　In London day by day:
Alas it doth not hurt us,
　We care not what you do;
For all you scoff, we'll sing and laugh,
　And yet be honest too.

　　＊　　＊　　＊　　＊

It grieves us much to see your wants
　Of things that we have store;
In Forests wide and Parks beside,
　And other places more:
Pray do not scorn the Windsor horn,
　That is both fair & new
Altho' you scold, we'll sing and laugh,
　And yet be honest too.

And now farewell unto you all,
　We have no more to say:
Be sure you imitate us right,
　In acting of your play:
If that you miss, we'll at you hiss,
　As others us'd to do;
And at you scoff, & sing, and laugh,
　And yet be honest too.

MS. penes Mr. Halliwell-Phillips, printed in The First Sketch of Shakespere's Merry Wives of Windsor, for the Shakespeare Society, 1842, p. 66

APPENDIX A.

LIST OF EXCLUSIONS.

I. *PASSAGES MISTAKEN FOR ALLUSIONS.*

The Schoole of Abuse: by Stephen Gosson   1579
("Some plaiers modest, if I be not deceived." Sig. C 6, *bk.*)

Letter from Sir Philip Sidney to Secretary Walsingham, dated "Utrecht, this 24th of March" . . 1586
(Mentioning "Will, my lord of Lester's jesting plaier." See Mr. Bruce in *Shakespeare Society's Papers*, vol. i, 1844, p. 88.)

An Epistle to the Gentlemen Students of both Universities: by Thomas Nash 1587
(This is prefixed to Robert Greene's Menaphon, 1589. It contains the famous passage on "English *Seneca*," and "whole *hamlets;* I should say, handfuls, of tragical speeches." (Sign. * * 3.) Compare an epigram "of one y^t had stolne much out of Seneca," in the Dr. Farmer Chetham MS., ed. Grosart, for the Chetham Society, 1873, Part I, vol. i p. 84. See also Mr. C. E. Browne in *Notes & Queries*, 5th S. i. 462.)

[The Rev. Mark Pattison kindly points out that this *Epistle* may have been written in 1587. Backwards, Nash mentions the recently-published Warner's *Albion* (1586); forwards, he speaks of the *Anatomie of Absurdities*, which was entered on the Stationers' Register, 19 Sept. 1588, as in the future,—"It may be. my *Anatomie of Absurdities* may acquaint you ere long with my skill in surgery." Lowndes and Hazlitt doubtfully put an edition of Greene's *Menaphon* in 1587. L. T. S.]

The Anatomie of Absurditie: by Thomas Nash (sig. A i, bk., of ed. 1590), is too early to refer to *Ven. and Ad.*   1589

The Teares of the Muses: by Edmond Spenser . . 1590
(Mentioning "Our pleasant Willy," in the complaint of Thalia.)

[Mr. J. W. Hales (Globe ed. of Spenser, pp. xliv—xlvi) believes that this referred to Shakespere, so also Mr.

and Mrs. Cowden Clarke (see their edition of Shakespere, 1878, p. xxv); Dr. Grosart now agrees with Dr. Nicholson that Lyly may have been intended, decidedly not Shakespere. (See too, Malone's *Life of Shakspeare*, 1821, Vol. II, p. 225. In 1590 Shakespere had written nothing but *Love's Labours Lost*, and possibly parts of *Titus Andronicus* and 1 *Henry VI*.) Mr. Collier points out proof that Sidney (who died 1586) may have been the "Willy" intended (*Introd. to Seven English Miscellanies*, p. xviii). Mr. Furnivall, who was lately in favour of Lyly, writes, May 27, 1879: "Having seen the contemporary entry of '*Tarlton*' opposite the Willy passage in the 1611 edition of Spenser's *Minor Poems* in the copy that Prof. Brewer gave Mr. Halliwell-Phillipps, and being convinced that Spenser referred to a comic *actor*, not a dramatist, I accept Tarlton as the Willy, though his name was Dick." As shown by Mr. Collier, Sir Philip Sidney was alluded to as "Willy," which seems to have been used as a term of affectionate reference. Mr. Furnivall finds that other MS. identifications in the same hand in this volume are correct. This seems to settle the question. L. T. S.]

[Four Letters, & certaine Sonnets: especially touching Robert Greene and other parties by him abused; Third Letter, pp. 48, 49: by Gabriel Harvey . . 1592

(It was conclusively pointed out by Mr. R. Simpson in a letter to the *Academy*, Oct. 17, 1874, that the supposed allusions in this letter are, not to Shakespere, but to one of the Harvey family and to Nash. Dr. Ingleby, convinced by the statement, printed a Postscript to his Introduction to the *Allusion Books* (New Sh. Soc., 1874), reproducing Mr. R. Simpson's letter, for circulation among the members of the New Shakspere Society. L. T. S.)]

Wits Miserie and the Worlds Madnesse, discovering the Devils Incarnate of this age: by Thomas Lodge . 1596

(The ghost, "Hamlet, revenge!" p. 56. This points to an older play on the subject of Hamlet.)

[Warning for Fair Women: a play . . 1599

("A filthy whining Ghost ✢ ✢ cries Vindicta! Revenge, Revenge!" *Induction*. Refers to the older Hamlet.) L. T. S.]

APP. A. PASSAGES MISTAKEN FOR ALLUSIONS. 423

The Poetaster : by Ben Jonson . . 1601
    (See *Note*, below.)

['Tis merrie when Gossips meet, by Samuel Rowlands . 1602
    (P. 22 of reprint of 1818 quotes the proverb,
        "blacke-bearded men
  Are precious pearles in beauteous womens eyes,"
  cited in *The Two Gentlemen of Verona*, Act V. sc. ii.)

The Tragedie of Darius : by W. Alexander, E. of Stirling 1603
    (Contains a passage in Darius' second long speech, sign. H,
    Act IV. sc. ii, resembling "The cloud-capt towers," &c.,
    Tempest, Act IV. sc. i.)

The Black Book 1604
    ("Can we not take our ease in our Inne," sign. B 4. A pro-
    verbial saying, *e.g.* J. Heywood's Epigrammes vpon Pro-
    uerbes 1562, Spencer Society's reprint, p. 132 ; Jonson's
    New Inn, Act I. sc. i ; and, earlier, *The Pilgrim's Tale*,
    printed in Thynne's *Animadversions*, Chaucer Society,
    1875, p. 77.) L. T. S.]

Paper's Complaint : by John Davies, of Hereford . . 1611
    (The words "there's one forthcoming yet," line 301, do not
    refer to Shakespere. See before, p. 96.)

Essayes and Characters : by John Stephens . . . 1615
    (He was friend to Ben Jonson, and himself the author of
    one long tragedy, *Cynthia's Revenge*. See *Notes & Queries*,
    4th S., iii. 550. The description of "A worthy Poet" is
    ideal, and the passages relating to his supposed works do
    not fit Shakespere's case.)

[The New Inn, by Ben Jonson, Act I. sc. i. . . . 1629
    (The passage beginning "all the world's a play," not neces-
    sarily copied from Shakespere, the idea being common to
    the times. See examples in Introd. to *As You Like it*,
    Clarendon Press edition, pp. xxxiii—xxxv, and particularly
    in Ward's *Hist. Eng. Dramatic Literature*, I. 402. It was
    used, too, by Cervantes in Don Quijote, see after, p. 428.)

424   APP. A. LIST OF EXCLUSIONS.

Silex Scintillans, or Sacred Poems and Private Ejaculations: by Henry Vaughan, Silurist . . . 1655
(Preface, sign. B 2, back. "Mr George Herbert, whose holy life and verse * * gave the first check to a most flourishing and advanced wit of his time." Dr. Grosart once thought this referred to Shakespere, but now believes Cowley was meant. Shakespere is impossible, because Herbert first published the *Temple* in 1631.) L. T. S.]

[Ben Jonson's Poetaster, acted in 1601.

[In the conversation upon Virgil],—
"*Tibullus*. . . . That, which he hath writ,
Is with such judgement labour'd, and distill'd
Through all the needfull uses of our lives
That could a man remember but his lines,
He should not touch at any serious point,
But he might breathe his spirit out of him.
 Cæsar. You meane, he might repeat part of his workes.
As fit for any conference he can use?
 Tibullus. True, royall Cæsar. *Cæs*. Worthily observ'd:
And a most worthie vertue in his workes.
What thinks materiall *Horace*, of his learning?
 Horace. His learning labours not the schoole-like glosse,
That most consists in *ecchoing* wordes, and termes,
And soonest wins a man an empty name;
Nor any long, or far-fetcht circumstance.
Wrapt in the curious generalties of artes:
But a direct, and *analytieke* summe
Of all the worth and first effects of artes.
And for his *poesie*, 'tis so ramm'd with life,
That it shall gather strength of life, with being,
And live hereafter, more admir'd, then now."
 (*The Poetaster*, Act V. sc. i. *Works*: 1616, [*fol*.] *p*. 332.)

This striking passage, which, taken by itself, seems so well to fit the description of Shakespere's works, having excited some discussion, I print it in full with some of the reasons for and against; Gifford and Dr. Sebastian Evans being in favour of the opinion that Jonson intended Shakespere; Dr. Ingleby, Dr. B. Nicholson, and Mr. Furnivall being against it.

Gifford says hereon, "It is evident that throughout the whole of this drama Jonson maintains a constant allusion to himself and his contemporaries; and were it not that it is fully settled by the critics, from Theobald to Chalmers, that the whole purport of his writings was to 'malign' Shakspeare, I should incline to believe that this speech, and that of Horace, which immediately follows, were both intended for him. Jonson could not think that Virgil was the poet of common life, as Tibullus affirms; or, as Horace,

APP. A. PASSAGES MISTAKEN FOR ALLUSIONS.

that he was unostentatious of literature, and averse from *echoing* the terms of others : whereas all this is as undoubtedly true of Shakspeare, as if it were pointedly written to describe him." (F. Cunningham's edition of *Jonson*, 8vo, 1871, Vol. I, p. 250.)

Dr. Sebastian Evans, in answer to Dr. Ingleby's objections, considers that, as Ben Jonson himself figures in the play as Horace, there is no impropriety in Virgil standing for Shakspeare, and that the question is, as the lines do not fit Spenser, who is there but Shakspere to whom Jonson would apply them ?

There does not seem to be anything to prove that, in the dialogue " To the Reader " at the end of the *Poetaster*, where Nasutus says,

> "Now for the Players, it is true, I tax'd 'hem,
> And yet, but some ;   *   *   *   *
>   What th' haue done 'gainst me,
> I am not mou'd with. If it gaue 'hem meat,
> Or got 'hem clothes. 'Tis well. That was their end.
> Onely amongst them I am sorry for
> Some better natures, by the rest so drawne,
> To run in that vile line ; "—

"better natures" was intended to refer to Shakespere. (See Cunningham's ed. of *Jonson*, 1871, Vol. I, p. 267.) But if Jonson, in this passage and in the famous pill scene (Act V. sc. iii) in the same play, can be shown to aim at Shakespere, then of course the first extract above cannot give Jonson's opinion of him in 1601, and may mean Virgil or anyone else suitable. And it is not likely that about the time Jonson was giving this praise, that Shakespere should, if it were intended for him, have acted towards Jonson as is implied by the words " our fellow Shakespeare hath given him a purge that made him beray his credit " (*Returne from Pernassus*, before, p. 48). This play, which was evidently written by a friend to Shakespere, was acted at Christmas, or New Year, 1601-2, not long after the appearance of the "Poetaster;" it does appear to point to a rivalry, if not a literary contention between the two poets at that time. On this side of the question Dr. Nicholson adduces that three of Shakespere's plays and one of Jonson's are found entered on the Stationers' Register, under presumable date 1600 or 1601, as ordered "to be staied " (*Malone*, Vol. II, p. 367), probably on account of a quarrel between them, just as in the notorious quarrel between Nash and G. Harvey we find on the same register, 1 June, 1599, the order "That all Nashes bookes and Doctor harvyes bookes be taken wheresoever they maye be found and that none of theire bookes bee ever printed hereafter." Dr. Nicholson further objects that the previous speeches of Horace and Gallus on Virgil and the first two lines spoken by Tibullus, are inconsistent with the rest of Tibullus' speech here given, as they cannot possibly apply to Shakespere, and also are inconsistent with Jonson's opinion of Shakespere's writing expressed 30 years later in his *Timber* (see before, p. 174); and that Gifford's statement as to Jonson's " constant " allusion to his contemporaries in this play is unsupported. I. T. S.]

II. ALLUSIONS IN SPURIOUS WORKS, AND SPURIOUS ALLUSIONS.

The British Theatre: 1750, attributed to William R. Chetwood.

>(Quotes (p. 9) lines from "the Interlude of" Robt. Armin's "Two Maids of More-clack," 1609, mentioning "our swan of Avon." They are not in that play, which has no "Interlude.")

Letter from Macklin the comedian.

>(Containing verses subscribed Thomas May and Endymion Porter, mentioning "Shakspeare" and "Avon's Swan," attributed by Malone to Macklin. Ed. 1821, Vol. I, 403-429.)

Song on Sir Thomas Lucy, attributed to John Jordan of Stratford-upon-Avon.

>(The Oldys Manuscripts are said to contain one stanza : other verses are quoted by William Chetwood in a Manuscript History of the Stage, 1730, published 1749. Also see *Malone*, ed. 1821, II. 565.

Epigrams by Ben Jonson and Shakespeare: quoted, and *nostro judicio* fabricated, by Steevens (see ante, p. 410).

[Accounts of the Book of Revells, giving lists of plays (including eight of Shakespere's) performed in 1605 and 1612, being spurious papers in the Public Record Office.

>(Printed as genuine in *Extracts from the Accounts of the Revels at Court* by Peter Cunningham, 1842, Shakespeare Society, pp. 203, 210. See *Athenæum*, June 20, 1868.)

To these may be added the names of those plays, not written by Shakspere, which were issued bearing on the title-page either his name or his initials :— The London Prodigal, 1605 ; Locrine, 1595 ; Life and Death of Thomas Lord Cromwell, 1613 ; A Yorkshire Tragedy, 1608 ; The Birth of Merlin ("written by William Shakespear and William Rowley"), 1662 ; First and Second Parts of the Troublesome Reign of King John, 1611 ; First Part of Sir John Oldcastle, 1600 (see before, p. 268) ; The Puritan, or the Widow of Watling Street, 1607. (See Rev. F. G. Fleay's *Introduction to Shakespearian Study*, 1877, pp. 42-46.) L. T. S.]

APPENDIX B.

SHAKESPERE'S INFLUENCE ON OTHER WRITERS.

BUT little has been done towards tracing the *Influence* of SHAKESPEARE's works on his successors of the seventeenth century. As a small contribution to such a work take the following, in addition to such writers quoted in the text as N. Breton, p. 457; Nicholson's *Acolastus,* p. 33; L. Barry, p. 95; Baron's *Pocula,* p. 279; and others.

[1. *The Civile Warres betweene the houses of Lancaster and Yorke,* by Samuel Daniel. The second edition of 1595 contains alterations made after the study of *Richard II.* See Grant White's ed. of Shakespere, vol. vi. pp. 139-142.

2. *Phillis and Flora,* 1598, a poem by R.S.; stanzas 56 and 57 (sign. C. 3) may perhaps have borrowed part of the description of the horse from *Venus and Adonis,* ll. 295-300. L. T. S.]

3. *The Two Angrie Women of Abington,* by Henry Porter, 1599, seems to quote from *Romeo and Juliet,* and has a trace of *Hamlet.*
(See Dyce's edition for the Percy Society, 1841, pp. 73 & 81.)

[4. *A Woman Kilde with Kindness,* by Thomas Heywood, 1607 (sign. G, back), the scene between Susan and Charles is thought to imitate Act III. sc. i. of *Measure for Measure.* The resemblance is, however, but superficial. L. T. S.]

5. *The Insatiate Countess,* by John Marston, 1613, perhaps imitates a line in *King John.*

> (See Malone's Shakespere, 1821, vol. xv. p. 261, *note.*)
> [Mr. Aldis Wright also suggests that the lines
> "A donative he hath of every God;
> *Apollo* gave him lockes, *Jove* his high front,
> * * * * *
> here they meete
> As in a sacred synod" (Act I. sc. i. sign. A 3)
> contain recollections of " the front of Jove himself" (*Hamlet*, III. sc. iv. l. 56), and *As You Like It*, Act III. sc. ii. l. 158.

6. *Polyolbion,* by Michael Drayton, 1615. In the description of how the bridegroom Tame was drest with flowers (Song 15), Mr. Furnivall thinks the expression " azur'd hare-bell " and two others are taken from *Cymbeline,* Act IV. sc. ii. (See the *Academy,* 29 March, 1879.) L. T. S.

7. *Don Quijote,* Parte II, 1615, has traces of *As you like it* and *Macbeth.*

> (See Mr. Rawdon Brown's letter in the *Athenæum*, July 5th, 1873.)
> [The connection with *As you like it* is founded on the idea that players and the stage figure human life, which, as remarked before, p. 423 (*The New Inn*), was not originally Shakespere's.]

[8. *The Witch,* by Thomas Middleton (in MS. till 1778. He died 1627), contains incantation and moonlight scenes resembling those in *Macbeth.*

> (See Middleton's Works, edited by Rev. A. Dyce, 1840, vol. i. pp. li-liv; and Johnson, Steevens and Reed's Shakespere, 1803, vol. ii. pp. 338—344. Other faint echoes of *Macbeth* are cited in Clark and Wright's edition, Clarendon Press Series, 1869, p. viii.) L. T. S.]

9. *The Legend of Cupid and Psyche,* by Shakerley Marmion, 1637, imitates a passage in *Hamlet,* Act III. sc. iv, and bears the trace of another in Act II. sc. ii, ll. 582, 583.

> (See Singer's edition, 1820, p. 33, lines 16, 17; p. 32, lines 1, 2.)

10. *Lucrecia,* part of *The Heroinæ,* 1639, by G. Rivers, appropriates some phrases from Shakespeare's *Lucrece.*

11. *The Unnatural Combat,* by Philip Massinger, 1639 (sign.

H, back), may possibly have followed a passage in *King John*, Act III. sc. i, fourth speech of Constance.
 (See Malone's Shakespere, 1821, vol. 15, p. 262 ; also Dr. Nicholson in *Notes and Queries*, 4th Ser., I. p. 289.)

12. *A Pastoral Dialogue*, by Thomas Carew (*Poems*, 1640, p. 77), offers some parallel in time and sentiments to Act III. sc. v. ll. 1-36, in *Romeo and Juliet*, of which it may be an imitation.
 (See *Carew's Poems* in the *Roxburghe Library*, 1870, p. 58, note.)

13. *The Cunning Lovers*, a comedy by Alexander Brome, 1654, contains two passages parallel to Shakespere, in Act II, p. 24, the conversation between Valentia and Prospero recalls that between *Romeo and Juliet*, Act II. sc. ii, ll. 33-61. In Act IV. p. 44, the scene with the Clown and Mantua as to "guerdon" and "banish" seems founded on Costard's "remuneration" in *Love's Labours Lost*, Act III.   L. T. S.]

14. *The Jews Tragedy*, by William Hemings, 1662, p. 29 (mispaged 37), imitates a line in *Hamlet* ("To be or not to be," &c.).
 (See Collier's *Bib. & Crit. Account*, vol. i. additions, p. xix*.)

[15. *Angliæ Speculum Morale ; the Moral State of England :* 1670. "The Friendly Rivals," one of three tales in this little volume, contains a "comical amour" in which two fat unwelcome wooers are tricked and caught by the lady and her maid ; spirits and satyrs sing, and "a company of Boyes dressed like Fairies come in dancing, and caper round them singing, and pinching them severely." The scene and the songs together seem to be a feeble imitation of the *Merry Wives of Windsor*, Act IV. sc. iv, and Act V. sc. ii-v. (See Mr. Elliot Browne in *Notes and Queries*, 5 Ser., I. p. 342.)

16. *The Nature, Use, and Abuse of the Tongue and Speech*, the second of two treatises by Richard Ward, Preacher, 1673, p. 208, quotes seven lines from the *Merchant of Venice* (Act IV. sc. i, l. 71) to enforce his example of "unprofitable and ineffectual Words."   L. T. S.]

SHAKESPERE'S INFLUENCE: COLLECTIONS OF POETRY, &c.

[And under this head, for they must have tended largely to the spread of Shakespere's *Influence* on the writers of the time, may be pointed out four popular collections of poems and extracts, one of which, *England's Parnassus* (to which Mr. R. Garnett of the British Museum kindly first drew my attention), demands more particular attention. The contents of the others can only be indicated.

17. ENGLAND'S PARNASSUS, 1600.

LIST OF PASSAGES QUOTED FROM SHAKESPERE
(including three attributed to other writers).

Page of
Eng. Par.

3 . . . . If Angels fight (2 ll.).
    Rich. II., Act III. sc. ii. l. 61.

7 Affection is a coale that must be coolde (3 ll.).
    Ven. and Ad., l. 387.

8 Things out of hope are compast oft with ventering (4 ll.).
    Ven. and Ad., l. 567.

12 Those which much covet, are with gaine so fond (7 ll.).
    Lucrece, l. 134.

14 All Orators are dumbe where Bewtie pleadeth.
    Lucrece, l. 268.

14 Bewtie it selfe doth of it selfe perswade (4 ll.).
    Lucrece, l. 29.

24 Care keepes his watch in every old mans eye (4 ll.).
    Rom. and Jul., Act II. sc. iii. l. 35.

48 Danger deviseth shifts ; wit waits on feare.
    Ven. and Ad., l. 690.

48 The path is smooth that leadeth unto Daunger.
    Ven. and Ad., l. 788.

54 . . . . The toongs of dying men (10 ll.).
    Rich. II., Act II. sc. i. l. 5.

55 . . Fearfull tormenting [commenting] (2 ll.).
    Rich. III., Act IV. sc. iii. l. 51.

APP. B. ENGLAND'S PARNASSUS, 1600. 431

Page of
Eng. Par.

89 The gift [*guilt*] being great, the reare doth still exceed (3 ll.).
Lucrece, l. 229.

111 Fat paunches have leane pates, and daintie bits (2 ll.).
Love's Labours Lost, Act I. sc. i. l. 26.

113 The purest treasure mortall times affoord (3 ll.).
Rich. II., Act I. sc. i. l. 177.

123 Griefe hath two tongues, and never woman yet (2 ll.).
Ven. and Ad., l. 1007.

123 An oven that is stopt, or river staied (6 ll.).
Ven. and Ad., l. 331.

124 . . . . Some Griefe shewes much of love (2 ll.).
Rom. and Jul., Act III. sc. v. l. 73.

124 True Griefe is fond and testy as a childe (6 ll.).
Lucrece, l. 1094.

125 Paine paies the income of each precious thing.
Lucrece, l. 334.

132 O rash false heat! wrapt in repentance cold (2 ll.).
Lucrece, l. 48.

137 True Hope is swift, and flies with swallowes wing (2 ll.).
Rich. III., Act V. sc. ii. l. 23.

143 Where love doth raigne, disturbing iealousie (8 ll.).
Ven. and Ad., l. 649.

154 . . . . Sparing Justice feeds iniquitie (1 l.).
Lucrece, l. 1687.

155 The baser is he, comming from a King (14 ll.).
Lucrece, 1002.

156 Not all the water in the rough rude sea (4 ll.).
Rich. II., Act III. sc. ii. l. 54.

157 . . . . No outragious thing
From vassall actors can be wipte away (3 ll.)
Lucrece, l. 607.

164 Love comforteth like sun-shine after raine (6 ll.).
Ven. and Ad., l. 799.

164 O deeper sinne then bottomlesse conceit (7 ll.).
Lucrece, l. 701.

171 . . . . love to heaven is fled (6 ll.).
Ven. and Ad., l. 793.

173 Love is a smoake, made with fume of sighes (5 ll.).
Rom. and Jul., Act I. sc. i. l. 196.

176 . . . . O brawling Love, O loving hate! (6 ll.).
Rom. and Jul., Act I. sc. i. l. 182.

180 Love keeps his revels where there are but twaine.
Ven. and Ad., l. 123.

182 O bold-beleeving Love! how hote [*strange*] it seemes (6 ll.).
Ven. and Ad. l. 985.

APP. B. SHAKESPERE'S INFLUENCE ON OTHER WRITERS.

Page of
Eng. Par.
182 Love goes toward Love, as schoole-boyes from their bookes (2 ll.).
Rom. and Jul., Act II. sc. ii. l. 156.
182 Love can comment upon every woe (1 l.).
Ven. and Ad., l. 714.
185 . . The sweetest honey
Is loathsome in his owne deliciousnesse (5 ll.).
Rom. and Jul., Act II. sc. vi. l. 11.
189 Against Loves fier feares frost hath dissolution (1 l.).
Lucrece, l. 355.
190 O learne to love; the lesson is but plaine (2 ll.).
Ven. and Ad., l. 407.
190 Love thrives not in the heart, that shadowes dreadeth.
Lucrece, l. 270.
192 Foule words and frownes must not repell a Lover (4 ll.).
Ven. and Ad., l. 573.
192 . . Lovers houres are long, though seeming short (5 ll.).
Ven. and Ad., l. 842.
192 A Lover may bestride the gossamours (3 ll.).
Rom. and Jul., Act II. sc. vi. l. 18.
204 . . Miserie is troden on by many (2 ll.).
Ven. and Ad., l. 707.
207 Soft pittie enters at an iron gate (1 l.).
Lucrece, l. 595.
207 Mercie but murders, pardoning those that kill.
Rom. and Jul., Act III. sc. i. l. 202.
217 . . markes descried in mens nativitie (2 ll.).
Lucrece, l. 538.
222 Opportunitie! thy guilt is great (7 ll.).
Lucrece, l. 876.
229 . . revels, daunces, maskes and merry howers (2 ll.).
Love's Lab. Lost, Act IV. sc. iii. l. 379.
241 A little harme, done to a great good end (5 ll.).
Lucrece, l. 528.
246 Princes are the glasse, the schoole, the booke (2 ll.) [attributed to Warner in E. P.]
Lucrece, l. 615.
248 Princes have but their titles for their glories (6 ll.).
Rich. III, Act I. sc. iv. l. 78.
261 Often the eye mistakes, the braine being troubled.
Ven. and Ad., l. 1068.
279 Sorrow breakes seasons and reposing howres (2 ll.).
Rich. III., Act I. sc. iv. l. 76.
279 Sad Sorrow, like a heavie ringing bell (3 ll.).
Lucrece, l. 1493.
280 Fell sorrowes tooth never ranckles more (2 ll.) [attributed to S. Daniell].
Rich. II., Act I. sc. iii. l. 302.

APP. B. ENGLAND'S PARNASSUS, 1600.

Page of
Eng. Par.
282 Teares harden lust, though marble weare with raine.
    Lucrece, l. 560.
283 Thoughts are the slaves of life, and life times foole (3 ll.).
    Hen. IV, Part I, Act V. sc. iv. l. 81.
283 Thoughts are but dreames, till their effects be tried.
    Lucrece, l. 353.
284 Unfainéd Thoughts do seldome dreame on evil (2 ll.).
    Lucrece, l. 87.
284 Mishapen Time, coapsmate of ugly might (5 ll.).
    Lucrece, l. 925.
286 Times glory is to calme contending kings (21 ll.).
    Lucrece, l. 939.
288 Treason is but trusted like the foxe (3 ll.).
    Hen. IV, Part I, Act V. sc. ii. l. 9.
291 Vertue it selfe turnes vice, being misapplyed (2 ll.).
    Rom. and Jul., Act II. sc. iii. l. 21.
293 What Vertue breedes, iniquitie devours (4 ll.).
    Lucrece, l. 872.
297 Foule cankering rust the hidden treasure frets (2 ll.).
    Ven. and Ad., l. 767.
306 Short time seemes long in sorrowes sharp sustaining (3 ll.).
    Lucrece, l. 1573.
306 . . Fellowship in Woe, doth woe asswage (2 ll.).
    Lucrece, l. 790.
306 Tis double death to drowne in ken of shore (7 ll.).
    Lucrece, l. 1114.
306 Distresse likes dumps, when time is kept with teares.
    Lucrece, l. 1127.
307 Windie atturnies of our clyent woes (5 ll.).
    Rich. III, Act IV. sc. iv. l. 127.
307 . . . Few words shall fit the trespasse best (2 ll.).
    Lucrece, l. 1613.
307 Deepe sounds make better [*lesser*] noyse then shallow fords (2 ll.).
    Lucrece, l. 1329.
311 . . . . Men have marble, women waxen minds (21 ll.).
    Lucrece, l. 1240.
313 Women may fall, when there's no strength in men.
    Rom. and Jul., Act II. sc. iii. l. 80.
327 Nights candles are burnt out, and jocund day (2 ll.).
    Rom. and Jul., Act III. sc. v. l. 9.
327 Loe! now the gentle Larke, wearie of rest (6 ll.).
    Ven. and Ad., l. 853.
327 Now fallen [*and solemn*] night with slow sad pace descended (3 ll.)
    Lucrece, l. 1081.
328 The gray-eyde morne smiles on the frowning night (4 ll.).
    Rom. and Jul., Act II. sc. iii. l. 1.

CENTURIE.

434 APP. B. SHAKESPERE'S INFLUENCE ON OTHER WRITERS

Page of
Eng. Par.

334 Now the world's comforter, with wearie gate (6 ll.).
    Ven. and Ad., l. 529.

348 This royall throne of Kings, this sceptred yle (15 ll.) [attributed to M. Drayton in E. P.].
    Rich. II, Act II. sc. i. l. 40.

382 Round hoof'd, short joynted, fetlocks shag and long (6 ll.).
    Ven. and Ad., l. 295.

396 Her Lilly hand her rosie cheekes lie under (28 ll.)
    Lucrece, l. 386.

407 O ! shee doth teach the torches to burne bright (6 ll.).
    Rom. and Jul., Act I. sc. v. l. 46.

423 Even as an emptie Eagle, sharpe by fast (6 ll.).
    Ven. and Ad., l. 55.

424 As through an arch the violent roring tide (7 ll.).
    Lucrece, l. 1667.

431 Looke, as the faire and fiery-poynted sunne (4 ll.).
    Lucrece, l. 372.

431 . . . . He shakes aloft his Romaine blade (7 ll.).
    Lucrece, l. 505.

431 As the poore frighted deere, that stands at gaze (7 ll.).
    Lucrece, l. 1149.

432 Like as the Snayle, whose hornes being once hit (6 ll.).
    Ven. and Ad., l. 1033.

446 This ill presage advisedly she marketh (6 ll.).
    Ven. and Ad., l. 457

451 Looke how a bright starre shooteth from the skie (8 ll.).
    Ven. and Ad., l. 815.

PASSAGES WRONGLY ATTRIBUTED TO SHAKESPERE.

56 Delay in love breeds doubts, but sharpe deniall death.[1]
    W. Warner's *Albions England*, 1597, B. IV. c. xxi. l. 35.

178 Most true it is that true love hath no power (2 ll.).
    Spenser's F. Q, Bk. I. c. iii. st. 30.

178 True love is free, and led with selfe delight (2 ll.).
    Spenser's F. Q, Bk. IV. c. i. st. 46.

---

[1] This line, attributed to Shakespere by R. A., appears to be taken from Warner's much weaker line,

"Delay he sayth, breedeth doubts, but sharpe deniall Death."

APP. B.   ENGLAND'S PARNASSUS, 1600.   435

Page of
Eng. Par.
307 Words are but winde, why cost they then so much ? (2 ll.)
                    Leg. of Lord Hastings (1610), p. 429.¹
307 Forth irreturnable flies the spoken Word (8 ll.).
                    Leg. of Lord Hastings, p. 429.
369 That time of yeere when the inamoured sunne (7 ll.).
                    Jervis Markham's Tragedy of *Sir Richard
                    Grinvile*, 1595, 1st stanza, sign. B 4.

*PASSAGES ATTRIBUTED TO SHAKESPERE,
BUT NOT IDENTIFIED.*

Page of
Eng. Par.
109 Like as the gentle heart it selfe bewraies,
        In doing gentle deeds with francke delight :
     Even so the baser minde it selfe displaies,
        In canckered malice, and revenge for spight.

178 Love alwaies doth bring forth most bounteous deeds,
     And in each gentle heart desire of honor breeds.

191 The lover and beloved are not tied to one love.

---

¹ The Legend of Lord Hastings is in the collection called the *Mirour for Magistrates*, and underwent several variations in different editions of that work. The above quotations are from stanzas included in the editions of 1574 and 1610; they are not to be found in the editions of 1578 (last part) and 1587.

436 APP. B. SHAKESPERE'S INFLUENCE ON OTHER WRITERS.

SPECIMENS OF VARIOUS READINGS.

The pureſt treaſure mortall times affoord,
Is ſpotleſtic reputation, that away,
Men are but guilded trunkes, or painted clay.
England's Parnassus, p. 113.

O raſh falſe heat wrapt in repentance cold,
Thy haſte ſprings ſtill blood and nere growes old.
p. 130 *(mispaged* 132).

Where loue doth raigne, diſturbing jealouſie,
Doth call himſelfe affections Centinell,

And in a peacefull houre, dooth crye kill, kill,
Diſtempering gentle loue with his deſire,
As ayre and water dooth abate the fire :
This found informer, this bare breeding ſpie
This cancker that eates up this tender ſpring,
This carry-tale, diſcentio's jealouſie.
p. 143.

Loue is a ſmoake made with fume of ſighes,
Being purg'd, a fier ſparkling in Louers eies
Being vext, a ſea nouriſht with louing teares,
What is it elſe? a madneſſe moſt diſtreſt,
A choaking gall, and a preſeruing ſweet.
p. 173.

The pureſt treaſure mortall times affoord
Is ſpotleſſe reputation, that away
Men are but guilded loame, or painted clay.
Rich. II (ed. 1598), Act I. sc. i.

O raſh falſe heate, wrapt in repentant cold,
Thy haſtie ſpring ſtill blads and nere growes old
Lucrece (ed. 1594), l. 48.

For where love raignes, diſturbing jealouſie
Doth call himſelf affections centinell;
Gives falſe alarms, ſuggeſteth mutinie,
And in a peacefull houre doth crie kill, kil.
Diſtempering gentle love with his deſire,
As aire and water doth abate the fire.
This foure informer, this bare-breeding ſpie,
This canker that eates up love's tender ſpring
This carry-tale, diſſentious jealouſie.
V. & A. (ed. 1599), l. 649, &c.

Love is a ſmoke made with the fume of ſighes
Being purg'd, a fire ſparkling in lovers eies,
Being vext, a ſea nouriſht with loving teares
What is it elſe? a madneſſe moſt diſcreet,
A choking gall, and a preſerving ſweete.
Rom. & Jul. (ed. 1599), Act I. sc. i.

APP. B. ENGLAND'S PARNASSUS, 1600.

The foregoing lists show the page of *England's Parnassus*, the first line of the passage, the number of lines quoted, and in what work of Shakespere (or other writer) the original passage is to be found.

The collection of poems entitled "England's Parnassus : or the choycest Flowers of our Moderne Poets," brought out in 1600 by an editor with the initials R. A. (usually considered to mean Robert Allot, though Mr. Collier inclines to Robert Armin), contains, besides three passages in reality Shakespere's, though given as from other writers, 97 extracts attributed to Shakespere. On carefully going through these, six are found to be wrongly so given; *Spencer's* Fairy Queen, *Warner's* England's Albion, the *Legend of Lord Hastings* in the *Mirror for Magistrates*, and *Jervis Markham's* Tragedy of Sir H. Grinville, being their originals. Three quotations to which Shakespere's name is attached I and others are unable to find in his plays or his poems ; one (*Eng. Par.*, p. 190), which escaped the searches of Mr. Collier, I have discovered in *Lucrece*. These last three, therefore, I print in full at the end of the above lists, leaving the reader to determine whether they lie hidden in any of the Poet's known works, or are relics of some lost poem of his, or whether they really belong to some other writer. The two first seem to me to bear the true Shakesperean ring.

In 1814 Mr. T. Park reprinted *England's Parnassus* in his *Heliconia*, vol. iii., with a few notes, but, as he says, he gives "these Parnassian reliques, with most of their 'imperfections on their head,'" that is (unlike Mr. Collier), he reprints the collection of 1600 as it stands.

Mr. Collier reprinted *England's Parnassus* in 1867 (among his Seven English Poetical Miscellanies) with a short Introductory Notice, and with a reference under each extract, identifying the source of nearly every quotation. His work does not appear to be an exact reprint of the *Parnassus* of 1600, but in a large number of cases I have found that he prints the passages, as corrected from their authors. Owing so greatly to his labours I have been sorry to note, in the course of verifying the quotations from Shakespere, many mistakes in reference, mistakes all of which (except one) occur in connection with *Venus and Adonis* and *Lucrece*. It is so easy to make errors in counting the stanzas of lengthy poems like these, that it is not wonderful perhaps that they should have been made ; I have hoped to avoid this difficulty by giving reference to the *lines* of the poems, which may be the more useful, as counting by lines instead of stanzas is the method adopted in the Globe and other editions of Shakespere. I have given the lines in these lists as they stand in *England's Parnassus*, not as they would be if taken direct from their authors (which last seems to be the method pursued by Mr. Collier) ; the reader will thus be able to gain an idea of the variations in reading which occur in the passages ; some of these are indicated between square brackets. A few passages are printed entire for the sake of further comparison of readings ; an examination of about a third of the whole shows the variations not to be numerous, though T. Park says (*Heliconia*, vol. iii., *Advertisement*) that "there is a pervading incorrectness in the excerpts themselves."

438 APP. B. SHAKESPERE'S INFLUENCE ON OTHER WRITERS.

This collection affords a strong proof that in 1600 Shakespere's popularity was based upon his love-writings more than on any other, while the connection between *Venus and Adonis* and *Romeo and Juliet* is also incidentally illustrated. Out of the 91 genuine Shakesperean extracts 63 are from *Venus and Adonis*, and *Lucrece;* while of the remaining 28, 13 are from *Romeo and Juliet;* the rest being from *Richard II, Richard III, Hen. IV.* Part I, and *Love's Labours Lost.* The classification into subjects by the compiler did not apparently affect his choice of the sources, in Shakespere's case, for the anthology.

18. *Belvedere,* or *The Garden of the Muses.* [Collected by John Bodenham, sign. A 7] . . . 1600

   In a list of twenty-five "Moderne and extant Poets, that have liv'd togither; [extracts being taken] from many of their extant workes, and some kept in privat," we find "William Shakspeare." (*To the Reader,* A 5, bk.)

19. *England's Helicon.* [Collected by John Bodenham] 1600

   Contains one piece, "On a day, (alack the day)," from Shakespere, out of *Love's Labours Lost,* Act IV. sc. iii. This collection also contains part of the song, "As it fell upon a day," and the song, "My flocks feed not," attributed to Shakespere in the *Passionate Pilgrim* (XVIII and XXI), but written by Barnfield; they are here signed "*Ignoto,*" Henry Constable's "The Sheepheard's Song of Venus and Adonis," the nearest parallel to Shakespere's *Venus and Adonis,* is also found in this collection.

20. *The English Parnassus:* or, a helpe to English Poesie. Containing a Collection of all Rhyming Monosyllables, the choicest Epithets, and Phrases: with some general forms upon all Occasions, Subjects, and Theams. By Josua Poole. (Second ed. 1677.) 1657

   Among "the Books principally made use of in the compiling of this Work" (p. 41) is "Shakespeare." In the third Part (p. 229), in which phrases and extracts are arranged under the alphabetical order of subjects, passages and lines from various poets are blended and run together in a way that is certainly ingenious,[1] though one not likely to have

---

[1] For example, under the head *Anchorite* we have a line and half from *Twelfth Night* with a strange jumble,—

   "Sitting like patience on a monument,
   Smiling at grief, uninterested in the worlds affairs:
   That onely lives, to learn well how to die."

APP. B. ENGLISH PARNASSUS, 1656.

tended to accurate knowledge by young scholars (Poole was a school-master at Hadley, in Middlesex). None of the extracts are subscribed, but a large number may be recognised as from Shakespere. Without pretending to make a complete list, bits from the following plays may be noted under the respective headings and pages in Poole :— *Twelfth Night*, p. 236 (Anchorite) ; *Romeo and Juliet*, p. 238 (Angels), 295 Oberon's Diet, 500 (Stars) ; *Henry V*, 259 (Bees)[1]; 1 *Hen. VI*, 285 (Comet)[1]; *Merchant of Venice*, 243 (Cruell)[2]; 1 *Hen. IV*, 245 (Dangerous)[2]; *King John*, 248 (Death)[2]; *Mids. Night's Dream*, and *Hamlet*, 275 (Embrace)[2]; *Hamlet*, 304 (Fear), 377 (Protestations of love) ; *Mids. N. Dream*, 290 (Fairies) ; *Richard III*, 320 (Gemmes) ; *Troilus and Cressida*, 336 (Hands) ; *Coriolanus*, and *Macbeth*, 345 (Honest) ; *Othello*, 362 (Kisse) ; *Tempest*, 414 (Nereides) ; *Love's Labours Lost*, 557 (Winter). L. T. S.]

---

[1] Pages 259, 285, of first paging ; the printer has mispaged the book and repeated from p. 239 to 288.
[2] Second paging, see last *note*.

APPENDIX C.

"*THE NEW METAMORPHOSIS*," by J. M.

THE manuscript poem quoted on p. 98, having been little noticed elsewhere, some short account of it may be thought worth having, because, written in Shakesperian times, it is full of allusions to the passing history and manners of those days, and in one or two places a possible reference to Shakespere or his writing may be traced.

Add. MS. 14,824, 14,825, and 14,826 is contained in three volumes quarto, in the contemporary vellum binding, of 88, 136, and 268 leaves respectively; the books are written in a close neat hand, leaving a considerable margin; few corrections are made, but here and there additional lines are put in the margin. The whole poem extends to about 34000 lines, divided into 24 Books, to each of which is prefixed an "Argument."

The first volume (Part I) bears two title-pages, one running thus: "The Newe Metamorphosis. Or a Feaste of Fancie or Poeticall Legendes. The first parte Diuided into Twelue Bookes. Written by J. M. gent 1600,"[1] with the motto,

"Hor: Aut prodesse volunt, aut delectare Poëtæ
aut simul et iucunda, et idonea dicere vitæ." (fo. 1.)

[De Ar. Poet, l. 333, 334.]

Then comes the Arguments for six books, then on fo. 3 the

---

[1] The title as originally written was: "The New Metamorphosis or Poeticall Legendes. Diuided into Twelue Bookes." "Or A feaste of Fancie," and "The first parte" were added afterwards.

APP. C. "THE NEW METAMORPHOSIS." 441

second title,—"An Iliade of Metamorphosis. Or the Araignement of Vice [*or Poeticall Legendes* having been written and then crossed out here] Devided into Twelve bookes. 1600.

"Parce tuum Vatem sceleris damnare Cupido
parce hos versiculos, contemptu impij serva."

"Tomus Primus" is crossed through on each title-page, but it evidently ought to be there. The other six arguments for vol. i. are prefixed to part ii. on fo. 1. "Tomus secundus," in vol. ii. also comprises twelve books, the arguments of which are not, however, set forth at the beginning of the volume.

Various conjectures may be made as to who J. M., the author, was. A former owner [1] of the Manuscript, who in 1806 (see vol. ii., fo. 138, back) went through it making frequent marginal notes in pencil, suggests on the title-page, *John Marston, Jervase Markham, John Mason*, and a fourth name which is rubbed out. Mr. Joseph Haslewood in his edition of Brathwait's *Barnabees Journal*, 1820 (vol. i. p. 96), quoting some lines from this MS. descriptive of Giggleswick Springs in Yorkshire, sets down the author as J[ohn] M[arston], but gives no reasons for so doing. Mr. Halliwell also quotes a few lines as to boy-players (from vol. ii., fo. 46) in his *Life of Shakespere*, 1848, p. 148, note; and in his edition of Marston's Works, published in the *Library of old authors*, 1856, vol. i, Pref. p. xix, he refers to the *New Metamorphosis* and says, "It is a long rambling poem, and parts of it resemble in some degree" Marston's style, but that it has slender claim to be considered his. The writer seems to have been of French name or extraction; he tells us on the fourth leaf (vol. i. part i):

"My name is Frenche, to tell yo^u in a worde,
Yet came not in with Conqueringe Williams fworde."

The author thus introduces his work in his "Prologue" (fos. 5, 6, back):—

---

[1] F. G. Waldron, see his initials "F. G. W.," vol. ii., fo. 234.

> " I here prefente my newe-borne poëfie,
> not with vaine glory puft to make me knowne,
> or Indian-like with feathers not myne owne
> to decke my felf, as many vfe to doe,
> to filchinge lynes I am a deadly foe.
>
> * * * * *
>
> Myne infante Mufe, longe ftudieng what to wright
> at first refolud fome bloody warres t'endighte
> but Loue caffierd that thought with his foft charme
> Sayeing that warre's beft, which can doe noe harme."

After weighing several subjects, he decides upon satire of the vices of the time :—

> " What then is fitter for thefe impious tymes
> then yrefull Satyrs, clad in rugged rymes,
> Harfh though my lynes be, you fhall fubftance fynde.
>
> * * * * *
>
> I haue noe Poëts pleafinge fmoth-fyl'd veyne
> but a ragg'd Satyrifts rougher hewen ftraine."

He cafts it under the guife of shewing to "the world infected with the goute," peftilence, pride, ingratefulnefs, witch-craft and other scourges, and "their strange mutation wrought by the Gods iufte Transformation."

Finally he invokes the assistance of

> " Matilda fayre, guide thou my wandring quill
> who rul'ft my harte, that vicious men & ill
> to their eternall fhame I may difgrace,
> & fo extoll of righteous men the race.
> My poore dull witte richly doe thou infpire,
> inflame my braine with Loues celeftiall fyre,
> that I may liuely in my rymes expreffe
> the fecret'ft actions of retyrednes,
> and fhewe the vglieft fate of horrid vice
> that fo hereafter it may none intice."

That either Marston or Markham could be the author may be doubted, for both had published several works before 1600, and would neither of them therefore speak of their "infant muse" in that year.[1] Marston's, too, were Satires: "The Scourge of Villanie, three bookes of Satyres," came out in 1598, and a second edition in 1599; his "Metamorphosis of Pigmalion's Image, and certaine Satyres," 1598, may possibly have suggested the subject of J. M.'s poem. Markham, of whom it is said that "his thefts were innumerable," is surely excluded by the declaration,—

"to filchinge lynes I am a deadly foe."

Whoever the author was, he seems to have kept his work by him, adding to it and correcting from time to time, for about twelve years. For though the title-page is dated 1600, and he evidently had intended to dedicate his poem to Queen Elizabeth (see the lines "The Author to his Booke," below), "tomus secundus" shows that he took up his pen again after the accession of James I, and after telling tales and dealing with a variety of subjects—among which is the taking of Cadiz in 1596—he describes the Gun-powder Plot of 1605, and finishes by touching upon Prince Henry's death, and the marriage of Elizabeth, daughter to James I, both which took place in the winter of 1612-13. See the Arguments to Books 1, 10, and 12 of Vol. II (after, p. 450, 451).

Prefixed to the book is a dialogue between Cupid and Momus, in which they contend for the patronage of the work. After some arguing, Momus says to Cupid:—

"Wherin this booke is matter of delighte
That patronize thou; that which is of fpighte
My felf will haue, I will his Patron bee
And let the envious freely carpe at mee.

---

[1] The dedication in his own hand of a masque by Marston (unique MS. at Bridgewater House) shows that his writing and that of the author of this poem differ entirely.

Take thou the one & I will haue the other.
C. Momus, that were to make thee Cupid's brother.
M. That I regarde not, nor doe clayme for righte,
Cupid is God of Loue, Momus of spighte." (*fo.* 4, back.)

After this follows—
 "The Authore to his Booke
 Nowe booke farewell, goe, take thine vnknowne flighte
 Synce th'art protected by two of fuch mighte
 that which was once vnto a Queene intended
 is nowe vnto two powerfull Gods commended
 When Gods doe thus poore Poëts workes defende
 what rude fatyrick fpirite dares then contende."

The following are the most interesting "Arguments"

[Vol. I, Part I. fo. 1]
Lib. 1. The Gods difpof'd to mirthe did for their Plotte
 make choife of Fayery: Quarels for the Lotte
 of Gouerment: Treafon 'gainft Chaftety:
 The Cloyfters exercife cald venerie:
 Venus ta'ne wafhinge by the Fifherman:
 Joues wronges he there expoftulateth than.

Lib. 8. Womans prefumptuous wifh, her pride abated:
 Fifh-ftealers: Loue-Nymphs: Empiric tranflated:
 Rare Glaffe: Strange thinges: Secrets difcouerers
 punifht: ¹with bufie bodie¹ Reformers.
 Gullions greate draughte: Xadleus iugling tricks:
 Murderers in priffon, loue Dice, Drinke, Meri-trix.

[Lib. 10. fo. 1, back] The Popes greate power: their Legends, Hiftories
 they keepe the Lawe, their feuerall Qualities:
 Rome is defcrib'd part of th' Popes reuenewes:
 Fantaftick fafhions: Blynd-Afinus enfewes
 The Ram-pie-feafte: Apollo, Mercurie
 two Faiery Nymphes, chofe for focietie.

---

¹—¹ These words are written above, the words " and those that would be needes" being crossed through.

APP. C. "THE NEW METAMORPHOSIS." 445

Lib. 12 Cupid & Venus parlie, ſhe him chides:
The Gods fall foule, the Parliament decydes
the Controverſie: Cupid is baniſhed.
Miſcheifes that followe: Merlyn propheſied:
Gunnes are invented: Th' Fleete Invincible
Sail'd back to Spaine, almoſt Inviſible.

Tomus Secundus.

Lib. 1. [Vol. II. fo. 2 back] England deſcrib'd, th' happineſſe in its Kinge:
Loue ſeekes a ſervice, ſure a wondrous thinge:
The crueltie of th' Tanner punniſhed:
Cupids ill happe is nexte deſciphered:
Loue conquers Conquerers: Men of beſt deſertes
are wrong'd by women that haue double hartes.

Lib. 2. [fo. 21] Arcadia's life & paſtorall happineſſe
reproofe of Moderne tymes ſo greate exceſſe:
The diſmall danger of immodeſt wiues,
Who chaſte ones haue, their treble happie liues:
The Merchants curſe, the Pyrats wickedneſſe
Rebellious miſcheife doth the next expreſſe.

Lib. 6. [fo. 94. back] Strange Fountaines vertues & their qualities,
Illiterate Prieſts their fooliſh ceremonies:
Dumbe Dogges once barking, & their pronunciation:
Th'abuſe of learnd Phyſitians vocation:
Children abuſing Parents reprehended:
Wiues runninge from their Huſbands are condemned.

Lib. 7. [fo. 110, back] Th' Incontinent doth the ſuſpected murther:
Luſt, Murther, Gaminge, doe their owne deaths further:
Cales voyage is deſcrib'd, their quick returne
Engliſh humanitie, they the Countrie burne:
A Lady mourninge for th' loſſe of her Sonne
Slayne in the Conflict when to th' Gates they run.

446   APP. C.   "THE NEW METAMORPHOSIS."

[Lib. 8.
(fo. 196)] Returninge home from Cales to paffe the tyme,
ech one muft tell his tale in Profe or Ryme.
About Plantations firſt they doe begin :
Of th' Lottery: next of The Wittols fin :
A Ladies chaſtety viuely fet out :
A Laſſes coynes puniſhed fans doubt.

[Lib. 10.
(fo. 194,
back)] Murder & Treafon, Romes Religion :
The Plotte defcrib'd of th' Pouder-Treafon :
The Traytors puniſhment, their goeinge to Hell :
Their change of office which became them well :
The Jeſuits vertue liuely is fet forth,
Tyburne the Antidote, 'gainft Tyburs wroth.

[Lib. 11.
(fo. 234)] Of drunkards here a ſtorie large you fee
and eke of thofe that their Abettors be.
Of Gluttony the next, exceſſe in Feaſtinge
which many after makes exceede in Faſtinge.
Contentious Knaues, next here muft haue a roome
Calumnious-viperous-tongues from Hell doe come

[Lib. 12.
(fo. 219,
back)] The Catalogue of ancient Brittifh Kinges :
Prince Henries deathe : Elizas Nuptiallinges :
Some ſtrange Mutations at the Princely Reuels :
Of Auarice the moſt vnmanly evils :
Falſe-play vnder the bourde next requires a roome
And Pride which heere doth for the laſt diſh come.

These "Arguments" give an idea of the variety of topics touched upon in the guise of allegory; the allusions to politics—the taking of Cadiz, the American Plantations, the power of Rome, the Spanish Armada, the non-marriage of Elizabeth, James I., Gun-powder plot, the death of Prince Henry, and marriage of Princess Elizabeth, and many others; the censure of manners, dress, excess, and drunkenness. Interspersed through the second volume are several tales—the tale of the Tanner, the

Master's Tale of Parson Darcie, the Surgeon's Tale, the Gunner's Tale, Tale of Mathilda, &c.; and in this volume the poet seems to have allowed himself to wander from his original scheme, to judge from the lighter subjects in Book VI, the first two pages of which are occupied with a description of nine famous springs and wells, beginning with Buxton and ending with Malvern, to which the author travelled in search of a cure for the colic;—a description worthy to be put beside William Harrison's account of our supposed medical waters (*Description of England*, ed. New Shakspere Society, 1876, pp. 333, 336).

The following passage, though it cannot be said to be an imitation, certainly recalls Shylock's enumeration of the dislikes of various men (*Merch. of Venice*, Act IV. sc. i). Accounting for the sudden and unexpected withdrawal of a certain captain from a feast, the writer says,—

    " It was becaufe a Pigge came to the table
    which to abide by no meanes he was able
    was not the Swan worthy t' be made a Goofe
    that fuch a dynner for a pigge would loofe.
    I thinke he was a Capten fine I
    of him good fir, I pray yo^u what thinke yee?
    I knewe the like by one that nould endure
    to fee a Goofe come to the table fure
    fome can not brooke to fe a Cuftarde there
    fome of a Cheefe doe ever ftande in feare
    & I knowe one, if fhe Tobacco fee
    or fmells the fame, fhe fwoones imediately
    the like of Rofes I haue heard fome tell
    touch but the fkyn & prefently 't will fwell
    & growe to blifters." (Vol. II. fo. 257.)

The phrase in *Othello*, Act III. sc. iii.,

    " I'd let her down the wind
    To prey at fortune"

finds an illustration in the lines upon ill fortune,—

> " if one goe downe the wynde he may be ſure
> the vttermoſt of evils to endure." (Vol. II. fo. 266, back.)

Scattered through the volumes are several words and phrases, which seem to be reminiscences of Shakespere without very certain reference, but they cannot be called either imitations or parallels. L. T. S.]

APPENDIX D.

SUPPLEMENTAL EXTRACTS.

WILLIAM LAMBARD, 1601.

That which paſſed from the Excellent Majeſtie of Queen Elizabeth, in her Privie Chamber at Eaſt Greenwich, 4° Auguſti 1601, 43° Reg. ſui, towards WILLIAM LAMBARDE.

He preſented her Majeſtie with his Pandecta of all her rolls, bundells, membranes, and parcells that be repoſed in her Majeſtie's Tower at London; whereof ſhe had given to him the charge 21st January laſt paſt.

* * * *

She proceeded to further pages, and aſked where ſhe found cauſe of ſtay * * he expounded theſe all according to their original diverſities * * ſo her Majeſtie fell upon the reign of King Richard II ſaying, "I am Richard II, know ye not that?'

W. L. "Such a wicked imagination was determined and attempted by a moſt unkind Gent. the moſt adorned creature that ever your Majeſtie made."

Her Majeſtie. "He that will forget God, will alſo forget his benefactors; this tragedy was played 40^{tie} times in open ſtreets and houſes."

Printed in *John Nichols' Progresses and Processions of Queen Elizabeth*, 1823, *Vol. III. p.* 552.

CENTURIE. G G

450 APP. D. SUPPLEMENTAL EXTRACTS: WILLIAM LAMBARD.

[A copy of the document from which this is an extract was sent to Mr. Nichols "from the original, by Thomas Lambard, of Sevenoaks, Esq." After the burning of the Birmingham Shakespeare Library in Jan. 1879, another copy of the same, from a manuscript, was anonymously sent to the Library Committee from Rugeley; there are probably therefore two MSS. of it in existence. William Lambard, a well-known antiquary and lawyer, at one time Keeper of the Records in the Tower, was a Kentish man, and died Aug. 19, 1601, a few days after his conversation with the Queen. His "Pandecta Rotulorum," probably the book presented to the Queen, was published in 1600.

The extract is important in its bearing upon the story of the Essex rebellion, and the use made by the conspirators of the tragedy of *Richard II.* See before, pp. 35—37. I am indebted to my friend Mr. Sam. Timmins of Birmingham for pointing it out. L. T. S.]

JOHN RAYNOLDS. 1606.

[The old Hermit, entertaining his guest at meat, takes a skull in his hand,—]

    He held it ſtill, in his ſiniſter hand,
    And turn'd it ſoft, and ſtroakt it with the other,
    He ſmil'd on it, and oft demurely faund,
    As it had beene, the head of his owne brother:
        Oft would h'have ſpoke, but ſomething bred delay;
        At length halfe weeping, theſe words did he ſay.

    This barren ſcull, that here you do behold,
    Why might it not, have beene an Emperours head?
    Whoſe ſtore-houſe rich, was heap'd with maſſy gold,
    If it were ſo, all that to him is dead:
        His Empire crowne, his dignities and all,
        When death tooke him, all them from him did fall.

       *   *   *   *

    And might it not, a Lady ſometimes ioye,
    T'haue deckt, and trim'd, this now rainbeaten face,
    With many a trick, and new-found pleaſing toye?
    Which if that now, ſhe did behold her caſe.
        Although on earth, ſhe were for to remaine,
        She would not paint, nor trimme it up againe.

    Why might not this, have beene ſome lawiers pate,
    The which ſometimes, brib'd, brawl'd, and tooke a fee,

And lawe exacted, to the higheſt rate?
Why might not this, be ſuch a one as he?
Your quirks, and quillets, now ſir where be they,
Now he is mute, and not a word can ſay.

Dolarnys Primerose, Or the first part of the passionate Hermit.
1606. *Sign. D* 4, *back, E. In Mr. Henry Huth's Library.
Reprinted for the Roxburghe Club,* 1816. [*Dolarnys=Raynolds*]

[Compare with this *Hamlet,* Act V. sc. i. Raynold's verses are perhaps a closer parallel than Thomas Randolph's reminiscences of the same scene in his *Jealous Lovers,* 1632, see before, pp. 187, 188.

If these verses may be taken as an undoubted allusion to Hamlet, not the least interesting is the first quoted above, which describes exactly the action of Hamlet on taking up the skull in use on the stage at the present day, and may fairly be supposed to bear reference to what Raynolds and the playgoers of his day had before their eyes in the grave-digger's scene. It is to be observed that no authority for this action, the turning soft, stroking, smiling, &c., is to be found in the play itself.

The last verse given above was quoted in the *Athenæum,* May 22, 1875, and in Mr. H. H. Furness' *Variorum Hamlet,* Vol. I. p. 386. Mr. Haslewood printed portions of the poem in the *British Bibliographer,* 1810, Vol. I. p. 153. L. T. S.]

* SIR THOMAS SMITH, 1605.

This falling away of them, * * haftied the laft breath of the once hoped-for *Prince*, as from him that muft notorioufly know * * that his fathers Empire and Gouernment, was but as the *Poeticall Furie in a Stage-aɛtion*, compleat yet with horrid and wofull Tragedies: a firft, but no second to any *Hamlet;* and that now *Reuenge*, iuft *Reuenge* was comming with his Sworde drawne againft him, his royall Mother, and deareft Sifter, to fill up thofe Murdering Sceanes.

> *Voiage and Entertainment in Rushia. With the tragicall ends of two Emperors, and one Empresse, within one moneth during his being there: And the miraculous preservation of the now raigning Emperor, esteemed dead for* 18 *yeares.* 1605. *Sign. K.*

THOMAS DEKKER, 1609.

[In his account of the Gipsies and their thefts, and killing of sheep, pigs, and poultry],—

The bloudy tragedies of al thefe, are only aɛted by yᵉ Women * * The Stage is fome large Heath, or a Firre bufh Common, far from any houfes: Upon which cafting them-felves into a Ring, they inclofe the Murdered, till the Maffacre be finifhed. If any paffenger come by, and wondring to fee fuch a conjuring circle kept by Hel-houndes, demaund what fpirits they raife there? one of the Murderers fteps to him, poyfons him with fweete wordes and fhifts him off, with this lye, yᵗ one of the women is falne in labour. But if any mad Hamlet hearing this, fmell villanie, & rufh in by violence to fee what the tawny Divels are dooing, then they excufe the faɛt, &c.

> *Lanthorne and Candle-light. Or, The Bell-Mans second Nights-Walke. Sign.* H 2.

*SAMUEL ROWLANDS, 1620.

I will not cry *Hamlet Revenge* my greeves,
But I will call *Hang-man Revenge* on theeves.

The Night-Raven. Sign. D 2.

[These three allusions were classed in Dr. Ingleby's first edition as "irrelevant," or mistaken. But it seems to me that considering their dates, it is open to doubt whether they do not as likely refer to Shakespere's play as to the older *Hamlet*, and that therefore they are of sufficient interest to warrant my printing the extracts in full. Our authorities for the existence of the pre-Shakesperian play of *Hamlet* are Nash's *Epistle* prefixed to Green's *Menaphon* (referred to in Appendix A, p. 421), and Lodge's *Wit's Miserie* (see before, p. 294). Professor Dowden, agreeing with me that there is no sufficient reason for setting down the above three passages decidedly as mistaken references, or for deciding that they refer to the old *Hamlet*, remarks upon the latter, — "I think, considering the probable date of the old *Hamlet*, and the remarkable impression apparently made by the ghost crying 'Revenge,' that it is not unlikely to have been a bloody drama in which the central *motiv* was revenge, and that the Hamlet of that old play was a close kinsman of the Hamlet of the *Historie* [of 1608, translated from Belleforest's *Histoires Tragiques*], capable of all kinds of vigorous action. In the old play he probably assumed his antic disposition manifestly for a purpose" (*Private letter*). He therefore thinks it possible, though not certain, that the two "revenge" passages above given may be connected with the old play. L. T. S.]

Anonymous, about 1613.

All yow that pleafe to underftand,
  Come liften to my ftorye,
To fee Death with his rakeing brande
  'Mongft fuch an auditorye :
Regarding neither Cardinall's might,
Nor yet the rugged face of Henry the eight.

A Sonnett upon the Pittifull Burneing of the Globe Play House in London. Second Stanza. First printed by Mr. Haslewood in the Gentleman's Magazine, Vol. 86, p. 114. Reprinted in W. C. Hazlitt's Roxburghe Library, The English Drama and Stage, 1869, p. 225.

[See the Letter from Thomas Lorkins, before, p. 102, as to the burning of the Globe Theatre, which took place on 29 June, 1613. L. T. S.]

GEFFRAY MYNSHUL, 1617.

[Addressing a creditor].--

If nothing will make thy ftony heart relent, thou in being cruell to thy debtor art worfe then the hang-man; * * But it may be thy eftate is ficke, thy credit much ingaged, and to fave thy felfe thou art forced to doe this. In fo doing thou doeft well; if another weare thy coate, and thou goeft cold, thou maift plucke it from his fhoulders. * * but if he which hath borrowed thy coate hath worne it out, and hath not a ragge to cover him with, wilt thou trample vpon his naked body? If with the Jew of Malta, inftead of coyne, thou requireft a pound of flefh next to thy debtor's heart, wilt thou cut him in pieces?

Essayes and Characters of a Prison and Prisoners. Of Creditors. 1618. *Reprint, Edinburgh,* 1821, *pp.* 30, 31.

[Mynshul wrote his Essayes while confined in the King's Bench Prison for debt, where he filled up his idle time by acute obfervations on the characters of those around him: he gives a melancholy picture of the miseries of unfortunate debtors in the seventeenth century. He seems to have confounded Marlowe's Jew of Malta with Shakespere in his memory, but the mention of the pound of flesh shows that it was Shylock to whom he referred.

The "Epiftle Dedicatory" is dated 27 January, 1617. L. T. S.]

NICHOLAS BRETON, died 1624.

The chattering Pie, the Jay, and eke the Quaile,
The Thruftle-Cock that was fo blacke of hewe.
The Arbor of Amorous Devises, 1597, p. 4, col. 2.

the gentlemans brains were much troubled, as you may fee by his perplexities; but with ftudying how to make one line levell with another, in more rime then perhaps fome will thinke reafon, with much adoe about nothing, hee hath made a piece of worke as little worth
Melancholike Humours: 1600. To the Reader, p. 5.

Mafter Wyldgoofe, it is not your huftie tuftie can make mee afraid of your bigge lookes: for I faw the Play of Ancient Piftoll, where a Cracking Coward was well cudgeld for his knavery: your railing is fo neare the Rafcall, that I am almoft afhamed to beftow fo good a name as the Rogue on you.
A Poste with a Packet of Mad Letters (Part I. 1603). [No. 22, A "coy Dame's" answer to a " Letter of scorne."] p. 11, col. 2.

Grimello. Why fir, I fet no fprings for Woodcocks, and though I be no great wife man, yet I can doe fomething elfe, then fhooe the Goofe for my liuing: and therefore, I pray you neither feare your Purfe, nor play too much with my folly.
Grimello's Fortunes, 1604, p. 5, col. 1.

An vnlearned and vnworthily called a Lawyer, is the figure of a foot-poft, who carries letters but knowes not what is in them, only can read the fuperfcriptions to direct them to their right owners. * * But what a taking are poore clients in when this too much trufted cunning companion, better redde in Pierce Plowman then in Ploydon and in the Play of Richard the Third then in the Pleas of Edward the Fourth; perfwades them all is fure when hee is fure of all!

The Good and the Badde, 1616, *No.* 19, *An Vnworthy Lawyer.*
The Complete Works in Prose and Verse of Nicholas Breton.
Rev. A. B. Grosart's Chertsey Worthies' Library, 1876-1878.

[In the third of the above extracts, Breton turns to good account the "swaggering rascal" of *Second Part of Henry IV;* in the fourth we have Polonius' contemptuous exclamation (*Hamlet*, Act I. Sc. iii. l. 115); in the first a line of Bottom's song in the *Midsummer Night's Dream*, Act III. Sc. i. l. 128. The others seem to name two of Shakespere's plays. The Rev. Dr. Grosart, who kindly points out these allusions, believes that Breton's works contain many words and phrases which bear the mark of Shakespere's influence. L. T. S.]

JOHN SWAN, 1635.

I conclude ; and with him who writeth thus, cannot but fay,

> Oh mickle is the pow'rfull good that lies
> In herbs, trees, ftones, and their true qualities ;
> For nought fo vile that on the earth doth live,
> But to the earth fome fecret good doth give.
> And nought fo rich on either rock or fhelf,
> But, if unknown, lies ufeleffe to it felf.
> Therefore who thus doth make their fecrets known,
> Doth profit others, and not hurt his own.
>
> *Speculum Mundi. Or A glasse representing the face of the world.* Cambridge, 1635, p. 299.

[Swan's work, a prose one, is somewhat on the plan of the first week of Du Bartas' Divine Weeks, and is a kind of epitome of the natural science of the day. He concludes that part of the "third day's work" which relates to precious stones, with these four lines quoted from Friar Laurence' speech, *Romeo and Juliet*, Act II. Sc. iii. 1. 15. The last four lines appear to have been added by himself. Swan has "good" instead of Shakespere's "grace" in the first line, "trees" for "plants" in the second, and "secret" for "special" in the fourth.

The quotation was pointed out by Mr. C. E. Browne in the *Athenæum*, 22 May, 1875. L. T. S.]

*JOHN MILTON, 1627.

Seu puer infelix indelibata reliquit
   Gaudia, & abrupto flendus amore cadit,
Seu ferus e tenebris iterat Styga criminis ultor,
   Confcia funereo pectora torre movens.

> *Elegia prima ad Carolum Diodatum.*
> *Elegiarum Liber primus. Poems of*
> *Mr. John Milton, both English and*
> *Latin, compos'd at several times.*
> 1645. *p.* 13 *of second paging.*

[Warton, in his edition of Milton's Poems, 1791, p. 425, points out that Milton, describing tragedy on the stage, perhaps intends *Romeo* in the first couplet here given; and either *Hamlet* or *Richard the Third* in the second. Warton, however, confesses that the allusions are loose and do not exactly correspond. Dr. Ingleby sends the passage for insertion. Cowper thus renders these lines :—

> "As when from bliss untasted torn away,
> Some youth dies, hapless, on his bridal day,
> Or when the ghost, sent back from shades below,
> Fills the assassin's heart with vengeful woe."

> *Latin and Italian Poems of Milton, translated*
> *into English Verse,* 4*to.* 1808. *p.* 11.

L. T. S.]

I. GENERAL INDEX.

Works to which no author's name is attached will be found under the head Anonymous.
The items to which a * is prefixed index the notes and general matter; the rest indicate "allusions," and include the Appendix on "Influence."

ACHERLEY, Thomas, 52
*Actor, vocation of, 58, 277, 411
*Actors of Shakespere, practices of early, 132, 451
*Alexander, W., Earl of Stirling, 423
*Allot, Robert, 437
*Alterations of Shakespere's plays after the Restoration, 324, 356, 365, 369-70, 380, 381, 389, 390, 391, 392
"Angliæ Speculum Morale," 429
ANONYMOUS—
  A Banquet of Jeasts, 181
  A Mournful Dittie, 56
  Antidote against Melancholy, 325
  Ballad on Duke of Monmouth, 387
  Brome's plays, Preface to, 308
  Characters, with Sir T. Overbury's Wife, 114
  Choyce Drollery, 134
  Elegy on death of Shakespere, 20
  Elegy on Lovelace, 313
  Epitaph on Jonson, 277
  Heraclitus Ridens, 388
  Hermeticall Banquet, drest by a Spagiricall Cook, 290

ANONYMOUS—
  *Histrio-Mastix, 200, 248
  Hudibras (Spurious), 329
  London Post, 251
  Meeting of Gallants at an Ordinarie, 65
  Mercurius Britannicus, 252
  Merry Divel of Edmonton, 73
  Of Education, 353
  "One friend to another," 40
  Perfect Occurrences, 273
  "Person of Honour," 386
  Pimlyco or Runne Red-cap, 89
  Prologue to Shirley's Love Tricks, 337
  Prologue to Rochester's Valentinian, 403
  Ratsey's Ghost, xix, 67
  Returne from Pernassus, 48, 68
  Rump: Poems and Songs, 244
  Song of 17th century, 419
  Sonnet on the burning of the Globe theatre, 455
  Ten Players' epistle, prefixed to first folio of Beaumont and Fletcher, 262
  Troilus and Cressida, Address prefixed to, 87
  The Hectors, or the False Challenge, 301

I. GENERAL INDEX.

ANONYMOUS—
   Verses prefixed to second Folio of Shakespere, 189, 190
   Vindex Anglicus, 256
   Willobie's Avisa, verses prefixed to, 6
   Wily Beguilde, 19
   Wits Recreations, 228
Anthropophagus, 159
Anton, Robert, 115
Aubrey, John, 383
Austin, Samuel, 309
Aylward, Paul, 257

B. (R), Greene's Funeralls, 3
Bacon, Lord, Conference of Pleasure xvi *note*
Baker, Sir Richard, 250, 315
*Ballads, 56, 63, 330, 387, 419
Bancroft, Thomas, 227
Banks, John, 395
Barkstead, William, 76
Barnfeild, Richard, 26
Baron, Robert, 279
Barrey, Ludovic, 95
*Bartas, Du, 142 *note*
Basse, William, 136, 151 *note*, 402
Beaumont and Fletcher—
   Knight of the Burning Pestle, 78 *note*, 89 *note*, 117
   Scornful Ladie, 117
   Booksellers' Preface to Works, 377
Bell, William, 288
Benson, John, 229
Berkenhead, J., 271
*Black Book, 423
Bodenham, John, 438
Bolton, Edmund, 91

Brathwaite, Richard—
   Strappado for the Divell, 112, 113
   The English Gentleman, 224
Breedy, Daniel, 257
Breton, Nicholas, 457
Brome, Alexander, 296, *429
Brome, Richard, 225
Brome's Plays, preface to, 308
Brooke, Christopher, 109
Browne, Thomas, 406
Buck, Sir George, 272
Burbadge, Elegy on, 131, xvii
*Burbage, 58, 62, 67, 84, 132
Burton, Robert, 161
*Bust of Shakespere, 125, 154
Butler, Charles, 243
Butler, Samuel, 276 *note*

C. (I), St. Marie Magdalen's Conversion, 57
C. (I), Epigrames, 63
Camden, William, 59
Carew, Richard, 20
*Carew, Thomas, 429
Cartwright, William, 270
Cavendish, Margaret, 332
Censure of the Poets, 168
Chamberlain, Robert, 226
Chapman, George, 69, 186
Chester, Robert, 43, 44
Chettle, Henry—
   Kind Hart's Dream, 4
   England's Mourning Garment, 55
Chetwood, Knightley, 399
*Chetwood, William R., 426
Chillingworth, William, 223

I. GENERAL INDEX.

Clarke, William, 15
Cleveland, John, 254
Cokaine, Sir Aston—
  To Philip Massenger, 196
  A Preludium to Richard Brome's Plays, 297
  To William Dugdale, 305
  To John Honyman, 306
  To Clement Fisher, 307
Condell, Henry, 143
Cook, J., 276
Cope, Sir Walter, 62
Corbet, Richard, 128
Cornwallis, Sir William, 41
Cotton, Charles, 336
Cowley, Abraham, 170, 303
Cranley, Thomas, 204
Crown, J., 389
*Current Elizabethan phrases, 19, 27, 54, 61, 82-3, 117, 155
DANIEL, George, of Beswick, 265, 266
Daniel, Samuel, 427
*Davenant, Charles, 398 note
Davenant, Sir William, 216
  *his abilities, 339 note
  *his operas and alterations of Shakespere, 323, 356, 397, 408
  *reputed son of Shakespere, 385
Davenport, Anthony, 281
Davies, John, of Hereford—
  Microcosmos, 58, *277
  Civill Warres of Death and Fortune, 84
  Scourge of Folly, 28, *94, *155 note
  Papers Complaint, 96, *423
Day, John, 82

Decker, Thomas—
  Satiro-Mastix, 50
  A Knight's conjuring, &c., 74
  Lanthorne and Candle Light, 453
*"Delighted" in *Measure for Measure*, 217
Denham, Sir John—
  Verses on John Fletcher, 263
  Poems, 343
*Des Maizeaux, P., 199, 397 note
Digges, Leonard, 154, 231
Don Quijote, 428
Dowdall, Mr., 417
Drayton, Michael—
  Legend of Mathilda, 13
  Barrons Wars, 53
  Elegies, 168
  Polyolbion, 428
*Drolls and Drolleries, 354
Dryden, John—
  Tempest, 211, 338, 339
  Essay of Dramatic Poesie, 341
  Lines to Congreve, 349 note
  Conquest of Granada, 352
  An Evening's Love, 352 note
  Prologue to University of Oxford, 357
  Prologue to *Aurungzebe*, 362
  Preface to *All for Love*, 368
  Prologue to *Julius Cæsar*, 348
  Preface to *Troilus and Cressida*: Criticism on Tragedy, 369—377
  Prologue to *Troilus and Cressida*, 376
  Prologue to C. Davenant's *Circe*, 398
  Prologue to Harris' *Mistakes*, 411
  Satires of Juvenal & Persius, 413
  To Sir Godfrey Kneller, 414

464 I. GENERAL INDEX.

Drummond, Sir William, 71, 111, 116, 129
*Du Bartas, 142 note
Dugdale, Sir William, 298
Dunton, John, 367 note

EDWARDES, Thomas, 17
"England's Parnassus," 430—438
*Epigram, supposed, by Jonson and Shakespere, 410 note
Epigrames by I. C., 63
Essex Rebellion, examinations—
Sir Gelly Meyricke, 35
Augustine Phillipps, 36
Evelyn, John, 326, 407
Evremond, St., 396

FELTHAM, Owen, 180, 213
*Ferrers, George, 22 note
Field, Nathaniel, 127
*Fitzgeoffry, H., 233 note, 290
Flecknoe, Richard, 314, 345
Fletcher, John (see Beaumont)—
The Woman Hater, 72
Wild Goose Chace, 135
The Woman's Prize, 135
Knight of Malta, 166
Noble Gentleman, 167
Fletcher, Joseph, 101
Folio, first, I. M.'s verses prefixed to, 155
Forman, Simon, 97
Freeman, Thomas, 106
*French writers, first notices of Shakespere by, 396, 415
Fuller, Thomas—
Worthies, 246, 249
Church History, 249 note
Fulman, William, 405

GAYTON, Edmund, 299
Gee, John, 160
Gell, Robert, 169
*German writer, first mention of Shakespere by, 342 note
*Germany, English Actors in, 342
*Gildon, Charles, 198 note
*Globe Theatre, burning of, 102, 455
*Gosson, Stephen, 421
Greene, Robert, 2
*Greene's Funeralls, 3
*Guzman de Alfarache, 155

H., Elegy on Burbage, 131
Habington, William, 200
Hales of Eton, John, 198, 208, 341
Harbert, Sir W. (?), 12
Harvey, Gabriel—
MS. note in Speght's Chaucer, 30
*Four Letters, &c., 422
Heminge, John, 143
Hemings, William, 429
Heraclitus Ridens, 388
Herbert, Sir Henry, 157, 173
Heywood, Thomas—
Fayre Mayde of the Exchange, 80
Apology for Actors, 99
Hierarchie of the Blessed Angels, 202
Woman killed with Kindness, 427
Hind, Capt. James, 291
Holland, Hugh, 153
Holland, Samuel, 302
Howell, James, 264
Howes, Edmund, 108

I. GENERAL INDEX.

Howes, John, 411 *note*
Hubburd's Tales, Father, 60

I. M. S., *see* S
Isham, Thomas, 355

J. (W.), Whipping of the Satyre, 47
James, Richard, Dr., 164
*James I., his letter to Shakespere, 217
Jefferies, Judge, 296 *note*
Johnson, John, 238
Jonson, Ben—
  Every Man out of his Humour, 31
  *Cynthia's Revels, 54, 151 *note*
  Bartholomew Fair,* 61, 105
  Eastward Hoe, 69
  Epicœne, 90
  Every Man in his Humour, 118
  *Sejanus, 119
  Conversation with Drummond, 129
  Verses on Dreshout's Portrait in Folio of 1623, 141
  Verses on Shakespere in Folio of 1623, 147
  Staple of News, 163
  Ode appended to the New Inn, 172
  Timber, 174
  *Epigram in his *Life*, 233, 234
  *Spurious Epigram by, 426
  *Poetaster, 49, 423, 424, 425
  *New Inn, 423
Jonson, Ben, MS. Epitaph on, 277
Jordan, Thomas, 330

KEELING, Captain, 79
*Kempe's jig, 27

Kirkman, Francis, 354

LAMBARD, William, 449
Lane, John, 32
Langbaine, Gerard, 408
L'Estrange, Sir Nicholas, 282
Ligon, Richard, 304
*Lodge, Thomas, 294 *note*, 423
Lorkins, Thomas, 102
*Lucy, Sir Thomas, song on, 426

M. (T.), Father Hubburd's Tales, 60
M. (J.), New Metamorphosis, 98
M. (I.), Lines prefixed to first folio of Shakespere, 155
*Mabbe's Guzman de Alfarache, 155
Machin, Lewis, 81
*Macklin the comedian, 426
Manningham, John, 45
Markham, Jarvis, 81
Marmion, Shakerley, 428
Marston, John—
  Scourge of Villanie, *3, 27, 29
  Malcontent, 66
  Eastward Hoe, 69
  What you Will, 77
  Parasitaster, 29 *note*
  Insatiate Countess, 428
Marvel, Andrew, 347
Massinger, Philip, 171, 185
  The Roman Actor, 171
  The Maid of Honour, 185
  Unnatural Combat, 428
Mathews, Sir Tobie, 40
Mayne, Jasper, 212, 289
Meres, Francis, 21, 24
Mervyn, James, 222

Middleton, Thomas—
  Blurt, Master Constable, 51
  Honest Whore, 51 *note*
  The Witch, 428
  Father Hubburd's Tales, 60
Milton, John—
  Epitaph on Shakespere, 176
  L'Allegro, 184
  Εἰκονοκλάστης, 274
  Introduction to Samson Agonistes, 275
  Elegy to Charles Diodate, 460
Morhoff, D. G., 342
Motteux, Peter,* 367 *note*, 415
Mulgrave. *See* Sheffield
Mynshul, Geffray, 456

Nash, Thomas—
  Pierce, Penniless, 5
  *Anatomie of Absurditie, 421
  *Epistle prefixed to Greene's *Menaphon*, 421
*" Nest," the term, 61
New Metamorphosis, 98, *440—448
Nicholson, Samuel, 33
*"Noise" in music, the term, 304 *note*

*Oldcastle, Sir John, 65, 127, 164, 249, 266—269, 294
Otway, Thomas, 381
Overbury, Sir Thomas, 114

Palmer, T., 272
Parker, Martine, 239
Peele, George, 75
Pepys, Samuel, 316
Percy, Charles, 38
*Performances of Shakespere's plays, 79, 93, 97, 103, 157, 158, 169, 173, 316-324, 326, 342, 355, 415
Phillips, Edward—
  Tractatulus de Carmine, etc., 344
  Theatrum Poetarum, 359
"Phillis and Flora," 427
Plaudite, at end of a play, 31, 156
*Players' vocation, 58, 277, 411
Poole, Josua, 438
Porter, Henry, 427
Prince of Priggs Revels, 291
Prujean, Thomas, 255
Prynne, William, 195, 200
Puritaine, or Widdow of Watling Street,* 3, 78

Radcliffe, Alexander, 393
Ramsay, H., 215
Randolph, Thomas—
  Jealous Lovers, 187
  Cornelianum Dolium, 224
  Hey for Honesty, 293
Ravenscroft, Edward, 404
Raynolds, John, 451
Raynsford, Sir George, 392
*Revells, Book of, spurious entries in, 426
*Richard III, King, traduced, 41, 402
Rivers, G., 428
Robinson, Thomas, 140
Rochester, Earl of, 364, 378
Rowlands, Samuel—
  Whole Crew of Kind Gossips, Meet, 85
  *Tis Merry When Gossips, 423
  The Night Raven, 454

I. GENERAL INDEX.

Rowley, William, 197 *note*
Ruskin, John, 247 *note*
Rymer, Thomas, 366, 367

SAINT MARIE MAGDALEN'S Conversion, 57
S. (J.), Prince of Priggs Revels, 291
S. (I. M.), Lines prefixed to First Folio of Shakespere, 190
S. (W.), The Puritaine, 78
S. (E.), Anthropophagus, 159
Scoloker, Anthony, 64
Scrope, Sir Carr, 363
*Scudery, Georges de, 386
Sedley, Sir Charles, 418
Shadwell, Thos., 365
*Shakespere's monument at Stratford, 298
Shakespere—
  *his wealth, 67
  *his native genius contrasted with art, 129, 314
  *his name *Will*, 203
  *as Godfather to Jonson's child, 282
  *his plays altered after the Restoration, 324, 356, 365, 369-70, 376, 380 *note*, 381, 389, 390, 391, 392
  *Inscription on grave-stone, 121
  *Inscription on Tablet under Bust, 125
  *His Epitaph on Jonson, 277
  *the play upon his name, 3, 227, 247, 300, 400
Sharpe, Lewis, 230
Sheffield, John, E. of Mulgrave, 394

Sheppard, Samuel—
  The Times displayed, &c., 120, 261
  Epigrams, 284, 285, 287
Shirley, James, 186, 201
  The Sisters, 236
*Sidney, Sir Philip, 421
Smith, Sir Thomas, 453
*" Sneak's noise," 304
Southampton, Countess of, 40
Southwell, Robert, 14
Speed, Samuel, 358
Spencer, John, 182
Spenser, Edmund—
  *Teares of the Muses, 421
*Spurious plays, 426
Stanhope, Lord Treasurer, 103
Stephens, John, 423
Stirling, Earl of, 423
*Stubbes' Anatomie of Abuses, 158 *note*
Suckling, Sir John—
  Fragmenta Aurea, 205, 208, 209, *218 *note*, *233 *note*
  Letters, 209
  Goblins, 210
*" Swan of Avon," 150, 262, 265
Swan, John, 459

TATE, Nahum—
  Loyal General, 379
  Richard the Second, 380 *note*
  King Lear, 390, 391
  Ingratitude of a Commonwealth, 392
Tatham, Jo., 295
Tailor, Robert, 107
Taylor, John, the Water-Poet—
  Three Weeks, three daies, &c., 126

H H 2

Taylor, John, the Water-Poet—
    The praise of Hemp-seed, 133
    Travels to Prague, 178
    To Nobody, 179
Temple, Sir William, 382
Terrent, T., 218
Thorpe, Thomas, 86
Tofte, Robert, 25
*Towers, W., 152
Trapp, John, M.A., 269 *note*

*VAUGHAN, Henry, 424
Vendenheym, H. J. Wurmsser von, 93
Verstegan, R., 247 *note*
Villiers, George, 2d Duke of Buckingham, 346

WALSH, William, 412
Ward, John, 327
Ward, Richard, 429
Warren, John, 235

Webster, John—
    *Induction to *Malcontent*, 66
    White Divel, 100
Weever, John—
    Epigrammes, 16
    Mirror of Martyrs, 42, 165
West, Richard, 214
Whipping of the Satyre, 47
Wild, Robert, 340
Willobie, Henry, 7
Wilmot, John, E. of Rochester, 364, 378
Winstanley, William, 400
Withers, George, 258
*Women players, 195 *note*
*"Works" and Plays, 233
Wright, Abraham, 219
Wright, James, 132
*"Wrong, king can do no," 174, 175
Wurmsser, Hans Jacob, 93

II. SHAKESPERE'S WORKS REFERRED TO IN THE EXTRACTS IN THIS VOLUME.[1]

(The line | between the figures denotes that the references on the *left* of it are between the dates 1591—1642. Those on the *right* are between 1642—1693.)

ANTONY AND CLEOPATRA, 115, 188, | 333
Comedy of Errors, 21, 45, 50, 74, 115, | 300 *note*
Coriolanus, 439
Cymbeline, 97, 118, 157
Falstaff, 2, 24, 40, 103, 114, 223, 233, | 254, 272, 280, 296, 299, 304, 309, 319, 329, 330, 333, 347, 378, 387, 388, 403, 412.
 fat, 31, 47, 126, | 325, 398
 Oldcastle, 65, 127, 164, | 249, 266—269, 294
Hamlet, 64, 66, 67, 70, 72, 73, 79, 117, 131, 135, 159, 160, 171, 185, 187, | 251, 316, 317, 322, 354, 373, 439
Henry IV., Part I, 21, 24, 31, 117, 157, 201, 209, | 254, 316, 320, 322, 354, 387
Henry IV., Part II, 31, 38, 50, 61, 90, 223, | 387
Henry V., 118, | 300, 319, 333, 439
Henry VI., 2, 33, 118, 436
Henry VIII., 102, 169, | 318, 322, 346, 396-7
Julius Cæsar, 42, 44, 53, 103, 157, 163, 174, 209, 232, | 333, 366, 367, 370, 374

King John, 21, 51, | 439
Lear, 131, | 380, 390, 391
Love's Labours Lost, 14, 21, 25, 62, 71, 432, | 351, 438, 439
Love labours wonne, 21, 23 *note*
Macbeth, 51, 78, 97, | 318, 319, 320, 321, 322, 351, 355, 439
Measure for Measure, | 351, 408
Merchant of Venice, 19, 21, 101, | 439
Merry Wives of Windsor, | 316, 317, 320, 333, 371, 406, 415, 419
Midsummer Night's Dream, 21, 71, 160, 179, 182, 232, | 317, 354, 439
Much Ado about Nothing, 103, 161, 233, | 408
Othello, 93, 103, 131, 173, 219, 232, | 316, 319, 322, 330, 366, 374, 412, 415, 418, 439
Passionate Pilgrim, 71, 99, 197
Pericles, 82, 89, 107, 113, 172, 173, 180, | 261, 295, 350, 398
Rape of Lucrece, 12, 13, 15, 16, 21, 26, 30, 32, 33, 44, 48, 57, 71, 106, 205, 430, | 261, 279, 344, 401

[1] For the purpose of this Index, the character of Falstaff and his sayings are taken as a "work."

II. SHAKESPERE'S WORKS REFERRED TO IN THIS VOLUME.

Richard II., 21, 35, 36, 79, 97, 173, 430, | 374, 380
Richard III., 21, 29, 41, 45, 48, 57, 77, 109, 112, 157, 188, 430, | 274, 380, 411 *note*, 439
Romeo and Juliet, 16, 19, 21, 27, 51, 52, 71, 95, 135, 154, 166, 167, 188, | 255, 317, 374, 430, 439
Sonnets, 21, 86, 116
Taming of the Shrew, 85, 157, | 300 *note*, 307, 320
Tempest, 103, 105, 118, | 321, 322, 346, 366, 372, 439
Timon of Athens, | 365
Titus Andronicus, 21, 60, 105, | 404
Troilus and Cressida, 57, | 369, 439
Twelfth Night, 45, 233, | 316, 317, 322, 438
Two Gentlemen of Verona, 21, 112, | 353
Venus and Adonis, 14, 16, 17, 21, 26, 30, 32, 33, 48, 71, 75, 80, 81, 87, 96, 106, 112, 140, 161, 186, 204, 224, 230, 238, 430, | 279, 344, 401
Winter's Tale, 97, 103, 118, 129, 157, 178, 214, | 331, 351, 408

THE following is the order of the most frequent mention of Shakespere's works (including the character of Falstaff as one) before, and after, the civil war-time, in one or other of the four manners described in groups 2, 3, 4, 5 (see before, p. xvii). The gauge of popularity afforded by this summary is only approximate, because it cannot take into account the proportions of extracts in the anthologies (Appendix B), and repetitions in notices like those of Pepys, Cavendish, or Dryden. (I am indebted to Mr. Furnivall for suggesting the list.)

	Before 1642.	After 1642.
Falstaff	13	22
Venus and Adonis	25	3
Hamlet	15	7
Rape of Lucrece	16	4
Romeo and Juliet	13	5
Othello	6	10
Richard III	12	4
Julius Cæsar	9	5
Henry IV—Part I	7	6
Macbeth	3	8

SHAKESPERE'S WORKS REFERRED TO IN THIS VOLUME. 471

	Before 1642.	After 1642.
Pericles	7	4
Winter's Tale	7	3
Love's Labours Lost ...	6	3
Midsummer Night's Dream	6	3
Tempest ...	3	6
Richard II	7	2
Merry Wives of Windsor		8
Henry IV—Part II ...	6	1
Twelfth Night	2	4
Comedy of Errors ...	5	1
Henry VIII ...	2	4
Henry V	1	4
Taming of the Shrew	2	3
Henry VI ...	4	
Merchant of Venice	3	1
Lear	1	3
Much Ado about Nothing	3	1
Titus Andronicus ...	3	1
Cymbeline	3	
Troilus and Cressida ...	1	2
King John	2	1
Two Gentlemen of Verona	2	1
Passionate Pilgrim	3	
Measure for Measure		2
Love's Labour Won	2	
Timon of Athens		1

[L. T. S.]

www.ingramcontent.com/pod-product-compliance
Lightning Source LLC
Chambersburg PA
CBHW020832020526
44114CB00040B/591